Philosophy, History, and Theology

Philosophy, History, and Theology

Selected Reviews 1975–2011

ALAN P. F. SELL

WIPF & STOCK · Eugene, Oregon

PHILOSOPHY, HISTORY, AND THEOLOGY
Selected Reviews, 1975–2011

Copyright © 2012 Alan P. F. Sell. All rights reserved. Except for brief quotations in critical publications or reviews, no part of this book may be reproduced in any manner without prior written permission from the publisher. Write: Permissions, Wipf and Stock Publishers, 199 W. 8th Ave., Suite 3, Eugene, OR 97401.

Wipf and Stock Publishers
199 W. 8th Ave., Suite 3
Eugene, OR 97401

www.wipfandstock.com

ISBN 13: 978-1-61097-968-9

Manufactured in the U.S.A.

To
Robert Pope,
Custodian of the Dissenting heritage, theological torch-bearer, good friend

It is impossible to have clear reasoning and judicious arguments from a writer who either will not tell you his meaning, or expresses it in such a manner that you cannot understand it.

—Job Orton to Samuel Palmer
in a letter of 26 April 1773

Contents

Preface / xi

Introduction / 1

PART ONE   PHILOSOPHY / 5

1. Seventeenth-Century British Philosophers / 7
2. Locke's Enlightenment / 9
3. English Philosophy in the Age of Locke / 13
4. Locke on Man, Person and Spirits / 15
5. Locke on Thinking Matter / 17
6. Locke and Burnet / 18
7. Locke and Christianity / 20
8. Locke on Depravity / 22
9. Locke and Religion / 25
10. Eighteenth-Century British Philosophers / 28
11. Joseph Butler / 32
12. Rational Dissent / 35
13. Richard Price / 37
14. Price's Correspondence / 43
15. William Godwin / 47
16. John Stuart Mill and the Religion of Humanity / 50
17. James McCosh / 53
18. Anglican idealism in the nineteenth century / 56
19. Henry Jones / 59

Contents

20 Oxford Idealism 1901–1945 / 62

21 R. G. Collingwood / 64

22 Philosophy of Education / 66

23 Philosophy of Religion / 72

24 Analytic Philosophy of Religion / 76

25 Theism Analyzed / 80

26 God's Nature and Existence / 82

27 Faith, Scepticism and Personal Identity / 86

28 The Philosophical Frontiers of Christian Theology / 88

29 Christian Theism and Moral Philosophy / 93

30 Asian Philosophy / 97

Part Two   History / 99

31 Medieval Thought / 101

32 Aquinas, Calvin and Protestant Thought / 103

33 The Unity of Brethren / 105

34 The Hutterian Brethren / 107

35 The English Sabbath / 109

36 The Enlightenment World / 111

37 Heterodoxy 1660–1750 / 119

38 British Intellectual History 1750–1950 / 121

39 Congregationalism in Wales / 124

40 American Congregationalism / 126

41 Baptist Covenants / 128

42 The Brethren / 131

43 The Evangelical and Reformed Church / 135

44 Evangelical Biography / 137

45 Evangelicalism in Modern Britain / 140

46 Methodism in Britain and Ireland / 143

Contents

47   Reasonable Enthusiast / 145

48   Locke, Wesley and Romanticism / 147

49   The Oxford Movement / 151

50   Congregationalism in Scotland / 153

51   English Dissent: Dissoluble or Dissolute? / 160

52   Conflict and Reconciliation / 164

53   English Baptists in the Nineteenth Century / 167

54   Strict Communion Baptists in Victorian England / 169

55   Cambridge Theology in the Nineteenth Century / 171

56   A Unitarian Theological College / 175

57   A Baptist Theological College / 179

58   Religion in the West Midlands / 182

59   Charles Grandison Finney / 185

60   Philip Schaff / 187

61   Revival in Wales / 189

36   The Crisis of Belief in Canada 1850–1940 / 191

63   The Social Gospel in Canada 1875–1915 / 198

64   Evangelical and Liberal Theology in Victorian England / 200

65   C. J. Cadoux / 201

PART THREE: THEOLOGY / 203

66   Origen / 205

67   Calvin on the Law / 206

68   Assurance / 208

69   The Existence of God in Dutch Theology / 210

70   Samuel Clarke and the Trinity / 213

71   Fletcher of Madeley: A Theological Biography / 217

72   Baptist Theologians / 219

73   Charles Hodge / 223

Contents

74 John Williamson Nevin / 225

75 Mercersburg Theology and American Religion / 227

76 Mercersburg Theology and Reformed Catholicity / 230

77 Reformed Confessionalism in Nineteenth-Century America / 237

78 Reformed Theology in America / 239

79 Thomas Chalmers and Mission / 242

80 God, Grace and the Bible in Scottish Reformed Theology / 244

81 Theology Through the Theologians / 251

82 John and Donald Baillie / 253

83 The Centenary of Lux Mundi / 255

84 Donald MacKinnon as Theologian / 257

85 Liberation Theology / 260

86 The Atonement / 264

87 Models of the Church / 266

88 On Being the Church / 270

89 Advancing Ecumenical Thinking / 275

90 Methodists in Dialog / 278

91 Art, Modernity and Faith / 282

92 On Christian Ethics / 284

93 Confusions in Christian Social Ethics / 286

94 Protestant Worship / 289

95 Pulpit, Table and Song / 292

96 Theology for Pew and Pulpit / 295

97 Reformed Spirituality / 296

Index of Authors/Editors of Books Reviewed / 301
Index of Sources / 303
General Index / 305

Preface

Since the rationale of this collection of reviews is explained in the Introduction, it is necessary here only to comment upon the arrangement of the material and to render thanks.

At the head of each review will be found bibliographical details of the work in question, though prices of books (many of them now out of date) will not be recorded. At the end of each review the original place of publication will be given. An Index of Authors/Editors of Books Reviewed, and an Index of Sources, precede the General Index. A very small number of editorial amendments have been made to a few of the reviews.

Thanks are rendered to the following editors and publishers for permission to reprint reviews which have appeared under their auspices: Leigh Andersen, *Critical Review of Books in Religion*; F. Christopher Anderson, *The New Mercersburg Review*; Alan Argent, *Congregational History Circle Magazine*; Maria Baghramian, *Philosophical Studies* (Ireland); Michael Beaney, *British Journal for the History of Philosophy*; Sarah Bennison, *Epworth Review*; Clyde Binfield, *Journal of the United Reformed History Society*; Isabelle Brochu, *National Bulletin on Liturgy*; Alastair Cheng, *Literary Review of Canada*; Michael Conway, *The Irish Theological Quarterly*; Martin Fitzpatrick, *Enlightenment and Dissent*; Theodore Gill, *Ecumenical Review*; Roland Hall, *The Locke Newsletter*; David Ceri Jones, *Proceedings of the Wesley Historical Society*; J. Gwynfor Jones, *Journal of the Presbyterian Church of Wales Historical Society*; Francis Landy, *Studies in Religion*; Arie C. Leder, *Calvin Theological Journal*; Patricia Methven, *King's Theological Journal*; Michael Parsons, *European Journal of Theology* and *Evangelical Quarterly*; Susan Parsons, *Studies in Christian Ethics*; Ian M. Randall, *The Baptist Quarterly*; Edna Rosenthal, *The European Legacy*; Alan Ruston, *Transactions of the Unitarian Historical Society*; David Sosa, *Philosophical Books*; David Steers, *Faith and Freedom*; Adrian Thatcher, *Modern Believing*; Iain Torrance, *Scottish Journal of Theology*; Douwe Visser, *Reformed World*; Anne Waites, *The Journal of Ecclesiastical History*; Brian Watson, *Friends of the Congregational Library Newsletter*; Robert Welsh, *Mid-Stream*; Roy Wolper, *The Scriblerian*.

The following publishers have likewise granted permission to reprint: Sage Publications: *The Irish Theological Quarterly*; Taylor and Francis: *British Journal for the History of Philosophy*, *The European Legacy*; *International Journal of Philosophical Studies*; Wiley-Blackwell: *Ecumenical Review*; *Philosophical Books*.

I thank all the authors who have supplied grist to my reflective mill. As on previous occasions it is my pleasurable duty to thank the editor-in-chief at Wipf and Stock, Dr.

Preface

K. C. Hanson, as well as my editor, Dr. Robin Parry, and all their colleagues, for their continuing support of my authorial efforts and for the care they lavish upon every stage of the publishing process.

Alan P. F. Sell
Milton Keynes, U.K.

Introduction

My first review was published in 1974; the second, published during the following year, appears in this collection. Over the years I have had the pleasure of reviewing numerous books, and I here present a selection of my findings. I have occasionally met academic colleagues who have regarded reviewing as a chore. To me it has never been so: on the contrary, I am always eager to learn from others, and I enjoy trying to balance out the several responsibilities that bear upon a reviewer. There is, first, the reviewer's responsibility to the author. I have always felt it my duty to let readers know what the book in question is about, and to deal as honestly as I can with the contents. It will not do to complain that an author has not written the book that I would have produced if only I had got around to it. Again, it is a dereliction of duty to heap false praise upon a work that is seriously flawed—after all, one has a responsibility to the readers and to oneself. It is even more important to give credit where it is due. One also has a responsibility both to the publisher, who may have invested heavily in the project and, at one remove, to the author's family who may, if many prefaces are to be believed, have suffered neglect during the writing process. Above all, I enjoy entering into conversation with authors on matters of interest to us both. In most of my reviews I strive not only to describe and apportion praise or blame, but also to reflect upon what I have read, in the hope that the discussion may be carried further.

The reviews in this collection (only a handful of which are as short as 'book notes') are among those of books that I have found to be of particular interest. It will be clear from the plan of the book that the reviews are the contributions of a borderland person who traverses the frontiers of philosophy, history and theology. While I by no means deny that work of high quality may be accomplished by those who pay microscopic attention to very specific fields of knowledge (I recall an eminent Church historian who would never venture an opinion outside of 'my fifty years'), I cannot easily regard our inherited departmental boundaries as sacrosanct. As a philosopher I could not disclaim all interest in the history of the subject, for we do not fully understand the major thinkers unless we know something of the intellectual world which they inhabited. Wearing the hat of a systematic theologian, and taking a firm grounding in biblical studies as read, I could not proceed without recourse to the techniques of linguistic analysis, or knowledge of the heritage of Christian doctrinal thought; and one of my favourite routes into history is to investigate what happens at the ecclesiastical grass roots when doctrines are espoused, modified or repudiated. I could not work satisfactorily with ecumenical partners unless I had accurate acquaintance with the history and polities of the several Christian traditions; and when exploring historical themes I cannot forget that

Introduction

Christians are people who believe things: they are not simply socio-political operatives, still less, statistics—though they can, of course, be hypocrites.

A practical consequence of what some may regard as my wanton eclecticism is that some of the books reviewed in this collection have been hard to apportion to the three parts: Philosophy, History and Theology. Indeed, in demonstration of the permeability of our inherited departmental boundaries, a number of them could be transferred to other sections without misrepresentation of their contents. With a view to making the work more than a random miscellany of unrelated items, I have selected and ordered the reviews in the hope of ensuring a degree of chronological and/or thematic progression within each part.

In Part One I set out from works which set the English Enlightenment in context, and I discuss studies of several aspects of the thought Locke, who has, somewhat misleadingly, been called the 'father of the English Enlightenment.' I should be greatly cheered if some of these studies encouraged those theologians who erect the Enlightenment as an Aunt Sally to be knocked down to be a little more discriminating when passing judgment. I then come to the eighteenth century, in my opinion one of the most philosophically and doctrinally interesting of all the centuries; and thence to the nineteenth, in which exotic philosophical interests increasingly require to be reckoned with—whether issuing from Kant, Hegel or Comte. The twentieth century saw both the laicizing of philosophy and the explosion of the 'genitive' philosophies. I have been especially interested in two of these: the philosophy *of* education, and, above all, the philosophy *of* religion. The former was the subject of my first two published reviews, of which I here include the second. I found the philosophy of education to be of great interest, notwithstanding that Gilbert Ryle pronounced it 'the last refuge of the incompetent.' I include this review both because the issues raised still bear consideration, and because I suspect that the philosophy of education is not as widespread in the curriculum followed by intending school teachers as once it was, with the result that many teachers of all age ranges reach the classroom without having encountered the subject. If this is indeed the case, I regret it. A discussion of works of analytical philosophy of religion follows, including one which undertakes the relatively rarely attempted task of bringing Christian theism into relation with moral philosophy—another particular interest of mine. The section ends with a work which reminds us of a world of philosophical reflection that is not Christian but which, by some of its practitioners, is being brought ever closer to the interests of at least some Western philosophers.

The books discussed in Part Two are arranged in roughly chronological order. We begin with a lucid survey of prominent aspects of medieval thought, and this is followed by the work of an author who brings Aquinas into relation with later Reformed and Protestant thought. There follow discussions of books on the continental and English Reformations, and on exports therefrom to the New World. The Evangelical Revival, the varieties of English Dissent, the Oxford Movement and Anglican theology, theological education, and revivals at home and abroad are among further themes treated. Christianity in Canada is the subject of two reviews, and the section ends with a consideration of Victorian evangelicalism and liberalism, the latter of which was kept alive not least by C. J. Cadoux, one of the doughtier, not to say angular, Congregational scholars of the first half of the twentieth century.

Introduction

In Part Three I turn to theology, and I set out from a book on Origen, whom I regard as one of the four greatest theologians of all time (the others being Aquinas, Calvin and Schleiermacher). We proceed through Calvin and Reformed theology to the evangelical Arminian, Fletcher of Madeley, and some Baptists. Thence to the rivals, Hodge and the Mercersburg theologians, and on to some Scots and Anglicans. The particular doctrines of assurance and atonement are considered and then we come to ecclesiology and ecumenism. Some reflections on aesthetics in relation to theology are followed by two items on Christian ethics, and the collection concludes with discussions of books on worship, and on that currently ubiquitous theme, spirituality.

As I ponder the academic interests I have developed over more than half a century I cannot but be grateful to that Providence which led me to the University of Manchester for my first degree in Arts, followed by the postgraduate degree of Bachelor of Divinity. I was privileged to sit at the feet of Desmond Paul Henry on traditional and symbolic logic; Eric Gilman on Plato, the empiricists and moral philosophy; Dorothy Emmet on Berkeley, and H. G. Alexander on the rationalists. Of these I owe a particular debt to Gilman, whose course in moral philosophy neglected neither Aristotle, the moral sense philosophers, Price and Kant, nor G. E. Moore, emotivist theories, and the then current metaethical analysis as represented by J. L. Austin ('Are cans constitutionally iffy?'), R. M. Hare, and others. Among the historians I encountered were W. Reginald Ward, who led us on a brisk and bracing tour of modern history, which in those days began in 1485 and ended in 1918; Albert Goodwin and R. G. Western on the French Revolution; and G. E. Aylmer and H. J. Perkin on aspects of English history. The classicists Vincent Knowles, A. J. N. Wilson and A. N. Marlow challenged me with two-way Greek translation, Euripides and Xenophon, while Desmond Leahy kindly made himself available for additional coaching. English Literature was in the hands of the bearded poet, Robin Skelton, who discoursed eloquently on Chaucer, the metaphysical poets and Dryden and Pope as he paced back and forth across lecture hall's extensive dais; our authority on Romanticism was Arthur Pollard; J. D. Jump's stimulating course was on the novel, and F. N. Lees chain-smoked his way through Shakespeare—all of the plays and some sonnets for good measure. The history of the English language was taught by R. F. Leslie and Dorothy Hignett, while William Haas told us all about phonemes and suchlike.

Thus primed I proceeded to Divinity, where I specialized in the philosophy and doctrine group of subjects and learned from John Heywood Thomas on the philosophy and psychology of religion, George Phillips on doctrine, and Ronald Preston on Christian ethics. In addition I took required biblical courses from T. W. Manson and Owen E. Evans on the New Testament, with Greek in the hands of J. H. Eric Hull; and H. H. Rowley and George Farr on the Old Testament. The Hebrew language lecturer was John M. Allegro, who took the class through Hebrew grammar in the most cheerful way possible, but clearly found his greatest delight in deciphering fragments of the Dead Sea Scrolls. P. Wernberg-Møller and Edgar Jones guided me through set texts in Hebrew. In Ecclesiastical History I learned from C. W. Dugmore on the Anglican Settlement and Prayer Books, W. Gordon Robinson on Dissent, and E. Gordon Rupp on the continental Reformation. Finally there was S.G. F. Brandon on comparative religion—ancient Egypt and Babylon as well as Indian

Introduction

religions and Islam; and D. Howard Smith on Chinese cults and philosophies. As if all of this were not enough there was the regular conduct of worship in churches near and far, summer student pastorates, and courses and examinations preparatory to the Christian ministry—all of this under the auspices of Lancashire Independent College which, during my sixth and final year became Northern Congregational College on its amalgamation with Yorkshire United Independent College, whose staff and remaining students came over the Pennines from Bradford to join us.

Into the ministry I went. During my first pastorate at Sedbergh and Dent I completed my research MA on the relations between Christian ethics and moral philosophy under the supervision of John Heywood Thomas and R. H. Preston; and during my second, at Worcester with Hallow and Ombersley, I gained the PhD from the University of Nottingham, for a thesis on Christianity and philosophy in twentieth-century Britain. This was supervised initially by Ronald Hepburn and James Richmond and, when Hepburn removed to Edinburgh, his successor, Jonathan Harrison, stepped into the breach. I was pleased that by enrolling at Nottingham my wish to be challenged at doctoral level by scholars all of whom were knowlegeable, but not all of whom were doctrinally persuaded, was more than amply fulfilled. In my early steps towards publication I was greatly encouraged and rigorously challenged by my former teacher, John Heywood Thomas, and also—especially with regard to comprehensiveness of references—by Geoffrey F. Nuttall. For the intellectual stimulus of all of those named I remain truly grateful.

Those who have been kind enough to review my own books (usually kindly, I am happy to say) have sometimes referred to, and even confessed to having enjoyed, what they call my 'dry wit'. Lest some of this should appear in what follows I shall explain myself. Whereas sarcasm is intended to wound, 'dry wit' is more like gentle teasing with a point, and it is not always understood. Occasionally scholars from other cultures have thought that I was 'not serious'. Well, if we have to beware of Greeks bearing gifts, perhaps we ought also to beware of English people wielding wit. Let me illustrate the point. Lancashire Independent College, Manchester, where I lived and studied during my Manchester days, had two principals, Alexander James Grieve and his successor and my Principal, W. Gordon Robinson, who between them served in that capacity for forty-six years. They were renowned for the sharpness of their wit, and many tales of both have flowed down the years; but I refer here to the former. Grieve was present at an early united service in Manchester, and the participating ministers were in the vestry sharing out the several parts of the liturgy. At once a very high Church priest of the Church of England said, 'The Blessing, of course, must be mine, as I am the only *priest* present.' As quick as a flash Grieve replied, 'I shall be happy to serve in the Sacrament of the reading of the Word.'[1] With wit of this kind it is necessary not only to hear what is being said, but to see what is being done: (a) the Word and sacrament are related, and (b) Grieve is responding to one who probably did not think that Congregationalists had valid sacraments or rightly ordained ministers; (c) Grieve speaks in terms of gracious willingness, whereas the priest demanded a perceived right; and (d) Grieve is almost certainly gently cutting a haughty cleric down to size.

1. Recounted by Grieve's son-in-law, Charles E. Surman, *Alexander James Grieve, MA, DD, 1874–1952*, Manchester: Lancashire Independent College, 1953, 45.

PART ONE

Philosophy

1

Seventeenth-Century British Philosophers

Andrew Pyle, ed. *The Dictionary of Seventeenth-Century British Philosophers*, 2 vols. Bristol: Thoemmes Press, 2000. Pp. xxi + 932.

With this handsome work Thoemmes Press further enhances its reputation as a publisher of eminently useful philosophical resources. The Press's eighteenth-century Dictionary has been cordially received by scholars in a number of fields, and we may confidently predict similar success in the case of the present work. Andrew Pyle has assembled a team of more than seventy scholars to handle over 400 entries (of which, to declare an interest, a few short ones are mine). The calibre of the contributors is on the whole high, the list including Stuart Brown, Vere Chappell, Sarah Hutton, N. H. Keeble, James Moore, Margaret J. Osler, Richard H. Popkin, G. A. J. Rogers and M. A. Stewart.

As is entirely appropriate to the century concerned, 'philosophy' is construed widely to embrace those from many fields who, in one way or another, pondered the state of things: scientists, theologians, such influential writers as Addison, Bunyan, Defoe and Milton, even Commonwealth sectaries—there is room for most if not all, wanton polemicists being shunned. The result is that we are immersed in the intellectual context in which those who subsequently became entombed in philosophy syllabi lived and, hence, we understand them better. In any case, as the editor points out (p. viii), 'it is usually the minor figures, not the luminaries, who are the typical representatives of the thought of the period.' 'British,' too, is understood with sufficient elasticity to include a few prominent continentals such as Comenius and De Dominis.

While, as might be expected, bare details only are supplied in the case of many obscure figures, the *Dictionary* generally rises above mere 'nuts and bolts.' Not only is criticism offered in some of the lengthier pieces but, for example, the neglected question of David Abercromby's status as a harbinger of the Scottish common-sense philosophy is addressed by Paul Tomassi in such a way as to turn one's feet in the direction of the library. Again, J. A. I. Campbell judiciously evaluates Charles Blount in such a way as to query the too easy labelling of him as a derivative plagiarist.

The decision to reprint the articles on Locke, Newton and some others from the eighteenth-century *Dictionary* is understandable and acceptable: indeed it exemplifies those inter-century intellectual continuities which our habit of carving up time into slabs of one hundred years can tempt us to overlook. Bacon, Cudworth, Hobbes and More are among major figures who receive ample treatment. Others who receive their due are William Ames, Isaac Barrow, Richard Baxter, Hugh Binning, Peter Browne, Gershom Carmichael, Walter Charleton, William Chillingworth, Samuel Clarke, Joseph Glanvill, Nehemiah Grew, John Hales, William Harvey, Richard Hooker, Bernard Mandeville, John Ray, Edward Stillingfleet, Thomas Tenison, John Tillotson, Matthew Tindal, John Toland, Isaac Watts and William Wollaston.

Articles on women include those on Mary Astell, whose 'Malebranchian orientation underlines her antipathy to the philosophy of John Locke' (p. 30); Margaret Cavendish, who used poetry and satire to convey her philosophical ideas, among them objections to Hobbes, More and others; Catharine Cockburn, defender of Locke and Clarke; and Damaris Masham, who evaluated the views of Norris, Locke and Leibniz.

Among numerous points noted in passing is the way in which Edward Bagshaw's Calvinism accorded with some of the newer scientific thinking. Readers unimpressed by this may be cheered to know that Bagshaw also fell foul of the appropriately named Busby for wearing a hat in church. That not all hastened to imbibe newer ideas is illustrated by Thomas Barlow, who advocated the use of Aristotelian logic as a weapon against the Jesuits. The article on Slingsby Bethel shows how, in revolutionary times, ideas coupled with rumbustious activities determined domicile. It is pleasant to make the acquaintance of the country gentleman Thomas Blundeville who, in addition to writing books on horsemanship, geography, cartography and navigation, also published *The Art of Logicke* for the benefit of zealous but unschooled ministers who sought ammunition against 'all subtill Sophisters, and cauelling Schismatikes.' Thomas Cole's anticipation of some of Locke's epistemological views is noted, as is John Dee's failed attempt to secure patronage by initiating Emperor Rudolph II into alchemical secrets. Henry Dodwell the Elder is interesting for the variety of responses to his eschatological opinions. R. W. Dyson does well to suggest that Robert Filmer was not as dim as has sometimes been alleged, while Ian Higgins brings out clearly the contemporary and longer-term significance of Charles Leslie's views on patriarchal monarchy *vis-à-vis* the Church. The way in which Morgan Llwyd's mysticism was expounded within the parameters of orthodox Calvinism, and with reference to the authority of Scripture, is clearly explained by R. M. Jones. The range of Joseph Mead's writing boggles the mind: the classics, Hebrew, Egyptology, theology, mathematics, astrology, botany and anatomy all falling within his purview. Perhaps the most elegant verdict in the *Dictionary* is that passed upon William Whiston, quoted from the *Encyclopaedia Britannica*: 'He was not only paradoxical to the verge of craziness, but intolerant to the verge of bigotry' (p. 876).

It is possible to question some judgements made along the way. One could wish that John Owen's part in the *Savoy Declaration of Faith and Order* (1658) had been noted; the bibliography for Jonas Proast might have been updated, while Beverley C. Southgate's article on John Sergeant and M. A. Stewart's on Stillingfleet appeared too late for inclusion as, perhaps, did G. A. J. Roger's piece on Stillingfleet (whose *Works* have recently been reprinted by this publisher).

The *Dictionary* is furnished with an index of persons which greatly facilitates cross-referencing, and the standard of production is high. It is, however, ironic that that most meticulous of scholars, Geoffrey F. Nuttall, should have his name misspelled, and ominous that the slip should occur on p. 666!

The International Journal of Philosophical Studies 9 (2001) 553–55.

2

Locke's Enlightenment

G. A. J. Rogers. *Locke's Enlightenment: Aspects of the Origin, Nature and Impact of his Philosophy*. Hildesheim: Georg Olms, 1998. Pp. xiv + 194.

Time was when, in some notable seats of learning, 'This is history, NOT philosophy!' was the most damning verdict which could be appended to a novice philosopher's essay. Contemporaneously, existentialists were, at best, deemed good for only novels and plays, while theologians (forsooth!) were irremediably blinkered and dogmatic exponents of nonsense. Such mentors were far removed in spirit from Whichcote: 'because I may be Mistaken, I must not be dogmatical and confident, preemptory and imperious.' Happily, during the last thirty years there has arisen a growing band of philosophers who are as well versed in the intellectual contexts of the arguments which interest them as in the arguments themselves. They understand that simply to abstract an argument from a philosophical work and to analyze its form may or may not yield an author's meaning, still less (*pace* certain literary critics) his or her intention in writing. For this we need some knowledge of semantics, and some acquaintance with the intellectual milieu (antecedents, opponents, historical context) of which the author was a part. Professor G.A.J. Rogers of the University of Keele understands this well. Indeed, he utters an implied rebuke to those modern commentators who tend to read Locke 'as if he were some secular representative of twentieth-century philosophy' (p. 157); and expresses his amazement that such a matter as the connection of Locke's work with the seventeenth-century revolution in science 'was so little highlighted in contemporary commentaries' at the beginning of his own career (p. ix). Few have done as much as Rogers to redress the balance, and he now ranks as one of our leading authorities in his chosen field. In the volume under review he presents the fruit of his assiduous researches, and although most of the chapters have previously been published, they do, following slight editing, together comprise a book rather than a collection of disparate fragments and, moreover, a book in which there is relatively little repetition.

Chapter 1, the product of a good deal of careful detective work on the sources, concerns the gestation of Locke's *Essay*. It also announces a running theme of the work, namely, that 'Modern science, political theory and theology, as well as modern philosophy were largely to be set within the epistemological parameters that Locke identified' (p. 1). But if Locke influenced others, he was himself a debtor—to Descartes (despite Locke's rejection of innate ideas, and his elevation of experience as the only source of knowledge), Boyle and, later, to Newton. Against any who may treat Locke almost exclusively as an epistemologist, Rogers reminds us of his commitment to an objective ethic grounded in theism. In chapter 2 the Locke-Descartes relation is pursued in greater detail, the author's suggestion being that the links were closer—concerning clear and distinct ideas, for example—than Locke later granted when replying to Stillingfleet's criticism of his views, and this despite the manifest distinction between Descartes' and Locke's theistic proofs.

Locke and scepticism is the next theme to occupy us, and here Rogers argues that although with the passage of time Locke became increasingly aware of the force of the sceptical challenge, he never thought that his epistemology could thereby be undermined. He faults sceptics for seeking demonstration and certainty where none may properly be found, and he is content with probability where that is all we may reasonably expect.

In the fourth chapter the Descartes-Locke relations are further delineated, this time in connection with the concept of infinity, and Henry More is helpfully introduced as a philosophical stepping-stone between the two. Locke's strategy is to argue that the concept of infinity can consort with his empiricism if we 'appeal to simple ideas of extension and duration combined with the idea of repetition' (p. 60). The Hobbes-Locke relationship is next reviewed, and Rogers illuminates this by enquiring how both viewed Boyle. He finds that whereas Hobbes remained with the classical sciences, with their tendency to dogmatism, Boyle was a Baconian experimentalist. Locke was with the latter—hence his repudiation of Newton's description of him as a Hobbesian—though at the same time Locke and Hobbes shared empiricism, a theory of perception, and similar anti-sceptical strategies. Locke's Baconian approach in science is next applied to anthropology, in which connection Hobbes is shown to supply the theoretical basis for field work which the positions of Descartes and Locke could never have yielded.

In chapter 7 the empiricism of Locke and Newton is under review. They were both influenced by Descartes, their ontologies were similar, they were mind-matter dualists, and they were unimpressed by scholastic doctrines of substance and properties. While Locke's focus was more theoretical and Newton's more experimental, they both 'placed the events of the world not in necessity, but in the will of God' (p. 111).

In the next chapter the question of toleration is treated in relation to Latitudinarianism. With reference to Chillingworth and to the Cambridge Platonists, Rogers shows how, since we have no right to require the commitment of others to claims of which we cannot be certain, ignorance became a ground for toleration. Not, indeed, that these writers, or Glanville for that matter, envisaged many distinct churches within one kingdom, the breakdown of church-state relations, or the removal of the civil magistrate from religious affairs. Locke's argument for toleration on the ground of the limits of knowledge went further in these directions, and was misunderstood by Jonas Proast and adversely criticized by Leibniz.

How did Locke and More understand liberty? Rogers finds (chapter 9) that they both regarded it as a moral concept, and as a gift peculiar to human beings. In the following chapter the early Stillingfleet is shown to have been akin to the Cambridge Platonists, and committed to the way of ideas, whereas when opposing Locke he seeks to distance himself from these positions. Rogers suggests that this is because Stillingfleet perceived Locke through the lens of Toland's deism—and Toland's position threatened orthodox Trinitarian doctrine. Nevertheless Locke and Stillingfleet were epistemologically closer than the latter found it prudent to admit.

In the penultimate chapter Rogers carefully shows how Locke's philosophical views modified his theological convictions; in particular, he rejected those theological opinions which did not accord with his position on knowledge and probable opinion. In so doing, and by repudiating innate ideas, he 'placed reason and religion unequivocally under the umbrella of empiricism' (p. 162). At the same time, he gave a 'central place' to revelation.

Finally, in a chapter entitled, 'Nature, Man and God in the English Enlightenment,' Rogers argues that seventeenth-century thinkers did not rush like lemmings towards secularization to the degree that Herbert Butterfield and others have supposed. There was always a place for 'Spirits' and, in many cases, for magic too.

It has been difficult, within a brief space, to indicate the contents and give the flavour of so rich a volume as this. Its strengths are many. Rogers well understands that whether Locke is purveying views on knowledge or toleration, his underlying interest is always religious and, especially, Christian. Indeed, Locke's philosophy, 'like that of the medieval schoolmen, was ultimately inextricably bound to his theology' (p. 48). Rogers is illuminating and properly discriminating on Locke's intellectual antecedents. He is judicious on Locke and the Trinity, and his claim that 'The history of Locke's thought in the eighteenth century is . . . an example of the way in which a philosopher's uncertain conjectures on religious questions can be taken and used to support positions probably much more radical than their author ever intended' (p. 172) is one for which I have elsewhere sought to supply some evidence (though I should prefer to describe Locke's conjectures as 'modest, restrained and honest' as well as 'uncertain'—one adjective seldom suffices when the subject is Locke). Rogers is also to be commended for the way in which he shows how, for Locke, the study of nature cannot yield the certainties of religion and morals—matters concerning which he was no sceptic.

If it is difficult to summarize this book, I find it equally difficult to disagree with its main thrust. The scholarship is careful, the judgements persuasive. The following, therefore, are reflections within a wide area of agreement:

1. Richard Ashcraft's portrait of Locke the radical (p. 17) requires now to be reviewed in the light of D.O. Thomas's paper, 'Richard Ashcraft on Locke's Two Treatises' (*Enlightenment and Dissent*, 14, 1995, 128–54).

2. It would be interesting to have more from Rogers on why Locke did not produce the ethics which Molyneux and Catharine Cockburn requested him to write. We know that Locke pleaded old age, the state of his health, and the sufficiency of the gospel revelation—but could it be that he was in a theoretical bind on this matter?

3. Those unfamiliar with English and Welsh dissenting history may find the following sentence opaque: 'For English thinkers of the mid-seventeenth century the problem [of authority] was of course a real one affecting the livelihood and even possibly the lives of those involved' (p. 114).

4. While it is true that Locke thinks of faith as *assensus* (p. 128), it is worth pointing out that the more his mind turned from science and medicine to theology, and especially as he worked on his paraphrases of New Testament epistles, he accorded a place to faith as trust (*fiducia*).

5. I have made bold to suggest that Locke uses 'Jesus is Messiah' (p. 168) as a portmanteau rather than a minimalist claim. (It would be interesting to know how far Professor Rogers agrees with me. Since, I understand, he has undertaken to review my book on Locke and the eighteenth-century divines, I may not have long to wait before finding out[1]).

The book is furnished with an index of persons, and the few editorial slips do not adversely affect the meaning.

Students and specialists alike will benefit greatly from paying detailed attention to this wide-ranging, carefully argued work. The scholarship on which it is based is thorough, and not the least attractive feature of it is the modest way in which John Rogers presents his findings.

The European Legacy, 4 (1999) 102–5.

---

1. See Professor Rogers' review of my *John Locke and the Eighteenth-Century Divines* in *Enlightenment and Dissent* 8 (1999) 263–70.

Part One: Philosophy

3

English Philosophy in the Age of Locke

M. A. Stewart, ed. *English Philosophy in the Age of Locke.*
Oxford: OUP, 2000. Pp. viii + 326.

It is a paradox that 'the Enlightenment project' (whatever that is—it is seldom defined) is subjected to repeated, ill-informed, denunciations by some theologians and even more postmodernists at the very time when there is less excuse than ever for such casual 'Aunt Sallying.' For genuine scholars are increasingly turning their attention to the Enlightenment in its several national guises, and of these the contributors to this volume are among the best.

While Hobbes and Locke are by no means neglected, this collection reinforces the conviction that if we wish to understand the history of philosophy we shall do well to pay heed to the varied intellectual soil in which the major figures were rooted. This necessitates paying attention to what I have elsewhere called the 'hinterland people' who, as Beverley C. Southgate rightly says, 'represent the muddled complexity of their times' (p. 282). Such people were frequently the foils to, stimuli and critics of, the 'big guns,' and they were in many cases more representative of their age than those who have subsequently become entombed in philosophy syllabi. Southgate's paper concerns the Roman Catholic John Sergeant, who ostensibly pits his reality-based logic against what he perceives as the creeping scepticism of his day, but actually rests on his faith in God.

Against the view that Hobbes sought to bolster the sovereign's secular power with the prestige of religion whilst at the same time undermining Christianity, Paul Dumouchel argues that Hobbes's reading of the biblical revelation as an historical process led him to justify the separation of politics from religion, thereby rendering redundant the religious legitimation of secular power. With Adam's expulsion from the garden God leaves humanity to create purely rational institutions within which 'men, through their representative, give to themselves their own laws' (p. 25).

With characteristic thoroughness Knud Haakonssen discusses 'The character and obligation of natural law according to Richard Cumberland.' He argues that Cumberland's Erastianism was grounded in 'a natural-law theory which made not only church government but civil government and the system of property, as it were, *adiaphora*' (p. 30). At the heart of Cumberland's moral philosophy are the concepts of 'the common good of all moral agents and of the natural law prescribing the actions involved in this common good...' (p. 41).

Ian Harris expounds 'Locke on justice'. He shows that in Locke's view political authority turns upon moral theory which, in turn, concerns God's rights-entailing plan: 'Justice, in short, secured men's rights' (p. 75). Different in kind is J. R. Milton's careful reappraisal of the Locke-Gassendi relationship. By means of a thorough analysis of Locke's notebooks Milton reaches the 'safest conclusion' that 'Gassendi's influence on Locke was much more limited than has commonly been supposed' (p. 107). It may he hoped that this paper will give pause to all who may he tempted to throw caution to the winds when pontificating upon the 'influence' of one thinker upon another. 'Influence' is a slippery term, and the evidence, when it is not ambiguous, is frequently slight.

Udo Thiel contributes an illuminating piece on 'The Trinity and human personal identity'. He pays particular attention to the impact of antitrinitarianism upon the Church of England during the 1690s, and to the diverse responses of William Sherlock and Robert South. He further shows that while Locke concentrated upon personal identity and not on the Trinity: indeed, upon personal identity through time and not on individuation, his discussion of consciousness is akin to that of Sherlock.

Readers of this journal may be expected to have a particular interest in chapters 5 and 6. John Marshall writes on 'Locke, Socinianism, "Socinianism", and Unitarianism'. He finds that Locke was at some points close to 'Socinianism' in its broader, polemical, sense, and suggests that he was probably a Unitarian in private. This extensive enquiry is worked out with ample attention to journals, notehooks and dates, and with reference to such issues as the resurrection of the same body and Christ's satisfaction for sin. Marshall reviews possible reasons for Locke's omitting antitrinitarianism from *The Reasonableness of Christianity*—always supposing that he was an antitrinitarian.

In the course of his study of 'Locke's theology, 1694–1704' Victor Nuovo concentrates upon Locke's constructive position so far as this may be determined. In expounding Locke's thought Nuovo queries Marshall' account of Locke's Socinianism (pp. 190–191) which, he thinks, diverts Marshall from paying sufficient attention to Locke's anti-Calvinism, itself fuelled by the antinomian controversy of the 1690s. Nuovo's view is that Locke, while holding positions on such matters as original sin and satisfaction with which Socinians concurred, did not have a Socinian agenda. He then proceeds to endorse a possibly innocent use of 'Socinian' by H. R. Trevor-Roper, according to which a Socinian is one who, like Erasmus, Hooker and many others—including Locke, stands in the 'Christian Renaissance' tradition. One may agree that there was such a tradition whilst also holding that the labelling of it as Socinian obscures more than it reveals.

Again, while Nuovo correctly affirms (pp. 195–96, n) that antinomians did not advocate lawlessness (though there were a few 'practical' antinomians), his silence on the fear which allegedly antinomian writings engendered in some orthodox and other hearts may suggest that he underestimates it. The fear was inspired by memories of Civil War, regicide, and the antics of wilder Commonwealth sectaries; and by concern lest civil unrest in their own time might lead to the snatching away of the measure of religious toleration so recently won, and still so stoutly opposed by some prominent churchmen. Although the full story is more complicated, this goes some way towards explaining the nervous twitching of doctrinal antennae on the republication of Tobias Crisp's sermons, Crisp's lambasting of licentiousness notwithstanding.

Among the most engaging papers is that of the editor himself. In 'Stillingfleet and the way of ideas' he discusses the bishop in relation to Locke, deists, unitarians and Descartes, and in a footnote he offers his verdict on the Marshall-Nuovo tussle: 'I see little ground to think that Locke was a Socinian in the historical sense, and he would clearly have rejected some individual statements emanating from English Unitarians in the 1690s; but he would have rejected just as many individual statements from trinitarians' (p. 255, n). At the heart of the discussion are the different ways in which Stillingfleet and Locke understood 'the way of ideas' and 'certainty'. In Stillingfleet's opinion Locke's position on the former led to scepticism, while his denial of certainty to faith (because it was not knowledge) was unduly restrictive.

These papers will foster discussion for some time to come.

Transactions of the Unitarian Historical Society, 23 (2003) 480–482.

4

Locke on Man, Person and Spirits

John W. Yolton. *The Two Intellectual Worlds of John Locke: Man, Person, and Spirits in the Essay*. Ithaca: Cornell, 2004. Pp. 180.

'Provocative' is one of the adjectives used by Vere Chappell in his commendatory blurb on this book's cover. Undoubtedly all readers will be provoked to admiration by Mr. Yolton's patient tracking and lucid exposition of such crucial, and slippery, terms as 'man', 'self', 'person', and 'soul'—the last mentioned being especially difficult to elucidate and relate to the other three. Although the spotlight here falls upon Locke's *Essay*, Mr. Yolton well understands how important it is to consider what Locke says in that work alongside what he says elsewhere: for example, in *Some Thoughts Concerning Education*.

This book will provoke thought. The following questions are among others raised in the first chapter alone: In having recourse to neurophysical explanation, did Locke intend to countenance epistemological reductionism? How far is it possible or useful to distinguish between 'self' as referring to personal identity and 'person' as bearing the moral connotation? How should we weigh what Locke says about the person's 'essential constitution' against his view that the person is constituted by character, the product of education? If the moral acts of man are directed by reason, what is there for the soul to do? As the work proceeds there is more intellectual provocation as we are introduced not only to the social and physical environments that Locke thinks human being occupy, but to the universe, the domain of God, angels and spirits, and the intellectual world. There are yet more questions: How may we form ideas of spirits? What is the temporal and eternal place and function of the soul? Running throughout is Locke's deep concern with the chain of being on the one hand and, on the other, with the goal of happiness in this life and the next—the latter in relation to morality and divine judgement.

In several places Mr. Yolton provokes the reviewer's responses. First, of Locke he declares that 'his Christianity was minimalist (a belief in Jesus as the Messiah and a few other notions).' Certainly Locke, seeking common ground in sectarian times, regarded the specified doctrine as the minimum qualifying belief to entitle a person to the name 'Christian'; but he did not think that this was all that there was to be believed; and since he himself believed in a good deal more than this, 'his Christianity' was more doctrinally robust than Mr. Yolton implies. Secondly, Mr. Yolton claims not to know whether Locke, given his aversion to enthusiasm, believed in legitimate divine inspiration of individuals. At the very least Locke could not deny the possibility (*Essay*, IV.xix.5). Thirdly, on Locke's claim that from the notion of 'an eternal, most powerful, and most knowing Being' all of God's other attributes may be deduced, Mr. Yolton remarks, 'He does not say what additional attributes could be deduced.' But Locke, living at a time of fairly intense confessional debate, could probably assume that his readers were aware of lengthy lists of God's so-called communicable and incommunicable attributes, these being understood as having been revealed to us.

Perhaps the most provocative question of all is: Does Locke really 'inhabit' two intellectual worlds—the material and the spiritual, or one world, some parts of the terrain of which are less accessible to us and therefore less confidently mapped by, and accessible to, our reason than others? Mr. Yolton declares that 'The two intellectual worlds of John Locke are closely linked.' But given Locke's concern for morality, judgement, immortality, and happiness, are they not, in his mind, inseparable?

The pedantry of one who toiled through Hebrew is provoked on p. 86, where the final s's should be dropped from the already plural 'cherubim' and 'seraphim.'

Will this book provoke irritation or dismay? Probably only in those philosophers who, when gazing into the Lockean pool, expect to see reflections of their hard-nosed empiricist selves, and are discomfited by a Locke encumbered with angels, spirits, and suchlike.

The Scriblerian, 39 (2006) 82–83.

Part One: Philosophy

5

Locke on Thinking Matter

John W. Yolton. *Thinking Matter: Materialism in Eighteenth-Century Britain*. Oxford: Basil Blackwell, 1984. Pp xiv + 238.

Few passing remarks have stimulated more literary activity than Locke's to the effect that there is no contradiction in the idea that God might superadd to matter the power of thought. The immaterialists perceived this aside as a threat to the doctrine of the immortality of the soul; for the soul alone, they held, could think. Accordingly they took to their pens and produced a plethora of publications, many of them now generally forgotten.

Professor Yolton serves us well in sifting through this material. He treats the whole of the eighteenth century, finding a point of departure in the pre-Lockeian Cudworth's *The True Intellectual System of the Universe*, and proceeding to Priestley's materialism. He provides detailed discussions of Hume, of space and extension, of the question whether matter is inert or active, of the concept of action, and of the physiology of thinking and acting. Locke is omnipresent. Among Yolton's concessions to the reader are the helpful and necessary synoptic recapitulations with which the book is punctuated. The work is further enhanced by a bibliography in which the lesser known are accorded brief biographical notes.

The themes are treated in such detail and yet with such economy that the book defies summary. Yolton draws a remarkable range of writers into his net, often allowing them to speak for themselves—though strangely he does not deal with the Locke-Burnet debate to which, as we shall see below, S A Grave devotes a monograph. As well as major philosophers of the period we meet both Isaac Watts and Philip Doddridge in their philosophical colours (and we may well prefer some of their hymns) We hear of Richard Bentley's 1692 sermon on 'Matter and motion cannot think,' and we wonder what his congregation made of it. But these examples underline how widespread was the anxiety engendered by Locke's suggestion. One of the ways in which the panic was expressed was in the liberal application of the label 'freethinkers' to groups as distinct yet as (sometimes) overlapping as the materialists, the deists and the Freemasons.

Among the highlights of the exposition is Yolton's account of Hume's 'startling and clever *tour de force*' to the effect that since the properties claimed by the immaterialists for the soul are identical to those claimed by Spinoza for his one substance, immaterialism is a variety of atheism! Intriguing too is the way in which, as the century progressed, materialism was aided by the development of the idea of matter as being not so much corpuscular as force and power. The 'odd divine out,' Robert Greene, is interesting, for he propounded his early force concept of matter in the context of a *defence* of religion against atheists, deists, Socinians and Arians. Again, Yolton's references to the *London* and the *Monthly* imply the importance of such journals in disseminating the views of the century's later authors among the cultured of the day.

For the most part Yolton remains within his century, though occasionally he takes issue with recent writers—Robert Schofield, for example, whose definition of 'materialism' as embracing the view that matter possesses forces is, according to Yolton, misleading, for that is what the immaterialists held.

To some extent the fears of the immaterialists were not fulfilled for, as Yolton points out in his conclusion, 'of the two writers in eighteenth-century Britain who were associated with the immaterialist's prophecy of automatism, Hartley and Priestley, neither eliminated the mental.' The main finding, that 'The nature of thought and of matter, as well as their connection, turns out to have been basic to most of the topics in science, philosophy, and religion' is amply justified by the author's review of this complex period in the history of thought. My one regret is the omission of any indication of the ways in which the ideas discussed here have a continuing, albeit sometimes unacknowledged, life. For one of the things which may confidently be asserted of the thought of the eighteenth century is that neither in science, philosophy nor religion are we yet done with it.

Philosophical Studies 31 (1986–1987) 438–39

6

Locke and Burnet

S. A. Grave. *Locke and Burnet*. Obtainable only from the Department of Philosophy, University of Western Australia, 1981. Pp. v + 40.

In this most useful, tightly-packed, monograph Professor Grave introduces us to the exchange of views between Locke and Thomas Burnet. Burnet's anonymous *Remarks upon an Essay Concerning Humane Understanding* (1697) drew an acid response from Locke in the same year. Burnet followed up with two further sets of *Remarks*, but Locke did not publicly notice them. He did, however, annotate his own copy of the final set, and Grave has examined this.

That Burnet occupied that fascinating 'in-between' period of thought is clear from his *Sacred Theory* (1681) in which he uses the Bible as a quasi-geological text book on the one hand, and exalts reason on the other. He maintains that we inhabit a ruined world; he sees no beauty in the mountains, and the stars lie 'carelessly scattered.' (Grave might have pointed out that the concept of 'landscape' had not yet arrived). Burnet's main evidence that we live in a ruined world is that the Genesis flood could not have taken place in the world as it is now—for where would sufficient water have come from to cover the mountains? Locke found Burnet's ingenious solution—an originally egg-shaped earth filled and water—wanting.

For his part Burnet had difficulties with Locke's account of the distinction between moral good and evil. To him this distinction is intrinsic and immutable; it does not depend upon our approving or condemning. Again, in partial accord with Butler, Burnet speaks of conscience as a law which distinguishes between good and evil by immediate perception, whereas to Locke the positing of such 'an inward distinguishing sensation antecedent to all sense or supposition of an external moral rule' leads straight to enthusiasm (a term whose eighteenth-century sense might have been defined). Grave then relates Burnet's view to that of the moral sense philosophers, showing that while Burnet used the analogy of a moral sense, he formulated no moral sense theory.

The next questions for review concern the immortality of the soul and the possibility of thinking matter. First, to Locke's suggestion that the soul may sometimes sleep Burnet poses the question, How can this be observed, for to observe is to think? Secondly, while allowing that spirit may act in matter, Burnet cannot conceive of thinking matter as such, and everything he knows about matter suggests that it is incapable of thought. Accordingly he refuses Locke's suggestion that God might add the power of thought to matter. Nor can he see how a doctrine of immortality could be built upon the two faulted presuppositions. For good measure Grave relates Locke's suggestion of the possibility of thinking matter to Priestley's subsequent confusing thoughts on the question.

The concluding chapter concerns innate knowledge. Grave maintains that nobody ever held the view of innate knowledge against which Locke protests and, with further references to Burnet, he proceeds carefully to the verdict that 'Locke denied innate and allowed self-evident truth. And deceived by appearances, as many of his opponents in the matter must also have been, he pounded on and on at a way of speaking with arguments appropriate, for the most part, only to a doctrine.'

In addition to elucidating the history of debate on important philosophical themes Professor Grave tacitly invites us to draw the inference that our understanding of prominent philosophers can be enhanced greatly by knowledge of their lesser-known—even anonymous—critics.

Philosophical Studies 31 (1986–1987) 439–40.

PHILOSOPHY, THEOLOGY AND HISTORY

7

Locke and Christianity

Victor Nuovo, ed. *John Locke and Christianity: Contemporary Responses to 'The Reasonableness of Christianity.'* Bristol: Thoemmes Press, 1997. Pp. xliii, 284.

One of the reasons why Locke is so intriguing, and sometimes so misunderstood—or only partially understood, is that he tends to consider one issue here, a related issue there, but declines to bring his thoughts together in a full-scale system. Accordingly, when reading him in one place we need at the same time to overhear what he says elsewhere. Epistemologists who look no further than the *Essay*, political theorists who major on Locke on government or toleration, educationists whose interest is confined to texts ostensibly treating that topic, may miss much. The point of these musings is to dissuade readers from supposing that everything Locke has to say about Christianity is here. The subtitle seriously qualifies the main title.

Locke's objective in the *Reasonableness* is to refute the deists and to defend the Christian doctrine of justification. This is made abundantly clear in Nuovo's lucid Introduction. The responses to Locke are varied, and have been judiciously selected, though one could wish that Locke's doughty defender, Catherine Cockburn, had not been omitted. What makes this volume in Thoemmes Press's enterprising series of 'Key Issues' more useful than it might otherwise have been is that we are given a taste of the *Reasonableness* itself, together with extracts from the writings of Locke's Dutch friend and correspondent, the Arminian Limborch, from the Socinian *Racovian Catechism* (1609), and from the Calvinist-turned-Unitarian Joshua Toulmin's 1814 'afterword' on the Trinitarian controversy of the previous century.

As is well known, Locke was suspected by many, and accused by some, of having aided and abetted Socinianism, and even of being a Socinian himself. The swashbuckling high Calvinist Anglican, John Edwards, was almost apoplectically persuaded that Locke was heretical on the Trinity, and equally convinced that Locke's indispensable minimum of belief— namely, that Jesus is the Messiah—attenuated the faith and scuppered the Calvinist *ordo salutis*. On the other hand, Edwards' fellow Anglican, Samuel Bold, was among those who rose to Locke's defence, while an anonymous Socinian replied directly to Edwards. Other authors here gathered are the convert to Roman Catholicism, John Gother, who seeks to correct the adverse view of 'papists' peddled by more polemical Protestants; the Presbyterian Daniel Williams, who pleads for doctrinal peace; Charles Blount, who presents his account of deism; (probably) Stephen Nye the Anglican with Unitarian leanings, who compiles extracts from William Chillingworth's *The Religion of*

Protestants a Safe Way to Salvation (1638) with a view to indicating the author's Socinian tendencies; William Sherlock, Dean of St. Paul's, who defends the Trinity and, against Edward Wetenhall who thought that doctrinal strife dishonoured the Reformation and gave Roman Catholics a stick with which to beat Protestants, deems the controversy unavoidable; and the Anglican Daniel Waterland who, in his rebuttal of Samuel Clarke's Arianism, grounds upon Edmund Law's Lockean epistemology and ethics.

To return to Nuovo's Introduction: he does well to sketch the doctrinal background—antinomianism, Calvinism *versus* Arminianism, deism—against which Locke wrote, though somewhat surprisingly he does not refer to Locke's friend the deist Anthony Collins, as a result of whose writings some deemed Locke guilty by association. Nuovo presents the antinomian controversy as having to do with the necessity or otherwise of faith for salvation, and fails to make enough of the point which wrecked the 'Happy Union' of 1691 between Presbyterians and Congregationalists, namely, the conviction that by virtue of their contention that for those who are saved by grace the divine law is abrogated, antinomians fostered moral laxity. Nuovo correctly notes that Locke stoutly opposed this doctrine.

Against Marshall, Milton, and others, Nuovo, in my view rightly, inclines to the view that the *Reasonableness* is not a Socinian book. He is right to say that Locke strives to avoid the trinitarian issue in the book, but does not suggest the possibility that to have done otherwise would have been to introduce a significant hostage to fortune in an anti-deist tract. Nuovo does well to show that 'Jesus is the Messiah' is a portmanteau belief for Locke, and he accurately draws Locke's distinction between this belief which qualifies those who espouse it as Christian, and the other important beliefs to which Christians ought to be committed. He also underlines the fact that Locke by no means thinks that the Gospel is discernible or verifiable by reason alone. Locke accords due place to revelation and Scripture. This latter consideration prompts the observation that Locke, the Socinians, and others utilized the principle of the sufficiency of Scripture long before (and in order to justify significantly different doctrinal points from) latter-day Christian fundamentalists. Of course, although they were among its harbingers, Locke and his contemporaries cannot be held responsible for the highly (sometimes mystifyingly) technical and ever-expanding hermeneutics industry which has come to flower only in our own time.

The Locke Newsletter 29 (1998) 181–3.

PHILOSOPHY, THEOLOGY AND HISTORY

8

Locke on Depravity

W. M. Spellman. *John Locke and the Problem of Depravity*. Oxford: Clarendon Press, 1988. Pp. 244

Contrary to the oft-reiterated thesis that Locke threw overboard the heavy baggage of morbid Christian anthropology, thereby impelling the good ship Education upon its enlightened way, Dr. Spellman demonstrates that although Locke did insist upon the character-forming influence of the individual's environment, the undertow of original sin was ever present to his mind. Our author is thus in recent good company, and the pirates in this story are those eighteenth-century thinkers and their successors, who have selectively plundered Locke's writings and have not taken them whole. The fact is that 'Throughout the corpus of [Locke's] published and manuscript writings there exists a definite strain of pessimism about human nature in general and about his immediate contemporaries in particular.'

The oscillations in Christian thought between man as handiwork of God and man as apostate are the subject of the first chapter. The Adamic theory of the Fall as the cause of original sin is shown to be Pauline rather than Pentateuchal, and the progress of this idea down to the Reformation is indicated. While appreciating Dr. Spellman's need to be selective, we should nevertheless have welcomed some 'rounding-out' paragraphs on, for example, Gottschalk (here confined within a note) and Bradwardine. It is characteristic of Dr. Spellman's eirenic approach that he articulates the measure of agreement between Augustine and Pelagius, both of whom advocated moral rigour; and that he reminds us that 'Man's utter helplessness in the face of sin was even acknowledged by that obdurate nemesis of the Puritans, William Laud.' Laud and the Puritans were further at one in opposing antinomianisnn.

In introducing Locke, Dr. Spellman finds scant evidence of his alleged Puritan upbringing, or of the influence upon him of John Owen's ideas concerning toleration. On the contrary, during his Oxford days Locke was deeply disturbed by religious enthusiasm—to him Quakers were 'mad folks'; and he was dismayed by the low intellectual capacities and the selfish proclivities of the generality of mortals. This distrust, together with his abhorrence of sectarian strife and his love of order in society, explains the welcome he accorded to Charles II at the Restoration of 1660. But—and here we recapitulate a running theme of his book—'Locke did not believe that man's proclivity for evil . . . could be overcome by individual merit alone; his "slavery to sin" was in effect irreversible without the redeeming work of Christ.' Locke set his face against both extreme Puritan pessimism and undue rationalistic optimism concerning human moral ability.

'The Broad Church Perspective' is delineated and discussed in the third chapter—a chapter notable for the sensitive analysis of Whichcote's influence upon Locke. Whichcote's thought appealed to Locke not only because of their shared rejection of the doctrine of predestination and advocacy of a minimal creed (in opposition to sectarian squabbles over 'non-essentials'), but also because the Platonist took sin with full seriousness. This measure of common ground was not shaken by Locke's eventual rejection of Whichcote's defence of innate moral knowledge.

The crux of Dr. Spellman's thesis is to be found in chapter IV: 'Creating the Moral Agent.' He shows that those who have viewed Locke's attack upon innate ideas as ushering in a new age of education and environmentalism can stand as comfortably as they do only because they overlook both the continuing impact upon him of the reality of man's sinful state, and the writings of those, generally regarded as more orthodox than Locke, who also emphasized the determinative power of good habits.

So to Locke's friendship with Limborch and other Dutch scholars—Arminian contacts which harmed Locke in Calvinistic eyes. Like found himself at the mercy of the Calvinist John Edwards' polemics, and when the deist John Toland drew from Locke, Locke became guilty by association in the opinion of conservative divines. By now Locke was devoting increasing attention to the study of the Bible, which he construed as affirming both the 'Pelagian' notion that sin is a matter of wrong choice, and the un-Pelagian view of sin's universality.

The quest of common ground surfaces once more in the sixth chapter, in which Dr. Spellman interestingly discusses John Norris, and shows how the original and final positions of Locke and Stillingfleet were direct opposites. That is to say, whereas Locke had started on the side of order and Stillingfleet on that of freedom, in later life Locke became the advocate of (limited) religious toleration, while Stillingfleet opposed it. Common ground remained, however, in that both continued to maintain the doctrine of depravity.

In the penultimate chapter Dr. Spellman shows that although Shaftesbury could not accept Locke's denial of innate moral ideas, he nevertheless inclined to Lockean realism and pessimism concerning natural man. Unlike Locke, however, Shaftesbury left natural man on his own, Locke's acknowledgement of the availability of saving grace notwithstanding.

In his conclusion, Dr. Spellman opines that Locke would not have welcomed the attentions of those eighteenth-century writers who turned him into an educationalist-environmentalist: Locke's view of man was closer to that of William Perkins than to that of William Godwin. Not indeed that he stood for sin as inherited from Adam; but he was convinced that Adam's sin had removed the possibility that unaided natural man could live up to his highest ideals. Education could not, by itself, remedy matters.

A useful bibliography and an index enhance this book.

Dr. Spellman's writing is generally clear and occasionally quaint (his textual studies have given him a fondness for the verb 'to espy'). He has closely studied his sources, and marshals his evidence with care. His notes are informative, though it seems a little slapdash to give Sydney Cave as the source of a widely-available position of Irenaeus. And how ironic that that famously meticulous scholar, Geoffrey F. Nuttall, should have his name misspelled in the bibliography! But these are small points. The cumulative effect of the following remarks is somewhat more serious:

First, as we have seen, Locke was not at the outset an advocate of toleration. Dr. Spellman informs us that by 1678 he had been a convert to the doctrine for many years. On what grounds? Was it simply, as our author states, that Locke reflected more upon 'the problem of natural law and man's knowledge of its contents'? Surely we must reckon with the history of the privations of Dissent under the Clarendon Code and, as an aspect of this, with the growing recognition on the part of many that a regime which hounds such non-subversive, educated, conscientious men as Richard Baxter, Philip Henry and Oliver Heywood eventually discredits itself. More important still was the Dissenting conviction that when Caesar usurps the place of God, the Christian's obedience is owed to God. Dr. Spellman does not sound this note.

Secondly, was Milton a Puritan or not? He is said to have been so on p. 49, while on p. 92 'Milton's Puritanism' is qualified by the words, if in truth the appellation is at appropriate.' The reason given for the latter mode of expression is that Milton's Puritanism 'extended little beyond an intense disdain for Church of England discipline, civil interference in matters of opinion and religious practice, and perceived monarchical tyranny.' He was a biblicist, and he was serious about sin. Now these are all significant matters, and they are not to be brushed aside on the ground that Milton could not assent to some of the formulae of scholastic Calvinism. A closer analysis of the ethos of Puritanism would have assisted at this point.

Thirdly, Dr. Spellman blandly states that 'The nub of Reformation theology, we know, centred on its understanding of man's depraved nature.' But did it? There is a strong line in Reformation theology which insists that we do not truly see ourselves until we have seen the holy majesty of God. In a further onesided statement we are informed that 'Each respective Reformed Church found itself putting together its own inviolable code of orthodoxy, an exclusive confessional dogma.' The term 'inviolable' is unfortunate, given the prefaces which were sometimes written by those who composed confessional statements, in which they declared their openness to correction if it could be shown that they had misinterpreted Scripture. Again, the suggestion that within the Reformed family the several confessions were used as weapons of exclusion cannot be supported. On the contrary, there is a high degree of accord between the Reformed confessions, and this is attributable in large measure precisely to the fact that there was cordial contact between the churches, that they shared their ideas, and that their scholars visited one another from Hungary to Scotland.

Fourthly, we are correctly told that the Calvinist John Edwards agreed with the Puritan Increase Mather and with the Latitudinarian John Locke that the depraved were to be exhorted to 'strive to enter in at the strait gate.' But the point is not made that the Bible itself is the source of the antinomy, 'You shall and you cannot . . .' Similarly, Dr. Spellman explains that Whitby held that 'The gift of free choice magnified . . . the seriousness of all offences in a manner that he believed was impossible under the *Calvinist* reading of Romans (which appeared to make God the author of man's hardness of heart)' (my italics). But it is Paul who says that God hardens the heart: this is no Calvinist 'reading,' the apostle's statement is unequivocal. How it is to be construed is, of course, another matter.

Taken together these remarks suggest that at times Dr. Spellman does not quite 'get under the skin' of some of those about whom he writes. They do not, however, controvert his main thesis.

We may conclude by noting two stimulating remarks—one from Dr. Spellman, one from Locke:

> (a) 'To rely on others for our religious precepts was, for Whichcote, to follow in the steps of the Roman Catholics.' This is the salutary face of Enlightenment individualism—that face which forbids us to take our faith at second hand. This part of the Enlightenment heritage is not to be overlooked by those who (with reason enough) lament the erosion of ecclesiology to which that same individualism could lead.

> (b) 'The great disputes that have been and are still in the several churches have been for the most part about their own inventions and not about things ordained by God Himself, or necessary to salvation.' Precisely because of the questions begged here the ecumenical machine trundles on.

Enlightenment and Dissent 9 (1990) 134-37.

9

Locke and Religion

John Marshall. *John Locke. Resistance, Religion and Responsibility.* Cambridge: CUP, 1994. Pp. xvi + 485.

It is a pleasure to welcome this substantial, meticulously-researched account of the historical context of Locke's thought concerning three prominent, intertwined and conveniently alliterative themes, by an Assistant Professor of History at the University of Denver. John Marshall's objectives are (1) to provide an 'historical explanation of the composition and intended meaning of the Second Treatise [of Government]' (p. xvii); (2) to depict the socio-political context in which Locke worked, and to specify the kind of English society he sought—especially its ethical desiderata; and (3) to demonstrate the formative influence of, and not simply to recognize the importance of, Locke's religious views in the development of his thought. It is a bold plan—especially considering the intricacies of dating some of Locke's writings—but the author proceeds confidently and achieves a considerable measure of success.

The Locke of the *Two Tracts upon Government* is revealed as a legalist and a voluntarist, albeit with theistic undergirding: 'without law there would be no moral good or evil. Without God there would be no law' (p. 15). The civil magistrate has absolute and arbitrary power even over things indifferent, otherwise society would disintegrate. At this early period the spectre of anarchy haunts Locke, who appears as thoroughly conservative. By 1667/8 however, the Locke of the 'Essay on Toleration' takes a significantly modified approach to the questions of power, authority and the civil magistrate. The monarchy is no longer deemed *de jure divino*, the magistrate's powers are limited to securing the public good (which, even the Latitudinarians notwithstanding, does not entail enforcing true religion), and the passive resistance of rulers who exceed their authority is justified. Marshall rightly observes that parts of this programme were as unwelcome to those nonconformists who did not object to the enforcement by magistrates of *their* favoured religious order as they were to the Anglicans: on both sides of the ecclesiastical divide the advocacy of undue liberty of conscience was perceived as a threat. It is in the *Second Treatise of Government* that Locke carefully distinguishes between religion and morality. People are under a primary obligation, and are at liberty, to do those things which they believe will lead to eternal felicity; force should not be applied in connection with such *beliefs*, and if it were it would not be effective, for such beliefs cannot be changed at will. The disruption of peaceful religious activities by hostile civil powers should be resisted peacefully only, otherwise anarchy and strife will ensue. On the other hand, there is moral *knowledge* which is as available to magistrates as to every moral agent; and liberty according to knowledge is an implicate of human rationality. Accordingly, magistrates may utilize force to coerce the will of citizens when public order is at stake, for what is then required is not the consent, but the obedience of the citizen. In the church people must consent only so far as they deem it in accord with God's will, and they are at liberty to leave any church which does not adequately serve their religious interests.

For the politically conservative Locke of 1660, the civil magistrates are concerned with both the temporal and spiritual good of the citizens, and 'There is no sense that freely-chosen worship was seen . . . as a rewarding form of religious experience for anyone' (p. 16).

However, in the course of his diplomatic mission to Cleves in 1665 Locke discovered that Roman Catholics, Lutherans and Calvinists managed to live together in peace, though he still lamented priestly domination of the faithful; and in the 'Essay on Toleration' he argues that short of the onset of civil disturbance, there should be toleration of such speculative matters as appropriate forms of worship and differing moral views, and that civil magistrates are to preserve societal peace. Although he remained disinclined to accord toleration to Roman Catholics on the ground that they honoured an alien power and were thus potential traitors, Locke's increasing acquaintance with and respect for Dissenters from 1679 onwards, and his own hesitations concerning the Trinity, are said to have fuelled his support for toleration in the 1690s. (Though in an uncharacteristic lapse Marshall, when referring to tolerable speculative opinions, both refers to Locke's 'doubts about or actual disbelief in the Trinity' at the end of his life, and says 'he did not disbelieve any of these doctrines' in consecutive sentences on p.64). By that time he had, in the *Letter Concerning Toleration* (1685), argued that toleration was incumbent upon Christians. The underlying ethical motifs are Locke's ideal (which he himself sought to realize) of the vocation of a Gentleman, and the Ciceronian ethical principle that it is legitimate to pursue one's own ends provided this be done justly, recognizing the right of others to one's beneficence. Not that Locke supposed that all could be sweetness and light here below: hence to immortality, heaven as our 'great interest and business,' and doctrine.

'Between the 1660s and the early 1690s [Locke] changed from being a trinitarian who very probably held a strong view of the Fall and of original sin . . . to becoming at the least heterodox in his expressions about the Trinity and original sin and very probably in private an unitarian heretic' (p. xv). This judgement, however, is properly tempered by the realization that 'Locke's intellectual commitment to eclecticism throughout his life invalidates any simple description of Locke as Socinian in a systematic, dogmatic sense' (p. xx; cf. p. 426). The fact remains that by 1684 the exiled Locke who, in his 'Essay on Infallibility' (1661/2) had professed belief in the Trinity whilst confessing that he could not understand how it was true, was delving into the works of the Dutch Arminians, a number of whom—notably Limborch—were his friends. His hesitations concerning the doctrine of the Trinity; his denial of inherited guilt, deemed by so many to be an implicate of the traditional doctrine of original sin—a doctrine with which Locke became increasingly less enamoured as his view of humanity moved from regarding people as 'beasts' to 'sheep' to 'potentially rational' beings (p. 64); and his reflections upon personal identity as residing not in continuity of substance but in consciousness—with their implications for the doctrine of immortality and the resurrection of the 'same' body: all of these were factors in the progression of Locke's doctrinal thoughts.

From one point of view Marshall's work may be read as an extended commentary upon one of his footnotes: 'There is an important sense in which many of Locke's commitments and changes of views were very significantly influenced by his friendships with individuals who helped him to question his received views' (p. 78). Latitudinarians, Arminians, Shaftesbury, Firmin and the Unitarians—these and others flit in and out of the story, leaving their marks upon Locke's developing positions. Nor should Locke's antagonists be overlooked. Marshall is as even-handed in his treatment of Stillingfleet, Filmer and Proast, for example, as he is when criticizing such a present-day Locke scholar as Ashcraft, whose work he values, but to some aspects of which he takes detailed exception. But Locke's Bible was equally, if not more, important to him than his friends. Marshall is to be complimented on showing (not least by reference to Locke's notes and fragmentary manuscripts) the degree to which Locke's thought was steeped in Scripture.

It would be surprising if, when considering so vast and complicated an undertaking, the attentive reviewer did not raise an eyebrow from time to time. More might have been made of the significance (if largely for subsequent theology) of Locke's increasing interest in faith as *fiducia* (p. 128; cf. p. 454), and not merely as intellectual assent to non-demonstrable propositions. While Marshall does well to emphasize the fact that 'Locke's political and religious individualism was not based on social or ethical egoism (p. 294), there is a social strand in Locke's ecclesiology which to some extent tempers the individualism, and of which more might have been made. Theologies usually being better than their polemical points, it is as odd to call the Remonstrants' five points of disagreement with the Calvinists the 'essence' of Arminian theology (p. 333), as it would be to suppose that the Calvinists' five-point riposte is the essence of Calvinism. And John Owen is an unfortunate choice of Calvinist to illustrate hostility to a working faith (p. 429), for he contended that 'Our universal obedience and good works are indispensably necessary, from the sovereign appointment and will of God; Father, Son and Holy Ghost,' and stoutly declared that 'no Protestant ever opposed the Christian doctrine of good works' (*Works*, II, p. 182; XIV, p. 200).

John Marshall has had to deal with Locke's intellectual antecedents, his socio-political context, the dating of his works, and divergent current scholarly opinion on all of these matters. Overall he has been remarkably successful and, rooted as it is in original sources, *au fait* with Locke's entire extant corpus, and abreast of much of the relevant secondary literature, his work will stand as a bench mark for years to come.

Enlightenment and Dissent 15 (1996) 112–16.

10

Eighteenth-Century British Philosophers

John W. Yolton, John Valdimir Price and John Stephens, eds.
The Dictionary of Eighteenth-Century British Philosophers. 2 vols.,
Bristol: Thoemmes Press, 1999. Pp. 1013.

Even if personal integrity did not prompt the admission, the prevailing public mood would suggest that I must declare an interest: I have myself contributed two modest articles to this sizeable work, which I should warmly have welcomed even if I had had no part in it. At a time of growing interest in the Enlightenment(s) there was a real need for an authoritative reference work covering the British context. Thoemmes Press have, with these handsomely produced volumes, amply met this need.

The bald facts are that the *Dictionary* contains over six hundred articles; there are almost one hundred contributors; and the editors have supplied a full Introduction and

Part One: Philosophy

a most useful index of persons. The careful cross-referencing will greatly assist users of the work.

Before turning to the articles themselves, some general observations may be made. First, since ideas cannot be constrained by chronology, the editors have rightly concerned themselves with the 'long eighteenth century,' Locke and Dugald Stewart being the main boundary persons. Secondly, 'philosophy' is wisely construed generously in order to accommodate that variety of natural philosophers, divines, 'thinkers'—some of them polymaths—which the century threw up. Accordingly, we find comment upon a range of topics from metaphysics to chemistry, theology to medicine, around which we nowadays too readily build disciplinary walls. Thirdly, 'British' in the title is understood as including a number of Irish thinkers and some from the dominions (though none who were born, or started writing, in America after 1776); and others who, though born elsewhere, worked in the British Isles. Fourthly, while critical observations abound, especially in the longer articles, the primary objective is expository. Such an ordinance is understandable in the case of the Berkeleys and Humes, since critical works on them proliferate—some of them listed in the helpful bibliographies provided here; and it is essential in the case of most of the forgotten thinkers, of whom some are here recorded here for the first time. It is a major strength of the *Dictionary* that many 'hinterland' intellectuals have been rescued from oblivion: not even the blessed Anon. has been overlooked. Apart from the intrinsic interest of some of the 'lesser fry,' we have not fully understood the big fish until we have had some acquaintance with their intellectual environment, comprising as it did those who frequently stimulated the enquiries of the well known and/or entered into the discussion—even into pamphlet wars—with them. Lastly, the index is instructive from the point of view of frequency of reference. It is no surprise that Locke has most entries, followed by Newton, Hume and Hutcheson; it is interesting that the names of Clarke and Priestley occur more frequently than those of Berkeley and Reid; while Philip Doddridge, William King, Benjamin Hoadly, Edward Stillingfleet, Jonathan Swift, George Turnbull and Isaac Watts are among others who flit in and out of a number of articles.

Mere sampling being unavoidable, I shall refer first to some articles on the big names; then to some on the lesser known; and finally to some of those 'fancy that!' nuggets of information which help to sustain reference-work authors and readers alike.

David McNaughton's fine article on Butler is typical of the best in the *Dictionary*. We have a concise account of Butler's life, and a balanced treatment of his thought—balanced both in the sense that the moral philosophy and the apologetics are given due place, and in the sense that the critical remarks are constructive—as, for example, in relation to Butler's anti-deist apologetic. McNaughton notes that both Butler and the deists presuppose that the world was created by an intelligent and generally benevolent agent. This starting-point having come under attack from Hume, those who decline it may be thought impervious to Butler's arguments. But Christian apologists may offer new or revised arguments for the deist premise; and those who are already Christians may invoke Butler's arguments defensively, 'For what Butler sought to show, in part, was that, if Christian doctrines were true, we should expect the world to be much as it is. That conclusion is, at the very least, sufficient to defend Christianity from the charge that its doctrines are implausible or absurd (p. 166b).

To handle Locke in small compass is the challenge posed to G. A. J. Rogers. He offers a biographical sketch, a careful account of the *Essay*, briefer treatment of the *Two Treatises of Government*, and a penultimate sentence on the 'considerable impact' made by Locke's writings on education, theology, and economics. Among indications of ongoing discussions is Rogers' judicious summary of the issue surrounding Locke and ideas: 'it is far from clear that ideas are for Locke . . . substantial entities. To have an idea is certainly to have an experience of some kind. But the experience may itself be of a physical object. It is far from clear that Locke's language commits him irrevocably to a "veil of perception" doctrine' (p. 562b).

The polymath Richard Price—minister of religion, actuary, moral and political philosopher—is in the competent hands of John Stephens. At the heart of the article is a lucid account of Price's *A Review of the Principal Questions in Morals*. Stephens brings out the importance to Price of his epistemological starting-point, reveals his indebtedness to Cudworth, Clarke, Butler and others, and shows how his rationalist ethic was refined by interaction with the views of Locke and Hume. Mention is made of Price's Arianism, and of his libertarianism—though neither here nor in the same author's piece on Priestley is the Price—Priestley discussion of freedom and necessity referred to.

In his perceptive account of Reid, Knud Haakonssen does well remind us that Reid's common-sense rebuttal of Hume was (a) not Reid's only preoccupation: 'Reid should be seen as a well-rounded Enlightenment figure occupied with a continuing philosophical agenda, rather than focused narrowly on one theory' (p. 739b); and (b) not entirely original, for behind him lay the moral-sense theories of Shaftesbury, Hutcheson and others. The formative aspects of Reid's intellectual inheritance are a providential naturalism, a Christianized stoicism, and a pervading rationalism. His wide-ranging influence down to our own time is noted. Reid set his face against 'a phantom world of so-called "ideas" that were caused by objects of observation so-called' (p. 742a); he contended that sensation is suggestive only, and that the mind is judgementally active in the perception of both internal and external sensations. We thus proceed to a clear statement of Reid's common-sense theory, and thence to an outline of his ethics. Some remarks on Reid's social vision justify Haakonssen's verdict that Reid 'was a man of uncommon sense' (p. 746b).

It may safely be said that while all the major British philosophers are discussed in this work, a large number of secondary figures are also included. We find deists such as Chubb, Collins, Tindal and Toland and Anglican divines such as Hoadly, Edmund and William Law, Sherlock, South, Stillingfleet, Warburton and Waterland; the ranks of Dissent produce Belsham, Doddridge, Grove, Jennings, Kippis, Lardner, Lindsey, Priestley, Taylor and Watts among others; John Wesley and George Whitefield are here (though relatively few other Methodists, whether Arminian or Calvinistic—their energies at the time being, no doubt, consumed by evangelistic activity); there are the Scots, Baxter, Beattie, Ferguson, Oswald, Robert Simpson and Dugald Stewart; women writers include Mary Astell, Catharine Cockburn, Damaris Masham, Hannah More and Mary Wollstonecraft;

Part One: Philosophy

literary figures such as Addison, Blake and Johnson and a number of artists, medical men and scientists receive due attention.

Not the least valuable aspect of the Dictionary is the space accorded to many who are little studied—even little known. Many of these fell into the editors' 'difficult to assign' tray, and frequently the three stalwarts have borne the burden themselves. In this category are such interesting characters as John Abernethy, a 'new light' Irish Dissenter, a campaigner for religious liberty, who was influenced by Hoadly, and whose moral philosophy, indebted to Locke and Clarke, was akin to that of Hutcheson; Manasseh Dowes, a barrister, who opposed universal toleration and, against Locke's view of a compact between governor and governed, held that a supreme power, antecedent to any government, derived from God, belongs to the people; Samuel Jones, the Dissenting tutor, whose pupils included Thomas Secker, Joseph Butler, Samuel Chandler and Andrew Gifford; Martin Madan, the erstwhile dissolute who became a Methodist preacher and then an advocate of polygamy; John Oldmixen, the poet and playwright who published *An Essay on Criticism*; Thomas Ruddiman, Latinist, antiquary, and defender of the divine right of kings and episcopacy against such 'wicked men' as George Buchanan and John Milton; George Stubbes the aesthetician, whose argument that beauty is exemplified by order, proportion and regularity, while deformity is exemplified by the opposite qualities, was characteristic of the period; and Benjamin Worster, a natural philosopher in the line of Francis Bacon, whose experimental interests ranged from optics to electricity.

Amongst a wide variety of miscellaneous information picked up along the way we recall Peter Annet's view that prostitution is a social convenience rather than a moral evil; Thomas Beddoes' accusation that the Bodleian Librarian was not buying enough foreign books and journals; A. Betson's caution (against Masquerades) that "Tis monstrous, in civil Life, as well as moral, to be in a perpetual Frolick' (p. 91b); Simon Browne's conclusion in 1723 that he had lost his soul and was now a brute animal with no mental life—whereupon he devoted himself to compiling dictionaries, spelling books and grammars, and to defending Christianity against the deists Woolston and Tindal; and Butler's regret that at Oxford he had to 'mis-spend so much time here in attending frivolous lectures and unintelligible disputations' (p. 162a). All this and more in the As and Bs alone . . .

It is always possible for reviewers of dictionaries to query the relative amounts of space accorded to particular individuals, and to raise an eyebrow at certain points: why, for example, are Thomas Amory and Richard Price designated High Arians when, unlike the Arian Micaijah Towgood, Price at least did not offer worship to Christ? It is a question of definition. Again, those in search of fuller biographical information might wish that references to the ODNB had been given where appropriate. But these are minor points. This *Dictionary* will serve its purpose for years to come. General readers will be informed, students in a number of fields will be provided with many useful leads, and specialists will find themselves happily enticed away from all manner of pressing duties. A notable achievement!

International Journal of Philosophical Studies 7 (2000) 266–69.

11

Joseph Butler

Terence Penelhum. *Butler*. London: Routledge, 1985. Pp. x + 221.

'One does not remove confusions, if they are really present, by banging the table.' It is perfectly understandable that one who has tarried long with a Bishop should on occasion exhort us to mend our ways; and it is not surprising that one who has immersed himself in the eighteenth century should habitually write with *Candour*. From the series within which this volume falls, (*The Arguments of the Philosophers*, ed. Ted Honderich), we have the right to expect close textual analysis, the careful sorting sifting of arguments, and assessments of the continuing worth of the positions under review. Our expectations are fully met here. For good measure, we have in addition a brief Introduction on 'Butler's life, personality and objectives,' which places the Bishop in the context of his time.

Since much has been written on Butler's ethics in our century, Professor Penelhum justifiably resolves to focus upon his philosophy of religion, which he ranks second only to that of Hume's. Not indeed that ethics are ever far from Butler's thought: his overriding objective is to stimulate his hearers and readers to the practice of virtue and religion. To this end he propounds arguments which, he hopes, the men of reason of his day will not be able reasonably to reject.

As is well known, Butler has the deists much in view (and we are rightly reminded that they were not all of one kind). Without denying the force of other approaches, he selects the argumentative weapons most likely to induce the deists to reach different conclusions. He will use premises to which he himself is not necessarily committed; he will 'bracket' doctrines in which he actually believes if they would only divert his opponents. As far as possible he adopts the presuppositions of the deists, and seeks to show that, beginning where they do, they ought to end somewhere else.

Professor Penelhum is well aware of the temptation to anachronism. Thus, any moderns who would say that to assume a theistic teleology is to assume the morality which Butler is commending, are reminded that in the eighteenth century, when atheism was rare, this assumption would not have been made. Again, we are not permitted to fall into the trap of thinking that Butler was aware of the challenges which Hume was yet to pose regarding apologetic method.

The book falls into two parts, of which the first is entitled, 'The advocate of virtue.' The opening chapter, 'Moral conduct and human nature,' makes plain Butler's view that conscience is our 'approving and disapproving faculty,' and that to obey its dictates is to act in accordance with our real nature; to act otherwise is to violate that nature. The dictates of conscience are 'by Nature a rule to us'; they are also divine commands. In the next chapter, 'The reality of benevolence,' Butler is shown to be victorious over Hobbes' selfish analyses of charity and compassion, and as making a strong, though not an absolutely watertight case against egoism and hedonism. Chapter three, on 'The case for virtues,' is concerned with Butler's view that virtue consists in obeying conscience. Butler believes that we are able to do this, and seeks to persuade the lethargic actually to do it. Professor Penelhum regards the judgement of naturalness or otherwise as a supplementary consideration which may assist in persuading the actor: he does not accept Sturgeon's Full Naturalistic Thesis concerning Butler, to the effect that such a judgement is a necessary component of all conscientious judgements, for this would violate Butler's principle of the supremacy of conscience. No doubt in the last resort the natural is what is right, and the unnatural is what is wrong; but conscience advises us here, albeit not infallibly. Butler will endorse the view that happiness follows the practice of virtue as a clinching argument *vis à vis* those who may be impressed by the compatible account of human motives, but he is not one to ground ethics in psychology. He is, however, far too confident that we all know what virtue requires. Professor Penelhum considers that any such confidence is 'eroded by the sheer variety of moral opinion in our present society.'

Part Two, 'The apologist,' opens with a discussion of 'The nature of Butler's apologetic.' Butler's minimal position, which is advocated throughout, is that 'in the first place, the case against Christianity is much weaker than its critics in his day maintained, and the evidence for it is significantly better; and that, in the second place, it is frivolous and imprudent not to give the most serious consideration to assenting to it in the light of these facts.' His metaphysical and epistemological model 'is of a God whose laws, both within and beyond observed nature, are through and through intelligible, but only partially known *to us*.' We gain insights into God's plan for us by analogy—a term which Butler does little to elucidate. The form of analogy which Butler employs is, however, supplemented by the deistic assumption of God's authorship of nature. Professor Penelhum rightly sees that any continuing value in Butler's arguments will appear only after that assumption, which cannot nowadays be made, is set aside. He therefore discusses Butler's arguments both as over against the deists, and from the standpoint of their worth as more general apologetic devices.

In his chapter on 'Identity and human life,' our author finds that as they stand, Butler's arguments establish the possibility, though not the probability of some form of life after death. They do suggest, however, a logically possible way of supposing an (and to that extent a non-Butlerian) afterlife: the case turns upon the realization that the subject of consciousness need be neither simple nor immaterial. Butler presupposes his own version of the future life when considering the case for natural religion, to which the chapter on 'Divine government and human probation' is devoted. If Butler does not make out his case that by attending to observable features of the world we may conclude that God's pedagogical governance is likely, he does illustrate the more successful apologetic procedure 'of showing how the revelation he is defending can interpret salient features of human experience.' However, what one may argue in face of deists, namely, that we are here under probation and that rewards and punishments will appropriately be distributed hereafter, will cut no ice with modern sceptics who do not make the deistic assumption of a divine moral order. Nevertheless, a probationary view of our condition may still make some appeal if it is proposed defensively: 'Should we not expect that the world would be in the ambiguous state it is if a probationary view of human nature were true?' (My formulation of the question).

The chapter on 'Revelation and miracle' reviews Butler's case for revealed religion. He discusses miracles, not as the basis of a system of religion (which Hume later said they could not be), but by way of showing that those who have accepted part of the Christian scheme on philosophical grounds 'have no good reason to deny that the miracle-stories of Christianity support the remainder of that system.' So to the concluding chapter, 'The ignorance of man.' Can a person who makes no presuppositions about God properly be persuaded by Butler? Professor Penelhum offers his reasons for thinking that despite defects of argumentation, Butler shows that the Christian revelation as a whole is more likely to be true than its deistic alternatives, and considers that modern scepticism may still be challenged by Butler's appeal to prudence. He also reminds us that to act upon the claims of Christianity requires that we believe those claims, for our calling is to do God's will as God's will, and that entails believing that God has dealings with us in such a way that the commands of conscience are the commands of God.

Professor Penelhum scatters many intriguing ideas in passing. Thus, for example, when Butler offers as a ground for refusing to equate benevolence and virtue the fact that if they were identical we would be morally indifferent concerning the distribution of goods among people, whereas, he says, we judge it morally better that the deserving (friends, benefactors) should have priority, Penelhum remarks in parenthesis that this collides with the New Testament command to love (cf. Matt. 20:1–16). Now Butler is not deceitful, and he knows the gospels. Is he here simply using an argumentative ploy to which he is not necessarily committed (we have been warned that he does sometimes do that); or is this an illustration of the power of the eighteenth-century intellectual climate, with its passion for the ordered, the duly proportioned and the equitable, over the practical urgings of the gospel which Butler supremely wishes his readers to heed, and which he with his unfailing generosity to unfortunates actually followed?

Again, Butler would take it for granted that we would not be given the command to love if we could not obey it; and Professor Penelhum refers to some modern theologians who contend that apart from special divine grace we cannot obey the command. He supposes that Butler would regard such theologians as sacrificing the evidence of their eyes to a theological system, and as having to construe examples of selfless love after the fashion of a psychological egoist. This prompts us to speculate upon other avenues which may be open to theologians. They may, for example, agree with Butler (and with Paul) that our problem is frequently not that we are unclear as to what we ought to do, but that we lack the strength or will to do it. They may then invoke the concept of common, or restraining (as distinct from saving), grace: that favour of God towards all, which accounts for the good which 'natural man' actually does, and which prevents the worst excesses to which he might otherwise go. Which only bears out what Professor Penelhum says in another connection, that Christianity is *resourceful* (even if its theologians sometimes have recourse to theories which appear redundant to those who seek the simplest and most 'natural' explanations).

This admirable book is furnished with a bibliography and an index; and is only slightly marred by proof-reading slips on pp. 123 and 184. Students of Butler (may their tribe increase—and it should, now) will be indebted to Terence Penelhum for years to come; and those who are inclined contemptuously to dismiss 'old-fashioned apologetics' will need to show with which arguments they will counter the careful case here presented. Certainly it will not suffice to bang the table—least of all now that so many confusions have been removed.

Philosophical Studies 33 (1991–2) 398–401.

12

Rational Dissent

Knud Haakonssen, ed. *Enlightenment and Religion. Rational Dissent in Eighteenth-century Britain.* Cambridge: CUP, 1996. Pp. xii + 348.

In recent years a considerable amount of scholarly effort has been devoted to qualifying Peter Gay's conclusion of thirty years ago that the Enlightenment, anti-Christian and anti-Church, marked the transition from Christendom to irreligion and atheism. A good deal of this work has been done and encouraged by the editor of this volume. On the evidence now before us, neither he nor his chosen contributors have succumbed to the idle life which, said Priestley. 'is the great inlet to the most destructive vices.' On the contrary, these are thoroughly researched papers, all of which increase our knowledge of the British Enlightenment, and some of which propose revised understandings of it. The authors share the conviction (*pace* Gay) that in different national contexts the Enlightenment takes on different hues. They seek to expound the views and elucidate the attitudes of that sub-set of English Dissent, the Rational Dissenters who, unlike some of their continental contemporaries, were by no means irreligious, anti-Church or hostile to Christianity, and who, as R.K. Webb shows in the second of his two papers, inherited and maintained a long and strong tradition of piety.

In his other paper Webb sets the book's scene by recounting the story of Dissent from the first Elizabethan era to the emergence of those who repudiated (at least) Calvinism, upheld the dignity of humanity, and were suspicious of enthusiasm. These English

Dissenters were influenced not only by Scottish Moderates—as Martin Fitzpatrick demonstrates in his detailed and perceptive discussion of the shared and contrasting views of the friends James Wodrow, the Moderate of Ayrshire, and Samuel Kenrick, the Unitarian of Bewdley—but also by the Irish Dissenters who, as M.A. Stewart shows in an admirable discussion of matters too frequently overlooked, were sufficiently motivated by civil disabilities to seek the expansive theological views then being purveyed at Glasgow University: they did not, as has sometimes been assumed, first learn of liberty in Glasgow and then return with the message to Ireland.

The burden of David Wykes' paper is that those who conducted the Dissenting academies did not set out to spawn Rational Dissenters, though they did foster a climate of free discussion which permitted those so inclined to move in that direction. The point is well made, though perhaps Dr. Wykes is over-zealous in wishing to revise the conclusion of some scholars (which he presents baldly) that 'Presbyterian congregations were converted from orthodox Calvinism by their ministers, who having adopted heterodox opinions at the academies, descended upon their unsuspecting congregations and proceeded to carry them into Unitarianism' (p. 99), and that this happened because influential trustees assumed the power of appointing ministers to vacant Presbyterian pastorates. There is, however, firm evidence that this did happen on occasion. On the other hand, some heterodox ministers maintained united, theologically diverse congregations by keeping silent on disputed points; while many church members, far from being 'carried over into Unitarianism,' seceded on trinitarian and/or church polity grounds. All of this can be granted without denying Dr. Wykes' positive point, namely, that 'a significant part of the membership of the leading Presbyterian congregations during the eighteenth century was willing to support ministers who had departed from orthodox Calvinism' (pp. 99–100). I am pleased to note that Alan Sanders independently endorses my view that church polity considerations played a large part in conserving Congregational orthodoxy (pp. 246–47).

John Seed argues that such Rational Dissenters as Price, Priestley, Kippis and Towers were far more than 'a noisy metropolitan clique of intellectuals of little influence on, or connection to, the wider culture' (p. 142); while in the context of illuminating reflections upon 'Law. Lawyers and Rational Dissent,' Wilfrid Prest discusses Dissenting lawyers and Priestley's writings on law and legal institutions. A.M.C. Waterman writes on 'The Nexus Between Theology and Political Doctrine'; John Gascoigne on 'Anglican Latitudinarianism, Rational Dissent and Political Radicalism'; Alan Sanders on 'The State as Highwayman: From Candour to Rights'; Alan Tapper on 'Priestley on Politics, Progress and Moral Theology'; and Iain McCalman on 'New Jerusalems: Prophecy, Dissent and Radical Culture in England. 1786–1830.'

Among many issues raised are marriage (the Irishman John MacBride argued that it is irrational to promise to remain faithful 'till death do [us] part,' since we cannot predict whether our spouse will 'turn Papist. and fly to a monastery or nunnery' (pp. 58–59); patronage; prudentialism; candour; millenarianism; American Independence and the French Revolution. Benjamin Hoadly, William Leechman, William Enfield and Harriet Martineau are among many of whom vignettes are provided. A good deal of evidence is adduced to show that the English Enlightened Dissenters had more in common with Enlightened members of the clerical establishment than with the Enlightenment radicals of the continent; and we are reminded that many of the Enlightened Dissenters did not permit a strong disjunction between reason and inspiration *vis à vis* biblical interpretation. That Rational Dissenters could unite in extolling reason and repudiating the establishment and Calvinism, whilst at the same time launching forth from significantly different philosophical starting-points (in this case Neoplatonist and materialist/associationist) is well brought out with reference to Price and Priestley.

It remains only to add that the editor's Introduction exposes the running theme of the collection and relates the ensuing papers to it in a skilful way. Intellectual historians whose view of the Enlightenment remains monochrome; church historians whose minds fly too quickly to Wesley and Whitefield when eighteenth-century religion is under discussion; social historians who too readily squeeze all Dissenters under over-elastic socio-political-economic rubrics; and philosophers whose eighteenth-century courses are exclusively concerned with Berkeley, Hume and (possibly) Reid, will have their horizons broadened and their consciences pricked by this admirable volume.

At their best the Rational Dissenters knew, in Stewart's words, that 'To be convinced and wrong is excusable; to profess anything without conviction is not' (p. 63). It is an intriguing epitaph—and a good discussion topic for an examination paper.

International Journal of Philosophical Studies 5 (1997) 142–43.

13

Richard Price

D. O. Thomas. *The Honest Mind. The Thought and Work of Richard Price.* Oxford: Clarendon Press, 1977. Pp xvi + 366.

How fitting that this stimulating work on a Welshman who became a founder-member of the Unitarian Society (1791) should emanate from Aberystwyth in the county of Cardiganshire, in the south of which Welsh Unitarianism made its greatest impact. Richard Price (1723–91) emerges from Dr. Thomas's remarkably comprehensive account as a distinguished philosopher, and as so much more besides. Indeed Price, extolled by his friend Priestley for his 'real candour' (p. 342) was a polymath; and the consequent demands upon the candid author—not to mention the candid reviewer—are considerable. Happily for both, Price's many spheres of interest and activity followed one another in relatively orderly sequence—he was not battling on all fronts at once. Today we are most likely to think of Price as a moral philosopher, or as the one whose political ideas Burke set out to demolish. In his own day he crusaded for human rights; he demanded toleration and freedom of worship; he was a financial expert; and he supported in turn the American colonists and the French revolutionaries.

Dr. Thomas undertakes to lay bare the principles which guided Price in all his varied enterprises and, on the basis of his rounded view, he is able on occasion to advocate the revision of received opinion. Thus he shows that Price was not concerned only to defend rationalist ethics against such empiricists as Hume and Hutcheson, but that he was no less anxious to counter those who adopted a legislative or voluntarist stance in ethics. Again, he shows how Price's stand for liberality in politics and religion is wedded to a complex of Puritan values and ideals, and this to a degree not always appreciated.

Thomas begins with an account of Price's family and upbringing, noting the contrast between his liberal views and the 'gloomy' opinions of his Calvinist father, Rice Price (p. 4). Price acquired his intellectual foundations from Locke, Clarke and Butler; he became, and remained, an Arian. Thomas tells us that 'he believed that salvation depends upon an unremitting struggle to obey the moral law' (p. 6); if *that* kind of relentless 'Pelagianism' does not make for real gloom your reviewer does not know what does. After training for the ministry Price served the Presbyterian cause at Newington Green, and later at Hackney where he delivered his last sermon on 20 February 1791. He died on 19 April, and was buried at Bunhill Fields on 26 April (p. 340).[2]

The preliminaries over, Dr. Thomas turns to the theologico-metaphysical framework of Price's thought. He outlines Price's position on the existence of God in relation to the problem of evil, reminding us of Price's conviction that because of its rectitude the moral law is binding even upon God; he elucidates Price on providence, discusses his Arianism, and shows that whilst denying the doctrines of original sin, total depravity, absolute predestination, particular redemption, and justification by faith, Price did not go to the Socinian extent of holding that Christ saves only by precept and example. Rather 'Price holds that it is the Cross that makes pardon available to those who repent' (p. 37). Thomas doubts whether Price successfully harmonizes his theology and his moral philosophy, and he puts the crucial point well: 'If men can determine the content of the moral law solely by the exercise of reason, if the individual is always free to choose to do what he believes to be his duty, if conscientiousness is of supreme moral worth, and if God always rewards the virtuous, it would seem as though the Christian elements of revelation, grace, and the interposition of the Saviour are not essential to the good life' (pp. 38–39).

Next, Dr. Thomas skilfully interprets Price's defence of the objectivity of the moral judgement against Hume and Hutcheson, but does not find him completely victorious. Price shows how the belief in this objectivity 'is implicit in the opinions which we hold

---

2. Dr. Thomas quotes from Priestley's *A Discourse on the Death of Dr. Price*, and mentions other tributes paid to him. I like that of Mrs. Barbauld, to whom Price was 'a man on whom blessings and eulogiums are ready to burst from all honest tongues.' See Robert Spears, *Record of Unitarian Worthies*, London, 1876, 173. In 1841 a tablet to Price was placed in Stoke Newington Unitarian Church. The text of the inscription is quoted by R. V. Holt, *The Unitarian Contribution to Social Progress*, London: Lindsey Press, 1952, 77.

Part One: Philosophy

about moral judgement [but] he does not succeed in showing . . . that this belief is well grounded' (p. 61). Price holds that by intuition we know what the moral law requires of us, and the honest man is he who follows his judgement notwithstanding his liability to error (p. 67). Chapter 4 carries this thought further and makes clear how much of the Puritan ethic remained with Price after he had jettisoned so many of its undergirding doctrines. Against those who, like Hutcheson, grounded virtue exclusively in benevolence, Price argued that virtue is of intrinsic rectitude (p. 72), though he did grant that the ways of applying moral principles will vary in accordance with custom, education and example.

On the question of conscience, Price is more aware of its fallibility than was Butler (p. 87). He distinguished between abstract and practical virtue, yet held the two in balance by maintaining that we are duty bound practically to accomplish what our convinced conscience informs us is fitting to be done; all of which entails our determining as accurately as possible the nature of our abstract duties. We must not rely uncritically upon received opinion, still less yield to prejudice; nor must be mistake unworthy self interest for that reasonable and calm self-love which is our duty (p. 101). A virtuous action proceeds from that reflection whose inspiration is genuine regard for rectitude (p. 105). Here again Thomas suggests that Price is not entirely consistent, for the place he accords to our proper inspiration by the thought of divine rewards of virtue seems to admit prudence as well as rectitude (p. 108).

Having considered what Price thinks it right for us to do, Thomas now comes to those things which we have a right to do. He shows how Price's conviction that all our energies are to be devoted to the service of God influenced his position on freedom of worship and political liberty. For Price 'liberty itself has an intrinsic value quite independently of the needs of the dutiful agent' (p. 120). The individual's liberty is not, however, absolute. The State has duties too, notably those of protecting the weak and preventing infringements of liberty; but the magistrate may not control our spiritual or cultural welfare (p. 125).

In a chapter entitled 'New Vocations' we learn of Price's publishing the papers of the late Thomas Bayes (minister of religion and FRS) on probability theory; and of the way in which Price was thereby inspired to write *inter alia* on demography and reversionary payments. Meanwhile America was seething and Price, who stood with Benjamin Franklin in support of the colonists, increasingly turned his mind to the concept of liberty as bearing upon both politics and worship. These themes are treated in detail by Thomas, particular attention properly being paid to the friendly exchanges between Price and Priestley on the freedom-necessity problem: Price denied what Priestley maintained, namely, that motives are causes of action (p. 161). It does not follow, thinks Thomas, that Price was a determinist; on the contrary, and against some interpreters, he finds the weight of evidence on the other side, notwithstanding the fact that Price 'sometimes appears to hold a form of psychological determinism' (p. 162).

Price went further than Locke in seeking religious liberty for all;[3] and he also advocated the disentanglement of Church and state. We may surmise that his work behind

---

3. Thomas quotes from a paper Price addressed to Chatham on 13 May 1772 (177). It is interesting to compare the sentiments here expressed with those of the General (i.e. Arminian) Baptist, Thomas Helwys, the first advocate of universal religious liberty on Engish soil. See his *The Mistery of Iniquity*, 1612, 69. Alike

the scenes indirectly fuelled Chatham's outburst in the Lords against the Archbishop of York's attack on Dissenters: 'we have no system: we have a Calvinist Creed, a Popish liturgy, and an Arminian clergy' (p. 179). Price's testimony against confessional tests was that 'in general they bind only honest men' (p. 185). On the question of political rights, Price maintained that apart from these men have no safeguard for their natural rights: to life, and to the security of person, property and reputation (p. 192). He thus advocated the extension of the franchise and the equal representation in Parliament of the several parts of the land (p. 204). Ideas on human rights and dignity underlay Price's activities in the field of private and social insurance, to which chapter 11 is interestingly devoted. Financial matters occupy chapter 12 too, and here we see Price, as a self-appointed but respected adviser to Pitt and others, defending his not entirely practicable objective of redeeming the national debt.

There follows a chapter on Price's involvement with the Americans, whose independence he supported, though with the proviso that the liberty which American leaders sought ought to be extended by them to the negroes (p. 268). Price rejoiced in the American victory—not least because of the failure of so many of his causes nearer to home (p. 283). Undeterred, he threw his lot in with the movement for parliamentary reform which emerged in 1779 (p. 284), though as his advice to Irish reformers demonstrated, 'he did not hold an absolutist conception of natural rights' (p. 292). By no means a republican (pp. 305, 306), Price welcomed the moves in France towards government by the people, and saw events surrounding the coming of William of Orange, American Independence and French Revolution as inspired by common motives. None of which pleased Burke, to whose 'assassination' of Price Thomas devotes his final chapter. Our author's rescue of Price from the unbecoming role in which Burke had cast him is welcome. It seems to me that Price's entire life and work is the answer to Burke's accusation that Price sat lightly to practical and historical experience (p. 326).

Burke did not see Price whole. Dr. Thomas does, and therein lies the value of his book. Price cannot be left to those philosophers who treat history with disdain on the ground that they are philosophers! Undeniably the great strength of this book lies in the perceptive and balanced philosophical analyses it contains, and this is as it should be; but the rest is a necessary and fascinating bonus. It is gratitude for what Thomas has done, together with a desire to stimulate further thought on Price, which prompts me now to raise some questions, to ask for more, and to share one or two things I have discovered.

First, two philosophical requests. In view of the interest in miracle in recent philosophy of religion and biblical theology, more discussion of Price's dissertation on that subject would have been welcome—especially since Hume, so widely famed for having demolished the claim that miracles have evidential value, provisionally thought that Price's position was 'new and plausible and ingenious, and perhaps solid.' Similarly, I would have

---

in breadth of tolerance, Price positively asserts the right of freedom to worship; Helwys staunchly denied the right of the monarch to prevent it. For this Helwys was imprisoned in Newgate on his return from exile in Holland, where his book was written. The standard work on toleration is W. K. Jordan, *The Development of Religious Toleration in England*, 4 vols., London: Allen & Unwin, 1932–40.

welcomed more than the tantalizingly brief footnote on p. 52 concerning the extent to which Price was a harbinger of Kant in moral philosophy.

Now to history. In a book whose subtitle refers to the 'work' of Price one would expect to read rather more about his work among his congregations. Was he a good minister? Was his preaching well received? Did the churches grow under his ministry? Is much known in this area? Are the Newington Green MSS (listed in the bibliography) silent? I have found that one of Dr. Thomas's sources does mention the 'large and delighted audiences' to which Price preached;[4] and that another writer notes that 'he was easily accessible, and most kind to the humblest, who never sought his aid in vain.'[5] I was rather surprised that Price's association with Lindsey and Priestley in the provision of the first avowedly Unitarian meeting house (opened in Essex Street, London on 17 April 1774) is not mentioned; and I should have welcomed something on Price's encouragement of the moves towards the formation of the Unitarian Society of which he was a founder member. It will be recalled that until 21 July 1813 those who professed unitarianism in England were liable to lose their citizenship, and that in Scotland such profession was a capital crime; yet Price 'sent in his guinea, saying that he could not allow a Unitarian Society to exist without his name.'[6] Again, the much appreciated assistance which Price gave to John Howard the prison reformer is worthy of mention. So to points of detail:

Dr. Thomas informs us (p. x) that the first draft of his book was 'much longer.' This may explain the compressed style of certain portions of the history. Even so, readers unfamiliar with lesser-known figures in dissenting history may wonder, for example, who the thrice-mentioned Caleb Rotheram was. Readers with a slight, possibly rusting, knowledge of dissenting history may wonder which Caleb Rotheram he was. The answer is that both Caleb Rotherams, father and son, ministered at Kendal in what is now the Unitarian Church; that the father conducted a Dissenting Academy; and that it is the son to whom Thomas refers.[7] We should hardly dare to make this small point did Thomas himself not pursue other equally small points. Thus he provides (p. 143 n.) evidence to support DNB's correction of the statement of Price's biographer, his nephew William Morgan, to the effect that Price received his DD from Glasgow. In fact he was so honoured by Marischal College, Aberdeen. It would seem, however, that in turn DNB requires correction, since according to Thomas's information the degree was conferred in 1769, not 1767.

In a work of this kind a measure of intelligent guesswork is inevitable and legitimate. Thus Thomas follows Ogborn (p. 128) in surmising that Price may have become acquainted with Thomas Bayes *via* John Eames, by whom both men had been tutored, albeit at different times, at Moorfields Academy. It is not impossible, I suggest, that Price would hear of Bayes from his uncle Samuel Price, Isaac Watts's co-pastor. For Watts had connections with the Tunbridge Wells Dissenters, to whom Bayes came as minister in

---

4. Walter D. Jeremy, *The Presbyterian Fund and Dr. Daniel Williams's Trust: with Biographical Notes on the Trustees, etc.*, London: Williams & Norgate, 1885, 151.

5. R. Spears, *Record of Unitarian Worthies*, 174.

6. Alexander Gordon, *Heads of English Unitarian History*, London: Green, 1895, 49, 45.

7. See Further Francis Nicholson and Ernest Axon, *The Older Nonconformity in Kendal*, Kendal: Titus Wilson, 1915, chapters 15, 16, 18, 39.

1731: he is said to have preached in a hired ballroom there in 1712, and he certainly preached there in 1729. My source further reports the Rev. Mr Onely of Speldhurst as saying of Bayes that although he was 'the best Greek scholar he had ever met with, he was not a popular preacher, nor evangelical in his doctrine.'[8] This last fact would not commend him to Samuel Price, though it would give him something in common with Richard, as Thomas would agree (p. 10).

Finally to a matter of theological balance. Dr. Thomas appears to see no need to question the popular mythology surrounding Calvin and Calvinism. Thus, he does not challenge Price's view that Calvin's teaching leads ultimately to an understanding of moral judgement as arbitrary (p. viii, cf. 6). But Calvinists are not necessarily necessitarians.[9] Again, when commenting on the 'remarkable characteristic' of many English Dissenters that they 'did not believe that the pursuit of knowledge is detrimental to religion; on the contrary, they thought that the exercise of reason is a duty owed to the Deity' (pp. 12–13), Thomas omits to mention that those thus praised were echoing Calvin himself.

'The honest mind' is a phrase which aptly epitomises Richard Price. But it is not the only thing. There is also the warm heart. With the latter Price's slightly older contemporary compatriots Daniel Rowland (1713–90) and Howel Harris (1714–73) had much more to do. (And, be it noted, they, like Whitefield, were Calvinists.) As Thomas points out (p. 2) Price entered the Academy of Vavasour Griffiths. This Academy had been established in Carmarthen, and Griffths agreed to assume responsibility for it on condition that it moved away from that liberal centre. Thus it came to Llwynllwyd near Hay in 1735, and by 1738 it was in Talgarth, where Price enrolled as a student Talgarth, whose Vicar, Pryce Davies, had, on 30 March 1735, preached a sermon which marked the first step towards Howel Harris's conversion.[10] We may therefore say that the little town of Talgarth was a locus of a major divide in nonconformity: that between head and heart. Richard Price gave his countrymen works of intellect which relatively few of them could appreciate; Harris and the evangelicals gave the Welsh masses something to sing about—and, as everybody knows, they have not yet ceased to sing.

Philosophical Studies 26 (1979) 305–10.

---

8. See Thomas Timpson, *Church History of Kent . . . comprising . . . IV Records of the Independent Churches in Kent*, London: 1859, 464.

9. For a classic discussion of the point see William Cunningham, *The Reformers and the Theology of the Reformation*, (1862), London: The Banner of Truth Trust, 1967, 471–524.

10. See G. F. Nuttall, *Howel Harris, 1714–1773: The Last Enthusiast*, Cardiff: University of Wales Press, 1965, 7, 45; W. T. Pennar Davies, 'Episodes in the history of Brecknockshire Dissent,' *Brycheiniog* 3, 1957, 11–65.

Part One: Philosophy

14

Price's Correspondence

D. O. Thomas and W. Bernard Peach, eds. *The Correspondence of Richard Price. Volume I: July 1748-March 1778*. Durham, NC: Duke University Press, and Cardiff: University of Wales Press, 1983. Pp. xxix + 294.

Richard Price would surely have applauded the sentiments which prompted two leading students of his work to combine forces on discovering that they were both engaged in collecting and editing his correspondence. That one scholar is from his native Wales and the other from the erstwhile 'colonies,' whose independence he advocated, would have pleased him even more. For the abiding impression which remains after studying the correspondence is of a series of co-operative networks which span academic disciplines, barriers of social class (the majority of the episcopal bench notwithstanding), and the Atlantic itself. This co-operation is at many levels: from the gathering of testimonies to secure a friend's honorary DD or admission to the Royal Society, to general championship in moral causes and specific assistance in academic research. A focal point of co-operation is the ubiquitous Club of Honest Whigs and, as the footnotes make clear, the part played by such more liberal Dissenting academies as Warrington, Kendal and Taunton in fostering rational enquiries and nurturing broad sympathies cannot be underestimated.

The letters and notes together introduce us to a galaxy of persons and issues, and bear witness to Price's polymathic range. Thus he writes to John Caton first on probability theory, later on actuarial matters pertaining to insurance; and in an appendix Price's correspondence with John Edwards, actuary of the Society for Equitable Assurances, is noted and extracted. Demography was among the themes on which Price wrote to Benjamin Franklin. On another occasion he was able to refer Franklin, then in London, to 'eleven preachers of Christianity on the rational plan,' though he had ruefully to add, 'But the Congregations of many of them are very thin, partly perhaps for this very reason.'

There are examples of the advice Price gave the Earl of Shelburne on financial matters, and a series of letters to the Earl of Chatham—a supporter of attempts in Parliament (which proved abortive) to remove the remaining legal disabilities suffered by Dissenters. For his part, Price consistently supported the American rebels, and the letters pertaining to the War of Independence are of considerable historical importance. As early as 1773 he informed Henry Marchant that 'I am in a country that is, I am afraid, declining . . . May our *American* brethren guard us against the evils [i.e. the denial of civil and religious liberty] which threaten us with ruin . . . *America* is the country to which most of the friends of liberty in this country are now looking; and it may be in some future period the country to which they will be flying.' Two years later John Winthrop of Harvard declared that 'All America is greatly indebted to you for . . . your exertions on their behalf.'

Joseph Priestley maintained regular contact with Price from their first meeting in 1766, their disagreement over the doctrine of necessity notwithstanding: 'I greatly differ from him,' wrote Price to William Adams, 'and I think he has got on very dangerous ground.' Priestley's experiments with air, involving rotten vegetables and decomposing mice, almost attain the status of a saga; and the wicked hope raised by Priestley on 12 October 1771: 'If I were to tell you how much time I have spent on this subject you would hardly believe me. I believe I must desist for the present'—is dashed seven days later. David Hume writes a gracious letter in response to Price's apology for his intemperate treatment of Hume's view of miracles; grants that Price puts the matter in a 'new and plausible and ingenious, and perhaps solid' light; and thanks him for not resorting to the 'illiberal language' of the Bishop of Gloucester (William Warburton). In the second of two letters Thomas Reid challenges the axiom which, he believes, derives from Descartes and is expounded by Hume, that 'whatever we can distinctly conceive is possible'; and with reference to Priestley's criticisms of his own *Inquiry*, Reid writes, 'I confess that in his late examinations he seems to me very lame as a Metaphysician as well as in some other Qualities of more Estimation.' If only Priestley had 'taken a Lesson of Meekness, good Manners and Candour' from 'Dr. Hartley his Paragon.'

Price himself writes lucidly and concisely to Miss Ashurst on divine providence; and to Miss A. Burrows in favour of the annihilation of the wicked at death, as against their eternal punishment. On the latter point Charles Chauncy, who favoured 'ultimate restoration' took issue with him. For what he called Jonathan Edwards' 'Doctrine of Fatalism' Chauncy had no room at all: 'I believe you never saw the Supreme Being . . . so explicitly and directly made the author and planner of moral evil.'

Where the human condition is concerned Price is a realist: 'God remembers we are dust: perfection is above human capacity, and cannot be the condition of our acceptance.' There is a prudential cast to some of Price's observations too. Following a period of sickness he writes to Miss Ashurst, 'What I have felt in myself, though little compared with the experience of others, has convinced me of the vanity of the world, of the power God has over us by the various capacities of misery he has given us, and consequently of the great importance of being on good terms with him . . .' Again, writing to Shelburne concerning the Americans—a subject on which the two men differed—Price says, 'We have indeed no way left of making them useful to us, but by making ourselves as useful to them as possible . . .'

Among the minor delights of such a collection as this is that one occasionally sees old friends in a new light. Thus for the reviewer John Howard will no longer be simply the prison reformer. He is also the man who diligently prodded Vesuvius with a thermometer four years after the eruption of 1766, and recorded his findings in *Philosophical Transactions* (1771).

The editorial notes are more than ordinarily full, and are of great assistance. It is not, however, clear why some relatively minor persons are indexed while others are not. A further indexing puzzle surrounds the name 'Rotheram.' According to the index Caleb

Part One: Philosophy

Rotheram (1694–1752) is mentioned on pp. 159 and 169. In fact a Caleb Rotheram appears on the latter and not the former; and also on pp. 187, 240 and 276. In every case the person referred to can only be Caleb Rotheram the Younger (1738–96). For good measure, an unindexed Dr. Rotheram is mentioned on p. 270, but this is John Rotheram (1725–89) the Anglican.

On 23 November 1771 Priestley wrote to Price, 'I have just received the printed sheets of my history, and the view of the margin makes me regret exceedingly, that the work could not have the benefit of your revisal before it was printed.' Drs Thomas and Peach can have no such regrets concerning this excellently-produced book. Philosophers, historians, and historians of thought and of science will all find things of interest here. We congratulate the editors and greatly look forward to the promised volumes II and III.

Philosophical Studies 31 (1986-7) 431–35

D. O. Thomas, ed. *The Correspondence of Richard Price. Volume 11: March 1778-February 1786*. Durham, NC: Duke University Press, and Cardiff: University of Wales Press, 1991. Pp. xxv + 348.

W. Bernard Peach, ed. *The Correspomdence of Richard Price. Volume III: March / 786-February 1791*. Durham, NC: Duke University Press, and Cardiff: University of Wales Press, 1994. Pp. xxxi + 382.

In this journal's predecessor (*Philosophical Studies*, 31 (1986–87) 432–35) I cordially welcomed the first volume of Price's *Correspondence* which covered the period from July 1748 to March 1778. With the two volumes now to hand the editors complete their major undertaking, and they and the publishers are warmly to be congratulated on the result.

A man of varied interests, Price was in touch with a correspondingly wide range of intellectuals and others. For this reason not only philosophers, but political theorists, theologians, and historians of ideas, of America and of France will find much of interest in these volumes. There are letters to and from Joseph Priestley, Benjamin Franklin, the Earl of Shelburne, Lord Monboddo, Thomas Jefferson, William Pitt, Benjamin Rush, the Marquis of Lansdowne, Theophilus Lindsey and the Duc de la Rochefoucauld, to name but a few. Letters from John Howard to Price are included, as are Price's to Ezra Stiles, the Comte de Mirabeau and others. Subjects range from the colonies and slavery to philosophical necessity; from the public debt and the financial arrangements of the Equitable Assurance Society to the French Revolution.

The letters reveal much of Price the man. As he wrote to his sparring partner Priestley, it was ever his conviction that 'in the end, the interest of truth will he promoted by a free and open discussion of speculative points' (2 p. 23); and to William Adams he explained that he and Priestley differed 'much in Metaphysics and Divinity, but with perfect respect for one another' (2 p. 327). Immersed in public affairs as he was, he could nevertheless confide, 'When I am in my study and among my books, and have nothing to encumber me I am happy' (2 p. 35). His integrity emerges in a comment to Lord Monboddo on the possibility that the soul is extended: 'The truth is, that I am much at a loss how to frame my Ideas on this subject' (2 p. 66). He nicely balances understatement and deference (note the words 'little' and 'entirely') when he informs the Earl of Shelburne that 'Some of the

Dissenting ministers are a little alarmed by your Lordship's recommending Sunday as a proper day for learning the use of arms. I cannot say I entirely agree with them' (2 p. 129). He pulls no punches with Benjamin Rush concerning Pennsylvania's legislature: 'That is a miserable legislature which relies much on the use of tests; for in general they bind only honest men' (2 p. 294). 'I derive my chief comfort from believing Christianity,' he told the Marquis of Lansdowne: 'Those who reject it lose a fund of unspeakable satisfaction; but they will not in my opinion be sufferers hereafter if they are honest enquirers and practice virtue' (3 p. 106). Never one to fawn, Price was disappointed when Kippis and three other Dissenters went, in 1789, to Windsor to present addresses to the King and Queen: 'I am ignorant what sort of addresses they are; but such simple and manly addresses as I should have been for would not have suited the general disposition which now prevails to an abject and most disgusting adulation and therefore, I am glad that I have never chosen on this occasion to meet my brethren' (3 p. 210). In a number of letters Price expresses concern at his wife's deteriorating health, and to William Adams he writes on 10 December 1786: 'The loss of the companion of my life to whom I owed a great part of its happiness has lately given a dreadful shock to my spirits' (3 p. 99).

Price was adept at summing up others. Of Isaac Newton he declares, 'certainly Sir Isaac was no Atheist, though by following too much the Mechanical Philosophy of Des Cartes, he has laid down Principles which have a tendency that way' (2 p. 94). More effusively: 'General Washington's name must always shine among the first, in the annals of the world' (2 p. 196). As for Bishop Hoadly, 'His name as a Divine stands very high; but among the writers on civil and religious liberty it stands next to the names of Sidney and Lock and Milton' (2 p. 212). Price did not think so highly of some of his fellow Dissenters: Isaac Watts's 'first Catechism is not short and simple enough, and has expressions in it not well adapted to the conceptions of a child and which have a tendency to give very improper Ideas of the Deity. The second Catechism is still more liable to these objections, and at the same time full of a very absurd system of Divinity' (2 p. 249).

These last remarks may serve to remind any who think of Price as primarily a moral philosopher or a political theorist that he was throughout his working life a Dissenting minister. Possibly his least successful venture, conducted in tandem with his pastorate, was as tutor at New College, Hackney (3 pp. 47, 80, 99, 109, 143, 157, 188). Not surprisingly, much of the prevailing religious atmosphere is detectable in his letters. He laments the decline of the Dissenting interest (2 p. 199); he is relieved that an Anabaptist preacher of Calne 'is zealous without being a methodist' (2 p. 229); he endorses the right of the Baptists not 'to contribute towards supporting a religious worship from which they dissent' (2 p. 274); and he is persuaded that 'church-controversies have driven many into Deism; nor indeed do I think there is a more contemptible character than that of a furious polemic Divine who, not satisfy'd with argument, calls for the aid of the State and consigns heretics to damnation' (3 p. 105). He is sure that bigotry 'generally defeats its own end by promoting discussion and spreading liberal and just principles' (3 p. 270). Interestingly, concerning the suggestion that he publish some of his sermons, Price is more apprehensive of attacks from Socinians (he himself being an Arian) than from Calvinists and Churchmen (2 p. 305), and he is guarded when writing to Lindsey: 'If contrary to my apprehensions the Socinian doctrine is true, I wish you success in your endeavours to propagate it' (3 p. 174). Following the publication of his sermons he answers Rush on the question of final restitution and universal salvation: 'No doctrine can be more congenial to the feelings of a benevolent heart. But I am not so well satisfy'd that extermination may not be inflicted as a punishment for vice' (3 p. 147).

Having, I trust, whetted the appetite of others for these volumes it remains to praise the editors for their industry, patience and skill. They have spared no effort to make this as exhaustive and as fully annotated a collection as possible. They put flesh on allusive bones; wherever possible they provide biographies of persons mentioned; and they even track down works referred to but unnamed in the letters. Each volume contains a list of the short titles of Price's published works, a chronology of Price's life for the period covered by the volume, and a most useful index. For good measure there are portraits of some of the leading personages.

In the Preface to Volume 3, W. Bernard Peach graciously quotes D.D. Raphael's remark concerning his co-editor: 'D. O. Thomas's knowledge of the thought and work of Richard Price exceeds that of any other scholar, living or dead' (3 p. xvi). The judgement is indisputable, but equally certainly Professor Peach was the ideal collaborator. It can with complete confidence be asserted that all who peruse these admirable volumes will come to know Richard Price a good deal better than they did.

International Journal of Philosophical Studies 3 (1995) 213–15.

15

William Godwin

Don Locke. *A Fantasy of Reason: The Life & Thought of William Godwin*. London: Routledge & Kegan Paul, 1980. Pp 398.

William Godwin had an engaging way of being hoist with his own petard—frequently. As Hazlitt wrote of him: 'He writes against himself. He has written against matrimony and been twice married. He has scouted all the common-place duties, and yet he is a good husband and a kind father. He is a strange composition of contrary qualities . . .' (p. 184). To put his predicament in another way: Godwin was a man whose faith in reason continued unabated to the end, but whose prudence in face of changing circumstances prompted him to sit loose to his axioms from time to time. Such is the all but forgotten thinker now resurrected by Professor Locke of the University of Warwick.

PHILOSOPHY, THEOLOGY AND HISTORY

Godwin's political views had, theoretically, the most far-reaching possibilities, but no one was less likely to organize for their practice than Godwin himself. Socially, he came into contact with many of the notables of his day: Southey, Coleridge, Lamb, Paine, Hazlitt, Shelley, Byron, Priestley, Harriet Martineau, Carlyle, and others; and his fairly regular impecuniosity led him into more than one pocket, until a government pension (a thing anathema to his *theory*) eased his old age.

There is Godwin the spiritual pilgrim from Calvinism through Sandemanianism, Deism, Socinianism, and Atheism to Pantheism; there is Godwin who caught the mood of the times with his *Political Justice* (1793)—a work which he subjected to subsequent revision and undermining; there is Godwin the earnestly rational lover to whom 'The supposition that I must have a companion for life is the result of a complication of vices' (p. 129); there is Godwin who, though awkward in society, was nevertheless pursued by Mary Keys, to whom he wrote, 'I am sorry . . . that the nature of my avocations restrains me from entering into regular discussions in the epistolary mode' (p. 112); there is Godwin the opponent of the institution of marriage, who became a distraught widower, and whose early confidence in the sufficiency of reason was shattered by his personal experiences of love and loss; there is Godwin, believing that men have duties but no rights, but yet helping to secure the acquittal of three men convicted on charges of treason; there is Godwin, attacked but never embittered; there is Godwin the philosopher, the author of novels, essays, histories, children's stories and a disastrous play.

Godwin comes alive under Professor Locke's hand. He is treated with the proper mixture of deference, irony and disbelief. There are occasional stylistic lapses, and some of the material in parentheses would more appropriately have appeared amongst the notes. On the whole, however, Locke writes well—occasionally with the wit and in the manner of Sir Leslie Stephen.

Introduced by a local tradesman to the French *philosophes*, Godwin imbibed their enlightened spirit and argued that if only men would become more rational the ills of society would be cured, and government would no longer be necessary. He was not so much a revolutionary (he opposed Paine) as an evolutionary, with faith in the perfectibility of man, in the intrinsic purity of the human mind, and in his apocalyptic vision of what society ought to be: 'There will be no war, no crimes, no administration of justice, as it is called, and no government . . . Each man will seek, with ineffable ardour, the good of all' (p. 8). He did, however, see the need of an educated elite to lead the masses in this direction.

In all of this we see how far removed Godwin became from the Calvinism in which he had been bred. There is no original sin here; and in place of irresistible grace he puts irresistible truth (p. 94). Against Hume he argues that reason alone motivates action, contending that 'passion' is the expression of a judgement for or against a course of action. He cannot show, however, that a man who knows the truth will necessarily do the right.

Godwin gradually came to face the difficulty that although the demise of governments was desirable, anarchic behaviour was not. He also had perforce to reckon with the emotions. As his confidence in the rationality and perfectibility of men diminished, Godwin fell into the role of a harbinger of utilitarianism: 'that life ought to be preferred which will be most conducive to the general good' (p. 169). Professor Locke finds the important theme of the desirability of justice in Godwin's writing (p. 178). But none saw more clearly than Godwin that men do not in fact desire justice before all else, and so he set about the vain endeavour of retaining the conclusions of *Political Justice* whilst undermining its premises (p. 200).

Political theorists, students of literature and culture, and philosophers will all find things of interest in this book. Theologians will note that Godwin's position *vis à vis* Christianity was about the only area in which a *volte face* did not occur. His mother wrote that 'your broken resolution in regard to matrimony encourages me to hope that you will ere long embrace the Gospel' (p. 124). But he never did. Perhaps his misfortune was that, theologically, he lived between the times. Persuaded of the barrenness of the older apologetic, wherein miracles were conceived as evidence (p. 18), and appalled by the predestinarian excesses of *scholastic* Calvinism (Professor Locke might have made the emphasis), wherein inscrutable eternal decrees coupled with a doctrine of covenants contractually conceived minimized grace, Godwin had no inkling of such alternative starting-points in theology as were already (unknown to the English) being proposed by Schleiermacher and others.

Professor Locke writes interestingly on Godwin's controversy with Malthus, rightly maintaining that by allowing himself to become embroiled in his opponent's statistical game the force of Godwin's better argument was lost; he writes with sympathy of Godwin's second marriage, family trials and financial misfortunes; and he presents a balanced account of Godwin's position *vis à vis* the later radicals. For good measure a useful Chronology is appended.

So to four points of detail: (1) The nature of Hoxton Academy's 'unorthodoxy' (p. 18) might have been spelled out. Rationalistic Arminianism was the culprit, and it led some towards Socinianism and thence to Unitarianism. On this matter Martin Fitzpatrick's illuminating article. 'William Godwin and the Rational Dissenters' (*The Price-Priestlev Newsletter*, no. 3, 1979, 4–28) may now be consulted. (2) Godwin's sermons are said to have been 'fervently evangelical, but not notably Calvinist' (p. 18). Godwin's then current Sandemanianism may go some way towards accounting for the latter fact; but to say that his sermons were 'evangelical' is misleading given that the period in question is that of the Evangelical Revival. The *Monthly Review*'s description of Godwin's sermons (pp. 18–19) underlines the point. (3) Professor Locke refers to Coleridge, 'deep in Spinoza and a religion which identified God with Nature itself' (p. 181). Coleridge did thus immerse himself, but the unwary should not be allowed to infer that Coleridge himself identified God with Nature. Coleridge is more complicated—and more interesting—than that; not least because of his keen sense of the reality of moral evil and of conscience, which prevented his blurring the creator-creature distinction. (4) Although one must concede that in general Godwin is 'remembered not at all' by philosophers (p. 350), we should not overlook D. H. Monro, *Godwin's Moral Philosophy* (1953) and P. H. Marshall, *William Godwin: A study of the origins, development and influence of his philosophy*, DPhil. thesis, University of Sussex (1977).

Among the welter of ambiguities which surround Godwin there is one constant feature: he worked hard. 'I was famous,' he wrote of his days at Hoxton Academy, 'for calm and impassionate discussion; for one whole summer I rose at five; and went to bed at midnight, that I might have sufficient time for theology and metaphysics.'

One of the most reassuring implications of this book is that, on occasion at least, a Professor of Philosophy can find a person as interesting as his arguments, and can accept the fact that 'it is not that [Godwin's] theories have been tested and refuted; the objection is that they cannot be refuted because they cannot be tested' (pp. 352–53). Doubtless the early Godwin would not have agreed that persons are as important as ideas; but that Godwin would surely have applauded Professor Locke for having the requisite knowledge to do him justice. Even so, it reflects no discredit upon Locke to surmise that no one knew Godwin better than Godwin himself: 'I have, perhaps, never been without the possession of important views and forcible reasonings; but they have ever been mixed with absurd and precipitate judgements, of which subsequent consideration has made me profoundly ashamed' (p. 63).

Philosophical Studies 30 (1984) 325–27.

16

John Stuart Mill and the Religion of Humanity

Linda C. Raeder. *John Stuart Mill and the Religion of Humanity*. Columbia, MO: University of Missouri Press, 2002. Pp. xi + 402.

It is interesting to observe that as the mainline churches in the West suffer numerical decline, the interest in the religious thought of certain prominent Western philosophers grows. Locke, for example, has been well served in this respect in recent years, and now it is the turn of Mill. With this sumptuous volume Linda C. Raeder, the associate editor of *Humanitas*, adds significantly to the corpus.

The thesis is succinctly stated: 'Neither Mill's philosophy nor his politics can he adequately comprehended without taking into account his religious views and purposes' (p. 1). The Mill here presented is one who was deeply hostile to traditional, supernaturalist, Christianity: indeed, he wished to destroy it and replace it with what he deemed to be the morally superior Religion of Humanity.

Part One: Philosophy

In prosecuting her case Raeder wisely draws upon Mill's letters (especially those to Comte) and diary entries as well as his published works. She is thereby able to support her contention that not the least difficulty in determining Mill's genuine views on religion in general and Christianity in particular is his way of holding back in public opinions which he was willing to communicate in private (pp. 55 59, etc.)—this with a view to securing a more favourable hearing for his new religion and its utilitarian 'creed' (his word). She also shows that for public consumption Mill prudently and as a matter of tactics did his best to suggest that the difference between Christianity and the Religion of Humanity was not so much that they advocated contrasting moral stances, as that they referred morality to different sources. This, in turn, enabled Mill to exploit Christianity to his own ends, sometimes to the point of annexing God.

We set out from the early influences upon Mill and here, notoriously, his father, James, looms large. Raeder is pointed: 'Mill seems to have regarded the religious beliefs he absorbed during his childhood and youth as simple objective truth, uniquely free from prejudice. This was pure self-deception. Mill was bound by certain granite prejudices against traditional religion, and especially against Christianity, almost from first to last' (p. 11). Bentham, from whom Mill gained the 'creed' he modified, is fully discussed, as are French writers, notably Henri de Saint-Simon and Auguste Comte. There follow discussions of Mill's essays, 'Nature' and 'Utility of Religion,' and Raeder then offers a stimulating assessment of the issues between Mill and Hamilton and Mansel. Raeder counters Alan Ryan's judgement that the nub of the Mill-Mansel controversy was that Mill's temperament was 'utterly secular' and 'this-worldly' by saying, 'Mill . . . was driven throughout his life by the most intense, if misdirected, religious impulses. There is nothing remotely "secular" or areligious in his thought or being' (p. 157 cf. p. 326).

Raeder proceeds further to illustrate her thesis by reference to Mill's 'Theism,' *On Liberty* and *Utilitarianism*. In a concluding chapter she ponders some 'Consequences and implications.' As compared with her generally careful exposition of Mill's writings this is the most problematic chapter in the book. For example, we have the inadequately supported claim that 'Mill's Religion of Humanity and the concomitant social morality he absorbed from both Bentham and Comte have been more or less assimilated by large segments of contemporary Anglo-American society and, arguably, constitute the dominant public ethos.' She even invokes the former president George H. W. Bush as an unwitting exponent of 'the new humanitarian ethos' on the ground that he declared, 'From now on, any definition of a successful life must include service to others' (p. 329). Here, surely, lurks the fallacy of incomplete enumeration. Again, we are informed that 'One result of Mill's endeavour to "immanentize" spiritual aspirations has been the growth of a centralized government charged with godlike powers and duties and the thoroughgoing politicization of social life' (p. 334). Even if this he true (and the case is not thoroughly argued), it seems odd to hold Mill entirely responsible for it.

At other points, too, it is possible to question the author's reliability, judgement and balance. As to reliability, she introduces associationism without explanation (p. 12), or any reference to Hartley, and her casual linking of it to equally unexplained Skinnerian behaviourist psychology obscures more than it reveals (pp. 34, 259). The throwaway line,

'Atheists and agnostics are typically indifferent to the religious question' (p. 66) is, in view of the history of philosophy of religion in the twentieth century, hard to justify. The passing characterization of deistic views (p. 108) is undiscriminating and problematic. As to judgement, she attributes the 'softened temper' of Mill's late essay, 'Theism' to the fact that by the time he wrote it his 'radically antireligious' wife, Harriet, had died (p. 364). But it may more plausibly be suggested that Mill's profound sense of loss on the death of his wife was the crucial factor here, and one compatible with his increasing wistfulness concerning the possibility of immortality. Where balance is concerned we might have expected closer attention to Coleridge and the Romantics, as well as to the influence on Mill of Malthus's work on population.

The book is furnished with copious notes, some of them very full and informative, a substantial bibliography, and an index from which some expected names (for example, Coleridge, Ryan) are omitted. Raeder's style is generally fluent, though her habit of beginning sentences with 'As said,' jars. She quotes extensively from Mill and other writers—too frequently at length, and in some cases repetitively.

The above comments notwithstanding, Raeder makes out her case that religion permeates Mill's thought and writings, and she does this on the basis of a careful reading of all relevant texts. On the last page of the final chapter she shows her hand: 'It may well he . . . that both truth and liberty require the recognition of precisely that which Mill took such pains to deny—whatever its merits, Humanity is surely not God' (p. 344). This remark prompts the observation that the voice of the Christian opposition to Mill, which was at times vociferous, is muted in this book. There are, it is true, passing references to a few such critics, but there is more to he said regarding not only philosophico-theological points, but also Mill's views on the Church as an institution. Again, we should not overlook the fact that in Christian circles no less than outside there was opposition to 'immoral' doctrine—in this connection the pioneering work of the eighteenth-century 'Arians' comes to mind. Not all believers were as benighted as Mill on occasion suggests. It would not be fair to Linda Raeder to regard these as culpable omissions from her hook, for she makes it quite clear that hers is the limited task of demonstrating the pervasiveness of religious concerns throughout Mill's writings, published and unpublished, and in achieving her objective she has served her readers in general well. More than that, and with reference to my concluding observations, she has cheered this reader in particular by leaving room for the book on Mill's religious thought which I am contracted to write.[11]

International Journal of Philosophical Studies 11 (2003) 356-58.

---

11. Alan P. F. Sell, *Mill on God: The Pervasiveness and Elusiveness of Mill's Religious Thought*, Aldershot: Ashgate, 2004.

Part One: Philosophy

17

James McCosh

J. David Hoeveler, Jr. *James McCosh*.
Princeton, NJ: Princeton University Press, 1981. Pp xlv + 374.

James McCosh (1811–94) was born in Scotland, educated at Glasgow and Edinburgh universities, and ordained to ministry within the Church of Scotland. He served in Arbroath, and then at Brechin. Whilst he was at Brechin the Disruption of 1843 occurred, when many evangelicals, who objected to the intrusion of 'Moderate' ministers under the patronage system, 'came out' of the Established Church to form the Free Church of Scotland. In this dispute McCosh sided with his mentor, the evangelical Thomas Chalmers. He continued as Free Church minister at Brechin until 1853, when he accepted a call to the Chair of Logic and Metaphysics at Queen's College, Belfast. In 1868 he became President of Princeton College, New Jersey, and in that position he remained until his retirement twenty years later. Standing in the line of Reid and Dugald Stewart, and not uninfluenced by Sir William Hamilton, McCosh was 'the last major voice of the Scottish Enlightenment and the philosophical realism for which it is best known.' Philosopher, evangelical Christian, minister, teacher, author, academic statesman—McCosh deserved a thorough study and, some minor slips notwithstanding, he has now received it.

The author of this handsomely-produced book has set himself a large task. He is not concerned only with intellectual biography: he seeks to show 'the relation of thought to its extended milieu.' More than that, he wishes to address the question: Did American universities and colleges take on the characteristics of their amorphous surroundings, or were they shaped rather by their remaining aloof from those surroundings? We intend no disrespect in regarding the latter theme as a sub-plot.

We begin with the Scottish Reformation—Knox, his heirs, and the emergence of the Scottish Enlightenment. The influence of Shaftesbury upon Hutcheson did much to rescue Scotland from 'the glacial age of Calvinism.' The moderate party in the Church, reared upon Hutchesonian moral decorum and confidence in a benevolent deity, were weighed and found wanting by McCosh. He approved of the way in which Scottish philosophers in general upheld the moral nature of man, but thought that they failed to see that nature as it really was—sinful and in need of supernatural grace. He could never tone down the distinction between the divine and the natural. This same evangelical thrust inspired his opposition to the Patronage Act of 1712 which, he believed, enabled the Establishment to usurp the rights of the congregations, and leave unsatisfied the needs of the soul. A major case in the book is that in his thought McCosh wove evangelicalism and Moderatism together, and it is well sustained. The way in which the lines were set for McCosh's work in this direction by his university training and his pastoral ministry is illuminatingly described in two chapters.

Part II of the book deals with McCosh's Belfast period, during which his most notable philosophical treatises were written. The chapter on 'Intuitional realism' is a careful account of the way in which McCosh sought to rescue philosophy from downright materialism and intuitionism alike. In the process he had to do battle with J. S. Mill on the one hand and with tendencies emanating from German Idealism on the other. (Some students will draw comfort from McCosh's remark that he could hardly bear to read Hegel). He welcomed the stand which transcendental and idealistic systems took against advancing materialism, but they paved the way to Fichte's unacceptable conclusion that the world is but a projection of the mind.

'Protestant scholasticism' is the theme of the next chapter, and Dr. Hoeveler shows how McCosh sought to sustain the position that notwithstanding the mind's limitations *vis à vis* the being of God, the mind can secure the foundations of belief. He was accordingly unpersuaded by Mansel's divorce of intellect from faith. In Mansel the revolt against German speculation was paving the way for scepticism. McCosh did not, however, offer an intellectual proof of the existence of God. In his moral philosophy he was with the Scottish moderates in defending the existence of a moral faculty, though he had serious reservations concerning the ability of that faculty apart from grace.

Chapter six on 'Nature and nature's God' relates McCosh to such pioneering evolutionists as Robert Chambers and Hugh Miller, and shows how for him the dynamic universe was shot through with purpose, and was orderly and illustrative of final causes. Like many another McCosh pursued Herbert Spencer, and gradually accommodated himself to Darwin's theory of natural selection.

Part III, 'America,' reveals McCosh the 'Academic reformer,' the 'Academic politician,' and gives us an insight into 'The New Princeton' which was his legacy. The factions within American Presbyterianism, the tussle between McCosh's Princeton and Unitarian Harvard, the internal faculty strife over evolution—all of these receive detailed treatment. For good measure we have insights into student discipline, faculty appointments, building projects, financial crisis, and the (not unrelated) alumni societies. One might think that this section of the book stands on its own (and, indeed, many may value it who would not be so enthused by the detailed philosophical exposition of Part II). But the moderate-evangelical blend of McCosh's thought is manifest—and at times on trial—throughout, as Dr. Hoeveler makes abundantly clear.

So to the sub-plot: Did Princeton under and immediately after McCosh reflect its environment, or did it remain aloof from it? What emerges is that by setting up alumni groups, instituting regional entrance examinations, and supporting private feeder schools McCosh did much to *form* Princeton's environment. But in meeting the challenge to make of Princeton a national centre of excellence he had to engage staff not all of whom were committed evangelicals. Princeton shortly after McCosh's days assumed more of the manners of the old Scottish Moderatism than McCosh would probably have liked.

Philosophers, church historians, and historians of thought and of education will find much of value in this book. McCosh's importance as one who strove to sustain a middle way in philosophy, and to hold in relation gospel and thought, faith and life is clearly shown. The jibe of Mark Pattison concerning 'the professed contempt of all learned enquiry which was a principle with the Evangelical school' is shown to be far too sweeping. Many half-or-more-than-half-forgotten philosophers are mentioned, and some—notably Hamilton and Brown—are vividly brought to life.

Sometimes, however, the lines are too sharply drawn. Dr. Hoeveler seems to have a somewhat disjunctive cast of mind. Not all Scottish evangelicals could be called pietists—especially when the latter term is not defined; nor can Paley be summarily dismissed as one who 'rested theology on little more than expediency and morals' (as a matter of fact, morals are quite a lot to rest it on). Again, by no means all Calvinists were for the 'harsh determinism' of Calvinism's 'glacial age.' There was, undeniably, a profound move away from scholastic Calvinism in the nineteenth century—and it is somewhat surprising that Dr. Hoeveler does not allude to Erskine of Linlathen and Mcleod Campbell in this connection. But it is too much to imply that all Calvinists came to place 'salvation in the will of the Believer.'

The educational significance of England's dissenting academics is overlooked (p. 18), though the omission is made good later (p. 216). It is nowhere made clear that the Free Church of Scotland (unlike England's nonconformists) maintained the Establishment principle: they regarded themselves as the Church of Scotland, Free. It is inadequate to say that the World Alliance of Reformed Churches (in which the reviewer has a vested interest and which was founded in 1875, not 1877) 'remains today the institutional centre of World Presbyterianism'; it does, but it is more than that, for in 1970 the international Presbyterian and Congregational bodies united and, further, in the Alliance there are a number of member churches which result from transconfessional unions.[12]

The book is enhanced by illustrations, and marred by a few slips. Thus we have some redundant Words (p. 50); and we should read F. D. Maurice (p. 155) and Alfred Russel Wallace (p. 207). The English style is idiosyncratic at times, and ranges from highly sophisticated (in the philosophical sections) to mundane travelogue: 'Here [Southwest Scotland] for centuries farmers had struggled to wrest a living from stubborn but not unfruitful soil, and here shepherds tended their numerous woolly flocks' (p. 33). Some slang expressions jar the ear.

The picture which emerges of McCosh is of a man of broad sympathies, keen intellect, considerable organizing ability, and overweening personal vanity. But he seems to have had the right wife. On complaining that his portrait made him look as if he had no teeth Isabelle retorted 'James, you hae non an' it's a fine picture.' As for Mrs. Hoeveler, she is thanked for being a '*masterful* historical sleuth' (my italics). Another Mrs. McCosh, perhaps? More likely this is a further illustration of 'two nations divided by a common language.' Either way it is, as Dr. Hoeveler might say, time to 'Call it quits' and conclude this review of a stimulating book.

Philosophical Studies 31 (1987–8) 435–37.

---

12. In 2010 the World Alliance of Reformed Churches united with the Reformed Ecumenical Council to form the World Communion of Reformed Churches.

18

Anglican Idealism in the Nineteenth Century

Timothy Maxwell Gouldstone. *The Rise and Decline of Anglican Idealism in the Nineteenth Century.* Basingstoke: Palgrave, 2005. Pp. xvi + 235.

If the title of this book accurately encapsulates the author's theme, the opening sentence of his Introduction makes it clear that his underlying agony is that from the 1850s onwards the Church of England's 'institutional framework failed to adapt to cultural changes, despite continual attempts at structural reformation.' In rapidly changing times, the ritualist and other preoccupations of many in the C. of E., and its continuing refusal to advocate the removal of those disabilities which both irked, and to some extent defined, the Nonconformists, were a dissuasive against any lively interest which Parliament might otherwise have shown in ecclesiastical affairs. This gloomy picture was somewhat brightened by the authors of *Essays and Reviews* (1860), whose stance was less dogmatic than that of either the Tractarians or their Evangelical opponents, and whose objective was to face up to the challenges to faith posed by scientific advance and recent biblical scholarship. In a different key, the authors of *Lux Mundi* (1889), for all that they evinced 'High Church' sympathies, were progressive in intention, drawing inspiration from T. H. Green's theistic idealism, which seemed to them compatible with their incarnational doctrine and their endorsement of the evolutionary theme.

The scene set, we step back to the beginning of the nineteenth century, when the universities of Oxford and Cambridge were 'effectively seminaries of the Church of England,' and the attitude towards scholarship of many students and staff alike left much to be desired. Not surprisingly, J. H. Newman wrote in 1829 that 'The talent of the day is against the Church,' while Thomas Arnold contended that 'The Church, as it now stands, no human power can save'—a view which many Broad Church Anglicans endorsed. Whately and the Noetics had seen the need for change, but if there was a wide measure of agreement on the diagnosis of the malaise, the remedies proposed were poles apart. We thus have the rise, and the squabbles, of parties within the C. of E.

The contributors to *Essays and Reviews* threw down the gauntlet in the interests of spiritual freedom, and in opposition to dogmatic 'fundamentalism' and the imposition of doctrinal tests. Where they sought to relate Christian thought to the rapidly changing culture, H. L. Mansel, in his Bampton Lectures of 1858, elevated the divine revelation above the pretensions of human reason, thereby, according to Leslie Stephen, siting faith 'only in the void of agnosticism.'

A number of Anglicans found what they deemed to be a viable way forward in the idealism flowing down from Hegel. Here, they felt, was a way of honouring reason, opposing Mill's utilitarianism, anchoring morality, siding with progress and accommodating their incarnational-immanentist thrust. Coleridge and Whewell were to some extent, and in their different ways, harbingers of this approach, as was Benjamin Jowett, whose resurrection of classical studies serviced the revival of patristics.

The theistic idealism of Green exemplifies that of those who sought that secure foundation for morals which, they felt, was denied to eighteenth-century empiricists and nineteenth-century utilitarians alike. They also thought that idealism provided a basis for faith that did not depend upon assent to specific dogmatic assertions. Notwithstanding the opposition of Henry Sidgwick of Cambridge, who was unpersuaded by Green's 'spiritual principle' and 'eternal consciousness,' and unimpressed by the 'tower of Babel' he had erected upon them, Green's non-dogmatic and ahistorical stance was influential, and that not only in scholarly circles, for it found popular and anguished expression in Mrs. Humphrey Ward's widely-read novel, *Robert Elsmere*. That not all were content to hover between undogmatic theism and agnosticism is clear from the position adopted by Frederick Temple. He advocated doctrinal tolerance, faulted the Tractarians for their acultural antiquarianism and, in headmasterly fashion, proposed the union of Church and State as the means to educate and civilize the nation and even the human race at large.

For his part, the Anglican idealist Aubrey Moore, was, no less than Mill (and the eighteenth-century 'Arians'), utterly disinclined to espouse any view of God that would affront the human conscience. Eager to embrace scientific advance, he was equally concerned to maintain orthodox doctrine. Mingling incarnationalism, immanentism and the idea of progress, he understood the cosmos teleologically and as pervaded by moral purpose.

From across the Irish Sea, Charles D'Arcy, though influenced by Green, feared that idealism would swallow up the individual. Accordingly, he balanced immanence with transcendence and repudiated pantheism. His view of cultural progress prompted him to bracket the doctrines of sin, judgement and atonement, and to construe evil and pain as stages on the way to a greater good. The propagation of this view in the wake of the agonies of the First World War did nothing to dissuade the growing number of opponents of idealism from judging that that philosophy had shot its bolt; and D'Arcy was not inclined to tackle philosophical arguments hostile to his own; but such arguments were advanced with increasing force by G. E. Moore and Bertrand Russell, while in the broader culture the anti-idealist mood was exemplified in the novels of Thomas Hardy. In so far as the C. of E. appeared wedded to a *passé* philosophy, it was increasingly perceived as antediluvian, if not redundant.

Even from the highly compressed account just given, it will be apparent that Dr. Gouldstone has explored a vast terrain. In providing a careful survey of complex, intermingling, theologico-philosophical ideas and ecclesiastical motives, he has served his readers well. His bibliography (though it does not include all of the works referred to) will further assist them. The way in which he follows the philosophical discussions into the wider literature of the period is illuminating. Within the overall length of the work, he was forced to be selective when considering his principal authors. Nevertheless, I think he could have made more use of J. R. Illingworth (though he is kind enough to refer to this reviewer's account of him[13]). The degree to which Anglicans of many stripes put great faith in elites who would, they thought, lead the masses to the promised land of educated harmony and morality is clearly brought out; and one might note that this aspiration was held in common by Mill (whose second name is wrongly given as 'Stewart' on p. 39), who thought it would be an uphill struggle. It is also good to be reminded that for all their allegiance to their chosen parties, the memberships of the several groups comprised many notable individualists.

Dr. Gouldstone has so many interesting things to tell us that at certain points the mass of information all but crowds out argument. Again, he is inclined on occasion to quote from secondary sources, not because he wishes to challenge the authors, or because they are saying something in a striking way, but simply in order to move the narrative along. In such cases referenced reported speech would have served him better. In one instance it would also have saved him from an anachronism, for he quotes with apparent approval a writer who declares that logical positivism was rife in the first decade of the twentieth century. Some garbled English on p. 168 gives the impression that J. H. Buckley, whose book was published in 1967, was active in the 1850s and 60s; and it was the old century, not the new, which turned on 31 December 1900 (p. 194).

In view of the geologist Adam Sedgwick's conservative attitude towards the Bible, it is odd to list him as a 'liberal [Cambridge] divine' alongside Connop Thirlwall and J. C. Hare. Again, the distinction between Berkeley's idealism and that of Hegel might have been more clearly drawn, this being of some relevance to the discussion of Moore and the idealism he refuted. When Dr. Gouldstone speaks of 'the problems that can result from imposing an alien philosophical framework [namely, idealism] on the Christian revelation,' a subtler approach is called for. To put it crudely, it was not that the idealism was in one bucket and the revelation in another, and that on being mixed together, the former tainted the latter. Rather, idealism was in the air the author's protagonists breathed as they assimilated and interpreted the given revelation. Some readers would have been helped by fuller accounts of the way in which Green viewed Hegel through Kantian eyes, and of the impact of the 'higher criticism' of the Bible, which engendered in some a troubled scepticism regarding the historicity of the biblical narratives which, they felt, idealism could assuage—as when Green, slipping in the weasel-word 'merely,' came to regret that 'the eternal act' had been reduced to 'a merely historical one . . .'

The foregoing gentle criticisms in no way invalidate my judgement that this is a welcome and informative study, which amply reveals the benefits to be derived from the attempt to place ideas in their cultural setting. Dr. Gouldstone makes it clear that, over and above their doctrinal attenuations, the Anglican idealists had insufficient theoretical purchase upon the changing culture of their day. There is, indeed, a certain irony in the fact that for all the social good works in which Green and some other idealists engaged,

---

13. Alan P. F. Sell, *Philosophical Idealism and Christian Belief*, Eugene, OR: Wipf and Stock, 2006.

their philosophical position was, at crucial points, as abstracted from history as was the philosophical method of the analysts who all but drove them from the field (at least temporarily, since ideas are notoriously difficult to kill outright).

In line with the diagnosis recorded in his Introduction, Dr. Gouldstone ends on an apocalyptic note: 'Ours is a time when theology must re-invent itself in the context of contemporary culture, or it will not survive except as the pursuit of marginalised sectarians.' Whereupon I offer him the lukewarm comfort that it is not an unmitigated disaster when sectarians are marginalized. Not the least of the Church's present problems is that too often sectarians, whether of the biblicist or ecclesiological sort, seem to hold centre stage.

The British Journal for the History of Philosophy 13 (2005) 807–10.

19

Henry Jones

David Boucher and Andrew Vincent. *A Radical Hegelian: The Political and Social Philosophy of Henry Jones*. Cardiff: University of Wales Press, 1993. Pp. x + 267.

How appropriate that in the centenary year of the University of Wales, this Press should publish a volume by lecturers at Swansea and Cardiff on Henry Jones (1852–1922) who taught philosophy at the colleges at Aberystwyth and Bangor before the University was constituted, and who proceeded thence to St. Andrews, and finally to the Chair of his old teacher at Glasgow, Edward Caird.

Henry Jones epitomizes the Welsh commitment to popular education. From humble, devout beginnings he became by hard graft a man of affairs and the most mellifluous, if not the most rigorous, exponent of absolute idealism of his generation. As titles of his books suggest idealism was to him a faith, a practical creed, a springboard to social reform.

A few decades ago Jones's idealism would have been declared *passé* by most professional philosophers in Britain, and it is perhaps a sign of the times that Drs. Boucher and Vincent should feel it appropriate to turn again to the thought of one for whom society was an organism, and citizenship entailed ethical responsibilities. However this may be, the primary objective of the authors is to expound Jones's thought in relation to his times, and this they do with considerable clarity, and with reference to a wide range of books, pamphlets, journal and newspaper articles (from *Mind* to *John O'London's Weekly*), and unpublished manuscript letters.

It is correctly perceived that Jones' socio-ethical contribution can be evaluated only after due account has been taken of the idealism, the liberal-religious convictions, the commitment to 'spiritualized' evolutionary thought, and the passion for education and communication which fuelled it. For Jones, as for Hegel, we begin from the reality we experience; and reality is 'a rational, evolving, spiritual unity.' Reflection upon this ordinary experience of reality yields philosophy. Kant, thought Jones, had done well to identify thought and reality, but he requires the correction of Hegel, who preserved the proper distinction between them within a wider unity. Jones made no secret of the idealistic ground on which he stood. As if to answer later positivists as well as sceptics of his own day he affirmed that the choice is between 'a conscious metaphysic or an unconscious one.'

Jones's faith enabled him to surmount personal tragedy and to remain optimistic despite the catastrophe of World War I, though, as the authors point out, his account of evil and sin *vis à vis* God is not entirely satisfactory. Undeterred, he pitted his evolutionary spiritualism against all comers; but by Jones, as by others, Spencer, 'the philosopher who more than any other represented the stupidity of the English people,' was singled out for particularly adverse treatment. Jones strongly repudiated the idea that evolution could justifiably be construed exclusively in scientific terms; it must, he thought, be treated in a manner compatible with morality and religion. Moreover, like Hegel, he endorsed the procedure of seeking to understand the lower in terms of the higher, rather than *vice versa*. In their progress towards the higher, human beings were free and responsible—Jones was no ethical determinist.

The groundwork completed, Drs. Boucher and Vincent pass to detailed discussions in four chapters of 'Citizenship, the enabling state and education,' 'Political reflections: socialism, liberalism and syndicalism,' 'Nations and the imperialism of moral ideals,' and '"German philosophy" and the morality of states.' Jones emerges as a liberal who modified the public/private dichotomy, and who emphasized duties and the common good more than individual rights narrowly conceived. That Jones, far from being an armchair theorist, was actively involved in numerous causes is made abundantly clear, as is his position, and those of other idealists and their opponents, on international affairs. From first to last, 'A citizen, for Jones, is not just a legal category or body of economic or social entitlements. It [sic] is an ethical and metaphysical state of mind or being.' Both individual citizens, societies, states, and humanity at large are grounded in 'colligating hypotheses,' which influence and are implicit in thought and practice.

There is something endearing about Henry Jones—his reservations about taking up a post in the 'little squabbling, scandalmongering' town of Aberystwyth notwithstanding![14] But integrity prompts the recognition that, philosophically, he could be a scamp. On occasion, when argumentative rigour is called for, he will supply a rhetorical flourish ('Spirit comprises the differences without annulling them') or treat us to a few lines of poetry, and then move swiftly on. I fear that our authors do not impede his escape as often as

---

14. The reviewer was cheerfully employed in that pleasant town at the time of writing.

they might. Again, they occasionally make his victories seem too easy and too complete. Thus, for example, Jones is permitted to trounce Andrew Seth for maintaining the distinction (inimical to Jones) between epistemology and metaphysics, but Seth is not granted a reference to his published reply. Again, when Jones is reported as saying that no one with any philosophical acumen could subscribe to a Lockean or Humean view of mind, some comment upon this sectarian remark might have been expected.

Queries concerning some points of interpretation and balance include the following: Edward Caird is said to have 'relied more heavily than Jones upon revealing his philosophy in the course of a critical exegesis of past philosophers.' In fact Caird characteristically noticed only those forebears who contributed to his own philosophical vision, and they tend to take on a somewhat Cairdian hue. Of Caird's lectures Jones said that 'No Scottish name later than that of David Hume passed his lips' (so much for the common sense philosophers). And when the authors rightly say that Albrecht Ritschl's theology was less prominent in Britain than in America, they might have noted the stream of Jones's contemporaries who expounded Ritschl—not least the Scots Denny, Garvie, R. Mackintosh and Orr—all of whom had connections with Glasgow.

But these minor points should not detract from the achievement of Drs. Boucher and Vincent in presenting so thorough and well-founded an account of the political and social philosophy of Henry Jones. Their book includes full notes, a classified bibliography, and indices of subjects and names (the latter of which might with advantage have been fuller). It also includes the engaging reminiscences of Jean Hunt, Jones's granddaughter.

In characteristically 'onward and upward' style Jones declared that 'College education should be available to the majority of people and within their reach throughout their life'—an idea whose time now seems to have come. But what would he have made of modules, semesterization, and that gross management-speak which transforms education into a matter of delivering products? Assuredly, the temptation to yield to the *backward* glance is sometimes strong.

British Journal for the History of Philosophy 3 (1995) 201–4.

20

Oxford Idealism

James Patrick. *The Magdalen Metaphysicals. Idealism and Orthodoxy at Oxford, 1901–1945*. Macon, GA: Mercer University Press, 1985. Pp. xliii + 190.

In this illuminating work James Patrick deploys his considerable learning skilfully, and succeeds in evoking an all but forgotten period in English philosophico-religious intellectual history. His elegant style (*pace* a 'final shove' on p. 121) is more than a little reminiscent of that of some of his subjects. Consider the opening sentence of the Preface: 'While the Oxford realists—Cook Wilson and his disciples H. A. Prichard and H. W. B. Joseph—celebrated their increasingly frequent victories over the ghost of Thomas Hill Green, other Oxford philosophers, having tried Wilson's realism, quietly returned to the work of renewing classical metaphysics and clarifying the relations between theology and philosophy that the Neo-Hegelian followers of Green had obscured and the realists denied.' Clause is built upon clause in a somewhat Latinate manner, and the operative term is the adverb 'quietly'.

Though not constituting a school, C. C. J. Webb, J. A. Smith, R. G. Collingwood and C. S. Lewis were united in believing that 'philosophical questions provoked theological answers'; and they were 'metaphysicals' in the sense that 'their philosophy tends deliberately towards poetry, complementing the achievements of the seventeenth-century metaphysical poets.' Their common debt to T. H. Green and Ruskin is clear, but so are Lewis's 'affection for Aristotle,' and the sympathies of Smith and Collingwood with Vico, Croce and Gentile. All were convinced of the importance of classical studies, of the discipline of history, of the literary character of philosophy, and of the priority where religion was concerned of truth over experience.

Patrick does not proceed by way of detailed philosophical analysis of texts, though ample references are given; rather, he engagingly introduces us to a circle. He says enough to make plain the characteristic themes and lines of approach of his metaphysicals, and by tracking down and describing J. A. Smith's fugitive work he has performed a real service; but it is in delineating their inter-relationships that he excels. Their stances *vis à vis* both Kant and the new realism are well depicted, and the non-judgemental footnote to the effect that 'The Magdalen metaphysicals perpetuated the Oxford custom of ignoring German scholarship apart from Kant and summaries of Hegel' speaks volumes. The Church of England, both in its High and Modernist aspects, forms another part of the backcloth, and the dispositions of the metaphysicals towards it are clearly indicated. Flavour is added by such observations as that 'Francis Herbert Bradley, whose *Appearance and Reality* (1893) made him the most important intellect among the idealists, was partly by disposition, partly for reasons of health, a recluse. Collingwood, whose house was a few hundred yards from Bradley's for sixteen years never saw him . . .' (p. 6). Bradley was, however, sufficiently in touch with affairs to name his dog Pusey in protest against Anglo-Catholic medievalism (p. 32).

A chapter on 'Edwardian Idealism' is followed by one chapter for each of the four metaphysicals. Dr. Patrick's judgements are sound: 'If Webb erred in his description of the relation between grace and nature, theology and philosophy, it was by identifying too closely the realms of revelation and reason. Nonetheless, he wrote amidst the debris of a century of eccentric and intemperate denials that any relation existed . . . (p. 38). Again: 'Collingwood always looks like a rationalist when he insists on rendering those [ultimate] presuppositions intelligible. He looks like a fideist . . . when he is insisting that the ultimate presuppositions are simply given' (p. 106). Yet again, 'Lewis was perhaps the single most effective spokesman for supernatural religion in England or America after 1940' (p. 133). But Patrick can be provocative too: 'John Alexander Smith had made the great questions live when philosophy was gripped by that failure of course called realism' (p. 75).

Such contemporaries and disciples as H. J. Paton, G. R. C. Mure, Austin Farrer and Willmoore Kendall are duly noted, and three sentences in the concluding chapter dramatically raise the entire question of theological method *vis à vis* philosophical 'isms': 'The religion to which idealism led most effortlessly (one might almost say the religion into which idealism naturally degenerated) remained after a century a religion to which the deep things—grace, glory, sanctity, the virtues, the vision of God, sin, Jesus, his cross, his resurrection and ascension—were strangers. Idealism had been capable of inspiring a search for truth and for God in the lives of men like Lewis, Webb and Collingwood. It was equally likely to produce an atmosphere of high-minded gnosticism and abstracted natural piety' (p. 168).

This handsomely-produced book is enhanced by portraits of the four metaphysicals and others, and by a useful bibliography—though James Bradley's helpful account of Hegel's reception in Britain seems to have escaped Dr. Patrick's net. A few indexing omissions, and slips on pp. 17, 81, 84, 85 and 106 do not seriously spoil a fine book; neither does the addition of ten years to A.J. Ayer's age when *Language, Truth and Logic* was first published (p. 137). We can even forgive the familiar (and snooty) description of Elgar's music as, though glorious, 'a little banal' (p. 1).

Philosophical Studies 32 (1988–1990) 350–352.

PHILOSOPHY, THEOLOGY AND HISTORY

21

R. G. Collingwood

David Boucher, James Connelly and Tariq Modood, eds. *Philosophy, History and Civilizations: Interdisciplinary Perspectives on R. G. Collingwood*. Cardiff: University of Wales Press, 1996. Pp. xviii + 388.

This welcome collection of papers constitutes evidence of the revival of interest in the thought of R. G. Collingwood. With contributions from philosophers, political theorists, historians of ideas and archaeologists it also demonstrates the diversity of Collingwood's interests. Relatively few twentieth-century British philosophers have stimulated the enquiries of such a variety of academic professionals. But Collingwood was no ordinary philosopher. Indeed, he sometimes felt that he was so against the prevailing stream of analytic philosophy as to be isolated and alone. On the other hand, his contacts with a number of philosophical contemporaries, including Ryle, Prichard and Mabbott, temper the impression of loneliness gleaned from more sombre passages in his *Autobiography*.

David Boucher's paper on the subject's life, times and legacy is followed by chapters on Collingwood's idea of philosophy (Tariq Modood); aesthetics and philosophical method (T. J. Diffey); faith and reason in the philosophy of religion (the late D. M. MacKinnon); Collingwood on some Italian philosophers (James Connelly; H. S. Harris; B. A. Haddock; Rik Peters); history and metaphysics (Leon Pompa; Adrian Oldfield; Rex Martin); process, progress and civilization (Jan van der Dussen); education and society (D. Boucher; A. J. M. Milne); and archaeology (Margot Browning; Ian Hodder). Comment upon every paper being precluded, I shall exemplify a random selection of particularly interesting discussions and then offer some general observations.

T. J. Diffey's forthright and stimulating paper on 'Aesthetics and philosophical method' distinguishes Collingwood's view that the philosopher may advise how the term 'art' should be used from that of the Wittgensteinians, who will ask only how the term is actually used (am I alone in having met one or two prescriptive Wittgensteinians?). Collingwood's contention that we should determine the meaning of terms by asking 'What are we trying to mean?' and not 'What do we mean?' is a suggestion worthy of wider discussion, as is his understanding of imagination as an emotional response to art and magic which comes between feeling and intellect—something to which Boucher refers in his paper on education.

The later Donald MacKinnon's elucidation of the 1935 debate between Ryle and Collingwood is illuminating. Awarding points to both sides, MacKinnon agrees with Ryle that while the ontological argument for God's existence fails because existence is not a predicate, it was nevertheless grounded in 'the confused recognition that the divine reality must be self-authenticating.' On a related matter, does not a thesis lurk in MacKinnon's observation that 'Kant's *point de départ* is curiously akin to a secularized transcript of that of Anselm's work'?

Leon Pompa's fecund paper will surely be a catalyst of further reflection upon historical consciousness as the historian's inheritance—a subject to which, he feels, Collingwood paid insufficient attention.

A number of themes run through the book, some more strongly than others. Among them are Collingwood's philosophical method and his engagement with Italian thinkers; his ambivalent relation to Wittgenstein; his view of history; and the status of absolute presuppositions. Not the least interesting aspect of the volume, and the one which encourages the expectation that more studies of Collingwood are imminent, is that diverse interpretations are offered at crucial points. How far was Collingwood an historical relativist? MacKinnon finds him closer to this position than does Boucher. Again, whereas Connelly, Peters and Haddock advert to the Italian inspiration of Collingwood's view of History, Browning would have us note Collingwood's archaeological work as evincing a significant empiricist interest. On the other hand, Hodder judges that Collingwood's archaeological 'interpretations often wandered too far from the data.'

Quite apart from potential skirmishes between Collingwood's interpreters, Collingwood himself at times needs to be checked. For example, he contrasts his own view that 'My fundamental doctrine is that reality is becoming, that is to say reality not so much is as happens' with that which he ascribes to the British idealists of his period, namely, that theirs is a static, Spinozistic, reality unable to accommodate process and becoming. In order to query this sweeping claim one need look no further than Edward Caird's attempt, when contemplating God as ultimate reality, to unite the idea of God as 'a self-determining principle manifested in a *development* which includes nature and man, with the conception of Him as in a sense eternally complete in himself'; or in Henry Jones's view of God as 'the *perfect in process*.'

With his view (as recounted by Haddock) that 'The philosopher who disregards the historical dimension of his work is . . . in the position of trying to argue that Plato was right (or wrong) without having ascertained what he was trying to say,' Collingwood seems to throw down the gauntlet before thinkers yet unborn: philosophers who proceed as if it were possible satisfactorily to treat the arguments of past thinkers as if the thinkers themselves (with their contexts and meanings) did not exist; and those who would nowadays prohibit the question 'What did this past author intend to say?' in favour of the practice of offering their own 'readings' of texts.

Some of the papers in this volume have been published previously, but the reprinting of them is justified both as giving them a wider readership and as making the collection as a whole more completely representative of the many lines of discussion flowing from Collingwood's writings. At point after point the attentive reader will wish to challenge Collingwood, his interpreters, or both—a further indication of the stimulus to be found in this hitherto neglected thinker.

Slips or stylistic barbarism were noted on pp. 12, 38, 39, 41, 197, 289 and 341; and an otherwise handsome production was marred by smudged pp. 372–73 and 384–85. Indexes of persons and of references to Collingwood's writings are supplied, though an index of subjects would have enabled the reader more easily to track topics common to more than one paper.

Whether in philosophy, historical method or archaeology, Collingwood was his own man. Such a person, as these papers clearly demonstrate, is not immune to oscillations between the inspired and the perverse. Collingwood was often right, sometimes wrong, and always forthright. He thus elicits that mixture of admiration and provocation which is the inspiration of such interpretative volumes as this.

International Journal of Philosophical Studies 6 (1998) 302–4.

22

Philosophy of Education

R. S. Peters, ed. *The Philosophy of Education*. London: OUP, 1973. Pp 278.

The philosophy of education appears to be engaging the attention of an ever increasing number of philosophers, and it is good that a collection of articles on the theme has been included in this most useful series. An Introduction outlines the present state of philosophy of education: contemporary philosophers of education, though not narrowly analytical in approach, do nevertheless understand that 'it is important to distinguish philosophical questions about education from the old mix of historical exposition and recommendations about policies and practices.' Not indeed that philosophy of education is an isolable branch of philosophy: 'it draws on . . . established branches of philosophy and brings them together in ways which are relevant to educational issues.' The articles are grouped under four headings; I shall briefly describe each group in turn.

I. *The Concept of Education*. In 'Aims of Education—a Conceptual Inquiry' R. S. Peters defends the distinction between 'education' and 'training.' Whereas 'education,' like 'reform,' suggests 'a family of processes "aiming at" a norm,' 'training' has to do with particular kinds of competence. Thus to ask 'What are the aims of education?' is to make a request that the achievements which constitute being educated be accurately specified. For example, an educated person will delight to pursue activities into which he has been initiated for their own sakes, and not simply as means to ends; he will aspire to such knowledge and understanding as will render him more than 'highly skilled,' and which will transform his outlook. Very often to state an educational aim is to highlight a neglected priority. Indeed 'the function of talk about aims in education is usually to clarify the minds of educators about their priorities.' More than that, 'aims' talk in the context of 'the education of the whole person' bears heavily upon educational procedures, for the procedures presuppose attitudes to the content of education, and to the concept 'education' itself. The task of the philosopher of education is 'to produce some kind of ethical foundations of education, the guiding lines for which are provided by the above analysis of "aims of education".' It is not, however, the philosopher's task to adjudicate upon the respective weights to be accorded to the several components of the curriculum.

Two commentaries follow: John Woods charges Peters with having presented recommendations concerning usage under the guise of analysis; and W. H. Dray wonders what it would be like to get an analysis of education 'right.' We cannot present the criticisms in detail, nor can we rehearse Peters' reply. Suffice it to say that he yields little ground, though in some further reflections he refines his comparison between 'education' and 'reform.' Since we have here the original paper, two commentaries upon it, the author's reply, and his further reflections, we are justifiably left with the impression that we are in the midst of an ongoing debate. The mode of presentation does, however, make for somewhat cumbersome and occasionally repetitive reading. One would welcome a fresh treatment in which critics were treated *en passant*. On the main issue, the reviewer is left wondering whether the discussion of aims in education will ever have the appearance of anything more substantial than border skirmishing unless participants are prepared to be explicit concerning their ideological bases. Does not the matter become truly engrossing when such adjectives as 'Christian' and 'humanist' are prefixed to 'education'? (Cf. this reviewer's penultimate sentence.)

Professor P. Herbst contributes a paper on 'Work, Labour, and University Education' which all engaged in higher education would do well to ponder. He utilizes Hannah Arendt's distinction between 'work' and 'labour'—the former being that which is intrinsically satisfying; the latter, that which is primarily instrumental—and suggests that 'the pleasure of labour . . . (if any) is always extrinsic to it.' Education, being work rather than labour, is threatened by the consumer society and, potentially, by those who provide research monies, with the result that 'for a teacher who has the education of his students at heart (as distinct from their careers) there may be tension, a case of divided loyalties.' Much of the research which multiplies in certain quarters is more properly designated 'labour.' It may have useful 'pay-offs' but commitment to enquiry for its own sake may well be lacking. In fact 'the education of a student is an end in itself. . . This work requires no further justification, and by attempting to justify it further, in terms of the values of the consumer society, we only succeed in undermining it.'

In 'Reflections on Educational Relevance' Professor I. Schemer fastens upon a concept which the preceding article throws into prominence. He sketches three ways in which 'relevance' may be understood. There is, first, the classical view that a relevant education will foster a state of union between the knower and the known such that attention is withdrawn from the immediate world and focused upon the world of ideal essences. This approach has now largely been abandoned in favour of the even more primitive view that it is with the ordinary world that the union between knower and known has to do. What then becomes of that needful transcendence of the phenomenal with which education ought to be concerned? Secondly, there is a psychological interpretation of 'relevance' according to which thought is conceived as problem-orientated, and education's task becomes that of problem solving. This position is held as normative and not merely as descriptive. What then of the need to go beyond a student's initial problems and to widen his view? Finally, there is the moral interpretation of 'relevance.' It is held that the school exists to be a means of improving society, and consequently instrumental values come to the fore. Schemer would not have us shun the practical altogether, but the dangers inherent in the moral stance should be heeded. Of these the chief is that 'the potential ramifications of knowledge cannot be determined in advance . . .' without exempting the goals 'from the critical scrutiny that schooling itself may foster.' The primary task of education 'is not to be relevant but to help form a society in which its ideals of free inquiry and rationality shall themselves have become chief touchstones of relevance.'

II. *The Content of Education.* The articles in this section provide a conspectus of views for and against the position that breadth of curriculum is an essential component of an adequate education. In 'Liberal Education and the Nature of Knowledge' Professor Paul Hirst argues that 'liberal education' is 'the appropriate label for a positive concept, that of an education based fairly and squarely on the nature of knowledge itself . . .' He finds much of value in the Greek emphasis upon education's function of 'freeing the mind from error and illusion and freeing men's conduct from wrong.' By way of some pertinent criticisms of the Harvard Committee Report, *General Education in a Free Society*, Hirst comes to a consideration of the forms of knowledge, that is, of those ways 'in which our experience becomes structured round the use of accepted public symbols.' The forms of knowledge may be classified as (a) distinct disciplines such as mathematics; and (b) fields of knowledge, whether theoretical or practical (which may or may not include elements of moral knowledge). A liberal education may be devised along either line, though some of the distinct disciplines must eventually be studied if the education is to be adequate. Although 'liberal education' as here defined represents only part of the education a person needs (since specialist education, physical education and character training are excluded from the definition), the outcome of such an education ought to be 'the growth of ever clearer and finer distinctions in our experience.'

Mrs. Mary Warnock pulls no punches in her article, 'Towards a Definition of Quality in Education.' She maintains that 'a good education must, above all things, be directed towards the strengthening of the faculty of imagination.' By 'imagination' she means 'that which enables one to perceive things, not isolated, but connected, in a wider field. It is what enables one to see things as *significant*.' And (*ex* Sartre) the imagination is necessarily free—it is that by means of which one is able to 'modify' what is seen and to envisage things as they are not. Mrs. Warnock is thus led to welcome the growing realization on the part of educational psychologists that children are capable of dealing in abstractions; and she deplores the stultifying effect of 'play research' when it is carried on for too long—even as far as some CSE projects. Children need to be interested in a subject, and to be provided with the tools with which they will be able to pursue on their own those things which have enthused them at school. This they will do only if their imagination has been fired. Since one cannot learn everything in depth, and since the imagination is cramped and the pupil bored if the attempt is made to include too many disparate elements in the curriculum, we need more specialization not less. These considerations apply equally to university education. The most important distinction between school and university is that 'university students should feel that they are in a place where real, not play, research goes on.' Quite so; but when Mrs. Warnock appears to hesitate on the question whether such research should be a major concern within polytechnics, this reviewer wishes to proclaim the desirability of surrounding all students in higher education with those who are pushing back the frontiers of their several disciplines.

In 'Curriculum Integration' Richard Pring pertinently examines one of the most fashionable concepts in educational circles. He suggests that much of what goes by the name of integrated studies is simply interdisciplinary, and that the epistemological presuppositions of a truly integrated approach in education are all too frequently unexamined. He distinguishes between a 'strong' thesis which holds to the unity of all knowledge, and a 'weak' thesis, according to which there is unity of knowledge within certain broad fields of experience. His view is that 'the unity which is built in, as it were, to the very concept of knowledge is manifest in the different disciplines and forms wherein knowledge is developed, and that this unity must find its logical basis ultimately in the "categorical" structure that underpins or provides the essential conditions for any thinking whatsoever.' Mr. Pring raises a number of questions which clamour for attention—not least those concerning instrumentalism, and concludes with the philosophically 'therapeutic' suggestion that if to speak of curriculum integration is but a grandiose way of speaking about that interdisciplinary inquiry which entails no necessary synthesis, we may simply be chasing a chimera. In which event if the philosopher does 'a few mistaken curriculum reformers out of business, this may be a good thing.' It is to be hoped that Pring's article will haunt any who may be tempted to promote new courses before they have done their philosophy.

This section concludes with 'Curriculum Planning: Taking a Means to an End,' by Hugh Sockett, whose name escapes the book's 'Notes on Contributor.' We have here a salutary criticism of the notion of behavioural objectives from the philosophical rather than the technical point of view. Sockett contends that much talk of behavioural objectives overlooks the complexity of the relations between fact and value in education. By means of a careful analysis of the idea of taking means to ends he concludes that 'the contingent relationship alone, which is at the heart of the [fundamentalist behavioural objectives] dogma, is inadequate since it simply does not do justice to the range of interconnections of significance in the educational enterprise.'

III. *Teaching and Learning.* First, Professor Hirst asks 'What is Teaching?' He advances a number of reasons for the desirability of a clear answer and argues that there is so tight a conceptual connection between teaching and learning that the one cannot be understood apart from the other: 'A teaching activity is the activity of a person A (the teacher), the intention of which is to bring about an activity (learning), by a person, B (the pupil), the intention of which is to achieve some end state (e.g., knowing, appreciating) whose object is X (e.g., a belief, attitude, skill).' One cannot help feeling that Hirst tends to labour the obvious in reaching this unexceptionable definition. There follows a discussion of the activity of teaching. The teacher must make plain what he intends shall be learnt, and the content 'must be indicatively expressed so that it is possible for this particular pupil B to learn X.' Not indeed that teaching necessarily implies learning, 'but it does necessarily imply the intention of bringing about learning by someone . . .' There remains the question of differentiating successful from good teaching, but until the criteria for what teaching is are agreed, this question is premature.

In 'Human Learning' Professor D. W. Hamlyn discusses the empiricist and rationalist approaches to learning, and maintains that although knowledge may take many forms there is no learning apart from the acquisition of knowledge. He subjects Piaget's Kantianism and Chomsky's rationalism to such close scrutiny that to summarize would be to caricature, and the upshot is that 'I do not think that it is intelligible to speak of innate knowledge and understanding, and therefore of innate ideas, at least in any sense that makes the notion of any use for the explanation of the acquisition of the rest of our knowledge of a common and objective world.' Hamlyn takes Chomsky's point that language learning could not begin if empiricist theories of learning were correct, 'for the possibility of learning X presupposes the existence of prior knowledge in terms of which X will make sense to the learner.' This need not, however, land us back in rationalism, for 'there is . . .no need for the prior knowledge . . . to be *temporally* prior.' An individual's learning is 'his initiation into a framework over which there is wide agreement'; and such factors as the influence of the individual's own personality and that of those around him, together with the nature of the learning and the circumstances in which it takes place, conspire to ensure that the decisions as to which forms of learning are appropriate at any one time will ever be a matter of compromise and art. All of which 'inevitably imposes limits on education as a discipline in its own right.'

The next contribution, also by Hamlyn, is on 'The Logical and Psychological Aspects of Learning.' He fastens upon the fact that the subjects into which knowledge is divided are not 'block entities laid out, as it were, in a Platonic realm,' and observes that to have learned is to have an idea of what a subject is about, and not merely to be able to recite general relevant propositions concerning its subject matter. The familiar psychological-developmental obstacles to learning are noted, but Hamlyn is especially concerned to draw attention to the less frequently treated epistemological or logical obstacles. We need to decide the principles of ordering the curriculum of a subject and this 'demands that very knowledge and understanding of the subject itself, plus an ability and willingness to reflect upon the exact relationships between the concepts presupposed within it. This is not a matter for psychology.' Taking Piaget's biologism to task *en route*, Professor Hamlyn shows that the relation obtaining between concept and instance is not one between the subjective and the objective, for a concept is not mine in any private sense, since to have a concept is to have a knowledge of what it is to be an x, and to have a knowledge of what things conform to the criterion. In short, 'the objectivity of a concept is bound up with the idea that it must be inter-subjective, interpersonal, just as knowledge is.' When all the psychological points concerning personality traits, intelligence and the like have been considered, there remains the philosophical task of reflecting upon what learning and education are.

IV. *The Justification of Education*. The first contribution here is by Mrs. Pat White, who writes on 'Education, Democracy and the Public Interest'. She seeks to show that a democrat is required to believe that an appropriate political education is in the *public* interest. And 'a policy in the public interest is one which benefits every member of a given public under the description member of the public. It is not necessarily the policy which is best for any individual considered as an individual'. The determination of what is in the public interest in the educational sphere cannot be left to experts, for *value* judgements concerning what the public ought to have are not matters of particular expertise. Furthermore, the criterion of public interest stands as a bulwark against those who would wish to press sectional interests only. In a pluralistic society there can be policies in the public interest—but *must* there be? Mrs. White answers: 'there is one policy about which there can be no choice in a democratic state . . .[that of] ensuring the provision of a political education. This is necessary because for a democracy to survive the citizens must know how to operate the democratic institutions.' It is not that individual citizens in a democracy will possess all the relevant knowledge for taking all the political decisions; but along the lines of Hirst's approach to liberal education the citizen may acquire knowledge of all the kinds of considerations which could bear upon political problems. The primary objective of a political education will be 'to get pupils to acquire the values which underlie the democratic system.'

The concluding essay is R. S. Peters', 'The Justification of Education.' He reviews instrumental and non-instrumental approaches to education, and argues that since to be educated is 'to have one's view of the world transformed by the development and systematization of conceptual scheme,' a one-sidedly instrumental approach to the definition of 'education' will not suffice. Education 'is the attempt to actualize the ideal implicit in Socrates' saying that the unexamined life is not worth living.'

The book is furnished with a useful brief bibliography and an index; it is marred by the presence of wrong words or misprints on pp. 126, 129, 188, 210 and 251. Among the more memorable—and sobering—statements in the book is that of Professor Schemer who says of education that 'its job is not only to provide persons with techniques but, more importantly, to provide techniques with critical, informed, and humane persons . . .' The collection as a whole fairly accurately reflects the state of current philosophy of education, and to have these papers conveniently to hand is a boon. The volume also provides grounds for assenting to the truth of a judgement expressed in the Introduction: 'philosophy of education is, at the moment, suffering from too little fundamental divergence in points of view.' If the book inspires the remedy it will have served the philosophy of education doubly well.

Philosophical Studies, XXIII (1975), 255–60.

Philosophy of Religion

Philip L. Quinn and Charles Taliaferro, eds. *A Companion to Philosophy of Religion.* Oxford: Blackwell, 1996. Pp. xvi + 639.

This sturdy tome is greatly to be welcomed. Sadly, it is not possible to comment upon, or even to list, all of its seventy-eight chapters. Happily, the editors have gathered the contributions into eleven sections, and a few remarks may be offered upon each of these.

Part 1, 'Philosophical Issues in the Religions of the World,' while it does not cover all the religions, is nevertheless illuminating upon those treated. The section exemplifies a characteristic feature of the book as a whole, namely, that while the articles are severally informative, when placed side by side they thrust to the fore significant general questions—in this case: If we do not wish to fall for blinkered sectarianism or atomistic relativism, what are we to do about the fact that some religions (the monotheistic and Hinduism, for example) seem much more amenable to the quest of interreligious doctrinal common ground than do others (such as Confucianism and the African religions)? The chapter on Islam tantalizingly ends in the eighteenth century, though with the assurance that the tradition is still being mined with profit. Some examples of this would have been welcomed. The important question of contrasting philosophies of history seems to slip between the chapters of this section.

In Part 2, 'Philosophical Theology and Philosophy of Religion in Western History,' David Burrell does well to show that, given its commitment to the one God who freely creates, medieval Islamic philosophy's failure to provide a coherent account of primary and secondary causality bequeaths a problem that has too frequently been neglected in subsequent philosophical theology.

Merold Westphal, in 'The Emergence of Modern Philosophy of Religion,' characterizes the Enlightenment fairly (a refreshing change indeed, since some in our time uncritically lambaste it), though he might have noted that there was more than one Enlightenment, and that some of them were not as anticlerical as others. My feeling that this chapter, which runs from the Hume and the deists to Kierkegaard and Nietzsche, stops too soon (presumably an editorial decision), will be explained below.

At times there are lacunae in this historical section that are made good in later, more thematic chapters. This applies, for example, to Duns Scotus, whom we might have expected to meet under 'Medieval Christian Philosophy.' Helpful cross-referencing frequently mitigates one's initial surprise.

Part One: Philosophy

'Some Currents in Twentieth-Century Philosophy of Religion' is the subject of Part 3. Some will wish to query the sharpness of the disjunction that John Hyman proposes between the 'early' and the 'later' Wittgenstein, and an indication that scholarly opinions diverge on the matter would have strengthened his piece. Ralph McInerny might have noted the extra-Roman Catholic influence of Thomism, upon the later A. E. Taylor and E. L. Mascall, for example. And how could Longergan have been altogether passed by?

What are we to make of the chapters entitled, 'The Reformed Tradition' and 'The Anglican Tradition'? On the face of it, philosophical interests are even less amenable to confessional circumscription than, as we increasingly discover, are doctrinal ones. Be that as it may, by a wanton hijacking of the adjective, 'The Reformed Tradition' in the hands of Nicholas Wolterstorff turns out to concern a variety of Christian philosophizing that, though having its roots in Calvin and others, is more immediately indebted to Abraham Kuyper, descending from him via Dooyeweerd in Holland, Stoker in South Africa, and Jellema in Grand Rapids; and that, among the heirs of the last named, it is occupied with the epistemological questions surrounding the notion of properly basic beliefs (though, as Alvin Plantinga later admits, so is William Alston, who is said to hold out for 'Episcopalian epistemology'—as well he might). A more confessional understanding of Reformed (assuming the term had to be used at all) would have admitted the contribution of older and more recent evidentialists, whom Wolterstorff passes over too quickly, as well as such encounter theologians as John Baillie and H. H. Farmer (and their critics), and such a doggedly against-the-analytical-stream writer as H. D. Lewis—none of whom appear in the index of this book. In addition, a number of ecclesiastically Reformed existentialists, process philosophers, and others are here excluded. Clearly, within the Reformed tradition a diversity of philosophical positions is held, and readers should be advised of this fact.

Perhaps the editors' intention was to oppose the allegedly anti-natural theology stance of the Reformed (but which Reformed?) to the more favorable Anglican disposition toward it. If so, the omission of many who are ecclesiastically, if not epistemologically, Reformed was only to be expected. As for 'The Anglican Tradition,' Brian Hebblethwaite opens with an accurate remark that seems to imply a rebuke to those who offered his assignment: 'It can hardly be claimed that philosophy of religion, as undertaken by twentieth century [*sic*] Anglicans, both clerical and lay, constitutes a particular identifiable school.' This is part of the problem; the other part is that the confessional embargo again excludes many—Edward Caird, Henry Jones, John Watson, and A. S. Pringle-Pattison among them—who were prominent in the discussions to which the restricted Mr. Hebblethwaite refers; and, again, these names are absent from the index as, unaccountably, is that of R. G. Collingwood. To revert to my earlier remark: There was a case for concluding Westphal's historical chapter with the Anglo-American idealists, against whom many twentieth-century philosophers of religion were in reaction. Not surprisingly, Mr. Hebblethwaite deals with the diversity of Anglican philosophers of religion in other parts of the world by saying little more about them other than that they exist and that their number includes, notably, William Alston.

Part 4, 'Theism and the Linguistic Turn,' concerns religious language, the verification challenge (Michael Martin is commendably even-handed here), and theological realism and anti-realism—Roger Trigg making it abundantly clear what a parting of the theoretical ways these options imply.

'The Theistic Conception of God' is the theme of Part 5, the longest section in the book. Richard E. Creel is thoughtful on 'Immutability and Passibility,' and honest too, for he records a change of opinion reached under the impact of criticism. This article in particular, but also the section as a whole, endorses my view that many philosophers are nowadays treating substantive theological issues with a degree of critical-analytical seriousness that ought to put even some quite well-known theologians to shame.

Descending from my soapbox, I turn to Part 6, 'The Justification of Theistic Belief,' in which classical and modern theistic arguments, miracles, fideism, and Reformed epistemology (again) are reviewed. In the following section, the problem of evil, naturalism, and atheism are proposed as 'Challenges to the Rationality of Theistic Belief.' Here we have the trinity of Michael L. Peterson, Kai Nielsen, and Antony Flew. How Christian philosophers of religion need the challenge of Nielsen and Flew, the former of whom in particular impresses by being fair—and he is tough-minded! Next we come to 'Theism and Modern Science,' where the subjects are cosmology, evolutionary biology, the mind, and technology as requiring an organismic theism.

In Part 9, 'Theism and Values,' the volume seems to lose its way a little. There are chapters on divine command ethics and natural law ethics, but nothing on religious ethics *vis à vis* philosophical ethics. Again, why the environment, politics, and medicine but not the family, education, pastoral care, and business? On specific essays I can remark only that it is unfortunate that in 'Theism and Toleration' Edward Langerak fails to distinguish clearly between 'toleration' = (historically) the right under the law for doctrinally orthodox Protestants to worship other than in the parish church, the legal penalties being not repealed but held in abeyance; and 'tolerance' = the disposition to tolerate views and practices other than one's own. Blending the two meanings, Langerak misleadingly informs us that 'Locke notoriously argued for intolerance of Catholics and atheists.' In fact, while Locke did not think that Roman Catholics should be tolerated under the law (for the political reasons correctly cited by the author), he was personally tolerant of beliefs and practices that did not threaten civic order. For example, 'if a Roman Catholic believes that to be really the body of Christ, which another man calls bread, he does no injury thereby to his neighbour.'

A cluster of doctrinal themes is gathered in Part 10, 'Philosophical Reflection on Christian Faith.' I could wish that Thomas P. Flint, writing on 'Providence and Predestination,' had adverted more directly to the theologico-moral protest against some formulations of predestination. (Happily, he does not refer to God's inscrutable will in his definition of predestination—a topic on which certain of the saints have seemed to know far too much!) One may regret that in her paper on 'Petitionary Prayer,' Eleonore Stump does not discuss the views of D. Z. Phillips (though his relevant book appears in her bibliography).

The final section, Part 11, 'New Directions in Philosophy of Religion,' opens with Sarah Coakley on 'Feminism.' Some readers may feel that of all the contributors, this one seems to be the most cross—or, at least, that she is on the shadow side of jolly, for this is not a temperate piece of reasoning. She wonders how some Calvinists can legitimately mount a free-will defense in connection with the problem of evil, for this defense requires 'the sovereign, unconditioned freedom of the individual to do evil (as well as good)'; but she does not stay to engage with those Calvinists who have declined to identify the philosophical doctrine of necessity with the theological doctrine of predestination. She spoils for a fight with Richard Swinburne, finding a subtext concerning the propriety of excluding women beneath what Swinburne himself would presumably regard as his use of conventional language. But she does not make it clear how, if Swinburne were to write while consciously thinking of the status of women or of the need to promote equality of the sexes, the validity of his arguments would be affected. If, indeed, 'masculinity' has become a privileged mode of interpretation (and Sarah Coakley does little more than assert this), it is not clear to what extent matters would be improved by replacing it with a different privileged mode of interpretation. And if an either-or is not desirable, how may we best accommodate a both-and? Is there a quite different starting point that would not involve the erection of particular kinds of human experience into *quasi*-absolute norms of interpretation? We need more help on such points than we are offered here. When the author turns to doctrine, she makes so many provocative statements that comment is here precluded. We are left in no doubt as to what Sarah Coakley abhors; but (at the risk of being accused of masculinity) I cannot help but feel that an opportunity has been lost to present the important positive insights of the several feminisms in a cogent, persuasive way designed to do justice to the subject and to win over waverers. As I read this chapter, a *mot* from Len E. Goodman's paper on 'Judaism' came to mind: '[R]adicalism, like heresy, limits catholicity, blunts synthesis, focuses attention sharply on a single issue or nexus, and may overstress it or press it to the breaking point.' Could this be a word to the wise?

The section concludes with lucid chapters on religious pluralism and comparative philosophies of religion. There follows a note concerning resources for further study, and an index. To every chapter a bibliography is appended. As might be expected, they are highly selective, but even so, some important books are conspicuous by their absence.

The editors and publisher are to be congratulated on the production of so useful and stimulating a volume. Almost without exception, we feel that we are in the hands of specialists who are so much at home in their subjects that they can write concisely and straightforwardly about them. 'Buddhism' (Paul J. Griffiths), 'Divine Action' (Thomas F. Tracy), 'Fideism' (Terence Penelhum), and 'Tradition' (Nasil Mitchell) are among a number of contributions to which I shall return again and again. Excitement is sparked not least by the way in which one article may serve as a foil to others. Thus, it is not fanciful to suppose that C. J. F. Williams' cheeky remark in his chapter on 'Being' to the effect that 'I pass over in silence works of other philosophers entitled *Being and Time* (Martin Heidegger) and *Being and Nothingness* (Jean-Paul Sartre). Of them, and of the whole tribe of existentialists, the less said the better,' will provoke *angst* in some quarters. Taken as a whole, the volume sets philosophy of religion in its historical and cross-cultural context, and provides an account of its current vibrant and varied state.

The chapters in this *Companion* will kindle the interest of students; refresh professionals who have been narrowed down by their own researches; and, to put it tactfully, serve as a revision course for those who have served their term in (or sold their soul to?) administration. Of course, not everybody will be pleased. For sectarian philosophers of all stripes a much slimmer volume would, no doubt, have sufficed.

Calvin Theological Journal 34 (1999) 221–25.

24

Analytic Philosophy of Religion

James F. Harris. *Analytic Philosophy of Religion*. Dordrecht: Kluwer, 2002. Pp. viii + 432.

To judge from the volume under review, Kluwer's *Handbook of Contemporary Philosophy of Religion*, under the general editorship of Eugene T: Long, will make a substantial contribution to the field. In this, the third volume in the series, James F. Harris of The College of William and Mary in Virginia begins by offering a bird's eye view of the ground to be traversed. While under no illusion that philosophers prior to the twentieth century were unconcerned with conceptual clarity, he justifiably claims that 'for much of the English-speaking world of philosophy, the first half of the twentieth century saw the concern with problems associated with the meaningfulness of language and with the clarification of concepts reach an unprecedented height' (p. 2). He swiftly (perhaps too swiftly) disposes of the philosophical idealism of the period 1875–1920, and introduces Moore, Russell and the American pragmatists, all of whom struck out in fresh ways. We next romp through the rise and fall of logical positivism (though noting that its ghost lingers here and there), and we come to ordinary language philosophy, Wittgenstein and Austin. Near the end of the chapter Harris doffs his cap to such philosophers as Gadamer, Habermas and Derrida, who are said to challenge Anglo-American analytical philosophy, but leaves them on one side (and perhaps to another volume in the series?). He concludes the Introduction with what, to be fashionable, we might call a mission statement: 'The ideal of the analytic philosopher of religion is to commit to an objective and neutral methodology that involves the analysis of language and concepts in a genuine attempt to understand and elucidate the claims and practices of religion.' He immediately adds, 'When the inquiry is conducted by theists and in defence of theism, we ought to be especially cautious to scrutinize both the method of enquiry and the results.' No doubt; but it would be foolhardy to assume that all non-theists are wholly innocent of bias.

Eight substantial chapters follow, of which the first is entitled, 'The problem of religious language.' Here the topics include A. G. N. Flew's falsification challenge and the responses thereto; Ian Ramsey's models and qualifiers, and Janet Soskice's attempt to retain the cognitive import of models by recourse to religious realism; analogy; R. B. Braithwaite's empiricism and Wittgenstein's language games; Paul Tillich's symbolism and Thomas McPherson's silence; eschatological verification as propounded by I. M. Crombie and John Hick; William P. Alston's desire to justify the making of literally true assertions about God; the problem of reference and the theory of speech-acts.

The question of 'The nature of God and the arguments for the existence of God' is next taken up. Omnipotence, omniscience and divine foreknowledge are discussed, and then we come to the ontological argument, with reference to Kant, Charles Hartshorne, Norman Malcolm, Alvin Plantinga, Richard Swinburne, and others. Harris shows himself as inclined towards a cumulative case for the existence of God.

We proceed to a chapter on 'Religious experience and epistemology,' which is concerned with the views of William James, Swinburne, Hick, Alston, the so-called Reformed epistemologists, the Wittgensteinian fideists, and D. Z. Phillips. To Chapter 5, 'Religion and science,' I shall return below. In Chapter 6 the problem of evil and suffering is discussed with reference to the free-will defence, contemporary moral theory and evil, probability theory and soul-making theodicies. The continuing challenges of humanism, naturalism and atheism occupy Chapter 7, and here the cosmological argument, personal identity and immortality are among the topics treated. Under the heading 'Religion and ethics' fall discussions of divine command theory, the autonomy of ethics and of human agents, deontology and God's will, duties (including conflicting ones), virtue ethics and feminist ethics. In the last main chapter the question of religious pluralism is investigated, with reference to Kraemer, Hick, Alston and Rahner, among others. In a conclusion Harris summarizes his main findings and, in view of the current diversity of method and approach among analytical philosophers, wisely declines the task of predicting the future of this way of philosophizing. An index completes the work.

Potential readers of this book would be quite wrong to conclude from my bald summary of its contents that the author has produced only a blow by blow descriptive account of one topic after another. He has done far more than this. Although on a number of occasions he is forced to reiterate the refrain that there are many issues with which he cannot here deal, he nevertheless advances the discussion of his chosen themes in stimulating and sometimes properly provocative ways. Certainly he is not averse to delivering a stern judgement when he deems it appropriate: 'If the epistemology in Reformed epistemology is derivative from and dependent upon Reformed theological claims that, in turn, are derivative from and dependent upon religious faith, then "Reformed" in "Reformed epistemology" does not modify or characterize a kind of epistemology but rather vitiates the substantive noun in the way that "counterfeit" vitiates the substantive noun in "counterfeit currency"' (p. 176). It is fair to say that Harris's writing style is marked more by clarity than by elegance, and that at times the constraint of space tempts him into undue compression, as when he refers to Cartesian dualism (p. 18), or hits the unsuspecting general reader with the need of 'a theory for subjective conditionals and counterfactuals' (p. 87).

Many good points are made in passing: for example, the recognition that 'some factual content and some literal meaning is necessary in order for a religious believer to choose the appropriate metaphors or other nonliteral uses of language' (p. 48); and the need for progress in the discussion of religious truth in the context of religious pluralism (p. 411). The chapter on religion and ethics is particularly welcome at a time when so many writers rush headlong into the 'issues' with undue regard for the theologico-philosopghical underpinnings.

There are some small regrets too. More might have been made of Tillich's analytical critics, among whom John Heywood Thomas was a pioneer; the question how far the Reformed epistemologists are true to Calvin where natural theology is concerned might have been raised; and it is surely anachronistic to judge that 'Jesus' selection of his twelve [male] disciples was not politically correct . . .' (p. 372). By a slip, an author discussed on p. 372 under the name of Linda Woodward appears in the footnote as Helen Woodward. Harris hopes that he has not omitted important contributors, and no doubt gap-hunting reviewers can be tiresome. Nevertheless, I could wish that Austin Farrer had not been passed over; that the encounter language of John Baillie and H. H. Farmer, belatedly analyzed by such philosophers as C. B. Martin and R. W. Hepburn, had been discussed in relation to religious experience; and that H. P. Owen's treatment of the moral argument for the existence of God had been noted.

The most problematic chapter is that on 'Religion and Science.' First, with its fairly extensive descriptive reaching back into history—to Galileo and Darwin in particular—it reads differently from the other chapters. Secondly, the stage is set in terms of conflict between religion and science, which is to overlook the fact that many of the early modern scientists were religious believers who understood their investigations of what they took to be God's handiwork as a divine vocation. Thirdly, some of the history is shaky. On p. 199 we are informed that 'the conflict generated by Darwin's theory of evolution by natural selection pitted science against Protestantism—the Church of England in Great Britain [sic] and fundamentalist Protestantism in the United States.' But the contexts are not equivalent. The work of many highly regarded British theologians who quite quickly persuaded themselves (rightly or wrongly—that is not the point here) that far from holding any terrors for the faith, evolution, as a theory of progress not of origins, provided an account of how God had gone about his work; together with the contribution of a number of 'believing biblical critics,' both Anglican as well as Scottish and English Nonconformist (the latter two categories being overlooked by Harris), coalesced to spare Britain the highly polarized fundamentalist-liberal debate which afflicted the United States, of which sometimes quite loud echoes are heard there to this day. Fourthly, in the section on creationism Harris's mask of objectivity is allowed to slip a little: he does not seem to care very much for fundamentalist creationists, and some of them may feel that at this point he has not been quite true to his stated objective of providing 'the strongest possible interpretation of the positions I criticize' (p. viii). Fifthly, and more quizzically, it is passing strange that one who draws his salary from the College of William and Mary, an institution not entirely unindebted to the English Reformation, should think that by contrast with the globally significant scientific revolution the Protestant Reformation was a 'domestic affair' among people in Western European countries' (p. 194). Harris here follows Whitehead, whose association with Harvard should have told him differently too.

At certain points in his narrative (when discussing Tillich, for example) Harris seems to wish to fight shy of theology. However, when discussing religious pluralism he makes no bones about raising the Christological question. Why, one wonders, does he not introduce soteriological considerations when treating the problem of evil? Many Christians find their *practical* answer to this in the Cross of Christ—and the current second revival of interest in the writings of P. T. Forsyth is not irrelevant in this connection.

Finally, as he reviews the journey he has taken Harris says that what Gilbert Ryle called the 'Revolution in Philosophy' was 'a revolution from idealism and abstract metaphysical speculation and a turn towards realism, empiricism, and common sense' (p. 414). No doubt many of the revolutionaries took a dim view of metaphysics and regarded themselves as taking a better way. The nagging question remains, How far was their judgement of metaphysics accurate, and were they as innocent of metaphysics as some of them (in public at least) supposed? This question throws into relief the fact that in Harris's book, while, in relation to the selected topics, many conflicting views are discussed, the voice of those concerned by what they perceived as the one-sidedness of the analytical enterprise as a whole is hardly heard. There was, however, a running critique, as represented by such philosophers as T. M. Knox, H. D. Lewis, H. J. Paton, S. Körner and others, none of whom was opposed to analysis as such, but all of whom questioned whether it was all there was to philosophy; and all of whom more than suspected that the analysts were covert metaphysicians. It would have made for balance had this voice been heard and the responses of those analysts who did more than stop their ears been recorded.

All caveats apart, this book can cordially be recommended to all who wish not only to follow the course of Anglo-American analytical philosophy of religion over the past century, but also to engage with the issues on their own account.

Philosophical Books 44 (2003) 285–89.

PHILOSOPHY, THEOLOGY AND HISTORY

25

Theism Analyzed

George N. Schlesinger. *New Perspectives on Old-Time Religion*. New York: Oxford University Press, 1988. Pp. 196.

Do not be misled by the title of this book. George N. Schlesinger is not (at any rate professionally) a student of revivalism, but a professor of philosophy at the University of North Carolina at Chapel Hill. By 'old-time religion' he means traditional theism, and of this he presents a defense which is lucid, demanding and, above all, fresh.

How far, if at all, can a being exemplify omniscience or 'omnibenevolence' *and* omnipotence? This is the question discussed in the first chapter. In addressing it Schlesinger displays one of his favorite techniques: he objects to the way in which a dilemma is posed, thereby drawing an opponent's sting. In the present case he argues that there are resources in the Anselmian approach to theism that may be deployed in such a way as to show that attributes A1 and A2 are of importance only insofar as they contribute to the divine greatness. Accordingly, we must 'ascribe just the degrees of A1, and A2 to God that are compossible, and maximize His perfection.' This proposed solution entails the rejection of the view that the divine attributes are 'independent, unique properties exemplified by God.' Rather, they are aspects of the primary property, absolute perfection. The 'alleged' problems concerning omniscience are deemed to evaporate in a discussion of petitionary prayer.

Enter evil. Schlesinger has no doubt that the problem of evil poses the strongest argument against theism. He discusses the Free Will Defense and argues that the 'Virtuous Response to Suffering' solution, while inadequate on its own, plays a vital part in a more complex theodicy. He refines his preferred defense, that concerning the Degree of Desirability of States which, uneasily as some have felt, relates the idea of the logically possible to that of the relative desirability of states. Throughout this discussion Schlesinger's pastoral concern is evident, but he will not be betrayed by it into unphilosophical rhetoric:

> It is hard to escape the conclusion that the very same horrors that served to reveal the enormity of human iniquity should also be instrumental in greatly enhancing the rectitude of those who chose to respond to them virtuously. This is specially so if we agree not to assume that the value of virtue which contributes to human welfare is only as great as the disvalue of wickedness that creates a comparable amount of misery . . . the positive value of virtuous acts by far exceeds the negative value of vicious acts.

Part One: Philosophy

We turn next to 'Religious and Secular Morality,' and to a spirited defense of the view that religion can provide 'an otherwise unavailable logical basis for ethics,' at the heart of which is a probationary view of life. Thence we turn to miracles, and to the distortion which occurs when Hume's critics and defenders are so wrapped up in confirmation theory as to be unable to relate miracles to 'the nature of theistic belief in general or the character and function of miracles in particular.' As with miracles, so with the argument from design: the application of probability theory is required if adequate treatments are to be given—all of this in the interests of the motivating conviction of this book:

> It is important to show that the believer can offer a rational justification for his position that is at least as respectable as that of his opponent's. And it is also important to show that he can do this without having to reinterpret radically, demythologize, or dilute traditional religious doctrines; without having to take shelter in impenetrably opaque metaphors and mystifications; and without claiming immunity from the testimonies of empirical evidence and logical argument by invoking the special, ineffable status of his beliefs.

There follows a chapter on 'Pascal's Wager' in which we are treated to a consideration of the grounds on which we may justifiably claim that 'theism is considerably more likely to be true than any pagan hypothesis.' Wagerers need not feel daunted by the problem of evil, for if there is a non-negligible chance that an adequate theodicy exists, the Wager is 'prudentially rational.' The idea of the reward of ecstasy is not to be ruled out, but this raises the question of the divine justice. What of those who cannot honestly make the Wager because they see no good evidence of God's existence, or because the circumstances of their lives have not favoured the raising and answering of the theistic question? Are such people excluded from salvation? Schlesinger argues that we are never absolutely free to choose any complete set of beliefs; neither are we ever without a measure of freedom. People have differing temperaments and aptitudes, and God's fairness is not thereby impugned. Moreover, God, being omniscient, is in the best possible position to make final adjudications.

The bald sketch here presented in no way does justice to the complexity yet clarity of Schlesinger's arguments, or to the importance of the topics treated which, as he rightly notes, roll into one another. In my opinion the rolling stops short at one important point. Those with a theological bent will note that Dr. Schlesinger, properly enough, conducts his case concerning the problem of evil along theoretical lines. But the Christian response has not fully been dealt with in the absence of some reference to the 'practical' response to the problem which is engendered by the Cross-Resurrection event. This is not a plea for a homily. Rather, the point is that an analysis of Christian claims concerning that event would have required Schlesinger to say more than he does concerning God's action in the world; and that in turn would have led us to the questions of the nature of history and the relation of time and eternity. Undeniably, not everything can be said in one book, but a fuller indication of our author's thoughts on these matters would have been welcomed.

As stated at the outset, this treatment of age-old problems is fresh. It is so in at least three ways. First, Schlesinger's work illustrates his conviction that 'The theist has been given an unprecedented opportunity to make substantial capital out of the new-wrought ideas of astro-physics' and of developments in logic and elsewhere. Secondly, as over against the kind of God with whom some philosophers deal—a god so emaciated as to be unrecognizable by believers—Schlesinger's God has attributes. A goodly number of these are paraded with a view to analyzing their relations within a coherent theistic worldview. Thirdly, the impression is conveyed that we are in the midst of a lively, current debate between Schlesinger and his critics. It would be an excellent exercise for students to be invited to suggest the possible next moves of his opponents, and to envisage his possible further responses. No doubt he himself will advise us of the latter when this intriguing book has received the close analytical attention it deserves.

Critical Review of Books in Religion III (1990) 398–400.

26

God's Nature and Existence

Richard M. Gale. *On the Nature and Existence of God*. Cambridge: CUP, 1991. Pp. 422.

This book, by a professor of philosophy at the University of Pittsburgh, is a significant contribution to the ever-growing body of literature on theism. In the first place—and refreshingly, since the question of the nature of the God whose existence is in question is sometimes overlooked—he focuses upon some of the classical divine attributes. His objective is to show that they tend so to 'over metaphysicalize' God that he is no longer a person, and hence is 'religiously unavailable.' Conceptual revision is thus called for. Secondly, he argues that neither epistemological nor pragmatic justifications of the proposition 'God exists' are unproblematic. While granting that the sceptical spirit of Hume's Philo pervades his book, Professor Gale's quest is of a God worthy of worship, even if the case for believing in his existence is inadequate.

In five chapters on atheological arguments Gale seeks to show why our concept of God must be 'redesigned' if God is to be it worthy object of worship. If, for example, we persist in maintaining that God is absolutely simple (that is, possesses every perfection to an unlimited or unsurpassable degree), we shall be vulnerable to atheological arguments which reveal the contradictions which ensue therefrom, of which a harbinger is God's creation of a stone so heavy that he cannot lift it. But, says Gale, no religious harm results from surrendering omnipotence thus construed. Again, consider absolute sovereignty: here ethical propositions constitute an important sticking-point, for they 'are not of the right categoreal sort to be made true by anyone's decision, even God's' (p. 34). Similar conceptual revision is required in connection with 'benevolence,' 'immutability,' and 'absoluteness'.

Chapter 2 concerns the creation-immutability argument. In its main versions this argument, bequeathed by Augustine, errs in temporally relating God's creative act to its worldly effects. Augustine wishes to claim that time comprises past, present and future, yet lands himself with an argument which yields the unreality of time. This is a gift to those who would advance atheological arguments; for the [Christian] theist is committed to a *past* creation and Incarnation, and to a *future* resurrection and judgement. How can these be if time is unreal? Professor Gale muses that had the implication of Augustine's argument been realized the Church 'would have tar and feathered rather than sainted him.' So to a discussion of the eternity of God, which clearly exposes classical theism's underlying problem, namely, that God is desired to play contradictory roles: 'to be both a person and a mystical reality that is beyond being, time, and distinctions' (p. 55).

The problem is underscored in the following chapter, in which the omniscience-immutability argument is investigated. Gale contends that the concept of a timelessly eternal God is not viable, and that the counter-arguments support the notion of an omni-temporally eternal God.

Chapter 4 concerns the deductive atheological argument from evil. Gale shows how, in seeking to defend God's omnipotence and omnibenevolence in face of evil, theists are liable to restrict their concepts of omniscience and sovereignty. This is argued *via* a substantial consideration of the free will defence, in which the views of J. L. Mackie, H. J. McCloskey and A. Plantinga are subjected to close scrutiny.

In the fifth chapter the indexical theory of actuality is weighed and found wanting. Accordingly, it cannot legitimately be mounted as an atheological argument. A positive result of this discussion is the demonstration that 'the actual world' is a nonrigid definite description and 'is actual' is a monadic predicate' (p. 197). The moral is that 'The actual world does not differ from other worlds in that it alone possesses the property of actuality, but in that it alone actually has existence' (p. 198).

Professor Gale next turns to theological arguments for the rationality of theistic beliefs, treating in turn ontological, cosmological, religious-experience, and pragmatic arguments. He carefully examines versions of the ontological argument, paying particular attention to those of Anselm, N. Malcolm and A. Plantinga ('Were it not for his brilliance and creativity, I never would have been moved to write this book,' p. 224). He concludes that none of the versions succeeds, and that if God were conceived as necessarily existing, he could not and would not exist.

In the course of his critique of cosmological arguments the author commends himself to this reviewer at least by taking Samuel Clarke seriously, and he has this *bon mot* concerning the Copleston-Russell debate: 'The cosmological arguer will rightly charge Russell with begging the question by assuming at the outset that all knowledge is scientific because only scientific explanations qualify as *real* explanations' (p. 252). This, he declares, is nothing more than a sentiment. The positions of P. Edwards and W. Rowe are examined, and two arguments in the form of ontological disproofs are mounted which serve to deny the existence of the sort of being whose existence is asserted in the conclusions of arguments of the cosmological variety.

Turning to religious experiences Gale questions whether they 'constitute evidence for reality being as it appears to the experients' (p. 286). To count as evidence experiences must be both veridical and cognitive. He argues that religious evidences, while possibly the former, cannot be the latter; and, further, that 'a religious experience . . . could not qualify as a veridical perception of an objective reality even if its apparent object were to exist and be the cause of the experience' (p. 287). The case is advanced in relation to the views of, *inter alia*, P. Quinn, W. Alston, R. Swinburne, W. Wainwright and P. Strawson, and language-game fideism of various kinds is deemed to be a *cul de sac*.

But what if there are desirable consequences of religious belief? Enter pragmatic arguments from prudence and from morality. An interesting discussion Pascal's wager concludes thus:

> Pascal's wager is not really a wager, since the people who will accept it do not see themselves as gambling at all. According to their scheme of preferences, they are not risking something finite, their worldly life, for the chance of gaining some infinite other-worldly reward, since the religious way of life is the one that has the greatest value for them. Pascal's 'wager' turns out to be nothing but a pep talk to those who suffer from a kind of weakness of will. (p. 353)

Again, from the fact that a believer may lead a morally better life as a result religious experience (and quite apart from the fact that there is no epistemic warrant for concluding to God from such an experience), we may not suppose that the believer has a sufficient reason for belief. Here Gale challenges the 'naysayer' to show that the believer brings about a moral evil that outweighs the realized good. He that 'While grounds were given for doubting that any of [the pragmatic arguments] succeed, no knockout was scored' (p. 387). This is not surprising, he thinks, for conclusive results in reasoning about normative issues are less likely than in areas of rational enquiry.

In his brief Epilogue Professor Gale affirms that if all we had were the epistemological and pragmatic arguments which he has reviewed, faith in God would lack rational justification. For his part he resonates with the Kierkegaardian view of 'faith as a subjective passion that outstrips our reason' (p. 387).

I am well aware that the foregoing bald summary does scant justice to the author's intricate analysis. His method entails the rigorous formulation of arguments, with ample use of the techniques of formal and symbolic logic. Equal space will be required and comparable logical acumen will be needed if chinks in his armour are to be found. I content myself with submitting three general remarks before proceeding to my conclusion.

First, as to Gale's distinction between 'hard core' descriptive properties of God—such as his being supremely great and eminently worthy of worship, and lower-level properties such as omnipotence, benevolence, and the like: the grounds upon which this distinction is drawn—other than the fact that it is convenient and seems to permit (a) such refurbishing of lower-level properties as may be required from time to time, whilst (b) permitting the claim that there is an identity of religious belief which persists through the ages—are not clear. Neither is it clear why properties (a), (b) and (c) should fall into one category, while properties (x), (y) and (z) should fall into the other. Again, it is not clear that 'being omnipotent' is not, to many believers, part of what 'being supremely great' means—and this would seem to render the promised distinction suspect. Yet again, can we, as readily as Professor Gale supposes, both redesign the lower-order properties and be sure that we are referring to the same being?

Secondly, the idea (to put it very crudely) that no matter what the philosophers and divines say about the divine attributes, the God-idea plays the same role in the same ongoing religious community, is open to question, since it would seem that until the God-idea is further specified (whether in classical, process or existentialist terms) it is hardly possible to worship (belief in God being inextricably interwoven with belief that God is such and such). When the God-idea is specified, significantly different attitudes and practices may (and surely do) characterize those who live with different specifications. It may well be that 'What constitutes sameness of a religious community over time is a deep issue that deserves a separate volume' (p. 11), but the positing of such sameness is so crucial to Gale's ultimate objective that a little more light on the matter in the present volume would have been welcomed.

Thirdly, may we hope that Professor Gale will be a little less enigmatic, and a little more constructive, in relation to the hints he drops in passing concerning his favourable dispositions towards process theology and Kierkegaard. Thus far, on these matters, he tantalizes.

There is evidence to suggest that fine writing is not our author's primary concern: indeed, on occasion his style renders his meaning opaque. For the most part, however, his language, if not always choice ('screw around'), is lucid—even pungent, as when he describes the non-cognitive language game of Hare, Phillips, *et al.*, as 'atrocious' in that it 'radically misdescribes the actual enterprise of religion.' Religious believers understand themselves as saying literally true things about God—otherwise their attempt to commune with God would make no sense; and 'Even the star of *Hervey* thought the big white rabbit to be real' (p. 292).

Readers of this deeply serious and often technically sophisticated book will be encouraged on their way by a delightful demonstration that Ronald Reagan is more powerful than God (because of what he can get away with); and by the recommendation that we play 'Pomp and Circumstance' whilst reading aloud the elevated cadences of the late nineteenth-century moralist W. K. Clifford. Nostalgia also plays a part. We have the invocation of boxers, band leaders and film stars: there is even the 'Gabby Hayes objection' (though the explanatory footnote supplied 'for readers who are too young to remember' Gabby is redundant, since that 'dentally challenged' eminence is ubiquitous on television screens to this day). As one adept at weaving into his text the titles of songs of which it is sometimes said that 'They don't write them that way any more,' Professor Gale would be the first to contest the first part of the proposition, 'T'ain't what you do, it's the way that you do it.' Certainly, what he has done was well worth the doing, and he has done it well. In view of its argumentative merits, and also because a number of those whom he rebukes are still in a position to, and have not in the past shown themselves reluctant to, reply to an adversary, we may expect that this book will provide a focus for discussion for some time to come.

International Journal of Philosophical Studies (1993) 143–46.

27

Faith, Scepticism, and Personal Identity

J. J. MacIntosh and H. A. Meynell, eds. *Faith, Scepticism and Personal Identity: A Festschrift for Terence Penelhum*. Calgary: University of Calgary Press, 1994. Pp. vii + 304.

The University of Calgary has, over its relatively short life, established an enviable reputation in both philosophy and religious studies. To no single person is this achievement more due than to Terence Penelhum, who, following a decade at the University of Alberta, became Head of the Department of Philosophy at Calgary (1964–70), and did much to found the Department of Religious Studies, which he served from 1978–88. The recipient of many honours, Terence Penelhurn continues to pursue his calling with integrity, wrestling with substitutive questions, utilizing his analytical skills, his knowledge of intellectual history, and his detailed acquaintance with the relevant texts. His gentle humour and his wry appreciation of the foibles of humanity help to maintain his equilibrium when confronted by philosophical ineptitude, the seamier ways of the world, and the faddishness of some of his co-religionists. He is among Canada's most respected philosophers, and is widely known around the world through his writings and his many guest lectures.

Since the establishment of Calgary's Department of Religious Studies, the local philosophers have never lacked for sparring partners, and it is entirely appropriate that this *Festschrift* should be edited jointly by Jack Macintosh (philosophy) and Hugo Meynell (religious studies). The latter contributes a Biographical Note an Introduction and a paper, the former a paper. To these are added the contributions of colleagues, friends and former pupils.

This is a disciplined *Festschrift*. I do not have the impression that any of the authors simply plundered an available stockpile of papers to be ransacked on celebratory occasions. On the contrary, the contributions both honour the recipient and concern his special interests—the philosophy of religion, Hume studies, and identity and self—frequently engaging directly with his thought. This makes possible what may without injustice to others be regarded as the highlight of the book: Penelhum's responses to his interlocutors, which are variously incisive and tentative, but always genial and modestly phrased. I thus feel both that a friend is appropriately honoured, and that the discussion is advanced.

The items already mentioned are joined by the following: 'Perceiving God,' (Kai Nielsen); 'On Religious Experience' (John Hick); 'Faith and the Limitations of Open-mindedness' (Basil Mitchell); 'Criticism of a Cosmological Argument' (Hugo Meynell); 'Hume on Religion: Stopping the Ocean with a Bull-rush?' (Annette C. Baier); 'Hume, Testimony to Miracles, the Order of Nature, and Jansenism' (Alasdair MacIntyre); The

Legitimation of Factual Necessity' (Anthony Flew); 'How a Sceptic may Live Scepticism' (David Fate Norton); 'Modern Work on Intentionality' (William Lyons); 'The Disunity of the Self' (Andrew Brennan); 'Personal Identity and Objective Reality' (Geoffrey Madell); 'Happiness and Personal Identity' (R. T. Herbert); and 'The Impossibility of Miraculous Reincarnation' (J. J. Macintosh).

A bibliography of Penelhum's works, an index, and a superb portrait enhance the work. It is quite impossible to comment upon all the points of interest raised by these impressive papers, but I should like to whet the appetite of potential readers by referring to Kai Nielsen's critique of William Alston's position on the way in which we perceive God, and to Penelhum's remarks upon both approaches. Penelhum's probing of Hick is of considerable current interest: "If I think that the world's major religious traditions, my own included, are culturally relative responses to the Real, and that it is not possible to conceive of, or have, culture-independent access to the Real, does not this have an inevitably adverse effect on the way in which I participate in my own religious faith?" (p. 234).

In entire sympathy with Basil Mitchell's view that in an ambiguous world cumulative considerations justify religious belief, Penelhum nevertheless wishes to foster a stronger natural theology than Mitchell proposes—one which would '*disambiguate* our situation by showing it to be irrational not to be believe in God' (p. 247). He values Meynell's attempt in this direction, but feels that his friend has not made clear the reason for believing in the existence of the divine creative will.

MacIntyre is applauded for observing the parallels between the epistemologies of Pascal and Hume; and in commenting on the papers on personal identity Penelhum brings Herbert, Macintosh, Madell and Brennan into creative tension. He emphasizes that personal integration is something to be achieved; that it concerns personal progress and regress on the way; and that these, 'though describable in the language of self-identity, are successes or failures of transformations *within a life*, and do not constitute breaks in the numerical identity of the individuals to whom, or within whose lives, they take place' (p. 277).

Among the most suggestive of Penelhum's remarks is this: 'The Christian is not
merely someone who thinks life will go on longer later, but someone who thinks a person is a different sort of being from the one that the unbeliever perceives' (p. 289). It is not difficult to imagine that this and other assertions will fuel philosophical discussion of this complex of issues for some time to come. If the anticipated responses are as thoughtful and constructive as those of Penelhum himself, 'the fair maid Philosophy' will emerge with her reputation untarnished, and the one here honoured will, once again, have served us well. May this collection receive the wide and discriminating readership that it deserves!

International Journal of Philosophical Studies 4 (1996) 363–65.

28

The Philosophical Frontiers of Christian Theology

Brian Hebblethwaite and Stewart Sutherland, eds. *The Philosophical Frontiers of Christian Theology; Essays presented to D. M. MacKinnon.* Cambridge: CUP, 1982. Pp 252.

With this important volume colleagues, pupils and friends of D. M. MacKinnon pay tribute to a philosopher whose work on the borderlands of theology has been widely influential. The preface incorporates biographical notes on MacKinnon, and the frontispiece portrait seems to speak of a brooding seriousness which is on the point of being overtaken by joy.

The collection falls into four parts, the first of which is entitled, 'Athens and Jerusalem.' C. F. D. Moule writes on 'The borderlands of ontology in the New Testament.' By means of the judicious examination of texts, and notably of *logos*, he shows that while the biblical writers, who do not set out to be philosophers as such, make minimal use of philosophical terms, they do record sayings of Christ's followers—supremely in connection with the resurrection narratives—'which imply an estimate not only of his function but of his being' (p. 9). In this way the New Testament presses those who study it up against ontological questions.

The late G. W. H. Lampe asks, 'Athens and Jerusalem: joint witnesses to Christ?' He reminds us that Christian apologists in the early centuries were prepared to grant that God had spoken to men in pre-Christian times. Christ, however, was the fulfilment of the highest pagan ideals, and there was ultimately but one source of divine revelation. The idea that this revelation was conveyed by God himself in propositional form was not contested. The theme is illustrated by reference to the fathers and to the gospels. In the latter connection Lampe finds that Matthew's Magi suggest that the first evangelist, no less than the third, believed in a preparation for Christ in pagan lands. All of this is interesting, but sadly the essay does not finally satisfy. Evidence is assembled which points to an affirmative answer to the question in the title, but a number of questions remain. For example: is the gospel in danger of attenuation when, in the interest of missionary strategy etc., bridges are built between it and other cultures? Perhaps such a question cannot easily be answered by, or even arise for, one whose avowedly 'liberal' theology enables him to 'envisage the possibility of many revelations ... The God of Islam, the God of Judaism, the God of Christianity [all monotheistic faiths, be it noted] may be understood as alternative ways of conceiving the one God, or perhaps as aspects, or modes of self-communication, of the same one God' (p. 18). Again, it appears that Lampe places his feet on the slope between 'The Bible is not a compendium of propositionally revealed truths' and 'We can manage without any revealed information at all' without making it clear where, or how, he stops. His recourse to the notion of encounter—as another contributor to the symposium. R. W. Hepburn would surely remind us, bristles with difficulties.

Part One ends with Christopher Stead's characteristically lucid essay, 'The concept of mind and the concept of God in the Christian Fathers.' He observes that although 'there is no biblical authority, in either Old or New Testament, for describing God as Mind . . . from the second century, at least, it was taken for granted by Christian apologists that the Greek word *nous* provided a convenient shorthand term to express their conviction of God as living and personal, and to link that conviction with the theism which was developing on its own lines among contemporary Greek philosophers' (p. 39). By means of a careful examination of Plato and of the later Platonism he reaches his (suitably qualified) conclusion that when Christians adopted later Platonism's view that the Ideas are God's thought, they did not make 'the proper adjustments to the concept of mind, whether in God himself or in us human beings . . . the mind is conceived as directed towards realities independent of itself; and the value of its apprehension depends on the values of the realities it contemplates . . . the Godhead [of active, outgoing love] cannot be pictured in this fashion' (pp. 52–53). This is precisely the kind of consideration which was inhibited by Lampe's presuppositions.

Don Cupitt opens Part Two, 'Theological enquiry after Kant,' with 'Kant and the negative theology.' His point of departure is MacKinnon's view that in his religious thought Kant stands in the tradition of the negative theology. Cupitt concurs to the extent: (a) that Kant 'strives to remain within the limits of thought,' and (b) that Kant insists that our inability to know God as God is a 'negative' witness to the Transcendent. But there are significant differences between Kant and the older negative theology. Where earlier theologians held that the existence of God was certain, but that his nature was unknowable, Kant demolished the proofs of God's existence. After Kant negative theology 'has to endure objective uncertainty about God' (p. 60). Other points of difference are discussed, the most important being encapsulated in the following words: 'The Greek Fathers, for example, invoke a sense of the mystery of the divine transcendence in order to awaken heavenly longings. Their language is designed to attract, whereas Kant's language is designed to repel. Kant wants us to renounce impossible and futile aspirations and be content with doing our duty. Do not aspire after the real God, he says, for that will only end in anthropomorphism and fantasy. Be content with the available God postulated by practical reason . . . (p. 63). Some concluding remarks in which the non-cognitive philosophy of religion of D. Z. Phillips is compared with that of Kant; and in which MacKinnon's descriptive-realist understanding of the negative way is said to be the Way of the Cross, are so brief as to be tantalizing to experts and opaque to general readers.

In 'Ideology, metaphor and analogy' Nicholas Lash shows how 'the forms of Christian discourse are set between the poles of metaphor and analogy, of narrative and metaphysics' (p. 72), and suggests that 'the distinction between narrative, metaphorical discourse, and those non-narrative modes of discourse to which reflection on the metaphorical gives rise appears, within Christianity, as a distinction between religious practice and critical reflection on that practice: between 'religion' and 'theology' (p. 73). In a closely-reasoned paper which defies brief summary he finds that 'the testing of Christian truth-claims occurs, or should occur, in the interplay between their practical verification and their exposure to historical, literary and philosophical criticism' (p. 87). This is perhaps the most stimulating and provocative essay in the book. The notes are full and suggestive—not least in connection with the alleged misinterpretation of Lonergan by the distinguished Anglican Thomist, E. L. Mascall.

Under the title, 'Theological study: the nineteenth century and after,' S. W. Sykes argues, with some justification, that 'The contemporary study of theology in English universities lacks...that kind of confident self-understanding without which it cannot begin to emerge as "a system of belief ", to which philosophical criticism can be applied' (p. 97). Agreeing with MacKinnon that 'what the Christian learns from his faith is that the study of the particular and actual takes precedence of the ideal or merely possible,' he adds that the force of this argument 'assumes the impact on the student of the doctrinal substance of the Christian faith itself, for the unified study of which this essay has pleaded' (p. 115).

Part Three, 'Metaphysics and Morality,' opens with R. W. Hepburn's sincere, serious and sensitive essay on 'Optimism, finitude and the meaning of life.' Avoiding the pitfalls (for, in his case, a non-theist) of undue optimism and undue pessimism, he finds that meaning can be found in life without the denial of life's finitude, and without the support of Christian or other religious hopes. He suggests that 'Through the balancing and mutual correcting of images we can come nearer to focusing on death ... We may see in that very human fragility an occasion for wonderment: exchanging, if we can, fear and resentment at the certainty of death for wonder at the life which it will close' (p. 141). Apart from its intrinsic worth Hepburn's paper cautions Christians not to bolster their own eschatologies by reference to the allegedly inevitable hollowness of the humanist's vision. As compared with shriller expositions of the Christian hope, Hepburn's religious humanism is remarkably sane and balanced. But in the quotation just given we are brought up sharp by the three little words, 'if we can.' Is there a word here for those whose experience—it may be of oppression, or guilt, or of utter frustration with life—prevents them from seeing in human fragility an occasion for wonderment? Is the serene religious humanist sufficient of a realist? Can we so easily 'bracket' the soteriological and eschatological concerns of western humanism's Christian seedbed?

Bernard Williams writes cogently on 'Practical necessity.' His argument turns on the recognition that 'To arrive at the conclusion that one must do a certain thing is, typically, to make a discovery—a discovery which is, always minimally and sometimes substantially, a discovery about oneself' (p. 151). He concludes: 'The recognition of practical necessity must involve an understanding at once of one's own powers and incapacities, and of what the world permits, and the recognition of a limit which is neither simply external to the self, nor yet a product of the will, is what can lend a special authority or dignity to such decisions...' (p. 152).

In 'Religion, ethics and action,' Stewart Sutherland sets out to refute those who maintain 'the transferability of ethical beliefs'—the thesis, that is, that when it comes to what is to be done there is common ground as between, for example, Christians and humanists. Sutherland denies that what makes Christian ethics distinctive is that it is 'secular ethics

+ X, and that if one doesn't like X, then one still may be said to share a great deal if not almost all of what constitutes an ethic, with a believer' (p. 157). But 'What is it to share an ethic?' 'What makes two actions the same (similar)?' These often unconsidered questions are here investigated, and the conclusion is that 'the description and classification of actions is not a matter for observers alone . . . identification of what a man does, that is, of his actions, cannot always be carried out wholly independently of identification of what he intended to do, and to state what he intended to do may not always be possible without reference to what his moral beliefs are' (p. 163). Such advocates of the transferability-thesis as Braithwaite, Hare and Cunningham err in representing human conduct 'as detachable from the thought that directs it' (p. 165). In a concluding paragraph Sutherland offers an agenda of matters arising which will occupy moral philosophers (including, one hopes, himself) for some time to come.

In Part Four we have three contributions under the general heading, 'Truth and falsehood in theology.' T. F. Torrance writes on 'Theological realism.' In the absence of a more suitable term he employs 'realist' 'to describe the orientation in thought that obtains in science, philosophy or theology on the basis of a non-dualist or unitary relation between the empirical and theoretical ingredients in the structure of the real world and in our knowledge of it (p. 173). Although the foundations of classical theology were realist in this sense, Torrance has sadly to record that the impact of Augustinian culture and the revival of Platonist and Aristotelian dualism is now, *via* phenomenalism, infecting contemporary Roman Catholic philosophy and theology. Schillebeeckx is taken as a test case, and Torrance's plea is for a return to the tradition of Nicene realism: for 'It is as our communion with God the Father through Christ and in his Spirit is grounded in and shares in the inner Trinitarian consubstantial or *homoousial* communion of the Father, Son and Holy Spirit, that the subjectively-given pole of conceptuality is constantly purified and refined under the searching light and quickening power of the objectively-given pole in divine revelation' (p. 193). No doubt some eyebrows will be raised at the way in which Torrance has Augustine and Aquinas playing not only in the same game but in the same team; but this is a learned piece of theological reflection. Such work is not to be taken for granted in these relatively rudderless theological times.

In his 'Notes on analogical predication and speaking about God' Roger White takes Wittgenstein on colour and Wrede on Christ's Messiahship as points of departure, and argues that whereas Aquinas and Barth agree that 'the words used to signify divine perfections are used in their primary sense in their application to God, and that their use when predicated of creatures is a derivative sense' (p. 202), Barth takes the further step of 'turning the traditional doctrine of analogical predication on its head: that it is from the use of words in talking about God that we may throw light on their everyday use and not *vice versa*' (p. 225).

Finally, Brian Hebblethwaite considers '"True" and "false" in Christology.' Eschewing the approaches of W. Cantwell Smith ('personal truth' signifies a quality of personal living), D. Z. Phillips (the sense to be given to 'truth' and 'reality' can be discerned only within the religious language-game), and idealist constructivism of all kinds, Hebblethwaite opts for realism which insists that the world is what it is irrespective of *our* knowing minds, and for theism which both humbles the intellectual (for God is in an important sense beyond our thought) and checks the sceptic (for we can know God—truly if not exhaustively). Hebblethwaite then examines certain Christological options in the light of his contention that 'Objectivity is secured both for actual and intended truth by reference to the creative will of God' (p. 232); and concludes that 'even in these profoundly religious contexts of incarnate, moral and practical truth the same basic sense of "truth" is still maintained— namely, that which expresses or shows how things are and were meant to be' (p. 237). Hebblethwaite has many interesting things to say but I would advert (the word, incidentally, which should have appeared halfway down p. 232) to the importance of something he *nearly* says. Having reviewed approaches to Christology 'from above' and 'from below' he writes, 'my point is that to see the Cross of Christ as God's Cross in our world implies an incarnational Christology' (p. 236). Quite so; and *my* point is that the air of unreality and of scholasticism which surrounds much recent Christological discussion would be dispelled if it were remembered that the severance in discussion of Christ's person from his work is fatal to sound Christology. It is salutary to recall that the early Christians found it impossible to withhold Christological titles from Jesus not simply because he came, but because of what he did when he came. The route to a sound Christology is *via* a sound soteriology.

This collection displays an internal coherence which works of this kind sometimes lack. Many of the contributions, by overt reference, testify to the stimulus received by the writers from the one in whose honour the essays were written. Paul Wignall's appended bibliography of 'Donald Mackinnon's published writings 1937–80' demonstrates the *breadth* of Mackinnon's *concerns* (both italicized words are important). We are here reminded that in 1966 MacKinnon published an article in the *Cambridge Review* entitled. 'Can a divinity professor be honest?' The answer must surely be, 'Yes—when the divinity professor in question is the recipient of the essays here reviewed.'

Philosophical Studies 30 (1984) 357–62.

29

Christian Theism and Moral Philosophy

Michael Beaty, Carlton Fisher and Mark Nelson, eds. *Christian Theism and Moral Philosophy*. Macon, GA: Mercer University Press, 1998. Pp. 319.

From time to time, when feeling more than ordinarily robust, I offer the advanced course in Christian Ethics. It is a risky undertaking, and it can be a debilitating experience, because the tendency is for more vocal students to dive straight for those 'issues' which, in common parlance, are deemed 'sexy', and to 'sound off' upon them in a faintly unproductive 'person-in-the-pub' kind of way. Genetic engineering, abortion, global warming: these are the current themes of choice, and it only needs the *Radio Times* to advertise a programme announcing that there is scarcely any difference between ourselves and chimpanzees and some of the D+ types will, if permitted, go on for hours. In such circumstances one needs, if not a theodicy, at least allies; for the quickest way to qualify for the label 'spoilsport' is to suggest that there are serious methodological issues underlying the ethical pronouncements to which we wantonly give vent.

The editors of the collection under review have assembled some allies. But what makes this volume especially stimulating is the fact that the contributors do not all see eye-to-eye on starting-points in Christian ethics. Indeed, the impression is conveyed that three of them, the late J. H. Yoder, Stanley Hauerwas and Charles Pinches, agreed to participate only on condition that they could challenge the editorial assumption that it makes sense to seek one theoretical starting-point in Christian ethics. Obligingly, the editors moved the goalposts.

Following an Introduction which takes the form of an editorial review of the papers presented, the work falls into three sections. Under 'The Metaphysics of Morals,' Ralph McInery writes on Aquinas, Robert M. Adams on divine commands and the social nature of obligation, C. Stephen Evans on a Kierkegaardian view of the foundations of morality and Marilyn McCord Adams on forgiveness. 'The Epistemology of Ethics' is the rubric under which Caroline J. Simon writes on Christianity and moral knowledge, David B. Fletcher discusses particular divine moral commands, Julius M. Moravcsik reflects on attitudes in ethics and John Howard Yoder proposes an alternative to methodologism. Finally, in a section headed 'The Ethics of Love,' James Keller proposes a consequentialist ethical theory, J. L. A. Garcia discusses norms of loving, Philip L. Quinn writes on the primacy of God's will in Christian ethics and Stanley Hauerwas and Charles Pinches combine to offer a Christian view of virtue. The book is furnished with a bibliography, notes on contributors and an index.

Every paper invites comment, but this is here precluded. Instead, some general remarks may be made first on the project as a whole, and then on a few points of particular interest or concern.

The editors' stated objective is to rise to a challenge laid down by Alvin Plantinga, who, in 1983, declared that 'we who are Christians and propose to be philosophers must not rest content with being philosophers who happen, incidentally, to be Christians; we must strive to be Christian philosophers. We must therefore pursue our projects with integrity, independence, and Christian boldness.' This quotation from the dust jacket is alluded to in the Introduction, but it is not closely scrutinized. Instead, the editors inform us that 'We selected and commissioned a set of essays that assumes of the respective authors either a commitment to a Christian worldview or an interest in how questions in moral philosophy should be answered from a Christian worldview' (p. vii). But this reinforces the question begged by Plantinga's use of the term 'independence.' Of what are Christian philosophers to be independent: of 'alien' worldviews? Of secular philosophical 'isms' or techniques? Of ecclesiastical authority? It would seem that when the terms 'independence' and 'worldview' are allied, a number of questions, here unresolved, are posed. Again, although I do not accuse him of writing pejoratively, some may be misled by Plantinga's use of the adverb 'incidentally.' Some of the acutest ethical reflection in the past fifty years has been offered by philosophers who regard themselves as Christians, and who are indeed Christians. They do not, however, set out to propound, defend or otherwise peddle a (still less the) Christian worldview; but from this it by no means follows that their Christian faith is 'incidental' in any casual, 'as it happens' sense.

It must not be supposed that the editors' attachment to worldviews leads them to deny epistemological common ground with those who do not embrace the Christian faith. However, in their very first footnote they do recognize the existence of some (more to be found, I suspect, in pockets in the United States, Holland and South Africa than elsewhere) who do deny that there is common ground. A 'dust-up' on this topic could have been quite entertaining if not altogether improving. In the event, while the editors admit those who query all 'one foundation' approaches in Christian ethics, there are limits to their welcome, and their conviction is that those who reflect and theorize upon moral questions share common ground which is 'so significant that it would be wrong to say of the Christian involved in the study of ethics that she is doing something fundamentally different from non-Christians in pursuing answers to these common questions' (p. 1; cf. pp. 178, 216).

While it would be unfair to complain that not every suggestion from moral philosophy is here pursued, it should be noted that the implications for Christian ethical discourse of linguistic analysis—so large a feature of moral philosophy during the past fifty years—are considered only *en passant*. This is a more serious omission than might at first sight appear, because the editors' project is to integrate 'theology and ethics into a coherent whole' (p. 2)—though Simon, following Peter Geach, appears to accord a greater degree of autonomy to ethics than the theology-*cum*-ethics school would allow (p. 130). Be that as it may, I understand the editors to mean that they wish to heal, or surmount, the theology–ethics bifurcation (to which Hauerwas and Pinches allude, p. 289) which in the West followed in the wake of Hobbes, and which was, for example, given early recognition in the curriculum of Henry Grove's Dissenting academy at Taunton. But this objective brings us directly into the realm of Christian doctrinal claims; and while we hear a good deal in this book about the norm of love, such matters as language concerning the guidance of the Spirit, or 'perfection' or 'eternal' in 'eternal life,' are not pursued, and this despite the absence of any general embargo against the supernatural and the eschatological.

A related question is this: if the healing of the theology–ethics divide can take place, what will be the consequences, if any, for our understanding of Christian ethical motivation? Shall we be able to endorse with renewed zeal Thomas Jackson's remark of 1857 (in *The Duties of Christians Theoretically and Practically Considered*) that whereas moral philosophy derives its motives from the reason and fitness of things, Christianity derives its most effective motives from the redeeming mercy of God? What difference, if any, would this make to the concept of ethical common ground? Might the desired healing be more certainly achieved if some of the contributors (pp. 24, 209, 279) remembered that 'love God, love neighbour' is the quintessence of Jewish ethics, while the distinctively Christian motive, 'as I have loved you,' entails discourse concerning the Cross, the atonement, and much else besides—all of which language is ripe for closer analysis than it sometimes receives.

When Evans proclaims, with reference to families, that 'Social relationships of this type carry with them ethical obligations' (p. 66), the spectre of Hume and the is/ought debate rise up before us. The nettle might more firmly have been grasped—not least by those who may feel that there is something faintly sub-human about an ethical theory which would appear to forbid a Good Samaritan's response on the ground that it violates a rule of formal logic. Evans's remark calls to mind an assertion of J. H. Godwin in 1885: 'abstract principles give no knowledge of real existence, and supply no motive to action of any kind. Fitness and agreement refer to some end or rule, and are most intelligible when referred to the capacity of the agent, and the welfare of all' (*Active Principles*, 301). Perhaps so, but a case needs to be made out.

The social context of ethical decision-making is brought strongly to the fore by Yoder. His approach is rooted in the Christian community's reasoning together and, no doubt, his experience of such activity prompts his bold assertion that 'Pluralism as to epistemological method is not a counsel of despair but part of the Good News (p. 188). He views with great suspicion what he calls 'the flight to methodology,' for it assumes that agreement on method at least partly resolves differences concerning concrete behaviour. In fact, he declares, we are under 'no obligation to reason the same way on all subjects' (p. 191; cf. p. 200). That, as Yoder says, Augustine was deontological about lying and teleological about killing seems clear; but is there anything that makes even a reasoned eclecticism cohere—and does it matter? If Yoder's frame of reference is the Christian society, his bedrock is the scriptural canon. It would therefore seem that despite his opposition to certain kinds of allegedly exclusive methodological foundations, he is not utterly bereft of somewhere to plant his feet.

In partial justification of their suspicion of the 'one foundation' approach, Hauerwas and Pinches deny that 'Christians have a place to stand to reflect about which way it would be "moral" for them so to be or to act' (p. 287). Whilst, for the sake of argument (because huge questions concerning personal identity are opened up), granting their general point that 'for Christians our lives are not constituted by what we (sometimes) do but rather by who we (always) are' (p. 289), may we not query their unqualified dislike of the question 'Now, I have become a Christian. How should I best express my Christian commitment in my moral life?' (p. 288). They deny that this can sensibly be said; but recent converts, for example, might perfectly properly address themselves in this way when, in a moral quandary, they ponder what as Christians they ought to do, in relation to what they might once cheerfully have done, but which now seems suspect.

Hauerwas and Pinches set their faces against the view that Christian ethics 'is a special realm of the Christian life that can be codified, encapsulated in a theory, and successfully translated into a particular language' (p. 289). Here 'Christian ethics' means 'the Christian way of life.' It is not clear to me from this joint paper whether the authors would allow the term to the meta-ethical analysis of Christian ethical discourse, which can be carried on by Christians or others without any adverse implication that morality is somehow separable from life as it is lived.

There is a contemporary feel to much of the writing here (and to some of the literary style)—so much so that some readers may greet Simon's reference to natural law as the return of an old friend. Against the suggestion that proponents of natural law have 'a perfect grasp of what morality requires,' she says, 'As the history of Catholic moral theology demonstrates, even if one sees the basics of morality as graspable by the "light of reason", the line of thought leading from this basis to particular applications may be neither simple nor easily discerned' (p. 129). Here one recalls Maritain's problematic remark concerning the 'imperceptible transitions' from the general deliverances of natural law to specific rules—an 'imperceptibility' which has caused greater concern to some than to others (some of whom have called in the ecclesiastical cavalry).

There is much else to reflect upon: Garcia's claim that 'our moral lives are our inner lives'—'a deep insight from which Christian ethics has strayed as it has followed modernist philosophies in attempting to understand morality on the model of commands of reason, social conventions, economic analysis, etc.' (p. 240); and the divergent views of some of the contributors on 'the immoralities of the patriarchs.' Suffice it to say that this is a most stimulating collection of papers. May the discussions be carried forward; may qualifications be made and gaps be filled as appropriate; and may jaded teachers of Christian Ethics take heart.

Studies in Christian Ethics 13 (2000) 108–12.

Part One: Philosophy

30

Asian Philosophy

Brian Carr and Indira Mahalingam, eds. *Companion Encyclopedia of Asian Philosophy*. London: Routledge, 1997. Pp. xviii + 1136.

When this hefty and most welcome volume reached me, I wondered how soon I should be able to attend to it. I then broke an arm and a leg and, behold, there was time.

The forty-eight chapters fall into six sections concerning Persian, Indian, Buddhist, Chinese, Japanese and Islamic philosophy. Each chapter is followed by references and by suggestions for further reading; there is a most useful glossary in which the terms are grouped according to the sections described, and a substantial index. The editors have chosen their contributors carefully: the chapters are authoritative and, with very few exceptions, the writing is clear and concise. The editing has been done to a high standard, though I did note two slips in one paper (pp. 471, 477). The several traditions are treated chronologically, from their origins to the present day, and we can thus see how they have developed through time—in some cases in relation to one another, and frequently in response to widely-differing socio-political contexts. Variety characterizes all of the traditions, Buddhism emerging as the most plastic, Islam as the most resistant to challenges to orthodoxy.

Detailed analysis being precluded, something of the flavour of the book may be conveyed by noting a few considerations which were brought forcibly to one's attention: the openness of some twentieth-century Parsis to theosophy, of some Chinese thinkers to continental European philosophy, of some nineteenth-century Japanese thinkers to Mill, Herbert Spencer and others, and of Radhakrishnan to Kant and Hegel; the way in which an appeal to tradition in Hinduism accompanies the transition from the more impersonal tendencies of the earlier *Upanisads* to a more theistic emphasis; the diverse ontologies of Indian philosophies, and the distinction between those which posit the existence of the soul and those which do not; the traditional concern of Thai Buddhist monks with community discipline, as over against the philosophical and doctrinal speculations of their Burmese counterparts; the unresolved Vedantic puzzle which makes God both 'the agent of action and the individual soul suffering for action'; the crucial part played by Śankara in Indian philosophy, his refutation of metaphysical dualism, and his likeness and unlikeness to Kant; the contrast between those Indian ethicists for whom the universal moral law operates in nature and in humanity, and those for whom it originates in god: the illuminating account of Buddhist philosophical training in Tibet the importance of Dignāga in the development of Buddhist logic and epistemology; the lucid account of

'Logic and language in Chinese philosophy', which sets out from a rebuke to the author of an *Encyclopedia Britannica* article who is charged with minimizing the importance of logic in Chinese thought; the impact of twentieth-century events in China upon that nation's thought; the philosophical implications for Japan of the difference between theoretically grounded Buddhism and Confucianism and the more exclusively ceremonial Shintoism native to the country; the contribution of such East-West bridge-builders as D. T. Suzuki; the disjunction in Islamic philosophy post-Avicenna between those like Al-Ghazālī for whom language mirrors reality, and those like Averroes (and also like the Jewish thinker, Maimonides) who, in order to accommodate diverse perspectives on the truth, emphasize ambiguity and equivocation; the conclusion that 'No Arabic writer after Averroes [deemed heretical by some] openly and confidently offers to declare, out of reason and critical thought alone, the true nature of being, the character of reality at large'; and the way in which in contemporary Islam tradition replaces traditional enquiries into epistemology, ontology and axiology.

Students will find this volume to be a mine of reliable information which makes many introductions to Eastern thought appear unacceptably slight; scholars whose natural habitat is Christian thought will be reminded of significant traditions which some of them may too easily be tempted to ignore; and it may be that specialists in some of the many branches of Asian philosophy will value a compendium which invites them to view the wood within which their several trees are set.

P. S. If you can lift this sturdy tome unaided, you have not broken your arm.

Modern Believing NS 39 (1998) 58–59.

Part Two
History

31

Medieval Thought

David Luscombe. *Medieval Thought*. Oxford: OUP 1997. Pp. 245.

While setting out from Augustine as the major precursor of medieval culture, Professor Luscombe of the University of Sheffield rightly warns against the temptation to fasten exclusively upon the great names of Western Christemdom. The pagan, Christian and Jewish thinkers of the Hellenistic world, where between AD 200 and 600 Plato and Aristotle were regularly studied, should not be overlooked. Nevertheless on any reckoning Augustine, Boethius and Denis the pseudo-Areopagite qualify for more detailed discussion, and this they receive here.

An introduction to the liberal arts in Carolingian Europe follows, and we briefly meet Alcuin, Hincmar, Ratramnus and Gottschalk, as well as John Scotus Erigena, whose importance is properly appreciated. The stimulus afforded by Boethius to logical studies is noted (indeed, it is a welcome feature of this book that logic is accorded its due place—something which does not always happen in general introductory books); and while, as might be expected, Anselm and Abelard are discussed at some length, John of Salisbury, Gilbert of Poitiers and William of Conches are not overlooked.

The twelfth and thirteenth centuries are aptly characterized as those of 'New sources—new problems,' though the author is too good a scholar to permit us to think that the new completely swept away the old. But the newly available Latin translations of Aristotle, as well as the contributions of Islamic and Jewish thinkers, had all to be reckoned with. Robert Grosseteste was perhaps the most successful in assimilating and sifting the new knowledge in the period up to 1277. His pupil, Roger Bacon, promoted experimental science, while Bacon's contemporary and fellow-Franciscan, Bonaventure, developed Augustine's doctrine of illumination in opposition to theories of cognition espoused by Arab philosophers. The Dominican Albert the Great, earnest student of Aristotle, paved the way for the comprehensive synthetic work of his pupil Thomas Aquinas.

The tensions in the Faculty of Arts at Paris over such positions as that of the Aristotelian John of Jandun to the effect that the tenets of Christian faith are one thing, what may be held in philosophy another, set Franciscan against Dominican, the former suspecting the latter of heresy, and led to the condemnations of 1270, 1277 and 1284. In the wake of the condemnations those still attracted to Arab and Greek thought fell somewhat inhibited, while those who mined older Augustinian seams—John Duns Scotus and Henry of Ghent among them—were viewed more favourably by the authorities.

In the fourteenth century we find considerable variety: the anti-'Pelagianism' of Thomas Bradwardine, the ongoing tussles between the realists and nominalists, the logic of the Benedictine monk Roger Swyneshead, the developments in natural philosophy associated with the names of Buridan, Oresme and Robert Kilwardby, and Blasius's doctrine of the materiality of the human soul.

The fifteenth century is represented by the polemics of Jean Gerson, the mystical theology of Nicholas of Cusa, and Lorenzo Valla and the humanists.

The work is supplied with substantial notes, a select bibliography and an index.

Professor Luscombe does well to challenge some of the received wisdom concerning medieval thought. For example, to see the period as one in which Platonism was supplanted in the thirteenth century by Aristotelianism is simplistic, both as minimizing the persistence of the former and as overlooking the inter-action of the two streams in the early Middle Ages. He rightly reminds us of a number of other traditions—not least the Stoic—which continued to influence intellectual life. Again, he places a large question mark against the notion that while the Thomists held that God ruled by reason, Duns Scotus was an arbitrary voluntarist; in fact Duns maintained that whatever God wills is rational. Yet again, while some fourteenth-century mystics—Thomas à Kempis among them—shunned philosophy, others, like Meister Eckhart, Tauler and Ruysbroek were important teachers of philosophy. And lest any are tempted still to think that to William of Ockham God was sheer power, Professor Luscombe reminds us that Ockham was well aware of God's infinite goodness and mercy. As for medieval humanism: here the cautionary word is that, however it may be for latter day humanists, medieval scholastic humanism required, rather than sought to exclude, the supernatural.

For the amount of detail presented in a small space (if occasionally at the cost of stylistic elegance); for the balanced interpretations offered; for the corrections and cautions along the way; and for the scholarly apparatus which invites further exploration, Professor Luscombe is warmly to be thanked.

Faith and Freedom 51 (1998) 77–78.

32

Aquinas, Calvin, and Protestant Thought

Arvin Vos. *Aquinas, Calvin, and Contemporary Protestant Thought*. Exeter: The Paternoster Press, 1985. Pp. xvi + 178.

In ecumenical circles ecclesiological discussion has become commonplace—indeed, it has become something of an industry. Questions concerning church order, ministry and sacraments are being keenly debated. But these conversations turn upon methodological presuppositions which are not so commonly analyzed. If it could be shown, for example, that the methodological divide between Aquinas and Calvin is not as great as has hitherto been supposed, what implications would this discovery have for the ecumenical process?

This is the profoundly important question which Vos's study prompts. He so skilfully demolishes Protestant stereotypes of Aquinas as to provoke the response, 'How could Protestants so easily have been misled?' Part of the answer, he suggests, lies in the conjunction of a certain reluctance to study the texts with due care, with a propensity for repeating what other (inaccurate) Protestant writers have said. The Professor of Philosophy at Western Kentucky University exposes all such, and leaves them without excuse.

With careful reference to Aquinas's writings Vos argues that the alleged difference between him and Calvin over the relation of faith to knowledge results from a terminological confusion only; for when Calvin claims that faith yields knowledge of God he is using certitude as a criterion of knowledge, whereas when Aquinas denies that faith yields knowledge his criterion of knowledge is comprehension. Again, Vos shows that Aquinas's implicit faith was by no means the blind trust in the Church for which Protestants have assailed him; neither is Aquinas's 'faith' to be reduced to mere assent. Vos makes plain that for Aquinas faith is to be distinguished from knowledge in that it is *not* based on rationally sufficient evidence; in this sense (though not as holding that faith alone yields knowledge of God) Aquinas is a fideist, not an evidentialist.

At the heart of the book Vos takes by the scruff of the neck those who impute to Aquinas the view that we must establish such preambles to the articles of faith as that God exists before we are warranted in believing. On the contrary, what Aquinas means is that some truths are in principle, and by some people, knowable by reason, whereas the majority may know the same truths by faith. Theology derives its basic principles immediately from God; the procedures of natural theology have a clarifying function: 'The key to understanding Aquinas's position is to recognize that when he speaks of the *praeambula fidei* he does not have in mind prerequisites to the act of believing but rather prerequisites to the objects of faith, the things that are believed.' On this point the 'entire

[Protestant] tradition' is mistaken. How can this be? Following G. de Broglie, Vos suggests that under Cartesian influence some theologians, both Thomist and Protestant, came independently to believe that faith could be reasonable only if it could be demonstrated that God is truthful and that he reveals himself. Moreover, it is the later scholastics rather than Aquinas himself that Calvin and other Protestants have opposed (in which connection some reference might have been made to Luther's anti-scholastic tracts).

We thus pass to the 'Protestant textbook tradition' on nature and grace, which is weighed and found wanting. It has been widely held in Protestant circles that Aquinas teaches that nature is good as far as it goes, but that grace is superadded. Aquinas has then been accused of laying the shaky foundation upon which 'autonomous man' subsequently finds that he can manage without grace. In fact Aquinas holds that while the *imago Dei* implies that man has a desire to know God, he cannot know him through nature, but only by grace.

There is a measure of repetition in this book—no doubt justifiable when one is attempting to open the ears of an entirely misguided tradition: the first hearing may prompt incredulity rather than penitence. Difficulties are occasionally passed over, as when we are advised both that for Aquinas 'human reason is simply not capable of arriving at certitude with regard to divine matters,' and that 'those who can grasp [the truths concerning the preambles] by reason have no need to grasp them by faith.' But our most serious query is whether, in a book purporting to relate Aquinas and Calvin, the latter is given as fair a hearing as the former. Granted that Protestant misconceptions concerning Aquinas (and Calvin) need to be removed (and not all Protestants are as benighted as those here discussed, some of whom are rather unrepresentative), the fact remains that we have not done justice to Calvin on the knowledge of God until we have taken account of his position of the Spirit in relation to Scripture; in other words, until we have dealt more directly with the problem of authority.

Philosophical Studies 32 (1998–1990) 377–79.

Part Two: History

33

The Unity of Brethren

Rudolf Rican. *The History of the Unity of Brethren*. Bethlehem, PA: The Moravian Church in America, 1992. Pp. v + 439.

Readers of English will find their knowledge of 'the first Reformation' greatly increased by this detailed study from the pen of the late Professor Rican, formerly of the Comenius Faculty, Prague.

The story begins with fourteenth-century protests against the perceived corruptions of the Roman Church. The Czech Reformers initially sought a renewed Catholic Church centred in Rome and, with feudalism disintegating all around them, their message was urgent and eschatologically-flavoured. They sought a society subject to the Word of God, and a Church prepared to meet Christ, her Bridegroom. Such was the position of Milicof Kromeriz (d.1374), the 'father of the Czech Reformation.' His student, Matej of Janov (d. 1393) understood the true Church to comprise the elect of God. The best known early leader was Jan Hus (martyred in 1416), and among exotic influences on the growing movement were John Wyclif, honoured by the Hussites as 'the evangelical doctor,' and the Waldensians.

The differences of emphasis as between Reformers in Bohemia and Moravia are spelled out, and it is made clear that the Czech Reformers had political as well as religious objectives—a source of tension, since some Hussites were more radical in both spheres than others. Clear accounts of the teaching of Petr Chelcicky and others are provided, and the beginnings of the Unity of Brethren are traced. Living under the Word, gathered in churches of congregational order (though with an over-arching council of elders), the Brethren practised the priesthood of all believers and repudiated such doctrines as transubstantiation. While the more conservative Hussites remained loyal to Rome—their criticisms of it notwithstanding—the Unity made a significant break in ordaining its own priests. In the ensuing strife the Brethren of Moravia suffered their first exile in 1481.

Under the influence of the theologian Lukas, the Brethren formulated their distinctive positions, among them this: 'Our separation from the Roman unity is good and just. Although this is true because of their evil deeds, it is, however, truer because of their wicked view of faith and because of much erroneous belief.'

With the turn of the fifteenth century the activities of hostile Roman Catholic noblemen caused problems for the Unity, but with the advent of 'the second Reformation' increasing contact with broadly like-minded Christians proved a source of strength. There were differences between the branches of the Reformation, however. For whereas the

Lutherans focused upon personal salvation, the Czechs emphasized rather the obligation laid upon the Church to be faithful to God in the world. Again, the Brethren carefully explained to Bucer their grounds for upholding the separation of Church from State. In 1536 they published a significant Confession of Faith.

The sometimes strained relations between the Brethren and the Utraquists; the severe restrictions placed upon the Bohemian congregations by the royal mandate of 1548; the exile in Prussia and the removal of some to Poland; contracts with the Reformed in Hungary from the mid-1560s; the Bohemian Confession of 1575; the publication of the Kralice Bible in 1596—all of these matters are carefully discussed. In general there was growing sympathy with Calvinism, especially with its view of the whole of society under the Word, and its teaching on the Lord's Supper.

The trials of the brethren under the Counter-Reformation, and the impressive contribution of Jan Amos Komensky (Comenius)—himself exiled—are faithfully recorded. By 1700 five Brethren congregations only were left, all of them in Poland. In the 1720s a congregation of Czech immigrants arose in Herrnhut, Saxony, on the estate of Nicholas Ludwig von Zinzendorf; it became Brethren, though now with the tincture of Zinzendorfian pietism. From the missionary zeal of these Brethren arose the Moravian Church as we know it today.

In a most illuminating concluding chapter the late Amédeo Molnár discusses Brethren theology in relation to that of 'the second Reformation.' Nor are the different societal contexts of the theologies overlooked: whereas the first Reformation was popular and sometimes revolutionary, the second was favoured especially by the young middle class, and was socially conservative. The Brethren sought always to ground in the Bible. They deemed confessions of faith to be revisible. They held Word and sacrament together, the latter never being regarded as a symbol only. They were silent on double predestination.

A bibliography and an index complete this most welcome book, whose translator, C. Daniel Crews, archivist of the Southern Province of the Moravian Church, supplies a rendering which is never less than intelligible and is for the most part fluent.

Journal of the United Reformed Church History Society 5 (1997) 642–43.

Part Two: History

34

The Hutterian Brethren

The Chronicle of the Hutterian Brethren,
Volume I. Rifton, NY: Plough Publishing House, 1987, 962pp.

When Georg Blaurock, Conrad Grebel, Felix Mantz, and probably others, baptized one another in January 1525 at Zürich, they inaugurated a movement which, though it soon diversified, continues to this day. The spirit of early Anabaptism survives especially strongly in the Hutterian Brethren, of whom there are now some 30,000 distributed among approximately 300 communities in North America, England and Japan. They take their name from Jakob Hutter who, on migrating from his native Tirol to Moravia, became in 1533 the leader of those Anabaptists who were already gathered there. Three years later Hutter was martyred, and this excellently-produced translation of *Das grosse Geschichtsbuch der*

Hutterischen Brüder commemorates the event. The discovery of this 'lost' work in safe Hutterian hands in 1908 caused considerable excitement in scholarly circles, and new German editions followed. Now, for the first time, we have an English version, and the Hutterian Brethren and their Mennonite and other helpers have rendered a signal service in making their *Chronicle* accessible to the wider readership it deserves.

The *Chronicle* opens with a sketch of history from creation to 1517, traces the rise of Anabaptism, and continues in detail to 1665. Historians, theologians, ecumenists, sociologists—all will find things of interest in these pages. All of life, and not a little of death, is here. The cases against the Roman mass and for believers' baptism are repeatedly made; brothers are hanged and burned; sisters are raped and imprisoned; officers of the law, Zwinglians, and Jesuits alike oppress; churchly discipline is exercised; agricultural work is done when conditions are sufficiently calm and settled; and by the end prices are rising and a pair of oxhides costs ten gulden. The collection includes letters, hymns and (and these are not found elsewhere) the five articles of faith which 'are the reason for the great controversy between us and the world,' namely, those concerning baptism, the Lord's Supper, true surrender and the Christian community of goods, pacifism, and the separation of believing and unbelieving marriage partners.

The translation preserves the direct, biblically-saturated, and often deeply moving language of the original. Thus, for example, at the end of a long list of martyrs we read the simple words, 'From the shedding of such innocent blood, Christians arose everywhere.' Again, after a brief respite in Hungary conditions worsened, until 'the believers were forced into the forest, even in the cold of wintertime, to live like wild animals. If only they had been allowed to do this unmolested, they would have been happy. But there was no sparing of anyone, no mercy for the old and gray, for expectant or nursing mothers and their babies. They had to go out into the unknown.'

Enemies without—and sometimes enemies within, too, such as that 'child of Judas' Jörg Früe, who infiltrated the community and then led judge, priests and magistrates to it, armed with swords and cudgels. This truly is a 'warts and all' record: Wilhelm Reublin, the 'unfaithful, malicious Ananias,' who withheld some of his money from the church; Georg Riedel, who was no nearer repentance after some years' exclusion, and who 'died in his sins'; and the three brothers who resorted to praying in secret when they should have been working the mill. On the other hand some, whose disciplinary zeal was overprominent, had to be reminded by Peter Riedemann that 'even the devout make mistakes'—something of which the Hutterians thought they had ample evidence when they contemplated the more pugilistic Münsterites, from whom they were at pains to distance themselves.

The first 'communistic' act; the ministry of Hutter himself; the faithful and effective leadership of Peter Walpot; the prayers of the martyr Hieronymus Käls—all are here, with so much more besides.

The work is furnished with editorial notes, and with appendices outlining the political and economic context of the *Chronicle*, and the subsequent history of the Hutterian Brethren. In addition we have a glossary of place names, maps showing the distribution of the Hutterian communities, a plan of underground hiding tunnels, facsimiles of the '1580' and '1581' codices, a glossary, a bibliography, and biblical and general indices. I earnestly hope that it will prove possible to publish an English translation of *Das Klein-Geschichtsbuch der Hutterischen Brüder* in due course.[1]

The *Chronicle* stimulates a number of reflections, among them the following: first, the age-old question, 'Who is a Christian' is raised afresh, both *vis à vis* state churches, and in relation to church discipline. Secondly, since the state imposes taxes, and if the Hutterians are correct in asserting that 'a believer does not owe taxes destined for bloodshed,' then we are forcefully reminded that church-state questions are inextricably interwoven with the peace question. Thirdly, the importance of memory in holding a people together is underlined by the *Chronicle*. For the Hutterians the heritage is inseparable from the present context, and we may well ask: 'Are we well advised to curtail confessional history (which need not and should not be blinkered history) in our seminaries and faculties in deference to the god Relevance, or to ecumenical "politeness", or to curriculum pressures?' But, above all, there is the humbling reminder that to this day many Christians find themselves in situations of oppression which will enable them to identify closely with the old Hutterians. They know the reality; but even to be with someone like Hans Schmidt in imagination is to be moved and inspired. As he was being led to execution he sang a hymn by Käls which begins:

---

1. Published as *The Chronicle of the Hutterian Brethren, Volume II*, by the Hutterian Brethren of Crystal Spring Colony, 1998.

In you, O Father,
Is my joy,
Though I must suffer here!
Let me be scorned
By everyone
If your grace still is near!

Against this, *some* of our current churchly concerns scarcely rise to the status of trivial pursuits.

The Ecumenical Review 40 (1998) 112–13.

35

The English Sabbath

Kenneth L. Parker. *The English Sabbath: A Study of Doctrine and Discipline from the Reformation to the Civil War*. New York: CUP, 1988. Pp. xii + 250.

Kenneth L. Parker has produced a piece of historical revisionism that greatly enhances our understanding of the continuity of pre- and post-Reformation English religious life. The evidence accumulated is formidable, and the style is as fluent as it is gracious. Some very distinguished historians are gently but firmly corrected.

The received interpretation, for which we are indebted to the Laudian Peter Heylyn's *History of the Sabbath* (1636), is that the idea of a morally binding Sabbath was a Puritan invention. It was devised by Presbyterians who had failed to secure a church establishment of their favored complexion, with a view to promoting further reformation from below. By the end of the first Elizabeth's reign, so it is said, a rift had developed between Puritans and the ecclesiastical authorities. Heylyn held that the fourth commandment was part of the ceremonial law abrogated by Christ; he attributed to the Puritans the view that the keeping of the Sabbath—albeit on the first and not the seventh day of the week—was a perpetual moral obligation. In all of this he was motivated by the desire to support Laudian 'catholicism' over against Puritan 'innovations'.

Parker adduces evidence to show that there was a developed pre-Reformation sabbatarian doctrine in England, that complaints concerning Sabbath abuses were especially common in the fourteenth and fifteenth centuries, and that Sabbath obligations were endorsed in sermons, cited in cases of ecclesiastical discipline, and extolled in popular art. Long-standing pro-sabbatarianism was reasserted in the Elizabethan church both by those who wished to uphold *sola scriptura* in Reformed fashion, and by those who wished to maintain a 'catholic' vision of the church that entailed discipline exercised by duly authorized persons.

Much fascinating information is brought to light. For example, Parker notes that as early as 1362 Simon Islip, Archbishop of Canterbury, was found complaining that while employees were pleased to have a work-free day, they did not 'sabbatize as they should, to the honour of God.' Popular pictures of the crucifixion show Christ assailed by the tools of trade and domestic implements. In 1413 Archbishop Thomas Arundel singled out barbers as particularly annoying Sabbath-breakers.

Where Heylyn (followed, for example, by Christopher Hill) claimed that medieval sabbatarianism was founded upon ecclesiastical authority, contemporary writers in fact upheld the divine institution of the Sabbath and distinguished that day from other holy days. Although many early Reformers, including Luther and Calvin, polemically rejected the scholastic idea of the morally binding Sabbath, Calvin did advocate the need of a day of rest and worship (he felt it would be one way of sustaining a Christian society). Beza and many others reverted to the idea of the Sabbath as a divine institution. Like many of their Lutheran counterparts, the early English Reformers rejected the medieval doctrine on polemical grounds, but with the *Bishop's Book* (1537) a cautious balance was struck. In 1563 the doctrine that the Sabbath was a divine institution was promulgated as the official position of the English church. The place of the Sabbath was not questioned until the 1630s. Holy days were more controversial, and Heylyn erred in arguing that they, together with the Sabbath, were established on the church's authority and that they were of equal importance. The Presbyterian Cartwright's exchange with Whitgift is illuminating in this connection. Cartwright, true to his conviction that what Scripture did not prescribe was forbidden, contended that God's law required six days of work and one of worship; Whitgift replied that while one day of worship was required, six days of work were *permitted* but not mandatory—with the consequent possibility of additional holy days.

Parker cites visitation articles and injunctions, consistory court records, and Parliamentary evidence to sustain his case that precisionists as well as many bishops and secular officials were equally dismayed by Sabbath laxity. Tragedies occurring on the Sabbath were widely regarded as signs of divine displeasure—as when an earthquake on a Sunday in 1580 terrorized some who were in theatres watching 'their bawdy Interludes.'

In Parker's later chapters the thesis that the doctrine of a morally binding Sabbath was a Puritan innovation sustains further blows. For example, the controversies of 1617 and 1618 over the *Book of Sports* (which specified permitted Sabbath recreations) 'generated debate over sabbatarian *discipline* [but] they were *theological* non-events.' In a word, assent to the notion of a morally binding Sabbath was widely regarded as a component of good Christian practice. Nevertheless, James I's *Declaration of Sports* (1618) did reinforce 'the prejudice of those who associated strict attitudes towards Sunday recreations with puritanism.' Following some years of consensus, and in the wake of the reissuing of the *Book of Sports*, this prejudice was exploited in the 1630s, when sabbatarianism became a war cry of those opposed to Laudian innovations. Indeed, 'sabbatarianism did not become a "puritan *cause célèbre*" until a few Laudians made it so.' Finally, in 1644, the *Book of Sports*, which had owed its authority to the King's position as temporal head of the church, was seized, together with other antisabbatarian books, and publicly burned by order of Parliament.

The English Sabbath is enhanced by an appendix containing tables of diocesan presentments and by an ample bibliography. It is difficult to imagine how the case that Parker presents on the basis of his diligently sought and carefully presented evidence could be overturned. He is to be congratulated upon a considerable achievement.

Calvin Theological Journal 24 (1989) 354–57.

36

The Enlightenment World

Martin Fitzpatrick, Peter Jones, Christa Knellwolf and Iain McCalman, eds. *The Enlightenment World*, London: Routledge, 2004. Pp. xxi + 714.

Had Isaac Watts suffered at the hands of a lazy reviewer, one wonders? According to Richard Yeo, he 'declared against superficial reading, . . .scolding those who went no further than the contents page or the index.' The fact that this reviewer found this remark on page 361 of this book suggests either that the sentence caught my eye as the book fell open at random, or that I have done something towards keeping the ghost of Watts at bay. The truth is that every word has been read. The difficulty would have lain in skipping over the pages, for this tome is as exciting as it is informative. The editors have assembled a team of thirty-nine authors, all of whom have the happy knack, not always in evidence among scholars, of wearing their learning lightly, and of distilling the essence of their several themes—many of which have attracted book-length studies—into concise, lucid and entertaining prose.

The publisher is equally to be praised for a sturdy, handsome, carefully edited, volume which is enhanced by eighty-two well-chosen and well-reproduced illustrations. The reader is further assisted by a glossary of terms (though I should prefer to define the Mennonites as a 'radical Reformation movement' rather than as an 'evangelical sect'), and by indices of persons and subjects. A list of references is appended to every chapter.

The work is divided into eight parts, each of which is introduced by one of the editors, and there are thirty-nine topical chapters. Detailed comment on every contribution being precluded, I shall attempt first to convey something of the flavour of the book—a risky undertaking given that the several chapters are already summaries of sometimes vast amounts of material, and then to offer some reflections arising from what I have read.

In a Preface the editors caution us that while it is sometimes appropriate to refer to *the* Enlightenment, the variety of intellectual and other strands which they have to encompass prompts them frequently avoid the definite article. They further make it clear that they do not offer a conglomeration of abstracted ideas; throughout, the several contexts of Enlightenment thought and activity are in view.

Part I concerns the 'Intellectual origins of Enlightenment.' Here a running theme is the importance of science as the supreme cognitive authority. This deference was fuelled by the optimism engendered by the ever-increasing number of discoveries made, and by the conviction that the scientific method of Bacon, Newton and others was impartial and 'objective'; all of this over against a Cartesianism which, while it had dispensed with Aristotelian substantial forms, nevertheless remained satisfied with an entirely speculative mechanical philosophy. Not, indeed, that the responses of debtors to Newton were identical: Hume's thought took a secular turn, whilst Hartley's retained a theological dimension. The epistemological enquiries which ran parallel to the scientific work are epitomized in the writings of Descartes and Locke, both of whom went in quest of philosophical certainty. Locke is shown to have been a 'critical and innovative' follower of Descartes. The scientific and philosophical activities noted could not but have implications for Christian claims to truth. Among the issues raised by external critics, among whom Spinoza was notable, and internal critics including the Remonstrants, latitudinarians, Locke and Clarke, was the place of revelation. Freethinkers and deists had their say, and from a variety of quarters the authority of Scripture, and the presumed evidential status of miracles and prophecy were questioned. Underlying much of this criticism was a sceptical attitude which could, negatively, call into question long-cherished beliefs and, positively, advance the cause of toleration, for since we have no direct access to the minds of others we cannot be certain of their beliefs. Scepticism concerning the foundation of morals prompted a variety of responses, notably that of Hutcheson and others, which rooted ethics in a moral sense. The significance of the Huguenots' experience and writings in the toleration debates is demonstrated, and the stimulus they provided to reflection on the limits of regal authority is noted.

In Part II, 'Aspects of Enlightenment formations,' attention is drawn to the clandestine Enlightenment of which Spinoza was a prominent inspiration, and to the way in which in England, in contrast to other parts of Europe, the Enlightenment was shaped more by the city than the court. The importance of the early Enlightenment in the Dutch Republic—a home to refugees (notably Huguenots), a source of ideas and a laboratory of social reform—is demonstrated, as is the contribution made by the Dutch publishers of books, pamphlets and newspapers to the dissemination of enlightened ideas internationally. In addition, the Dutch were leaders in the field of education: newer ideas and empirical scientific investigations were encouraged, though not at the expense of belief in divine providence, as witness the Dutch 'physico-theology.' Rearguard orthodox Calvinist action notwithstanding, the tide of religious toleration (Spinoza being a catalyst) could not be held back. England, too, was much influenced by its Dutch connections and its Huguenot immigrants, while the Revolution of 1688 introduced a monarchy destined to share power with Parliament. Although the civil rights provision of the Toleration Act of 1689 were limited, the Act did encourage outside observers, Voltaire among them, to perceive England as a pioneer of tolerance and pluralism. The coffee houses and print made their contributions to the flow of ideas, as did the numerous scientific and cultural societies, clubs and Masonic lodges which sprang up in many parts of the country. Through their reading, attendance at scientific lectures and membership of those societies open to them, women became increasingly able to share in the propagation of ideas. In Germany, with its strong natural law tradition, Christian Thomasius, though himself a Christian, strove to check theological influence upon civil jurisprudence, while pietists (whose mystical tendencies did not always preclude radical reformist inclinations), Huguenots, sceptics and Socinians all contributed to the ferment of ideas. In early Enlightenment France the court was central, cultural attainment in the higher reaches of society was high, and Louis XIV, the Sun King, was, by some, well-nigh divinized. But for all the national and provincial academies and the fashionable salons designed to bolster it, absolute monarchy was increasingly questioned, not least by the frequently clandestine but increasingly audible *philosophes*.

'The High Enlightenment' is the title of Part III. Questions concerning the nature of truth, humanity and God, the problem of evil, providential purpose, moral obligation and human perfectibility were raised by Christians and their critics. Also widely shared by deists, materialists, atheists and Christians (though not by Voltaire and Kant) was the goal of human happiness. If La Mettrie could declare that 'The world will never be happy until it is atheist,' neither Newton nor Locke could forego the hope of eternal rewards. The idea of progress and optimism that it may be achieved were further prominent strands in Enlightenment thought, though more naive convictions concerning these were shattered by the Lisbon earthquake of 1755, and Rousseau famously read human 'perfection' as 'decrepitude.' As a chronicle of scientific and other progress achieved, the *Encyclopédie* was of outstanding significance and, writing as I am in the week in which scientists have landed an exploratory device on Titan, it is pleasant to be reminded that among all the other scientific inventions of the eighteenth- century was the gravity-defying hot-air balloon. As knowledge of remoter societies increased it became ever clearer to some that human progress was relative to geographical location and historical context. So to increasing interest in the human sciences; also to such mutually contradictory views of humanity as Hobbes's pessimistic mechanism and traditional Christian views. Hume's writings on the psychology of knowledge stimulated discussion, and there were numerous attempts to answer the question how far human characteristics—whether moral or gender—were naturally given or socially and culturally acquired. Some pondered the uniqueness of human beings *vis à vis* other primates. The growing spate of historical writings is discussed with reference to the less-than-absolute distinction between 'conjectural' and 'philosophical' historians. The former, like Adam Ferguson and Adam Smith, sought to delineate the stages of human history; the latter—Hume and Gibbon among them—adopted a narrative approach to historical events and issues. The dissemination of knowledge and ideas was advanced by pedagogical notions derived from Locke's *Some Thoughts Concerning*

Education. Education was seen to involve the stimulation of curiosity in order that the mind, a *tabula rasa*, might be inscribed with ideas. The doctrine of the association of ideas was propounded—supremely by David Hartley—as an explanation of the mental process whereby sensations prompted ideas which could then be associated with further ideas. Rousseau's 'minority report' advocating the isolation of the individual child from society so that he can be taught unimpeded by 'nature' ill accorded with his view of what the education of citizens as social beings required. If, to Kant, the education of the young was a disciplined affair which inculcated good behaviour conceived as obligatory, to Pestalozzi the objective was autonomous agency achieved by child-centred learning. The political step was taken when educational method was employed as an aspect of the state's policing function—a practice which appealed more to the Germans than the English. It did not go unremarked that the levelling effect of Locke's epistemology removed the alleged grounds for distinguishing between the educational capacities of males and females. There ensued steps towards the democracy of knowledge—an idea advocated by Joseph Priestley among others.

Part IV directs our attention to 'Polite Culture and the Arts.' From the 1730s onwards more and more people gained access to art and music through salons, exhibitions and increasingly professional concerts. A few had opportunities for travel, and an interest in landscape was gradually fostered; eventually 'expression' replaced 'imitation' as the artistic goal. There was a multifaceted discussion of 'sensibility' in relation to medicine, philosophy, social reform, the place of women and the French Revolution. A further term, 'politeness,' was also a topic of debate in salons, universities, scientific societies and Masonic lodges (including those for women). As scientists revealed ever more of the secrets of nature, many artists drew inspiration from its continuing mystery, whilst seeking to emulate the accuracy of the scientists as far as the use of colour was concerned. More classically-inspired artists continued to produce idealized representations of nature. The French *philosophes* did much to stimulate reflection upon music, as did the Encyclopédie (to which Rousseau contributed a number of articles on music), and the debate over the relative merits of Italian comic opera and French tragic opera. Of particular interest was the debate between Rameau and Rousseau, the former exalting harmony, the latter melody, as of the first importance in musical expression. There were discussions of the 'meaning' of music, while a growing acceptance of the dictum, 'Art for art's sake,' prompted the opinions of an increasing breed of non-practitioner critics.

Part V concerns 'Material and Popular Culture.' It is a tale of a vastly-expanding print culture ever more accessible to all reaches of society (from learned tomes to handbills), of technological change, of consumer goods and social status. Encyclopedias played an important part in the transmission of (especially scientific) knowledge, the contribution of Chambers taking pride of place in Britain. Whereas English authorities adopted a more liberal stance, in France many printing activities were clandestine until the freedom of the press was deemed a natural and inalienable right in 1789. With changing ideas and social contexts, and growing economies, came changes in dress, the growing importance of the clothing trade, and a move towards washable fabrics on grounds of health and hygiene.

Some spurned the enticements of luxury and devoted themselves to folk culture which, as the gap between rulers and ruled grew wider, became plebeian culture.

'Reforming the World' is the title of Part VI. While ideas inspired many changes, the ideas themselves were the products of diverse contexts; there never was a single intellectual blueprint for realizing the widely-entertained aspiration that the world could be made a better place. If the *philosophes* were, so to speak, the engine of intellectual change in France, their component parts did not function without friction, and they were variously powered by deism, atheism and Christianity. Many of them, having persuaded themselves that a 'civilization' was known by its art and literature, were appalled when Rousseau found religion essential to virtue and branded the arts as a corrupting force in society. They were more gratified when their opposition to despotism and slavery was endorsed by increasing numbers, though none of them went so far as to contend for political or social equality. The enlightened despotism of Frederick the Great made a considerable impact, and did much to stimulate the study of government, notably at the universities of Halle and Göttingen. Republicanism, too, was revivified, not so much in the sense of popular anti-monarchical sentiment (though Paine was an exception here) as in relation to classical sources—a development typified by the writings of Machiavelli and Harrington. However, although it was classically-stimulated, eighteenth-century political thought was not for the most part inclined to the pessimism inherent in the backward-looking view that the pinnacle of political achievement had been reached in a non-recoverable past. On the contrary, there was, in some countries more than in others, growing optimism in the possibilities opened up by representative government. Diverse accounts were offered of the common good, and of the liberty deemed to be central to it. The accumulation of wealth was increasingly regarded as a sign of civic health, not as one of personal corruption. In the field of economics, the older mercantilism gave way to the realization of the importance of the colonies, and the question whether money was of value in itself, or only as a means to commerce, was widely debated. Developing markets (including those represented by those new consumers, women industrial workers) prompted much economic theorizing, amongst which Adam Smith's free market views were particularly significant. Philanthropy blossomed as the eighteenth century proceeded, but it was clear to those concerned that the provision of assistance to the needy and the establishment of new institutions was not, by itself, enough. The reform of the law was required, hence the relation of philanthropy to questions of human rights, and the ending of the slave trade, both of which had international implications. At the same time, and more problematically, humanitarians were tempted to grade societies and races according to their ability to match up to enlightened ideals. Those who agreed in general on the need to reform the law differed over whether pragmatic or more idealistic considerations concerning the individual's rights and the need to check the government should take precedence. Wilkes was among those who went to court with the latter view in mind. The natural law tradition continued prominently in Germany, while Montesquieu and Beccaria, respectively, proposed that laws should reflect the current age, and that they should be framed in accordance with the principles governing the human psyche. To Bentham, natural law was redundant, and should be replaced by laws designed to increase the stock of human happiness.

'Transformations and Explorations' concern us in Part VII. The growing interest in voyages and exploration was fed by print, theatrical performances and museum displays. Among the agents prompting the creation of a unified yet diverse world were many who were not members of social elites—soldiers, sailors, and missionaries, among them the Moravians. Intellectually, the Enlightenment concept of a universal human nature was reviewed by those who wished to come to grips with the variety represented by indigenous cultures. At the same time the baleful results of voyages—the importation of firearms and of Western diseases— gave some food for thought. Fascination with the exotic fuelled a Utopian literature and an interest in paradise which was reflected even in garden design. Accompanying this was millenarian speculation, from which Newton was not immune, though there was also a compensating repudiation of 'enthusiasm.' Burke thought that undue faith in human reason was itself a species of enthusiasm; but others, remembering the Civil War and the Commonwealth sectaries, upheld the rights of reason in relation to religious belief. Priestley brought reason to bear upon scriptural interpretation, but this in no way prevented his reading contemporary events in terms of biblical eschatology. Bicheno regarded reading the sign of the times as an Enlightenment exercise in free enquiry, itself a legacy, he (questionably) thought, of the Reformation.

We come finally to Part VIII: 'The Enlightenment and its Critics, Then and Now.' A general thesis of this book, namely, that the Enlightenment is a richly variegated phenomenon, receives its most particular demonstration in the account of the University of Halle, 1690–1730, where Thomasius advocated anti-scholastic civil philosophy, Franke espoused a version of pietism which did not entail quietism so much as the view that the world was reformable, and Wolff purveyed his anti-scholastic Leibnizian metaphysics. The very different critiques of the Enlightenment mounted by Rousseau and Burke are discussed in more detail, and a chapter is devoted to comparisons and contrasts between Enlightenment and current feminism, with special reference to Mary Wollstonecraft, Mary Astell, Mary Montague and Catherine Macaulay. Perceptive and balanced accounts of the neo-Marxist critique of the Enlightenment by Adorno and Horkheimer, and the 'post-modernist' critique of Foucault, Derrida (both of whom declined the label) and others, bring the main text to completion.

It would be surprising if, in a work of such breadth and complexity, a few errors did not creep in. There is, for example, the declaration that self love in the eighteenth century meant what we should understand as selfishness (p. 24); and the description of Birmingham as a city—a status it did not achieve until 1889 (p. 113). But I turn from such minor matters to some more substantive observations.

First, there can be no question that the volume as a whole demonstrates the thesis that thought influenced developments in many contexts, but that the influence was mutual: the diverse contexts—geographical, religious, socio-political, cultural—prompted reflection in many fields. It follows that the Enlightenment was no single phenomenon—least of all a philosophical one: for thinking otherwise Jonathan Israel is criticized by Ian Hunter (pp. 590–92). Wider cultural aspects apart, Martin Fitzpatrick rightly points out that 'Enthusiasm and reason found unusual combinations at the beginning of the Enlightenment as they did at the end' (p.83). He further observes that precisely because there were divergent strands of thought and popular opinion, some authors carefully tailored their writings to different readerships, and, as with Newton's Socinian ideas, omitted what might prove unpalatable from their published works (p. 85).

Secondly, I note the way in which toleration and associated themes rightly constitute a running theme of this book In their different ways Locke, Bayle and Spinoza are important here, but so are the numerous refugees of the period—especially the Huguenots, and the example of the Dutch Republic. The ripples resulting from the dissemination of ideas of toleration through print, educational institutions and travel reached to many parts of society and to many regions of Europe, albeit at different paces. The issue was not merely toleration under the law, but tolerance of diverse, even contradictory, beliefs. Conscience was elevated along with reason, and in this connection I should have welcomed a little more. Whereas we have discussions of 'sensibility', 'politeness' and the like, there is little on 'the right of private judgement' especially in relation to theology and Christian doctrine. The way in which all sides in the manifold (and, from our vantage-point, variously dispiriting and enjoyable) doctrinal disputes of the eighteenth century appealed to this principle is of more than passing interest; as is the more general impact of Enlightenment thought in this area: if it fostered an individualism which could adversely affect ecclesiology, it also encouraged a much needed moral critique of untoward statements of doctrine from whencesoever they came.

Thirdly, I would observe that many of the issues presented in this book are still with us: natural endowments *versus* socio-cultural influences; secular *versus* religious world views; human rights and the place of women; the legacy (now) of colonialism (in which connection the way in which many early missionaries sided with indigenous peoples against Western commercial interests should not go unnoticed); human rights in general and the place of women in particular. And what of those institutions which might be thought to have been especially concerned with enlightenment, the universities? Margaret C. Jacob writes, 'While hardly in the vanguard of the Enlightenment, universities also practised forms of politeness . . .' (p. 275). That throwaway first clause (though she notes the exception demonstrated by Ian Hunter in his excellent chapter on the University of Halle) prompts one to wonder whether present-day universities are in danger of ceasing to be the centres of enlightenment that the best of them had become. The inhibiting factor is no longer, in most places, a conservative clericalism, but a managerialism and quasi-commercialism at whose behest marketable 'products' are 'delivered' to 'customers.' I fear I verge upon homily—but then, so does Peter Jones, who may, and probably does, have in mind the problematic notion that the educational process should be entirely jolly and entertaining: 'Only security in skills enables each of us boldly to experiment, confidently to explore, unashamedly to revise,' he declares (p. 327). Such security is hard won, and sometimes part of the price is drudgery.

Fourthly, in a volume on the Enlightenment world it is interesting to see how, in some cases, even the most advanced writers seem now to have been singularly unenlightened. Montesquieu persuaded himself of global depopulation, and thought that in ten centuries the world would have become a desert (p. 190); Priestley thought that the role of education was to prejudice children 'in favour of our opinions and practices' (p. 220); while Kant opined that whatever was said by a person 'black from head to foot' could only be stupid (p. 651). Before we too hastily assume the role of judges, let us ponder the question how far our existing conventions are preventing us from seeing things of importance. We shall not be able to answer the question, but two hundred years hence our heirs and successors surely will.

So to some concluding remarks: Isaac Barrow believed that because 'one Part of Learning doth confer Light to another . . . he can hardly be a good scholar who is not a general one' (p. 351). Of course, it was easier to say that prior to the explosion of knowledge which has subsequently overtaken us. Martin Fitzpatrick and his editorial colleagues were wise to call upon the resources of such an authoritative team of authors, and skilful in planning a composite work which has so high a degree of unity. No liberal arts college, university or sizeable public library should be without it.

Benjamin Franklin said that he was 'almost sorry I was born so soon, since I cannot have the happiness of knowing what will be known 100 years hence' (p. 184). From the stereotypes of the Enlightenment which some writers peddle, it would seem that they do not have the happiness of knowing what happened 200 years ago. This impressive book will come to their aid.

From time to time the contributors adjust themselves to earlier commentators on the Enlightenment, and we may be sure that as the years go by fresh insights will be gained and new interpretations will be advanced. But however great the changes (and long after the last anti-Enlightenment postmodernist has bitten the dust) this book will have continuing value; for it will stand as a witness to the way in which a group of authoritative scholars viewed the Enlightenment world near the beginning of Christianity's third millennium.

On page 8 Peter Jones writes, 'It would be a mistake to think . . . that the names or achievements of those whom we discuss were known to more than a handful of their contemporaries or their descendants' But, two hundred years on, we are studying them. Here is consolation indeed for any scholars whose book sales disappoint.

Enlightenment and Dissent 21 (2002) 198–209.

Part Two: History

37

Heterodoxy 1660–1750

Roger D. Lund, ed. *The Margins of Orthodoxy. Heterodox Writing and Cultural Response, 1660–1750*. Cambridge: CUP, 1995. Pp. xiv + 298.

'What is orthodoxy, and how is it to be defended?' 'How are reason and revelation, conscience and authority (ecclesial, biblical, political), most satisfactorily adjusted?' These questions indicate the running themes in this collection of papers by four historians, three political scientists, two professors of English/humanities, and one philosopher.

While it may at first sight be supposed that orthodoxy has exclusively to do with adherence to such doctrinal standards as are enshrined in the ancient creeds and the Articles of the Church of England, it soon becomes apparent that cultural attitudes and socio-political assumptions are inextricably interwoven with theological claims. Hence, for example, J. G. A. Pocock's demonstration of the tensions between the notion of a Church as by law established, and the incarnational idea of a Church as the body of Christ in the world—views which, it was thought by many, must nevertheless be held together over against Romanism on the one hand and, on the other, the view that the Church is solely the creation of the secular power.

Orthodox believers and traditionalist divines alike were concerned that by regarding beliefs hitherto deemed mandatory as matters of speculative opinion, society's cement would be eroded—not least by the replacement of the idea of the Church as a divinely-constituted society with the view of churches as voluntary (possibly mutually-hostile and societally-disruptive) associations. In this connection Christopher Hill discusses the legacy of the seventeenth-century sectaries—especially its anticlerical aspects. Richard Ashcraft resumes the latter theme in relation to Lockean political thought, and Ronald Paulson does likewise in connection with Hogarth and such literary wits as Hogarth's friend Henry Fielding.

It is hardly surprising that the useful index to this work contains more references to Locke than to anyone else. In a characteristically lucid paper G. A. J. Rogers argues that Locke's inadvertent contribution to the onset of secularism derived from his views on knowledge and probable opinion, which became criteria for determining the acceptability or otherwise of theological positions. I welcome this endorsement of an as yet unpublished conclusion which I myself have independently reached.

Samuel Parker, Thomas Woolston and Thomas Curteis are also the subjects of papers. Gordon Schochet chronicles Parker's progression from Interregnum Presbyterian through persecuting Restoration divine to Bishop of Oxford, finding him more concerned with political power and ecclesiastical stability than with religious principles; while the editor shows how Woolston's wit antagonized clerics who believed that to ridicule religion was to threaten government, and led to his eventual imprisonment. Jeffrey S. Chamberlain shows how the politically Low Church Curteis, open to the toleration of Dissenters, could be as hot against deism (not least for its overestimate of the capabilities of unaided human reason) and infidelity as any High Churchman.

Shelley Burtt argues that institutional change does not always result from the clash of opposites, but may be the product of transformation from within, as commitments, approaches, concepts and languages are adjusted, and as opponents are co-opted or sidestepped. This is illustrated by reference to the Societies for the Reformation of Manners, which increasingly defended the place of the civil magistrate in enforcing moral behaviour, not on biblical or theological grounds concerning God's will and spiritual welfare, but on temporal grounds having to do with the maintenance of civil order.

In 'Deists and Anglicans' Joseph M. Levine shows how, in making their case against miracles and superstition, the deists manifested a 'stubborn recourse to history,' whereas their orthodox opponents' incipient progressivism and historicist reading of the Bible gave their writings a distinctly modern flavour.

The several papers are fully referenced, and a select bibliography both enhances the value of the work as a whole, and further underscores its thematic unity. In all, this is a most illuminating volume on a range of issues which are as important and intriguing as they are occasionally elusive. There is, however, a significant lacuna. While agreeing that 'orthodoxy' should be understood in a suitably elastic way, there were specifically doctrinal debates in the longer eighteenth century which caused distress to many, and which are scarcely alluded to here. I think especially of the 'Arianism' of the early decades of the century, and of the heterodox stimulus provided by Samuel Clarke (the title of whose celebrated book, *The Scripture Doctrine of the Trinity*, is mangled on p. 3). Nevertheless, more than enough evidence has been presented to justify J. G. A. Pocock's declaration that 'the conflict between orthodoxy and opinion provides the reason why the eighteenth century is a great age in the historiography of Christian doctrine' (p. 51).

British Journal for the History of Philosophy 6 (1998) 498–99.

Part Two: History

38

British Intellectual History 1750–1950

Stefan Collini, Richard Whatmore and Brian Young, eds. *History, Religion, and Culture: British Intellectual History 1750-1950*. Cambridge: CUP, 2000. Pp. viii + 289.

This illuminating volume is a companion to *Economy, Polity, and Society*. The pair comprise a tribute to John Burrow and David Winch, both of whom taught at the University of Sussex for many pioneering year, and both of whom retired, aged sixty-five, in 2000. All of the contributors have connections with Sussex, or with Burrow and Winch, or with both, and all are practitioners of intellectual history which, according to Collini, means not that they elevate things intellectual above all else, but that they happen 'to find the reflective and expressive life of the past to be of interest' (p. 2), just as other historians focus upon economic or political history. At the same time, the aspect of human activity upon which intellectual history fastens is so broad that it may be regarded as having 'a kind of "anti-specialist" identity, both because it cannot be equated with the history of one subject-matter or discipline and because it cannot he reduced to one methodology or vocabulary' (p. 10). The range of topics which find hospitality under this book's title amply demonstrates the point.

Collini admits that, owing to the withdrawal of one contributor and the illness of another, the second half of the specified period of interest is less fully covered than the first. He is also frank concerning such lacunae as the history of scientific thought and of popular culture. He further points out that there is 'little directly on the history of philosophy' (p. 20). Why, then, review the book in this journal? Because although we cannot claim that the contents will he 'bread and butter' to specialist historians of philosophy (least of all to those of the argument-abstracting kind), it will contribute to their understanding of the intellectual soil in which their primary concerns took root. More particularly, there are some pages on Hume and Mill, for example, which will repay the attention of philosophers of history and political theorists.

Indeed, in the first essay, 'Historical distance and the historiography of eighteenth-century Britain,' Mark Salber Phillips sets out from Hume's view of Clarendon's account of the execution of Charles I. To Clarendon, close to the event, the episode was so painful that he passed over it very quickly, whereas to 'a reader of another age' the incident is most interesting. In Hume's remarks, Phillips finds two kinds of distance: that which separates a later reader from an earlier event, and that which results from the fact that historical narratives not only reflect distance but construct it. Phillips focuses on the latter and, with reference to Macaulay, Carlyle and others, seeks to show that 'norms of historical distance are themselves products of history and they have changed markedly over time' (p. 33).

PHILOSOPHY, THEOLOGY AND HISTORY

The following two papers concern Edward Gibbon. In the first, J. G. A. Pocock confronts the puzzle why, in his *History of the Decline and Fall of the Roman Empire*, Gibbon kept Christianity out of his story until the Council of Nicea. He argues that chapters 15 and 16 constitute an unsatisfactory prelude to the story which became the ground upon which the work as a whole has been heavily criticized. Pocock notes that both Gibbon and his critics emphasized Christ the sanctifier of morality rather than Christ the redeemer of sins; he shows how the concepts of providence and miracle are woven into the story; he neatly contrasts attitudes towards religion in the English and French Enlightenments; and he suggests that political convictions conditioned Gibbon's responses to his critics. Thus, although neither Richard Watson the Anglican nor Joseph Priestley the Unitarian was doctrinally orthodox (something which was not particularly offensive in Gibbon's eyes), Priestley was dealt with in a hostile fashion because Gibbon loathed his politics. Pocock's concluding suggestion is that Gibbon found himself writing church history before he had a clear idea of how to go about it.

David Womersley tackles that most slippery of topics, 'Gibbon's religious characters.' How far is it justifiable to regard Gibbon as 'the English Voltaire'? Womersley pursues the question with special reference to Gibbon's lesser writings, and pays particular attention to the fact that he possessed a copy of the Enlightenment tract against Moses, Jesus and Mahomet, *Livre des trois fameux imposteurs*. He wisely concludes in tentative vein: did Gibbon's return to the Church of England in 1754 coincide with the onset of scepticism concerning religion which he camouflaged after 1776? Or did Gibbon first use religion as a goad to attract attention, and latterly use it as a defence when the attention turned hostile? Or was his primary running concern the achievement of literary fame, so that in his mind 'the life of writing and the life of religious faith' were parallel but separate—perhaps mutually exclusive?

Brian Young contributes a lively piece on '"The lust of Empire and religious hate": Christianity, history, and India, 1790–1820,' in which the historian Thomas Maurice emerges as the nineteenth-century equivalent of a daytime television playwright, while the Baptist William Ward (whose biography is alluded to but not referenced—it is by Samuel Stennett) appears, by reason of his righteous disgust at 'rude' Hindu gods and suchlike, as the Mary Whitehouse of the mission field. Blair Worden carefully discusses Oliver Cromwell's fluctuating reputation in the nineteenth century, noting in particular the part played by Carlyle as the 'galvanizing force of Victorian Cromwellianism' (p. 115), as well as by sundry Nonconformists from Robert Vaughan to Joseph Parker (who in 1899 was indeed 'soon to become chairman of the Congregational Union' (p. 121)—again: he had already served in that capacity in 1876). 'Religion and politics in the *Quarterly Review*' is William Thomas's subject. This is an intriguing account of politics and publishing, in which Thomas draws upon the archives of John Murray the publisher, and portrays the changing relations of the editorial mainstays, J. G. Lockhart and John William Crocker. In 'Ruskin's way: *tout à fait comme un oiseau*,' John Drury argues that Ruskin was not opposed to mass (that is, large forms) in art: 'It was just something which failed to claim the attention of his acute and widely roving eye' (p. 157). Drury attributes this partly to

Ruskin's predilection for Turner's style, and partly to his non-doctrinal way of reading the Bible. To Ruskin, Constable's work was 'greatcoat weather and no more' (quoted, p. 165).

Boyd Hilton's essay on 'The politics of anatomy and an anatomy of politics c.1825–1850' is notable for the careful way in which he distinguishes four scientific stances which turn upon two different understandings of providence. There were radical, reformist, uniformitarian and frequently Unitarian scientists; mechanistic natural theologians who saw 'God's clockwork machinery as working harmoniously' and were, like Paley, optimists; mechanistic natural theologians who saw 'the machinery as a process of moral trial,' and were, like Sedgwick, pessimists; and there were those who rejected natural and functional explanations of the body and had recourse to revelation, not balking at a 'meddling' God (p. 190). While ultra-Tory scientists with immaterialist beliefs opposed immanentist radicals, the two groups were at one in their opposition to scientists of the liberal establishment who resorted to natural law, natural theology, Newtonianism and utilitarianism.

In 'Images of time: from Carlylean Vulcanism to sedimentary gradualism,' John Burrow charts the movement 'from a characteristic (though far from universal) disposition to the representation of history in terms of eventfulness, even of a catastrophic, apocalyptic kind, to the subtler representation of it as a kind of sedimentary process, whose longer-term significance hay far beyond the knowledge of the actors engaged in it' (p. 198).

The former approach is exemplified by the spectacles put on by places of entertainment, the lurid paintings of John Martin and the pervasiveness of prophetic and millennialist ideas; the latter taking its cue from the geologist Charles Lyell. In all of this, Carlyle (almost omnipresent in this volume) is a transitional figure; for although his is the sensibility of the apocalyptic sublime, he is also attracted by a steady-state world and has gradualist sympathies.

The two remaining papers, '"Race" and "nation" in mid-Victorian thought' by Peter Mandler, and Juliet Stapleton's 'Political thought and national identity in Britain, 1850–1950' are interesting in themselves and for the way in which their apparent disagreement ushers in editor Collini to the role of umpire. Mandler argues that the mindset in mid-century England was that the country had providentially escaped the nationalisms which had ravaged European neighbours, and that the ideal of a multi-national empire in which Celts, negroes and aborigines would be weaned from their childish ways by the English was the ideal aspired to. This, he points out, did not preclude patriotism. For her part, Stapleton contends that nationalism was a pervasive force in English thought and society, and she demonstrates this by reference to such themes as Irish Home Rule and collectivist political philosophy, and to individuals from Tawney and Trevelyan, through E. M. Forster to Enoch Powell and John Betjeman. Collini's adjudication (necessarily abbreviated) is to the effect that whereas Mandler concentrates upon theories deemed to be explanatory of social change, Stapleton identifies recurrent English attitudes and loyalties over a longer period of time.

Prompted by the discussion of Ruskin, we may justifiably wonder whether, in view of the considerable amount of *detail* in these studies (not to mention the many yet to be written), a Gibbon *redivivus*, capable of handling the *mass*, is even remotely conceivable.

British Journal for the History of Philosophy 11 (2003) 161–64.

39

Congregationalism in Wales

R Tudur Jones. *Congregationalism in Wales*, ed. Robert Pope. Cardiff: University of Wales Press, 2004. Pp. xvii + 376.

With the sudden death of Tudur Jones on 23 July 1998 Wales lost it most distinguished church historian of the twentieth century. Many will recall his *Congregationalism in England 1662–1962*, which was published to mark the tercentenary of the Great Ejectment, but until now those who cannot read Welsh have been denied access to his companion work of 1966 on Welsh Congregationalism. This impediment is splendidly removed by this fluent translation, through which the author's voice may still be heard. As a most welcome bonus we have Robert Pope's concluding chapter which brings the story down to the early years of this century. Dr. Pope undertakes his task with that grace and skill which are necessary when some of the actors are still alive and (in one or two cases) kicking.

The editor tells nothing less than the truth when he declares that as well as its scholars, theologians, poets, authors and, above all, its preachers Welsh Congregationalism 'has its own heroes and martyrs, its villains and charlatans.' That they are all on display here makes for a lively narrative, whether the particular topic under review is inherently inspiring or depressing.

While acknowledging that throughout Christian history there have been those who have upheld the view that the Church is the gathered company of Christ's people, Tudur Jones sets out from Henry VIII and the English Reformation. William Morgan's translation of the Bible into Welsh (1588) is noted, as is the Presbyterianism of Thomas Cartwright, but the pace increases with the Presbyterian-turned-Separatist martyr, John Penry, and the harbingers of English Congregationalism, Browne, Harrison, Barrow and Greenwood. Due attention is paid to the Welsh Puritans, Wroth, Erbury, Cradock, Powell and Llwyd, and we learn that early Welsh Congregationalism was fluid, with some taking the radical Separatist line, some seeking a Congregationalism within the context of the Anglican parishes, and others tending in the direction of Presbyterianism, not least where a local church comprised a number of branches. In 1639 the first Puritan church on Welsh soil was gathered at Llanvaches. In their religious life the Puritans emphasized the personal relationship with God more than religious 'externals.' Some were more ecumenically-minded than others, and most purveyed the federal Calvinism of the *Savoy Declaration of Faith and Order* (1658).

The reactions to, and the deprivations following, the Restoration of the monarchy in 1660 are discussed, and the point is made that 'The Congregationalism of the age of persecution was far more flexible and inventive than the legalistic Congregationalism of the twentieth century.' Following the Toleration Act of 1689 the Congregationalists were accorded the right to worship unhindered, though at the same time they were subjected to a number of civil and religious disabilities.

In the early eighteenth century increasing emphasis was placed upon the Lord's Supper, while, in keeping with the covenantal polity, infant baptism was restricted to the children of church members. Baptism was regarded as a Christian, not an ecclesiastical, ordinance, and was normally administered in the home. The Dissenting academies claim their rightful place in the story, as do the doctrinal disputes over antinomianism, Arminianism and Arianism.

The influence of the Evangelical Revival in enlivening the members and increasing the number of churches was considerable, and we are informed that it was the Independents 'of all people, who developed . . . the Welsh *hwyl*.' There was an explosion of hymn writing, and the need to come to terms with the new breed of Calvinistic Methodist. But as many were swept into the churches by conversion, the local covenant and the church meeting began to assume less importance. Sunday schools and overseas missionary activity were among happier products of the Revival, while in the theology of Edward Williams, Calvinist and evangelical ideas were blended with such a degree of success that moderate Calvinism held sway through most of the nineteenth century.

That century was characterized by numerous revivals, the removal of most of the Nonconformists' disabilities, increasing political involvement, the embrace of the temperance movement, and of poetry competitions and Welsh culture in general. From having regarded the theatre as the sink of iniquity the Nonconformists now managed to accept Joseph Parry's opera, *Blodwen*. The preaching went on, often in an unhelpfully competitive spirit, and pastoral work suffered from the absence from home of the 'princes of the pulpit.' Towards the end of the century the Higher Criticism of the Bible began to make its mark, while post-Hegelian immanentist thought fertilized liberal theology—a fact which calls forth Jones's protest: 'there was hardly ever a narrower crib in which to place Christ than that philosophy.'

In the twentieth century, World War I, the theology of Karl Barth, and the growing sense of Welsh nationhood all made an impact upon the Congregationalists. But so did social and working conditions. Sadly, while Congregationalists had taught people how to stand firm against the rigours of life, it did not supply the theological critique of social practices which was required—so to the decline of the Liberal Party and the rise of Socialism, with its ambivalent attitude towards Nonconformity. Nor did the Congregationalists perceive that below the societal problems lay a much deeper crisis of faith: 'a fierce conflict had arisen between the people and their God.' In the midst of all of this the churches lost the rudder of their covenantal polity: 'In many churches the sovereignty of the local church became synonymous with the stubbornness of the main members.' The Union of Welsh Independents (1871) strove to support the churches in a variety of ways, but its efforts were not appreciated by all. Tudur Jones ends with a call to recover the concept of the gathered church as a springboard to service in the world.

Dr. Pope's chapter is entitled, 'Survival,' and Congregationalism in Wales has survived; but it has also declined. Institution after institution has been closed; ecumenists have been thwarted; and from 106,357 church members spread among 810 churches in 1962 the tally fell in 2001 to 33,452 members and 499 churches. During the same period the number of ministers fell from 399 to 114. The bifurcation of some—especially ministers—into those who were theologically liberal and those who followed the Martyn Lloyd-Jones brand of Calvinism went alongside a creeping anti-intellectualism in some quarters, and a partisan approach to theological education (and to the location of its institutions) which caused considerable sorrow. For many, the individual's free conscience took precedence over classical doctrine and Congregational polity.

For all that, Dr. Pope, good theologian that he is, rightly concludes that God will continue to work through history. The question is how much more of what many have cherished will be left behind along the way, and what will replace it?

Friends of the Congregational Library Newsletter 2 (2005), 16–18.

40

American Congregationalism

John Von Rohr. *The Shaping of American Congregationalism 1620–1957*, Cleveland, OH: The Pilgrim Press. Pp. xi + 499.

Wearing his considerable learning lightly, John Von Rohr, Professor Emeritus of Historical Theology and History of Christianity at the Pacific School of Religion, has written a book which admirably captures the spirit of his subject, and may be read with profit by a wide readership. It may be read either straight through, with the recurrent themes—history, theology, polity, worship and mission—jostling one another within each successive period; or by pursuing the five topics in a more single minded way.

All the great events are here: the arrival of the Pilgrims; the establishment of the Massachusetts colony; the Cambridge Synod; the Great Awakening; the Unitarian separation and the Second Great Awakening; the establishment of missions at home and abroad; the Congregational and Christian union of 1931, and the joining of this united body with the Evangelical and Reformed Church in 1957. The great people are here too: from William Brewster and John Cotton, through Jonathan Edwards and Charles Finney, to Douglas Horton and Wilhelm Pauck. The events and people are sensitively set within their socio-political-economic context, and due account is taken of Congregationalism's ecumenical contribution.

The thematic sections on polity and worship are particularly illuminating. The former clearly establishes the fact that American Congregationalist polity was never monochrome, but displayed in varying degrees local autonomy, consociation and (as Roger Williams and some Quakers found to their cost) religious establishments of various kinds and durations. The decreasing rigour in examining candidates for church membership is highlighted, but the place of the church meeting (which has no index entry) in the modern period—its importance, the degree to which it was honoured, its theology—is left vague. The development of worship is traced from the Puritan emphasis upon the importance of preaching to the influence of the modern liturgical movement. The changing fortunes of baptism, from its location within covenant theology, through its relative demise under revivalist conversion-orientated fervour, to its re-emergence in the twentieth-century as a family occasion are charted—as if in fulfilment of John Cotton's seventeenth century injunction, 'sit loose from the Ordinances.'

Professor Von Rohr excels in providing lucid accounts of theological topics as complicated and various as Jonathan Edwards and the New Divinity (the story of the modification of Calvinism); the new Theology (wherein the Cross attracts as being the supreme revelation of self-giving and suffering for others); Social Gospel theology; neo-orthodoxy; and neo-liberalism. The steps taken to fulfil the missionary obligation at home and abroad, and the challenge posed to that enterprise by a church culture imbued with local autonomy are likewise competently described.

Among many points of detail, it is interesting to note that even in New England's establishment Congregationalism the Lord's table was fenced against those who were not members of a Congregational church. The importance attached to theological education is revealed in the story of Harvard and (consequent upon that institution's increasing theological liberalism) Andover; and space is rightly accorded to the significant contribution of such frontier colleges as Oberlin. Divergent Congregationalist reactions to the revivalist Finney's 'new measures' are noted, as is James Davenport's self-proclaimed ability to distinguish infallibly between the saved and the damned. As the old practice of allocating pews in church by reference to social standing and the size of subscriptions was being undermined by the increasing democratization of society, the saints at Acton, Massachusetts, in 1757 advanced an additional motive for reform, namely, that the seats closest to the pulpit should be occupied by the town's leading sinners, who most needed to hear the preaching. The quest of freedom from the English yoke is well treated, as is the place of the laity in general and of women in particular. When exhorted to save her strength and forsake religious for more womanly pursuits, Sarah Osborn, a mid-eighteenth century church member at Newport, Rhode Island, retorted, 'Needlework overpowers me vastly more than the duties I am engaged in.' In 1853 Antoinette Brown became the first ordained woman in American Congregationalism. The variety and enrichment brought by successive waves of immigrants; the challenges posed by industrialization—these are among many other strands in the story. The abortive attempt at union with the Presbyterians in the early 1800s was eventually followed by increasing co-operation with other Christians through para-church organizations, fellowship with other Congregationalists through the International Congregational Council, and union with like- minded denominations in the twentieth century (though with those who constituted the National Association of Congregational Christian Churches and the Conservative Congregational Christian Conference declining to unite).

Many random questions are suggested along the way. How many votes would Thomas Hooker receive today for his view that 'Take away a Sabbath, who can defend us from atheism, barbarism, and all manner of profaneness'? How would the 'placement' services of today's denominational strategists accommodate a Moses Noyes, who was on trial at Lyme, Connecticut, for twenty-seven years before being ordained? In a time of financial constraint, what price a polity which proclaims that 'A little church with great godliness is far to be preferred to a great church (I mean for number) and small purity'? Do any of our present churches need recourse to the policy of two in 1889 which, 'as a relief from the strain of attention and the weariness of sitting still, have singing in the middle of the sermon'? Despite a century of universal education and the increasing 'professionalization of the ministry', do we have a solution to Henry Ward Beecher's fear, expressed in 1872, that 'the intelligent part of society [may] go past us'? Finally, recalling the widespread shock occasioned by the defection of a number of Yale professors to Anglicanism in 1772, one cannot but ruefully wonder what a late twentieth-century theological professor would have to do to shock, or even mildly to nudge, anyone at all.

Congregational History Circle Magazine 3 (1997) 50–52.

41

Baptist Covenants

Charles W. Deweese. *Baptist Church Covenants.* Nashville: Broadman Press, 1990. Pp. xiv + 239.

The director of publications and communications of the Historical Commission of the Southern Baptist Convention is warmly to be thanked for this well-referenced, timely, book. He opens with a foreword followed by five chapters in which the covenant idea and Baptist covenants in Britain, America, Canada and elsewhere are discussed. In chapter six we have the texts of seventy-nine covenants, of which the earliest is that of Broadmead, Bristol (1640), and the most recent that of Halawa Heights, Honolulu (1988).

Whereas Dr. Deweese notes (p. 200) that church covenants are responses to God's gracious initiative, he emphasizes (e.g., p. 81) the human aspect of covenanting. No doubt this is prominent but, happily, many of the texts he reproduces show clearly that the church members knew that their covenanting with one another was an enabled response to God, who had first moved towards them (see, for example, pp. 118, 132, 156, 184, 194). Again, although it is true that confessions of faith are more doctrinal, while covenants are more ethical and practical (p. viii), we should not overlook the substantial doctrinal assertions which appear in some of the covenants (see, of example, pp. 134, 140, 142, 158, 165).

It is interesting to observe that (as with Congregational covenants, which this reviewer has discussed elsewhere[2]) the wording of Baptist covenants reflects the wider theological and intellectual climate. For example, we may correctly infer from the phraseology of the Baptists of Great Ellingham—'a little handful of the meanest, both of the Children of men and of the Children of God'—that the question of assurance and the way of introspection were in vogue in 1699 (p. 121). Seventy-one years on the Baptists of Caerleon resort to Enlightenment language in declaring that 'it is the duty of all reasonable creatures to obey [God] in the whole of His revealed will' (p. 125).

Inner-Baptist differences of emphasis are also of interest. Thus, whereas the saints at Meherrin Baptist Church, Lunenburg County, Virginia, happily described themselves in 1779 as 'part of the Baptist Church of Christ (p. 144), those at Cherokee Creek, North Carolina, had in 1783 decided that there were Baptists and Baptists: 'There are Several Classes of Antepaedobaptists, with which we Cannot agree. Namely, the Seven Day Baptists, the no Sabbath Baptists, and those that Dip three times in Baptism . . .' (p. 146). Consider this: 'We promise . . . solemnly to renounce all evil words and actions, foolish talking, jesting, cursing, lying, malicious anger, extortion and fraud of every kind, covetousness, drunkenness and keeping evil company and to abstain from sinful whispering, backbiting, all wilful hypocrisy and dishonesty, all excess or superfluity to the gratification of pride and also resist from gaming, wagering, singing of carnal songs and all Carnal myrth, fidling, dancing and vain recreation and all sinful contentions and not wink at the disorder of and [sic: ? any] under our care, but prudently use the Rod of correction when necessary and not neglect family devotion . . .' (p. 150). It would seem either that it was not much fun being a Baptist in Dumplin Creek, Tennessee, in 1797, or that there was an excess of saintly sin to be combatted there, or both. More seriously, we are reminded how easy it is to cross the line between disciplining one another under grace, and policing one another under new laws of the saints' devising. For their part, the Freewill Baptists of 1858 balanced their negatives with socially-orientated positives: 'we will not traffic in, nor use intoxicating drinks, as a beverage, and . . . we will sustain the other benevolent enterprises of the day, as Missions, Sabbath Schools, Moral Reform, Anti-Slavery, Education, and all others which, in the use of holy means, tend to the glory of God and the welfare of man' (p. 163).

None was more enterprising than Peter Philanthropos Roots, who provided both prose and metrical versions of his 1806 covenant. Thus, according to taste, we may decline 'lacivious [sic] talking, foolish jesting, evil speaking,' or sing:

---

2. Alan P. F. Sell. *Dissenting Thought and the Life of the Churches. Studies in an English Tradition.* Lewiston, NY: Edwin Mellen, 1990, ch. 1.

> No frothy wit, nor tattling vile,
> Shall waste our time, our hearts beguile.
> (pp. 154–55)

The timeliness of this volume emerges in the following remark, which applies equally to others in the gathered church tradition, and not only to those in America: 'A dilemma facing contemporary Baptists in America is how to reconcile mounting trends towards an uncommitted church membership with doctrinal statements that require a committed membership' (p. vii). Dr. Deweese writes interestingly on the ways in which the preparation today of church covenants could foster the restoration of the ecclesiology which underlies them, and to which they give expression. He pleads for the imaginative use of covenants—not least in connection with the 'church covenant meeting'.

But why the decline in local covenants? The author's reasons (pp. 89–91) may be summarized thus: (1) The increasing availability of printed covenants. (2) Resistance to covenants legalistically applied. (3) The decline in moral standards accompanying secularization. (4) Weaknesses discerned in the widely-used Brown covenant of 1853. (5) Slowness to depart from Brown's covenant, which was often (wrongly) regarded as official. (6) Baptist failure to take seriously the ecclesiology of their confessions of faith. (7) More concern with numerical growth than with regenerate membership. No doubt these are pertinent points, but something important is missing. May we not say that in the wake of the Revival, evangelical individualism (which can be uncomfortably close to Enlightenment individualism in religious dress), aided and abetted by western consumerism, has led to the privatization of religion in many quarters? Is not this at least a partial explanation of Dr. Deweese's sixth point above? Is not the remedy that of proclaiming a Gospel whereby people are saved into a covenant community?

The collecting of covenants is time-consuming but not unduly difficult—a few elusive ones apart. The accurate placing of covenants in their intellectual and social contexts is a more demanding objective, and here Dr. Deweese has performed valiantly. It is to be feared, however, that his objective of restoring the covenant ecclesiology in all its richness and challenge will prove to be the most elusive goal of all.

The Baptist Quarterly 34 (1991) 142–43.

Part Two: History

42

The Brethren

Donald F. Durnbaugh, *et al. The Brethren Encyclopedia*. 3 vols., Ambler, PA: The Brethren Encyclopedia Inc., 1983–4. Pp. xiii + 2126.

Let us first be clear with which Brethren we are dealing. These are not those associated with nineteenth-century Plymouth, but those whose movement began at Schwarzenau/Eder, Germany, in 1708, and was largely transplanted to North America within the next thirty years. Today the main Brethren denominations are the Brethren Church (BC), the Church of the Brethren (CB), the Dunkard Brethren (DB), the Fellowship of Grace Brethren Churches (FGBC), and the Old German Baptist Brethren (OGBB).

The Reformed should be the last to rebuke a communion which has known internal secession, and the Brethren are acutely aware of the double irony of strife within a peace church tradition. Indeed, one of the objectives of this *Encyclopedia* was to mark the centenary of an unhappy division; another was to draw together contributors from the five churches, with a view to deeper mutual understanding within the family. The first objective has been met; we may have every hope that the latter is on the way to realization; we are utterly convinced that Donald F. Durnbaugh and his large team of assistants and contributors have rendered a signal service to the wider Church in making these volumes available.

Volumes 1 and 2 carry us from A to Z. Volume 3 contains a chronology, maps, charts and statistics; lists of congregations and annual gatherings; lists of ordained ministers and elders (1708–1980), missionaries, institutions and donors; and an extensive bibliography. The ethos of the Brethren is conveyed by numerous photographs, and by typographically-distinguished documents and anecdotes. There are 260 articles on family history, and some 2,600 accounts of all those local congregations of the five main bodies which have at least ten members and have existed for at least ten years. These, together with numerous biographies, and articles on historical, doctrinal, sociological and institutional matters fulfil the editorial hope of presenting a 'reasonably full coverage of Brethren life, belief, practice, and heritage'; and this despite the fact that 'Brethren have generally been reluctant to recognize the importance of documenting their archives'—a lament of wider appropriateness, one fears.

Scholarly disagreement persists as to the relative degrees of Brethren indebtedness to sixteenth-century Anabaptism and eighteenth-century Radical Pietism. The restorationist emphases of both persist, however, as do Anabaptist-like principles concerning the visible, disciplined local church, and separation from the world. Time would fail to tell the story through the wealth of material here provided—though your reviewer doffs his cap to elder James Arnold Sell, who lived to the age of 102 years, and salutes the not atypical church planting zeal of the mother church of North Dakota at Cando, which spawned nine daughters and survives to this day.

Although Brethren have not made much use of formal credal statements, their theology is orthodox, evangelical, conservative rather than liberal. It is not, however, entirely uniform. At least four, and perhaps six, of the original eight Brethren of Schwarzenau had been members of the Reformed Church. They continued to accept much of the Heidelberg Catechism on which they had been reared; but they denied the propriety of infant baptism, of state churches, and of oath-taking, and they asserted the place of the human will in salvation. We thus find that most of the Brethren groups are more Arminian than Calvinist, the exception being the FGBC, a product of the conservative-liberal debate of the 1920s and 30s which is largely inclined towards dispensational Calvinism. Other Brethren have been known to accuse the FGBC of antinomianism. The penal substitutionary theory of the atonement has traditionally been advocated in Brethren circles. Salvation, open to all who respond to Christ in repentance and faith is 'an accomplished fact, a continuing walk, and a future hope.' Whereas the CB includes premillenarians, postmillenarians and amillenarians, the OGBB and the DB are for the most part premillenarians.

All Brethren agree that the Bible is divinely inspired, and that its message comes home to us by the Spirit. The FGBC are, however, strongly committed to biblical inerrancy, and uphold 'biblical creationism' over against the theory of evolution. Some other Brethren share this position, though the OGBB and the DB lay more emphasis upon practices deemed to be scriptural than upon doctrines about the Bible.

Brethren Christianity is strongly Christ-centred, turning upon a personal relationship between the believers and their Lord, which is lived out in the household of faith. Entry to the household is by believer baptism (though some Brethren congregations will accept a letter of transfer from those who were baptized as infants) which is, in descending order of importance, for believers only, by immersion (*pace* the Mennonites) and triune. So concerned were Brethren over the mode of baptism—the subject of numerous controversial pamphlets in the past—that they were at times in danger of losing the meaning of it. (Not indeed that Brethren theologizing was always intense: William Beaham defined sin as 'a raspberry seed under God's denture').

Consistently with the foregoing, the Brethren advocate a high doctrine of the Church, as thus defined: 'Whereas a low view defines the church as a loose association of like-minded believers who are already saved, a high view places more emphasis on the church and its ordinances as a means of grace.' Within the corporate priesthood there has traditionally been no ministerial/lay distinction, baptism being held to include all the elements of ordination. In some circles today, however, ordination services have accompanied the increasing professionalizing of the ministry—this being one product of formal ministerial training programmes.

The Love Feast, incorporating feet-washing, the holy kiss, and the Lord's Supper, is traditional in Brethren circles. In the first half of the nineteenth century there were squabbles over the type and quantity of food to be served. (Incidentally, Brethren—or sisters—have probably published more cookery books in proportion to their size than any other Christian family). Some prescribed mutton, since Jesus was keeping the Passover; others advocated a less inhibited menu on the ground that the new covenant releases from former prohibitions. The laying-on of hands as a symbolic (not a sacerdotal) act is practised during the anointing of the sick, baptism, and the installation of officers. Fasting is generally considered to be a valuable, though a private, matter.

Among Brethren side-shoots was the Ephrata Community. Founded in the eighteenth-century by Johann Conrad Beissel (who had been influenced by English Seventh-Day Baptists), its membership observed Saturday as the Sabbath, encouraged celibacy whilst not excluding the married, maintained a notable publishing house, but gradually declined (typhus playing a part), ceased, and is now a tourist attraction. Beissel's successor as leader, J. Peter Miller (1709–96), had defected from the Reformed Church, to the chagrin of that body. Renewed interest in communitarianism has developed amongst the Brethren since the middle of the present (twentieth) century; some Brethren families, for example, have joined the Hutterian Brethren.

Along with high churchmanship as Brethren understand it has gone a keen interest in church discipline and a godly walk. Hymns and gospel songs have made their way at different rates among the Brethren groups, the OGBB still using the twenty-sixth edition of their 1882 hymnal only in their official worship. This group never accepted Sunday Schools—indeed, opposition to such was a factor in their secession of 1881. Other Brethren have produced numerous hymnals and courses of instruction, and the CB cooperates with twelve other denominations in producing educational materials. In 1955 the FGBC joined Carl McIntire's fundamentalist American Council of Churches. The CB is the only Brethren group to belong to the National and World Councils of Churches.

As to life-style, some Brethren groups continue to adopt a separatist policy of witnessing over against the world, rather than one of infiltration. This witness is signalled in part by dress. Thus, for example, the DB encourage men to wear beards, forbid hats to women, ties to men, and wristwatches to both sexes. Again, in 1913 and 1921 seceders from the OGBB held that the motor car, the telephone and other modern inventions constituted dangerous temptations to entanglement with the world. Traditionally, Brethren have been opposed to secret societies, but today the OGBB and the DB alone make non-membership of such bodies a condition of church membership. On the other hand, and unlike some other Brethren, the OGBB, who in 1980 cautioned against attendance at ice- and roller-skating rinks, are not opposed to drinking alcohol in moderation. The CB is more permissive than the FGBC regarding abortion; in the OGBB excommunication follows discovered pre-marital sexual relations. While the DB do not avail themselves of higher education, the Brethren P. J. Flory and H. C. Urey won Nobel Prizes for chemistry and nuclear physics respectively. Though many Brethren have retained connections with agriculture, some—the Studebakers, for example—have given their name to manufactured products.

The Brethren have been, and are, active in missions and in relief work, but it is as one of the historic peace churches that they command particular attention today. There is, however, diversity within the peace position. It encompasses the refusal to participate in, or train for, war; the readiness to suffer rather than to fight; the advocacy of non-violent ways of resolving conflict; and a general commitment to peacemaking in a threatened world. While the OGBB and the FGBC tend to endorse the view that the state has the obligation to take the lives of those proved guilty of dangerous crimes, other Brethren, as part of their over-arching pacifism, do not.

There is much of interest to the Reformed family in these volumes: not least the Brethren expression of the congregational polity, and their position (more homogeneous than ours) on church-state relations. We do not always appear in a good light. We have hounded the Brethren for their pacifism, and in 1858 Samuel Garber of the Brethren was arrested for preaching against slavery in a Tennessee Presbyterian church. In view of the Reformed family's increasing closeness to the Disciples tradition (with which we have already united in the United Kingdom and elsewhere) we may expect some interest in the early Brethren-Disciples struggles. The Brethren felt that what they regarded as the revivalist excesses of camp meetings—of which that at Cane Ridge in 1801 was the archetype—were 'not profitable'; and over against the Campbell-Stone restorationist movement some Brethren declared that an unbroken chain of authority flowed from the apostles *via* the Waldensians and the Anabaptists to themselves—a view now abandoned. Nevertheless, in some areas Brethren went over to the Disciples.

Since this review is written in Calgary at the onset of the Winter Olympics fever, it is not inappropriate to note that Robert 'Bob' Richards, then a CB minister, won an Olympic gold medal in 1956 for pole-vaulting. What the OGBB and the DB thought about that is left to the imagination.

So is the passing thought: with about half the membership of all the Brethren together, and with two more centuries to cover, could the United Reformed Church produce an encyclopedia to mark its jubilee in 1997? Have we the writers, the interest, the donors, the will?

Christian—and not only Brethren—disharmony will, no doubt, be overcome hereafter. That, at least, is one implication of the epitaph composed by Alexander Mack Jr. (1712–1803), Brethren historian and apologist (if not poet), which adorns his headstone at Germantown, Pennsylvania:

> GOD
> Who us of dust did make and us again to dust will take,
> His wisdom, like the sun, shall break
> When in his likeness we awake.

Journal of the United Reformed Church History Society 4 (1988) 161–65.

43

The Evangelical and Reformed Church

David Dunn, *et* al., [1961], with a new Introduction by Lowell H. Zuck. *A History of the Evangelical and Reformed Church*. New York: The Pilgrim Press 1990. Pp. xxx, 371.

As with natural families, so with churchly : we may well know more about our neighbours than about our relatives overseas. With the republication of this book the American Evangelical and Reformed branch should become much better known to its British Reformed cousins. For good measure, this new edition contains Lowell H. Zuck's account of the first thirty years of the United Church of Christ, the 1957 union of the E and R Church with the Congregational Christian Churches.

As its name suggests, the E and R Church was already a union of the old German Reformed Church (1725) with the Evangelical Synod (1840). The union was consummated in 1934, and there followed just twenty-three years of church growth and the increase of ecumenical zeal before the still wider union of 1957. Indeed, when less than ten years into its new life the E and R Church was already contemplating its death as a distinct denomination.

The bulk of the book is occupied by the prehistory of the E and R Church. It is a story of immigration from different parts of 'Germany' (with some Reformed coming from Hungary), in two very different centuries, to different regions of a vast 'new' country. The Reformed brought with them the heritage of Zwingli, the Heidelberg Catechisrn, the Palatinate Liturgy and consistorial church order; the Evangelicals, fortified by the Augsburg Confession, Luther's Catechism and the Heidelberg Catechism, were tempered by the eirenic spirit of Melanchthon. The latter had to make their nineteenth-century way in what was for them a dramatically new context of the separation of Church and State. In practical terms this meant that, in the absence of state funding, they had to learn to give voluntarily to Christian work.

Both traditions experienced the impress of pietism; neither succumbed to the excesses of frontier revivalism; both established schools, colleges and seminaries; engaged in home and foreign missions; undertook publishing and social welfare ventures; and struggled with the language issue (German or English?). If the German Reformed of Pennsylvania were divided in their response to Zinzendorf's attempts of 1736 to unite German confessionalists with pietists, Evangelicals (already of mixed Lutheran and Reformed heritage) had to carve out a path between German immigrant freethinking ministers who baptized in the name of Liberty. Fraternity and Equality, and the Saxon Lutherans of Missouri who 'consider it a sin to serve a united church, since, according to their opinion, the Reformed are the children of Satan.'

The theological contribution of the two streams is of particular interest. To the nineteenth-century German Reformed we are indebted for the catholic-incarnational Mercersburg theology of the former Presbyterian J.W. Nevin, and Philip Schaff;[3] from the Evangelical side in this (twentieth) century have come the Niebuhrs. Given the history of fracture within the Reformed family, it is cheering to note that no permanent secession had occurred when, following nearly four decades of strife between the Mercersburg party and their Reformed traditionalists opponents, among whom J.H.A. Bomberger of Ursinus College was prominent, the peace commission of 1878 brought matters to a conclusion.

The story is enlivened by such information as that 'When the British Army was approaching Philadelphia in 1777, Zion Reformed Church in Allentown ripped up the floors of its church to hide the Liberty Bell until the city was evacuated by the British.' We are treated to two lines of a nineteenth-century revivalist hymn:

> Once I was blind. I could not see.
> The Calvinist deceived me.

Eden Theological Seminary is named, not after the biblical garden, but after its nearest station on the Wabash Railroad; the London Missionary Society cooperated with the Basel Mission in securing German and Swiss missionaries for the American Mid-West; and, during the course of his sermon preached at the final pre-union conference of the Reformed Church on 26 June 1934, F. William Leich quoted P. T. Forsyth: 'The great issue within Christianity is not between systems and doxies, but a battle for the holy as the one all-inclusive gift of Christ.'

The Pilgrim Press is warmly to be thanked for reissuing this most informative book, the value of which is enhanced by portraits, statistical data, an updated bibliography and an index.

Journal of the United Reformed Church 5 (1993) 117–19.

---

3. See further reviews 60, 75, 76 and 77 below.

Part Two: History

44

Evangelical Biography

Donald M. Lewis, ed. *The Blackwell Dictionary of Evangelical Biography 1730–1860*. 2 vols., Oxford: Blackwell, 1995, pp. xxviii (repeated in vol. 2) + 1259.

To judge from the number of dictionaries and encyclopedias which roll (or thud) from the presses, there is an insatiable demand for packaged information. We have long since learned to value such tomes as *The Oxford Dictionary of the Christian Church* and *The New International Dictionary of the Christian Church* for their breadth of coverage. But of late numerous other volumes have appeared which are, however complete within their respective terms of reference, limited by confession (*Encyclopedia of the Reformed Faith*), or geography (*Dictionary of Scottish Church History and Theology*), or period (*The Blackwell Companion to the Enlightenment*), or discipline (*Biographical Dictionary of Twentieth-Century Philosophers*), or theme (*Dictionary of the Ecumenical Movement*). Were it not calculated to leave one open to the charge of evincing an unsanctified mind one might plaintively enquire how many potted Wesleys do we need? But, of course, he is too important to be omitted from appropriate works of reference. Moreover, fresh accounts of the well-known can, given adequate space and competent authorship, incorporate the latest scholarly interpretations and list the most recent relevant works. Badly done—in which case the longevity of such volumes is a disadvantage—a dictionary article can mislead those whose main recourse is to handy sources into perpetrating errors for years to come.

How does the *Dictionary of Evangelical Biography* measure up? The editor clearly states his objectives, which are (in brief): to fill a gap; to acknowledge the significance of evangelicalism during the period in question; to serve a wide range of professional and lay readers; and to package in convenient form a considerable amount of recent scholarship. The field of vision is not narrow: evangelicalism's impact upon society—not excluding the contribution of women—is constantly in view. The focus is on the period from the beginnings of the evangelical revival to the 'Prayer-Meeting Revival' of 1858–59; and the concern is largely with the English-speaking world. Following David Bebbington's characterization, contributors were asked to make the following definition their canon:

> Evangelical Protestantism was a movement marked by: conversionism (involving a call to personal repentance and moral transformation); crucicentrism (evangelicals have centred their theology on the cross of Christ, the doctrine of the Atonement being central to their theological understanding); biblicism (the Bible being taken as the supreme authority in matters of faith and practice); and activism (a commitment

to doing which springs from the moral radicalism rooted in a sense of personal responsibility).

Under this rubric are happily gathered ministers and missionaries, officers of evangelical organizations, numerous lay people in many fields of endeavour, and a selection of non-English-speaking evangelicals—César Malan and Zinzendorf among them—who could not be excluded. Anglicans, Baptists, Congregationalists, Methodists, Presbyterians, Quakers, and also members of such important but sometimes neglected groups as the Moravians, Plymouth Brethren and Strict Baptists—all are here.

The predictable people—the Wesleys, Whitefield, the Countess of Huntingdon, Howell Harris, William Carey, Jonathan Edwards, Adoniram Judson, Charles Grandison Finney, and many others are competently handled, as one would expect. But the particular value of such a focused volume as this is that due attention can be paid to many hinterland worthies who were insufficiently famous or notorious to qualify for admission to the general reference books.

Not the least encouragement to the conscientious reviewer of such a sizeable work is the miscellaneous information which jumps off the page along the way. Thus, the American Methodist itinerant, Benjamin Abbott, was converted following a dream, while the Episcopalian, Thomasia Meade, was similarly blessed during a bout of measles. James Acland, Principal of Bradford Baptist Academy, denied the right of the state to enforce observance of the Lord's Day, and the anti-slavery Quaker, Anthony Benezet, wished to be remembered as 'a poor creature, and, through divine favour, enabled to know it.' The picture of Elizabeth Bultitude, the itinerant Primitive Methodist preacher, with her 'large round rubicund face in a poke bonnet' and her 'ejaculatory prayers with many fervent repetitions' is difficult to dislodge from the mind. David Cargill, a Wesleyan missionary to Fiji, was one of a number of evangelicals who devised a written language for those amongst whom they went. It was good to make the acquaintance of Anna Gambold, Moravian, pioneer botanist, poet and musician, who engaged in mission to the Cherokees. The way in which the naval officer turned missionary, Allen Francis Gardiner, persisted in his calling despite numerous setbacks and hardships is as inspiring as it is humbling. The black Baptist preacher, John Jasper, freed from slavery after fifty years, presided over a church which grew from nine members to two thousand—despite a preaching style which incorporated 'grunts and heavings terrible to bear.' I welcomed the full article on the Plymouth Brother, George Müller, who devoted himself to orphaned children and to the financial support of missionaries. The least flattering verdict in the entire two volumes must surely be that passed upon the 'obstinacy and Puritanism' of Charles Perry, the first Anglican bishop of Melbourne: 'What a disaster it is when a Presbyterian or Dissenting minister who has missed his way and got into the church is made a Bishop. ' It would appear that few took more of the evangelistic opportunities which came their way than John Russell, the distinguished portrait painter, who pleaded for the conversion of his unsaved subjects during sittings. The house of the New York merchant and philanthropist, Lewis Tappan, a supporter of Finney, was wrecked by a mob who disapproved of his abolitionism. No such fate befell Octavius Winslow, the notable Baptist minister who seceded to the Church of England and was ordained by the Bishop of Chichester in 1870.

It is always possible to think of persons missing—my old friends, James Rooker and Henry Rogers, for example. And what of James Wells and Benjamin Wallin? But the *Dictionary* is as comprehensive as may reasonably be expected, and for the most part the authors are well chosen. Similarly, it is not difficult to find gaps in the information provided—R. S. Candlish's critique of F. D. Maurice, for example—but one appreciates that when word allowances are tight hard choices have to be made. Again, the relative length of articles prompts a raised eyebrow from time to time. Alexander Duff is allowed twice as much space as Philip Doddridge; Francis Asbury receives a column more than John Wesley, and two more than Whitefield. Three columns for Henry Bidleman Bascom seems over-generous, and fourteen lines for Benjamin Beddome niggardly. On the other hand, in cases where the present entry is virtually the only treatment of a lesser known but significant person (William Briggs, for example), a longer entry is fully justified. The fact that a number of bibliographies omit significant works, by no means all of which are so recent as to have appeared during the publishing process, is much to be regretted.

These sturdily-bound volumes contain some 3,500 articles and have occupied 360 scholars drawn from many parts of the world. An index assists the user to identify the geographical area, denomination (where known), and occupation of the several subjects; however, it contains a number of slips and should be used with caution: for example, the Baptist A. Austin is also listed as a Congregational minister.

As compared with the tomes mentioned at the outset, the distinguishing characteristic of this *Dictionary* is not its comprehensiveness in the ODCC sense, confession, geography, discipline or theme, but its depiction of a movement or party (very broadly conceived). This suggests that the work is least effective (because one-sided) in the field of intellectual history in general and polemics in particular; for some of those against whom the evangelicals sharpened their quills (not being themselves evangelicals) are not present. But for the many good things we have received we may return thanks to the editor, his specialist advisers, the legion of contributors, and the publisher. Since for many this *Dictionary* will provide the only source of information on a large number of evangelicals of the period 1730–1860, it may be hoped that theological and other libraries will make every effort to accommodate its cost within their increasingly strained budgets.

The Baptist Quarterly 37 (1997) 150–52.

Evangelicalism in Modern Britain

D. W. Bebbington. *Evangelicalism in Modern Britain.
A history from the 1730s to the 1980s*. London: Unwin Hyman, 1989. Pp. xi + 364.

'Surely no man ever had a mind so full of facts and so void of ideas.' I am not here concerned with the justice or otherwise of James Denney's verdict upon J.G. Frazer. I simply wish to point out that in Dr. Bebbington's latest book there are facts a-plenty, but they are skilfully deployed to illuminate ideas.

Dr. Bebbington sets out to provide a comprehensive account of a movement within British Christianity which has hitherto been neglected. More particularly, he wishes to show how Evangelicalism has shaped, but has first been shaped by, its historical and cultural environment. He suggests that conversionism, activism, biblicism and crucicentrism 'form a quadrilateral of priorities [more than one priority?] that is the basis of Evangelicalism.' The four concepts are carefully discussed, and we then pass to an account of the early Evangelical movement (1734 onwards). Dr. Bebbington describes the community life of the Evangelicals; he notes their social composition, remarking upon the importance of the place accorded to women; and he elucidates the several strands within the movement: Calvinism and Arminianism; Anglicanism and Dissent; and its Scottish varieties. He is especially concerned to show both the continuity of Evangelicalism with its Puritan past, and the place of such newer influences as High Church spirituality, the Moravians, and the modern call to mission. The prominent factor in the last-mentioned is the doctrine of assurance, which had undergone a significant shift of emphasis resulting from the sensationalist epistemology of the Enlightenment.

Dr. Bebbington is, with good reason, in the camp of those revisionists who hold that 'Evangelicalism was accepted along with many characteristic traits of the Enlightenment. Its emergence was itself an expression of the age of reason.' He notes both the continuing Puritanism of the Strict Baptists, and the impact in Scotland—not least upon Thomas Chalmers—of the common sense philosophy of Reid and his successors. The 'optimism of grace' and the modification of High Calvinism were among other results of the Enlightenment. The theological influence of Jonathan Edwards is properly, if briefly, brought out. The pragmatic spirit, the literary awareness, the humanitarian concern and the political interests of early Evangelicals are passed in review.

A constellation of impulses produced a change of direction in Evangelicalism *circa* 1830. Mission strategy, the revival of interest in Calvinism associated with the Haldanes and Henry Drummond, the contribution of Edward Irving, the impact of Romanticism, the growth of millennialism, concern with the advent hope, changing views of biblical inspiration—these were among the factors making for change. Doctrinal modifications in the wake of Erskine of Linlathen, J. McLeod Campbell and F. D. Maurice pleased some and alarmed others; and Irving's catholic experiment had a considerable influence upon many. Evangelicals found themselves in opposing camps on the Church-State issue, and they managed to irritate one another within such co-operative movements as the Evangelical Alliance. Anti-Catholicism became especially pronounced in some Anglican circles. The word which sums up the changed spirit and attitudes is 'Romanticism'.

Turning to Church and society, Dr. Bebbington discusses the 1851 Census, social class, the relative weakness of organized atheism, revivalism, philanthropy, education, and that Evangelical lifestyle which zealously sought to eradicate those sins of which it disapproved. The best is made of the Evangelical contribution to scholarship, and the theological Down Grade receives due mention.

The later nineteenth century was productive of Keswick and holiness teaching—to which Wesleyanism, Quaker spirituality, the Brethren and the Anglican Mildmay Circle were variously related, as were the American revivalists, Moody and Sankey. In the 1920s the [relative] unity of Evangelicalism was broken by 'liberal' theology, the 'higher criticism' of the Bible, and by disagreements over biblical inerrancy. Some Evangelicals pursued liturgical interests, while others felt that ritualism was coming too close to home. Science and religion, the use of leisure, the social witness of the Church—these were all areas within which Evangelicals could, and did, divide.

So to the charismatic movement, the Oxford Group, the emphasis upon self-fulfilment in the 1960s, the ecumenical movement, the revitalization of Evangelical scholarship, the Reformed and sectarian wings of Evangelicalism, and, finally, to a brief concluding chapter on this diverse but significant movement.

Our rapid sketch does scant justice to Dr. Bebbington's well-packed volume. We must, however, pass to some comments on an ascending scale of seriousness. First, there is material here to ease the reader's journey: the clergyman who was converted whilst preaching his own sermon; the image of Adam Clarke playing marbles; W.E. Orchard's 'wet' recommendation, 'On Ash Wednesday morning, say to your wife, "My dear, is there any virtue you would like me to acquire?"'

Well-provided though we are with information, at certain points I should like to know more: the results of the lack of Evangelical attention to those doctrines (including the Trinity) which were not emphasized by them; the varied motivations towards, and responses to, the establishment of ministerial training colleges; the often conservative and sometimes reactionary influence of the considerable amount of lay preaching which was undertaken; the Evangelical enthusiasm for merchandising the gospel; the impact of such large-circulation papers as *The Christian Herald*; the Gospel Standard Baptists in relation to 'duty faith'; the anti-'decisionist' Evangelicals; the post-1960 Reformed Baptists. If the minimal influence in Britain of Kuyper and Dooyeweerd (both of whom escape the index) is to be noted, we need to be told a little more about their position(s). And there is more to be said concerning Wesley's divergence from Lockean epistemology, and concerning the distinction to be drawn between the rationalistic and the Evangelical Arminians.

Next, there is the matter of balance. We have a good deal on Irving, much less on McLeod Campbell; the W. Robertson Smith case is mentioned, but not that of Dods and Bruce later, or of Samuel Davidson earlier; the Oxford Group receives considerable attention, Evangelical attitudes towards ecumenism too little.

Certain statements give one pause. For example, 'at the beginning of the nineteenth century Independent ministers were trained not in theology or Greek, but simply in preaching.' But they were trained in all of these at that period if the written accounts of the work of Edward Williams and James Bennett at Rotherham, Fletcher and Hope at Blackburn, Simpson at Hoxton, Bull at Newport Pagnell, and Pye Smith and Hill at Homerton are to be believed. Again, is it possible, as has sometimes been alleged, that Alexander Kilham's Methodist New Connexion polity was inspired as much by the Presbyterian church order which surrounded him during his formative years as by the egalitarianism of the French Revolution? Granted that Dr. Bebbington says only that Kilham was inspired 'in part' by the latter; was Presbyterianism another part?

Dr. Bebbington does well to remind us that the biblical inerrancy debate is a relatively recent phenomenon. He does not altogether convince me that Evangelicalism became unduly adapted to the high culture of the 1960s—a large number of Evangelicals stood sturdily against that culture. He makes good his case that Evangelicalism is in important respects a product of the Enlightenment. One of the lessons of this book is that labels such as 'Evangelicalism' can obscure more than they reveal. However, Christianity has no monopoly of labels. Dr. Bebbington attaches the philosophical label 'empiricist' to Locke. But Gilbert Ryle declared that 'Most of the doctrines which an Empiricist (as ordinarily defined) should hold are strenuously denied by Locke.' Food for thought…

It takes a certain courage to chart the choppy waters of Evangelicalism. Those prejudiced against the movement will not be able to understand Dr. Bebbington's balanced, eirenic approach. From within the movement some will question his 'soundness.' We may expect to learn something about the reviewers of Dr. Bebbington's stimulating book!

Enlightenment and Dissent 10 (1991) 115–18.

Part Two: History

46

Methodism in Britain and Ireland

John A. Vickers, ed. *A Dictionary of Methodism in Britain and Ireland.*
Peterborough: Epworth Press, 2000. Pp. 438.

Edwin Waugh's depiction of the adverse effects of drink on family life, *Come Whoam to thi' Childer an' Me*, sold 20,000 copies in a matter of days. It is pleasant to think that this *Dictionary* may enjoy like success, for it is unique, informative, authoratitive, remarkably comprehensive, and, by today's standards, reasonably priced. The editor and his advisers are to be congratulated on a work which will be valued by churchgoers, historians, theologians and ecumenists; and there may even be enough statistics here to satisfy scholars of the bean-counting sort.

The editor explains that the work is a 'first port of call' (in which case more consistent reference to the *Dictionary of National Biography* [now ODNB] would have assisted some readers to the next port), and that the objective has been to present basic information concisely. In such a work of 'bones' one does not look for fine writing, but for clarity and accuracy, and these are to be found. The bonus is that despite the constraints, writers such as David Carter and John Newton prove themselves to be fluent miniaturists, while one may be forgiven for suspecting that in his article on Eastern Orthodoxy Gordon Wakefield manages to show his colours: 'The doctrine of theosis (deification), though Protestants of the Barthian school have deemed it dangerous, is found in the Wesley hymns.' The several tribes of Methodism are in capable hands, as such names as Oliver Beckerlegge, Geoffrey Milburn and Alan Rose testify. The article bibliographies, though brief, will assist those who wish to enquire further, though very occasionally more authoritative references could have been substituted for some of those given. A comprehensive bibliography completes the volume.

The editorial claim that Calvinistic Methodism is included needs to be qualified by the observation that while the pioneers are there—Whitefield, the Countess of Huntingdon, Harris, Rowland and William Williams; and while there is a general article on Welsh Calvinistic Methodism (or Presbyterian Church of Wales), post-pioneer biographies are at best scarce.

But if not quite all of British Methodism is here, an enormous slice of it is. In addition to biographies we have articles on Methodism in the several geographical regions of Britain, on its missionary outreach, on its finances and property, on its doctrine, worship and church government (which last Susan Howdle manages to make less than soporific), and on its many institutions. The Methodists seem to have thought of everything: not only a Fellowship of the Kingdom and a Methodist Sacramental Fellowship, but also a Methodist Philatelic Society and a Worn Out Ministers Fund.

Readers unfamiliar with Methodist ways will welcome such articles as that on the Class Meeting, though they may remain a little confused as to the relation between Baptism and Membership (is it conceivable that the occasional Methodist is in the same puzzled state?). The differing ordination practices of the several branches of Methodism are theologically revealing, as is the remark of James Thorne the Bible Christian, that the term 'Reverend' is 'unscriptural and a badge of popery.'

In a work of this kind we expect to find the Wesleys, Alexander Kilham, Hugh Bourne, Jabez Bunting, and we are not disappointed. But the 'hinterland people' are very well represented. We have John Adams-Acton the sculptor; the soprano Ada Alsop who, no doubt, could have made mincemeat of Francis Duckworth's famous tune, 'Rimington'; numerous dynasties both ministerial—Moultons, Rattenburys; and business—Chubbs (locks) and Ranks (flour and films); Joseph Orton, advocate for Australia's aborigines; Joseph Arch the early trade unionist and Len Murray the latter-day one; Sarah Mallett who began preaching during epileptic fits; J. Agar Beet, 'the greatest "forgotten" theologian of British Methodism'; G. B. Evans, the BBC's 'Romany'; Elizabeth Bultitude of the 'large and rubicund face,' the last Primitive Methodist female itinerant and the only one to 'die in the work'; the ubiquitous David Frost; Billy Bray, 'the King's son'; William Pickles Hartley who made jam; and Howard Belben, the first minister your reviewer can remember. There is a sprinkling of MPs, among them Michael Foot, George Thomas and Michael Stewart; and the following are among academic Methodists to be found in a variety of disciplines: Geoffrey Rose (epidemiology), Herbert Butterfield (history), W. D. Wright (applied optics), C. A. Coulson (mathematics and science), H. Cecil Pawson (agriculture), H. F. Mathews and A. Victor Murray (education), and T. E. Jessop (philosophy). A sizeable number of Methodists was involved in the temperance movement: Peter Thompson bought the Old Mahogany Bar, 'a notorious gin palace,' and Wilton's Music Hall, and turned them into mission halls. On the other hand John Wesley Thomas opposed teetotalism and, for good measure, the Pope and J. Everett too.

The editor and his advisers clearly faced daunting problems of selection, and these are never more acute that when making decisions concerning the living. Thus we have the historians John Kent, John Walsh and Reginald Ward, but not Henry Rack and Peter Stephens; and might not Owen Evans have been included among the biblical scholars Barrett, Grayston, Hooker-Stacey, Marshall and Young—not least for his stalwart work on the Welsh Bible? Present-day British Methodism's most prolific philosopher of religion, David Pailin, is likewise absent.

Methodism's ecumenical contribution is inadequately treated. There should surely have been more than a passing reference to the Free Church Federal Council and its predecessors, to which Methodists have contributed with varying degrees of enthusiasm; and while the articles on the World Methodist Council and Geoffrey Wainwright note (without specifying them) that Methodists have been engaged in international bilateral dialogues, there is no indication of the results of this theological work, some of which bear directly upon such included topics as Calvinism and Arminianism. Again, I could find no reference to those numerous Local Ecumenical Projects in which so many Methodists are involved. No doubt one's occasional suspicion that at the point of ecumenical decision some Methodists become afflicted with a touch of the Buntings is to be devoutly repented of. It would, however, be sad if they really felt that the world is their parish—provided that it's Methodist!

Occasionally one queries the balance between articles. Thus the editor does well to confine John Wesley to just over five columns, but E. S. Waterhouse surely deserves more than nine lines, in none of which are his published works referred to. His article does, however, include an example of what used to be called a 'human touch'—the kind of miscellaneous information of no great significance which nevertheless eases the passage of dictionary writers and readers alike. We learn that Waterhouse, a railway enthusiast, 'often travelled on the footplate.' But Geoffrey Wainwright's fondness for Yorkshire County Cricket Club is passed over in silence—as well it might be, says this Surrey man.

Proceedings of the Wesley Historical Society 52 (2000) 245–47.

47

Reasonable Enthusiast

Henry D. Rack. *Reasonable Enthusiast: John Wesley and the Rise of Methodism.* London: Epworth Press, 1989. Pp. xvi + 656.

Since Wesley is probably one of the world's most famous half-known and inaccurately-known people, Henry Rack's comprehensive and truthful biography is greatly to be welcomed. In a 'Prelude' Mr. Rack sets his subject in his socio-political and religious context, thereby providing the basis for his overall view of Wesley as 'a "reasonable enthusiast", combining religious values in some ways as radical as anything in the sixteenth-century Anabaptists and seventeenth-century Puritan Separatists with aspects of High Church polity, and clothing the whole in the language of Locke as well as that of the Bible.'

Part One takes us to 1738. We expect to meet Susanna and her encouragements to perfectionism, but Mr. Rack can also tell us all we need to know about Westley Hall's temporary jilting of Wesley's sister Martha in favour of sister Kezziah. We expect to hear of the Holy Club, but its character and activities are here illuminated by recent research. Wesley's troubled relations with women, his obsessive private devotional discipline, the influence of the mystics—all are here. So too the Georgia adventure (and the 'selective and slanted' *Journal* account of it); the influence of the Moravians; and Sarah Hopkey, 'the worst of all the serpents in [Wesley's] Eden.' There follows an account of the Aldersgate Street experience in which the nature of the 'conversion' is closely examined, with special reference to Wesley's understanding of justification by grace through faith in relation to his earlier High Church convictions. An 'Interlude' on the origins of the Evangelical Revival follows. It is properly noted that the Revival did not begin with Wesley, and that there was more life in the older Dissent than has sometimes been allowed.

'John Wesley and the rise of Methodism (1738–60)' is the subject of Part Two. Wesley's practice, and his relations with evangelical Calvinists—notably Whitefield—are duly considered, and early frictions concerning the doctrine and order of the Church of England are noted. It becomes clear that although Wesley has been depicted as an organizational zealot, most of what he did as his movement spread was unplanned: he reacted pragmatically to ever-changing situations. Charles Wesley, 'sweet singer and uneasy colleague' next takes the stage, to be followed by more women and the unfortunate marriage. Thence, *via* mobs, controversies and Evangelical Anglican and Dissenting rivals, to an 'Interlude' on 'Society and revival in the later eighteenth century.' The renewal of the High Church tradition, Sunday Schools, hyper-Calvinist and Arminian Baptists—all receive brief mention here.

Part Three concerns 'John Wesley and the consolidation of Methodism (1760–91).' The crisis of the 1760s over perfectionism; Wesley's multifarious activities as evangelist, author, editor and educator, and his political stances, are deftly treated. Cold water is poured upon the notion that Methodism averted revolution in England. The careful chapter on 'Doctrine, devotion and social concern' contains a cautionary word to liturgiologists who might too swiftly assume generally high sacramentalism in Methodist worship. Further differences over perfectionism come into view. The Calvinistic and subscription controversies are next explored and Mr. Rack clearly demonstrates the increasing incongruity between Wesley's profession of loyalty to the Church of England and the actions he took in the cause of evangelization. The American 'problem' did much to bring matters to a head during the 1780s: the decade of Coke and the ordinations.

In a 'Postlude' Mr. Rack adjusts himself to several of the verdicts which have been pronounced upon Wesley and offers his own judicious assessment. The latter includes this characteristically honest statement: 'Although it may be felt that only by his hard-core character and commitment could Wesley have achieved what he did for Methodism, the human cost remained severe.'

Mr. Rack has served us well. He has made good use of his numerous sources—many of them obscure; his judgements are well-founded. After his detailed probing of both the Wesley legend and the 'smoke-screen' which Wesley himself created in his writings, our author emerges as neither an hagiographer nor a debunker—and Wesley deserves neither. Mr. Rack is cool—more reasonable than enthusiastic, perhaps—but not unkind. While he justifiably holds Wesley in high esteem, he also, understandably enough, finds him a most uncomfortable companion on occasion. Above all, this account is properly balanced. Historical, sociological, psychological and theological considerations find their due place, and on controversial points those who disagree with the author will be challenged to reconsider their positions.

To conclude: first, if this is who Wesley was (and impressive evidence will need to be adduced to convince us otherwise), Wesleyan Methodism's positive results can only have been of grace. Secondly, since Mr. Rack has done so well, it will be some time before we really need another biography of Wesley—but doubtless uncovenanted mercies will yet descend upon us.

The Baptist Quarterly 33 (1990) 396–97.

48

Locke, Wesley, and Romanticism

Richard E. Brantley. *Locke, Wesley, and the Method of English Romanticism*. Gainsville, FL: University of Florida Press, 1984. Pp. xi + 300.

The contemplation of the title of Professor Brantley's book alone suffices to conjure up a vision of extensive bibliographies, and suggests the need for a polymathic author. Locke and Wesley, taken individually, have proved too much for some; together they are daunting. Their combined association with the tangled web of English Romantic method encourages the hope that our author will be not only a voracious reader with an adequate grasp of philosophy and theology, but a student of literature highly skilled in ideological and linguistic detection. Reservations notwithstanding, Brantley is our man. His full notes and useful appendices testify to his wide and careful reading of primary and secondary sources; he is at home in the eighteenth-century intellectual climate; he is abreast of current literary theory. What does he produce from these formidable resources?

Brantley seeks to show the significance of John Wesley's dialectic of philosophy and faith for the method of English Romanticism. He argues first that Wesley's empirical theological method is derived from Locke's epistemology; and secondly that Wesley's 'mediation of Locke's thought is an immediate context of English Romantic poetry: Blake, Wordsworth, Coleridge, Shelley, and Keats, whatever their differences from each other, resemble each other in their formulations of experience, which echo Wesley's.'

The Wesley who thus emerges is not a narrow-minded pietist aloof from matters intellectual, but one who exercised a considerably more than religious influence upon Methodist contemporaries and literary successors alike. He transmitted a Lockean philosophical method to the poets under review, and communicated a Lockean idiom to their language. Brantley's trail takes us from things, through ideas, to words.

We first investigate Wesley's 'Lockean connection,' which was forged by Peter Browne's *The procedure, extent and limits of human understanding* (1728). Wesley spent more than three months abridging this work, and was impressed by the way in which Browne drew out 'Locke's implication that spiritual influx can supplement biblical truth and knowledge.' For Browne, 'faith,' construed as 'a mind based sixth "sense" which receives and interprets sense data, extends Lockean reason.' It thus transpired that 'Wesley's strange warming of the heart and his view of God's love as shed abroad therein parallel the view of sense perception as sufficiently accordant with the nature of the thing itself.' That is to say, that both spiritual and natural actuality are inward and outward.

In delineating Wesley's philosophical theology, Brantley draws attention to his sensationalist diction, and to his use of the analogy between faith and empirical observation. Faith, writes Wesley, is the 'feeling of the soul, whereby a believer perceives, through the "power of the Highest overshadowing him" . . . both the existence and the presence of him in whom he "lives, moves, and has his being" and indeed the whole invisible world, the entire system of things eternal.' Wesley's consistent denial of innate ideas is deemed to be a further indication of his radical empiricism.

With the fourth chapter we come to the 'Romantic' method, and to Brantley's demonstration that the intellectual aspect of the Evangelical Revival was 'present to' the English Romantic mind: the 'Lockean-Wesleyan continuum is background to, if not the context for, Romantic thought and expression.' We cannot here follow him in detail through his chosen poets, though the assertion that 'the subject-object, empirically rational dimension of "Tintern Abbey" is consistent with its "sense sublime" in the same way that Wesley's theology of immediate revelation is consistent with his Lockean epistemology,' typifies his overall case.

In 'A methodological postscript' the conclusion is underscored that the poets considered 'owe something of their theory, and much of their practice, to the relation between Locke and John Wesley. This mix, then, is English Romantic method.' We await Brantley's application of his method to Cowper, Shelley, Hazlitt and Lamb; and we may hope that references to Jonathan Edwards and to German Romanticism will be pursued further. Meanwhile Brantley has done well to throw his considerable weight behind those who would rescue Wesley from the intellectual oblivion to which some have too readily consigned him.

Professor Brantley is an enthusiast (at least in the modern sense of the term). He is quick to inform us of what has never been done before, and of what he is doing for the first time. He does a good deal of 'contending.' He resurrects archaic 'nays' for emphasis; he can outdo the most turgid older divine with a convoluted ten-line sentence. He picks upon those who have not seen what is so clear to him. No doubt candour is to be expected from one who has dwelt so long in the eighteenth century. But problems arise, and these may be classified under three headings.

1. Insufficiently close analysis of terms. (a) It is one thing to say that Locke and Wesley both employ the term 'assurance'; it is quite another to imply that 'assurance' *qua* 'the highest degree of probability' is synonymous with 'assurance' *qua* 'blessed.' (b) The assertion that Locke's 'primarily natural experience' coalesces with Wesley's 'primarily

spiritual experience' in Wesley's philosophical theology raises unaddressed questions concerning our ability to, and means of, making the posited distinction. (c) The reference to 'The fundamentalist absolute trust in the New Testament' of 'many evangelicals who followed [at the time, or in his wake?] Wesley' is anachronistic if the fundamentalists are his contemporaries, and is in any case question-begging. A similar question is begged when Brantley accepts Carl F. H. Henry's description of 'evangelical faith' as 'biblical essentials'.

2. Overstatement of the case. (a) The reference to Wesley's 'anti- ecclesiastical disregard of Church order' may lead some to infer that Wesley's outlook was radical. On the contrary, he was much in favour of order, and rebelled only when hidebound attitudes towards it obstructed the preaching of the Gospel. (b) When Browne's emphasis upon the continuing witness of the Spirit is said to be his 'most original contribution to Lockean thought, and to Anglican,' we may well suspect a failure to appreciate the Calvinist tradition. (c) The assertion that 'at no time before or since the eighteenth century did the interdiscipline of theology and philosophy flourish more luxuriantly than it did then' would seem to ignore patristic and medieval thought. (d) It is surprising that Brantley should declare that the OED definition of 'evangelical' (1791): 'those Protestants who hold that the essence of the Gospel consists in the doctrine of salvation by faith in the atoning death of Christ, and deny the saving efficacy of either good works or the sacraments,' fits 'pretty well' Whitefield, Evangelical Anglicans and 'rigid' Dutch Reformed, Presbyterian and Baptist Calvinists, but not Wesley. His point is that Wesley's evangelicalism included a philosophical component as well; but it is not shown that that of the other groups mentioned did not—frequently it did. (e) To 'draw a parallel between Wesley's conversion and such resurgences of empiricism as that of A. J. Ayer verges upon the fantastic. Indeed, the introduction of the inadequately-stated verification principle (not to mention the failure to note its subsequent modification) is a red herring. (f) Although Brantley's normal practice is to claim no more than that Wesley's philosophical theology was 'in the air' breathed by the poets discussed, he can also say that this philosophical theology informs a central dialectic of the poets,' and that Wesley's 'thought and expression counterpart, and largely account for, the poets' languages of philosophy and faith.' These linguistic oscillations from the generally influential to the causative throw into relief the distinction between 'harbinger' and 'generator.' In his better moments Brantley knows that he cannot opt for the latter. (g) Wesley's homiletic declaration that 'A full conviction of our ignorance may teach us ... to trust the invisible God, farther than we can see him,' is said to be 'Perhaps the most peculiarly Wesleyan statement in the sermon from which it is taken.' But Wesley has no monopoly here: the Puritans (properly agnostic where necessary) repeatedly remind us that although we may have a true apprehension of God, we may not have a full comprehension of him.

3. Selective argumentation. As he zealously forges ahead, Brantley on occasion fails to pay due heed to balancing considerations and to counter evidence. (a) The importance of the Toleration Act of 1689 should not be overlooked. On the one hand it inspired Lockeans to seek for a sweetly reasonable basis for religious harmony, enforced uniformity having failed. On the other hand it encouraged those who wished to think their own

thoughts, no matter how divisive the results. Brantley pays little heed to the rationalistic, as distinct from the evangelical, Arminians, who were a foil (and, on occasion, a thorn in the flesh) to Wesley—yet Arminians of both kinds were influenced by Locke. What are we to make of this? Was Wesley more selectively Lockean and/or was Locke more fecund than Brantley allows? In this connection more might have been made of Isaac Watts's vacillations in interpreting Locke's thought, to which Brantley adverts; and the importance of Locke in the curriculum of the more 'liberal' Dissenting academies might have been noted. (b) If Wesley had such a considerable methodological influence even upon his followers, why were so many Methodists beguiled by the deist Henry Dodwell's *Christianity not Founded on Argument*, which they (wrongly) construed as leaving the way open for faith? (c) Brantley notes Wesley's distrust of 'Behmen and a whole army of Mystic authors,' but when treating of Blake he omits to account for Blake's fondness for such writers. If important non-Wesleyan influences upon the poets are overlooked, the picture is skewed. (d) The suggestion that there is a 'frequently Lockean motivation underlying Wesley's choice of scripture texts' leaves one with the uncomfortable feeling that here the cart is put before the horse. Is post-conversion Wesley not more the biblical expositor who utilizes his intellectual heritage, than the Lockean philosopher who resorts to the Bible for bolstering texts? (e) Wesley's 'strictures against Humean attitudes towards religion' are mentioned, as is his acceptance of Hume's critique of causation; but the former might well have been explored further, especially in view of Brantley's demolition of V. H. H. Green, who argued that Wesley 'offered nothing that could satisfactorily meet the intellectual difficulties of his times.' To which Brantley retorts, 'But the reverse is true.' Whereupon this reviewer gently suggests that while Wesley met the perceived intellectual needs of some (and, humanly speaking, the religious needs of many more), he by no means satisfactorily solved the intellectual difficulties of his time: indeed, those difficulties linger still. Brantley does not show how far, if at all, Wesley met the challenge of Humean scepticism; neither does he show how, if at all, Wesley's sixth "sense" (the posited religious one) relates to Hutcheson's moral sense or Reid's common sense, both of which owed something to Locke. This is the more surprising when we are assured that 'Wesley, writing after it became smart if not fashionable to think that not even things, much less their secondary qualities, exist outside the mind, seems intent upon countering over-Berkleian subtleties.' Granted, a note introduces the matter (and, incidentally, describes Hutcheson, Hume, Ferguson and Adam Smith as English moralists), but we must ask for more: the question of the philosophical worth of Wesley's intellectual legacy may not be shirked, least of all by one who claims so much for it.

When detailed knowledge is combined with the zealous overstatement of a plausible case we have the makings of a stimulating and provocative book. Such a book has been written by Professor Brantley.

Enlightenment and Dissent 8 (1989) 140–144.

Part Two: History

49

The Oxford Movement

Peter Benedict Nockles. *The Oxford Movement in Context: Anglican High Churchmanship, 1760–1857*. Cambridge: CUP, 1994. Pp. xvi + 342.

Dr. Nockles of the John Rylands University Library of Manchester has delved deeply into a large number of neglected printed and manuscript sources, and has adjusted himself to scholarly opinion, with a view to demonstrating that the nineteenth-century Tractrian revival within the Church of England had its harbingers in those who, during the preceding seventy years, had worked for the restoration of the High Church tradition. His temporal boundaries are the High Church revival of the 1760s, which coincided with the accession of George III and the end of the 'Whig ascendency,' and the late 1850s (thereby accommodating both the Tractarians and the Gorham and Denison controversies). Within the general continuity of High Churchmanship there were differing views on many matters, and the author elucidates these with considerable skill.

We are first offered a substantial 'Historiographical introduction' to Tractarianism, which reveals that the primary focus, whether of friendly or hostile writers, has been on the leaders of the movement: Newman, Froude, Keble and Pusey. Evangelicals and Broad Churchmen have had their expositors too, but less attention has been paid to the older High Churchmen. Justification is provided for Mark Pattison's mid-nineteenth-century judgement that the Tractarians themselves conceived High Church history as jumping from Waterland and Brett to 1833. There was thus fostered nostalgia for a Caroline age deemed golden. Nockles redresses the balance by resurrecting the Hutchinsonians, named after an opponent of Newton's scientific theories, whose number included the influential George Horne (1730–92); and the 'Hackney Phalanx,' an amorphous group including John James Watson, which was active during the first three decades of the nineteenth century. These groups were linked not only by theology and churchmanship, but by friendship (Oxford University being a key factor), family ties and ecclesiastical patronage. There were in addition such custodians of the tradition as John Oxlee, who were more freelance, so to speak; while such contemporaries of the Tractarians as William Mascall manifested indebtedness to both the Tractarians and the older High Churchmen, and 'might best be described as advanced old High Churchmen' (p. 39). Relationships were further cemented by membership of such organizations as the SPG, the SPCK, the National Society and the Church Building Society.

The older High Church tradition did not flow directly into Tractarianism, but existed alongside it. Its representatives were those whom Hurrell Froude designated the 'Z's,' as distinct from the 'Y's' (the Tractarians) and the 'X's' or 'Peculiars' (the Evangelicals). The older High Churchmen held a doctrine of apostolic succession; and they maintained the supremacy of Scripture, and the value of the creeds, Prayer Book and catechism. They appreciated the writings of the early Fathers, upheld in a qualified way the primacy of dogma, and emphasized sacramental grace (normally stopping short of the Roman Catholic principle of *ex opere operato*). Their spirituality was practical, and they were suspicious of subjectivism and enthusiasm. Loyal to the establishment, they expected the state, as divinely ordained, to protect and promote the interests of the Church of England.

Dr. Nockles proceeds to disentangle the complex relationships, both ideological and personal between the Tractrians and their High Church forebears and contemporaries. He does this *via* well-documented and judicious discussions of the politics of Church and state; antiquity and the rule of faith; the apostolic paradigm; spirituality, liturgy and worship; and the sacraments and justification. A chapter summarizing the historical relations of the old High Churchmen and the Tractarians leads him to his conclusion, namely, that 'The Tractarians sharpened a sense of High Church party identity in the Church, but they did not and could not create it' (p. 307). He further observes that 'Ironically, it was the liberal Protestant comprehensiveness of the Church of England against which the Oxford Movement reacted, which ultimately ensured for Anglo-Catholics the freedom to protest and advance their views' (p. 319).

What accounts for the impact of the Tractarians? Dr. Nockles adverts to 'A unique combination of moral strength and religious dynamism, imbued with the spirit of Romanticism' (p. 325). Though initially partisan and disruptive, the Oxford Movement's spiritual influence 'overrode its increasing tendency towards a churchy sectarianism' (p. 327), with the result that the opposition of some Broad Churchmen and Evangelicals was softened.

Dr. Nockles excels in explicating the provenance and slipperiness of key terms. He reminds us, for example, that 'An Evangelical in the pre-Tractarian era was not a Low Churchman' (p. 32). He points out that since many Tractarians had been reared in Evangelicalism, they had a deeper appreciation of Evangelical spirituality than did some pre-Tractarian High Churchmen of the period 1805–30 (p. 318). He shows that whereas 'Anti-Roman Catholicism was intrinsic to traditional High Church ecclesiology' (p. 164), 'The emergence of a genuinely "Romanising" wing to the Movement in the early 1840s . . . marked an ideological watershed' (p. 143). However, the Tractarians were not directly responsible either for the interest in church architecture and furnishings, or for ritualism (pp. 213–14). The following is among many *mots*: 'The key to Newman's ultimate loss of faith in Anglicanism lay in his attempt to erect a coherent dogmatic edifice on a structure never designed to support it' (p. 129). Examiners will readily interpolate the words 'Discuss this statement.'

The bibliography is too 'select,' but the notes are full. Ecclesiastical and intellectual historians of the period will ignore Dr. Nockles' first rate study at their peril.

Enlightenment and Dissent 15 (1996) 128–30.

50

Congregationalism in Scotland

William D. McNaughton. *Early Congregational Independency in the Highlands and Islands and the North- East of Scotland*. Tiree: The Trustees of Ruaig Congregational Church; obtainable from The United Reformed Church Synod of Scotland. Pp. xxix + 659.

Having already served us well with *The Scottish Congregational Ministry 1794–1993*, W. D. McNaughton places us further in his debt with this sturdy and inexpensive volume. He has an important story to tell of a generally neglected episode in Scottish history: that concerning the Congregational pastor-and-student evangelists whose itinerant ministry did so much to propagate the Gospel in the eighty years to 1870. I said that McNaughton has an important story to tell, and certainly he interprets what is going on in a lucid and balanced way. But what especially delights is that wherever possible he allows the actors to speak in their own words. His investigation of sources, many of them scarce and all of them listed, is well nigh exhaustive, and his use of them is exemplary; the notes and indices are a boon, and the illustrations afford further illumination. But the story, told county by county, is the thing. What follows is an attempt to present something of the flavour of it.

The initial impetus towards the movement which became the Scottish Congregational Union (1812) came from the Evangelical Revival, one of the Scottish products of which was the Society for Propagating the Gospel at Home. Whereas the primary concern of the early English Congregationalists and their Separatist harbingers was ecclesiological, in post-Revival Scotland the quest was for vital religion—a quest which implied a critique of Moderatism. However, a number of awakened Scots became distressed by what they perceived as disciplinary laxity in the denominations to which they belonged, and their desire for a regenerate church membership led them towards the Congregational polity.

All was not plain sailing, however. The internal divisiveness which had characterized the earlier Berean, Old Scots, and Glasite versions of Independency was not unknown among the new breed of Congregationalists. A significant split occurred in 1808, when James Haldane, a major financial supporter of the Society for Propagating the Gospel at Home, embraced Baptist views and drew others after him. Thereafter a number of regional evangelistic agencies were established, and it became normal to release Congregational pastors, as well as students at the Glasgow Theological Academy conducted by Ralph Wardlaw, for summer itinerancy. The stated objectives of the Congregational Union were church aid and home mission.

PHILOSOPHY, THEOLOGY AND HISTORY

Following the publication of C. G. Finney's *Lectures on Revivals* (1835) some took to the 'new measures,' to the dismay of such moderate Calvinists as Wardlaw, who smelled the burning rubber of Arminianism. The associated theological issue concerned the extent of the atonement. Nine theological students were expelled from the Glasgow Academy over this and, more generally, there was a loss of members to the Evangelical Union (1843), whose principal leader was James Morison. The teaching of John McLeod Campbell was not without influence in some districts. In 1847 John Morison of Millseat used the occasion of an infant's baptism to defend the paedobaptist position, some members of his church having recently withdrawn following a visit of Alexander Campbell of America.

The Disruption of 1843 and the 'coming out' of 'the Church of Scotland, Free' resulted in the existence of a sizeable Church committed to evangelical theology—the very thing that the Congregationalists had organized to provide. Their growth was henceforth inhibited, not least because their terms of (regenerate) membership were stricter than those prevailing in some Presbyterian circles. Emigration made further inroads into their membership, and depleted the rural populations in which they had been evangelistic pioneers. It is also the case that not all of those who flocked to hear the evangelists became church members. At Thurso in 1836, for example, whereas 300 attended the morning service and 350/400 the evening, there were but sixty church members. Although Greville Ewing, the architect of Scottish Congregationalism, advocated the role of itinerant evangelist to the end, no revivals were heard of after 1874, the founding (c. 1873) of a college at Sannox for the training of Gaelic evangelists notwithstanding.

The dedication and self-sacrifice of the Congregationalists shines through. At Kintyre the landlord deprived them of their farms, and one man, 'while removing his effects in a boat, was drowned in the sea, leaving a widow and several young children.' At Knockando, the clergy influenced the 'Lords of the soil' and 'Several individuals were put out of their farms, and others have suffered a good deal from their relatives.' At Oban a large gathering, previously ignorant of the fact that such a text existed, heard the Act of Toleration read aloud. On Islay members were reluctant to provide hospitality to itinerant evangelists lest they 'incur the displeasure of some petty local authorities, lay or ecclesiastical, or both.' In some places ministers of the Church of Scotland refused to baptize the infants of, or grant burial spaces to, those who attended evangelists' meetings. At Inverness, on account of their voluntarism, the Congregationalists were represented as being in league with the Papists. By the 1870s, however, there was a degree of co-operation in some places, as at Oban, where the Congregational minister, Charles Whyte, and three Presbyterian ministers held regular united meetings in both English and Gaelic.

On the strength of a Sale of Ladies' Work in Edinburgh which raised £164, six Gaelic speaking Congregational ministers were sent as itinerants to Perthshire, Sutherland and the Western Isles. At Elgin, both the Lord's Supper and Church Meeting were held weekly, disciplinary cases being dealt with at the latter. From the account of Donald Galbraith of Campbelltown it appears that revivals could be something of a nuisance at times, and their results transitory: 'The Revival, which appeared in this district in a most exciting form, tended rather to interfere with our ordinary arrangements, especially our Sabbath evening sermons and lectures, which used to form a most interesting part of my winter work. . . . [M]atters are now getting quiet enough, and, as might be expected, a somewhat painful relapse is quite apparent.' When John Arthur had the temerity to tell the tongue-speaking Mary Campbell of the Gare Lock that she was deluded, he was met with 'much rolling of the eyes.'

A positive, response to the evangelists' efforts was not a foregone conclusion. One who heard the impressive James Kennedy preach 'thought that every person present would be converted, except a woman I noticed asleep.' On the other hand, a conscience-smitten young man who had been making malt illegally turned himself in to the authorities. A Highlander who walked nine miles to the services felt that he had a right to meetings lasting more than ninety minutes, while an old man, deprived of 'the terrors of the law,' rebuked a student who had majored on the love of God.

We need not doubt that William McGavin spoke for many when he said, 'It is a noble thing to preach the gospel in a cathedral; but I hold it more honourable to preach it in a hovel; because it indicates that humility, disinterestedness, and self- denial, which ought always to characterise the ministers of Christ.' The record of the evangelists is impressive. James and Alexander Dewar's dedication in preaching in all but three of the Gaelic parishes from Fort William to John o' Groats and round to Cape Wrath is representative of the commitment of many. Nor should we forget Tommy, James Kennedy's brown pony. He always carried his master directly to his preaching engagements, 'But on his homeward journey he knew well that there was no haste, and regardless of whip or spur he took his own wilful way, and traversed the road as best suited his own convenience.' What else should we expect of a Congregational quadruped?

Journal of the United Reformed Church VII (2005) 398–401.

William D. McNaughton. *Early Congregational Independency in Lowland Scotland, Volume I.* Glasgow: The Congregational Federation in Scotland, 2005. Pp. xvi + 681.

William D. McNaughton. *Early Congregational Independency in Shetland.* Lerwick: The Shetland Times, 2005. Pp. 151.

It is a pleasure to welcome the first part of *Early Congregational Independency in Lowland Scotland*, a companion volume to Dr. McNaughton's *Early Congregational Independency in the Highlands and the North-East of Scotland*. In all of his volumes the author is concerned with Congregationalism down to about 1867, by which time its youthful evangelistic zeal (this, rather than ecclesiology, being Scottish Congregationalism's *raison d'être*) had waned. He also takes account of early Evangelical Union causes, which were established in most of the counties here under review: Fife, Angus, Kincardineshire, Dunbartonshire, Stirlingshire, Clackmannanshire, West Lothian, Midlothian, East Lothian, Berwickshire, Wigtownshire, Kirkcudbrightshire, Dumfriesshire, Roxburghshire, Selkirkshire and Peeblesshire. He proceeds county by county and church by church.

On 20 December 1797, two years after the founding of the London Missionary Society, Scottish Christians established the Society for Propagating the Gospel at Home. This body, and Robert and James Haldane, were prominent in early evangelistic efforts in the region here under review. Among other prominent names in the story are those of Ralph Wardlaw and Greville Ewing, both of whom combined pastoral charge with theological teaching; John Aikman and John Campbell. Of the founders of the Evangelical

Union, James Morison, formerly of the Secession Church and John Kirk the erstwhile Congregationalist and former student of Wardlaw, take their rightful place in this record.

Like its predecessor, this book is the product of an immense amount of work, and there are many quotable passages, of which the following is a very small sample. When a lady complained to Matthew Wilks that the evangelist Francis Dick 'is so rough,' Wilks retorted, 'Rough! Madam, what of that? A rough diamond against polished glass any day!' At the height of the atonement controversy of the 1840s Ralph Wardlaw, determined to uphold limited atonement and to nip Arminianizing tendencies in the bud, faced his students with this question: 'Do you hold, or do you not, the necessity of a special influence of the Holy Spirit, in order to the regeneration of the sinner, or his conversion to God, distinct from the influence of the Word or of providential circumstances, but accompanying these means, and rendering them efficacious?' Nine students were expelled because of unsatisfactory answers and of these, seven who applied to the Congregational Union for preaching credentials were refused. When the Revd John Watson of Musselburgh, who was also Secretary of the Union and suffered frequent bouts of ill health, married into money, tongues wagged, and W. L. Alexander decreed in print that 'as a general rule, no man of independent income should occupy the place of pastor in a Christian church.' At Innerleithen, William Dobson's ministry was hindered in a different way: 'The Free Church minister uses his influence to prevent people attending Mr. Dobson's meetings.' Readers of this *Journal* will be interested in a quotation from W. B. Selbie's biography of A. M. Fairbairn, himself a product of the Evangelical Union. Recalling Fairbairn's Bathgate pastorate the writer, Andrew Law, reveals within a few lines something of Fairbairn's character, of the reactions to James Morison and the Evangelical Union, and of the degree of suspicion in which foreign theology was held:

> Living on the verge of the town and with easy access to the quiet hills, the Rev. A. M. Fairbairn was rarely seen in the public street. A hard student, a recluse, even then a great scholar, he naturally lived apart from the ordinary life of a country town. Sectarian lines were sharply drawn. The three Presbyterian ministers were friendly enough with each other . . . but the sect who called themselves the E.U.'s and who were called by their neighbours Morisonians, were outside the pale of brotherhood. As for their pastor, he was known to be a student of German theology, and [sic] proof in itself that he was dangerous. He was suspected of knowing something of Hindu philosophy, and it was even whispered that he had quoted in his pulpit passages from the Vedas. Plainly a man to avoid.

The attractively-printed and illustrated book, *Early Congregationalism in Shetland* is, as we might expect, smaller in scale. It is organized as a chronological narrative. Once again the Society for the Propagation of the Gospel at Home is in evidence, and in 1799 James Haldane was among the early preachers in Shetland. The population of 26,000 occupied 'thirty scattered parishes, placed under the care of twelve ministers, of whom not more than two or three preached the Gospel.' George Reid, who arrived in Shetland in 1806 and served there for thirty-three years, travelled the islands during the summer months and preached in Lerwick in the winter. In July 1808 a Congregational church was gathered in Lerwick comprising eleven men and five women. The Congregational Union of Scotland sent itinerants to Shetland, and by 1860 there were 'twelve chapels, in ten of which are churches more or less prosperous. Over these churches there are five pastors . . .' of whom three were Shetlanders. Gradually expansion ceased and decline set in. The Union was never able to supply sufficient funds or trained pastors. Whereas in 1867 there were seventeen Congregational places of worship on Shetland, today there are two, at Lerwick and Reawick.

Dr. McNaughton is to be congratulated on having produced these carefully referenced works. He is on a very worthwhile rescue mission. I very much look forward to volume two of Lowlands, and I hope that his work on *Early Independency in Orkney* will soon see the light of published day.[4]

Journal of the United Reformed Church History Society 7 (2006) 512–13.

William D. McNaughton. *Early Congregational Independency in Lowland Scotland, Volume II*. Glasgow: United Reformed Church Synod of Scotland and The Trustees of Ruaig Congregational Church, Tiree, 2007. Pp. xvi + 505.

This sturdy hardback, a veritable bran tub of information concerning Glasgow and the western Lowlands, has been produced at a remarkably favourable price. We are already indebted to Dr. McNaughton for biographical notes on Congregational ministers who served in Scotland from 1794 to 1993. With this volume he completes his Congregational and Evangelical Union trawl of church records covering the entire land, for good measure noting forays into northern England and Evangelical Union activities in Ireland and Canada.

In the two introductory chapters some important points are made: the *raison d'être* of Scottish Congregationalism was evangelistic, not sectarian or ecclesiological. Positively, the stimulus was provided by the labours of Whitefield, Bogue, Fuller and others; negatively, by the desire to counter Moderatism. Evangelists were sent to many parts by The Society for the Propagation of the Gospel at Home, which was constituted in 1798. Prominent leaders included James and Robert Haldane who, on embracing Baptist views departed, taking their funds with them, thereby leaving some of the Congregational causes in a financial plight. Long-term distinguished leadership was provided by Greville Ewing, and Ralph Wardlaw.

Some suffered for their convictions, as when farmers were turned from their land by landowners supposedly influenced by parochial clergy; or when quarrymen and servants were sacked on leaving their employers' churches. The importance of the Glasgow Theological Academy (1811) cannot be overstated. Although their motives were not sectarian, the Congregationalists did expect that their churches would comprise the regenerate, and be constituted in accordance with biblical principles, though they did not carry

---

4. See now, W. D. McNaughton, *Early Congregational Independency in Orkney*. Published as Supplement 1 to *The Journal of the United Reformed Church History Society* 7, 2006, and Supplement 1 to *The Congregational History Society Magazine* 5, 2006.

restorationism as far as the Bereans, the Old Scots Independents, and the Glasites. Charles Grandison Finney's *Lectures on Revivals of Religion* (1835) was influential in some quarters, but the idea of protracted revival meetings and the adoption of the 'new measures' were elsewhere regarded with suspicion. Whereas many Congregationalists upheld God's sovereignty in the matter of the salvation of the elect, others, tending in an evangelical Arminian direction, held that Christ's saving work had been accomplished for all, that all obstacles to salvation had been removed except the individual sinner's unbelief, and that whether individuals were saved or not turned upon their own free response to the Spirit's striving within. James Morison was in the latter camp, and on expulsion from the United Secession Church he and others formed the Evangelical Union in 1843. By 1867 (Dr. McNaughton's terminal date) the flames of evangelical zeal had largely been extinguished by conventional religiosity, and in 1897 the general coalescence of soteriologies permitted the union of the Congregational and Evangelical Unions.

There follow chapters on the churches in the area under review. Those interested in doctrine and church order will find much to interest them. I have already mentioned Calvinism *versus* 'Arminianizing' tensions. In addition there was a tussle at Wishaw EU church when some sixteen people who had become convinced that having a plurality of elders was the biblical way left to form a Brethren meeting. Greville Ewing found himself in a pamphlet war with John Robertson, the assistant minister at Cambuslang Parish Church, over the propriety of itinerant preaching—something which Ewing defended to the end.

Those who lament the all but lost art of godly discipline will enjoy reading the responses to the 1845 questionnaire distributed by the Congregational Union. From the answers it appears that ministers would baptize only the children of members of the church though George Simpson Ingram of Albion Street/North Hanover church, Glasgow, 'would not object to baptize the children of presbyterians or episcopalians provided he were satisfied that such were Christians.' The Lord's Supper was held weekly, except when the minister was away and a substitute minister could not be engaged; though Thomas Low of Inverkip said that he would not object to the Supper's being held in his absence. Unusually, the church at Stewarton was constituted when, on confessional grounds, two Wesleyans were refused communion at the Parish Church. It would seem that weekly church meeting was the norm.

Readers concerned with socio-ethical issues will find something to their liking here: Ralph Wardlaw's work for the abolition of slavery and the slave trade, for example; or the work of the Glasgow City Mission and the role of David Nasmith; or the temperance question, which reared its head in a number of churches. Strife over temperance prompted the resignation of the Evangelical Union co-founder and professor, John Guthrie, from the Greenock church, and explains the refusal of both Alexander Davidson and A. M. Fairbairn to succeed him there. Guthrie sympathized with the position of the Scottish Temperance League, namely, that moral persuasion should be the policy, whereas others supported the United Kingdom Alliance which advocated legal prohibition.

Ministers in pastoral charge will find a word of consolation that they may recall if ever they are told, half-accusingly, that 'the chapel used to be full.' For at Albion Street the attendance at services exceeded 700, but there were just ninety communicants. In other words, the chapels were seldom filled by the church; and nowadays the 610 would be in the shops, off to the football, caravanning in the summer or wintering in Malaga (a prospect which makes the most boring sermon seem strangely inviting). Again, ministers who feel oppressed by heavy duties may reflect upon the work-load of John Ward of Kilmarnock. He conducted public worship three times every Sunday, gave a lecture every Thursday, and conducted other occasional meetings. In addition,

> The minister seldom fails in seeing all the congregation at their own houses at least once or twice a-year. Some of them at a considerable distance he sees much oftener, and he always preaches in places where he can find accommodation. Since his induction, he has been in the habit of preaching in the towns and villages in Kilmarnock and surrounding parishes, especially where members of the congregation reside—often in the summer in the open air.'

There is a great deal of miscellaneous information along the way. During the opening service of the Glasgow Tabernacle 'The rails of the staircase giving way, some limbs were broken; but . . . no lives were lost.' Although Ewing could have been addressed as Dr. or The Reverend, 'His disapprobation of "religious titles" . . . was sacredly regarded by his family and friends. The only distinctive title which he liked, was "minister of the Gospel"' (What a fine man he was). At Bridgeton church thirty-five members including the precentor resigned when, on 9 February 1858, Nisbet Galloway appeared in the pulpit wearing a gown. Notwithstanding that the Trinity Congregational church stone-laying ceremony was 'gone through in due Masonic form,' the church ran into financial difficulties. David Livingstone 'gave himself to the Lord' at the Sunday Bible Class at Hamilton. When Mr. Wilson, a Secession minister, attended the Inverkip church and heard Thomas Low preach 'He was so pleased with the matter of the Discourse that he made me repeat to him the heads of it while he wrote them down, but he said it was very ill delivered, and strongly advised me to go and study elocution.' It would seem that the first organ to be used in worship was installed in North Dundas Street EU church, Glasgow, in 1853. When preparing the ground for Neilston/Barrhead EU church, John Kirk sadly recorded that at Neilston 'We have only conversed with four. One or two seem to have received the truth, but the general ear is shut . . . Perfect contempt appears in many of the faces.' The folk of Huddersfield gave Kirk a more enthusiastic welcome: 'Both men and women kept crying out at intervals—"Ay"'—"Yes"—"Bless the Lord"— "That's it!"' Finally, it was a pleasure to meet William Cunningham of Stewarton: 'Every night he dressed himself in a newly laundered white nightgown and night cap in preparation for the Advent, but as he expected it to be somewhat cold flying through the clouds he always put on plenty of woolens [sic] underneath.'

There are nearly a hundred pages of notes, tables supplying information on CUS and EU churches, and indices of persons, and of subjects and places.

Scholars will benefit greatly from Dr. McNaughton's works, while others will find much to interest and entertain them. With this volume a major project has reached a triumphant finale. What will Dr. McNaughton do for an encore?

Journal of the United Reformed Church History Society 8 (2008) 121–23.

51

English Dissent: Dissoluble or Dissolute?

Mark D. Johnson. *The Dissolution of Dissent, 1850–1918*,
New York & London: Garland Publishing, 1987. Pp. xxiii + 345.

In this welcome and provocative book Dr, Johnson seeks to show how English Dissent, as represented by Congregationalism, dissolved into a bland ecumenism as social impediments were removed, and as the desire to take their due place in society (exemplified by the story of Mansfield College, Oxford) undermined traditional dissidence. He anchors the intellectual history in the socio-political context of the times, thereby drawing our attention to important sources which those concerned only with the period's significant thinkers may leave uninvestigated.

There are five substantial chapters. The first, entitled 'From the Old Evangelicalism to the New: The Theological Education of Robert William Dale,' sets out from R. W. Dale's view that Evangelical individualism contributed to the slackening of the Dissenters' grip upon ecclesiology. Not least by subtly re-writing Dissenting history at crucial points, Dale managed to articulate a new Evangelicalism, attuned to the aspirations of the growing Nonconformist middle class, accommodating those modifications of scholastic Calvinism which recent evangelistic practice seemed to require. The theological transformation is illustrated by reference to the Carrs Lane succession of John Angell James and Dale. The influence of F. D. Maurice upon Dale is shown to have been formative; John Campbell's doomed rearguard action against the 'increase of German error' is noted, as is Dale's 'hearty admiration' of the socio-politically prophetic Edward Miall. The mood captured by Binney's declaration that 'It is not wrong to be rich,' and that Congregationalism's special mission was to the middle classes; and the Unitarian George Dawson's (undiscriminating) allegation that the ethical stance of the early Evangelicals was largely other-worldly, are revealed as further factors in Dale's formation. As Dale's theological position matured, he set the older Evangelical emphasis upon the Cross within the broader framework of the Incarnation; though with the passage of time he came to regret the loss of the sense that 'sin is an awful offence,' and that Christ is Lord and not only Brother.

In Chapter II 'The Leicester Conference' of 1877 (which A. J. Grieve later described as 'a small theological breeze') is described and analyzed. Johnson rightly views the episode as indicative of Congregational anxiety at the erosion of communal life in face of 'spiritual'-liberal (albeit internally discordant) emphases. The theological role of James Baldwin Brown, who mediated the thought of McLeod Campbell, Erskine of Linlathen (whose final 'e' and necessary qualifying phrase are omitted in both text and index) and, supremely, of Maurice, is carefully delineated. The pantheism of James Allanson Picton, and the tendencies towards, and the reactions against, Unitarianism are recorded, as is the impact of Edward White's preference for the annihilation, rather than the eternal punishment, of unbelievers. The crusade for disestablishment and the Bulgarian atrocities are likewise part of the picture.

'The Crisis in the Colleges' is the subject of Chapter III. The Congregationalists became increasingly concerned that their colleges, whose tutors were required by financial stringency to be polymaths even if they were not, were failing to produce doctrinally sound and culturally acceptable ministers. Hence the removal in 1886 of Spring Hill College from Birmingham to Oxford, where it became Mansfield College. In the establishment of Mansfield (Chapter IV), the part played by Dale, a belated convert to the idea, was crucial; as was the self-sacrificial resignation of Spring Hill's Principal, D. W. Simon—the originator of the Oxford idea. Simon became Principal of the Scottish Congregational Theological Hall, thereby easing Fairbairn's path from Airedale College to Mansfield. The activities of R. F. Horton within the University of Oxford are rightly given prominence (though his book, *The Dissolution of Dissent*—an outcome for which he saw no necessity—is not here discussed). Horton attempted, *via* the Oxford University Nonconformists Union, to promote the positive values of Free Churchmanship. The contribution of Mansfield's first Principal is accurately assessed; and the rueful conclusion is that, despite all the hopes surrounding Mansfield, its New Puritanism was in reality a further sign of the bankruptcy of Nonconformity: Nonconformists have 'no other well-defined purpose than to find an acceptable place for themselves in the mainstream' (p. 224).

So to a chapter entitled 'From the New Puritanism to Ecumenism: Mansfield College, 1886–1918.' Ritschlianism is shown to have been the theology which led towards ecumenism, for Ritschl attempted to divorce religion from theoretical knowledge, and this facilitated churchly co-operation. Mansfield's early days, its teachers, its financial difficulties, its failure to galvanize the University's growing number of Nonconformist students, the impact upon the College of the 'higher criticism,' the plea for social relevance, the implications of Hegelianism, Frank Lenwood and the Student Christian Movement—all of these and more are discussed.

Johnson concludes: 'As Congregationalists lost confidence in the validity of their polity and their political character by the end of the century, Mansfield sought legitimacy through the ecumenical movement, for ecumenism offered Nonconformity a form of official recognition and acceptance within a catholic federation of the Churches . . . Ecumenism was the final phase in the dissolution of Dissent' (pp. 299–300).

Dr. Johnson's work is based upon wide, if not exhaustive, reading, and we are greatly in his debt for his accounts of Dale, Horton and others; for his discriminating study of Mansfield's formative years; and especially for his perceptive treatment of the Leicester Conference. A handful of typographical slips does not unduly disturb; neither does the question of definition in the statement that the 1747 secession from the Old Meeting, Birmingham, was prompted by *Unitarian* influence (p. 12). More serious is the anachronistic assertion that 'Congregationalism represented the attempt to return to what Congregationalists believed to be the *democratic* polity of the first- century Church' (9; my italics). This is corrected overleaf by Dale: 'Each Christian assembly stood in the immediate presence of Christ, and was directly responsible to Him.' That is, Congregationalists sought to be Christocentric. We have here an example of a running weakness in this book: the lack of careful definition of terms, which leads to some one-sided judgements.

Consider the judgement: 'during the nineteenth century the largest English Nonconformist bodies possessed no outstanding theologians. There was no Coleridge or Maurice among them, nor even a Benjamin Jowett' (p. xvi). But how is 'outstanding' to be defined? There are occasions in Christian theology when new departures are made and, undeniably, Coleridge, Maurice and 'even' Jowett were catalysts in this respect. There are also times when what is required are highly-skilled theological 'middlemen,' who can assimilate, process and hand on a welter of new ideas in such a way that the Church is edified and not rent asunder. This was the work that was preeminently required in the second half of the nineteenth century. That during such a period the Nonconformists should have produced such thinkers as Dale, Fairbairn, Pope and Martineau is—especially give the inadequacies of their theological colleges, of which Dr. Johnson more than once reminds us—at least moderately remarkable. Moreover, after 1860 the Church of England did not produce another Coleridge, Maurice or 'even' Jowett, Oxford and Cambridge notwithstanding.

Again, Johnson advises that P. T. Forsyth was 'perhaps the last important theologian English Nonconformity produced' (p. xvi). It has seriously been suggested (by Emil Brunner, for example) that Forsyth was the greatest theologian to emerge from any English denomination this century. But what is the analysis of 'important'? It does appear that Nonconformists have, during the twentieth century, excelled in Biblical studies: (C. H. Dodd, T. W. Manson, V. Taylor, G. Caird, with the Baptists, H. W. Robinson, T. H. Robinson, H. H. Rowley and A. R. Johnson cornering the Old Testament market, along with the Methodist N. H. Snaith). There have been notable Nonconformist church historians: W. T. Whitley, E. A. Payne, A. G. Matthews, A. Peel, J. Wilkinson, and E. G. Rupp. Nevertheless, the varied contributions of such theologians as A. E. Garvie, C. J. Cadoux, R. S. Franks, John Oman, H. H. Farmer and others should not be underestimated.

Next, there is the question of method and perspective. Johnson fastens upon Congregationalism as being the most politically prominent Nonconformist denomination at the beginning of his period; and upon Mansfield College, 'the institution through which the best of the Congregational ministry was absorbed into the "mainstream" of national life' (p. 163). This poses unanswered questions. Were the more traditional Dissenting attitudes more faithfully preserved by other denominations and/or by other Nonconformist (including Congregational) colleges? Whether justifiably or not, Mansfield has been accused from time to time—even by a few of its alumni—of 'apeing the Anglicans,' of succumbing to 'liturgical fusspottery' and the like. How does the drop-out rate of Congregationalism's 'best' ministers compare with that of those from other colleges? By the outbreak of World War I, only 50 percent of the total of Mansfield's graduates remained in the ministry. (c) Without some reference to colleges contemporary with Mansfield, may not readers be left with the impression that Mansfield, which was raised upon the ruins of less adequate nineteenth-century colleges, failed to a large extent and all was lost? This would be to overlook positive developments elsewhere. At one period the General Secretary of the Congregational Union and four of the nine Moderators (none from Mansfield) were trained at Yorkshire United Independent College. At another period Lancashire Independent College, *via* its association with the University of Manchester, offered theological courses second to none in comprehensiveness and rigour. Nevertheless, Mansfield produced almost twice as many (14) English Congregational theological college Principals during the period from 1920 to the present as all the other colleges together. Of these, half were decently knowledgeable concerning Dissent, and two or three notorious for it! The list of Mansfield-trained scholars, principled ecumenists, missionaries and 'working ministers' is likewise not unimpressive.

The most serious difficulty comes when Johnson nominates ecumenism as an important culprit in the dissolution of (Congregational) Dissent. There are two main aspects of the problem, both questions of definition. 'Ecumenism' is not subjected to detailed analysis. He seems to encompass the unprincipled 'if you can't beat 'em join 'em' attitude, and the 'co-operation in good works' and 'huddling together for warmth motives (pp. 299, 290, 21, 253, 277). That these prevailed in some quarters cannot be denied, but there was something more. Johnson quotes Fairbairn accurately: 'It is perhaps harder to be a Nonconformist today than it has ever been in the history of England. The very decay of the disabilities from which our fathers suffered has made it harder for us than it was to them to dissent' (p. 169). However, he omits Fairbairn's next sentence: 'But while it has become harder it has also become more necessary: for the need of the testimony to a Church in which Christ is supreme was never so great as now.' No doubt the testimony was inadequately made; but Johnson's failure to give due weight to a more positive understanding prevents him from considering the possibility that Dissenters were right to seek the fulfilment of their Dissenting catholicity in an ecumenism in which the gospel of God's grace took precedence.

'Congregationalism' is defined in this book too much in terms of the autonomy of the local church. No doubt this is a slippery subject, and the oscillation between independence, interdependence, autonomy and catholicity has characterized Congregationalism through the centuries. Nevertheless the assertion that 'The independence of each individual church was the cardinal principle of Congregationalism' (p. 91) would have had a different ring in the seventeenth century from what it came to have in the nineteenth when the decibels of individualism were increased in the wake of the Enlightenment. If these subtleties are not teased out, it is impossible to understand why many Congregationalists have regarded the attempts of genuine ecumenism to manifest God's given unity in Christ as worthy of their support, and as consistent with their testimony that the one Lord of the Church gathers his saints into a catholic fellowship manifested locally.

Had there been no socio-political disabilities, the questions 'Who is a Christian?,' 'Who are the Church?,' 'How are the crown rights of the Redeemer to be honoured in his Church? and 'What are the proper relations between Church and State'—the questions of Dissent—would still have required attention, and they still do. Precisely because of the removal of most of the socio-political impediments, deep theological discussion of these questions is, in principle, possible. Over and above the abiding importance of the questions, such discussion is necessary now when societal marginalization afflicts all the English denominations, and the confessionally-varied established churches are in international dialogue with those of the Dissenting traditions. Will the questions be raised? This is to ask whether Dissent really has been dissolved, or whether it is simply, and perhaps temporarily, dissolute.

The Baptist Quarterly 33 (1990) 243–46.

52

Conflict and Reconciliation

John Munsey Turner. *Conflict and Reconciliation. Studies in Methodism and Ecumenism in England, 1740–1982*. London: Epworth Press, 1985. Pp. xiv + 306.

In a letter of 10 December 1777 John Wesley wrote, 'Though I am always in haste, I am never in a hurry.' That is precisely the attitude in which to approach this thought-provoking book. John Munsey Turner offers us the fruit of many years of careful reflection upon his theme, managing with apparent ease to be both learned and (which is by no means the same thing) wise.

We set out from the 'Eighteenth-century background,' and are reminded of the way in which Methodism so often filled gaps left by the parochial system of the Church of England. There is no hiding of the fact (full marks to a Methodist) that the renewal of English and Welsh religion was 'well under way' before Wesley's 'heartwarming' of May 1738 (pp. 7, 90). 'The separation of Methodism from the Church of England' is deftly handled, and something of the trauma of it is encapsulated in Charles Wesley's letter to John Nelson on the subject of the licensing of Wesleyan preachers: 'John, I love thee from my heart; yet rather than see thee a Dissenting minister, I wish to see thee smiling in thy coffin' (p. 15). Here too is the important reminder that in the matter of ministerial orders Wesley was in a liberal Anglican tradition deriving from Richard Hooker, which is no less Anglican because it is not 'Catholic.' The third chapter, on 'Methodism, Catholicism and patterns of Dissent,' is a brilliant socio-theological exposition of Newman's remark that 'Methodism and Popery are in different ways . . . the foster-mothers of abandoned children (p. 36). Not indeed that the two foster-mothers had much happy contact until recent years. On the contrary, Wesley's anti-Catholicism was a significant part of his legacy. Even so, 'it is sheer Anglican pretentiousness to suggest that the Church of England is in some way a bridge between Catholicism and Methodism' (p. 43).

In 'The theological legacy of John Wesley' the author claims enough, but not too much. Wesley was a people's theologian, not a professional systematician. Firm on the priority of God's universal love, and eager in the quest of holiness, he could also 'hedge his bets' at ticklish points in the doctrine of perfection; and his doctrine of sin was confused. When Turner refers to the Calvinist Toplady, 'who could with one hand write "Rock of Ages" and with the other call John Wesley "a low and puny tadpole in divinity"' (p. 47), one is almost tempted to mention Wesley's letter of 24 June 1770 to Mr. Merryweather of Yarn: 'Mr. Augustus Toplady I know well; but I do not fight with chimney-sweepers. He is too dirty a writer for me to meddle with; I should only dirty my fingers.' Matters are redeemed on the same page with one of the most urgent questions in the book: 'can [Wesley's] "Arminianism of the heart" [which Geoffrey Nuttall distinguished from the more rationalistic "Arminianism of the head"] withstand the impact of the reality of God in other religions or the almost total eclipse of hell in the mainstream Christian tradition? ... Perhaps at its lowest we can say that Wesley's point has been taken only too well and that the danger now is of an uncritical universalism with judgement drained away.'

There follow chapters on 'From connexion to denomination,' in which the interestingly different stories of Wesleyan and Primitive Methodism are told; and 'Methodists, Evangelicals and High Churchmen,' in which the notion that Methodists inevitably relate more closely to Anglican Evangelicals than to Anglican High Churchmen is shown to be false. There might be cooperation in the British and Foreign Bible Society but, for example, Charles Simeon could brook no interdenominationalism on the mission field. Among many sometimes overlooked points in 'The rise of the Nonconformist platform: Dissent, Methodism, the state and politics 1791–1852' is the distinction which needs to be drawn within Dissent between such cultured radicals as Price and Priestley, and the mass of Baptists and Independents. Again, Wesley's socio-political stance was much more that of Burke than of Locke. The differing political emphases within Methodism are well described, and the tale of increasing rights under the law for Nonconformists is informatively told.

In the chapter on 'Methodism and the Oxford Movement—Aggressive Anglicanism and militant Dissent' we learn how two parties with so much in common—Oxford, the quest of holiness, Arminianism—pulled ever further apart. Despite the efforts of a few, notably the theologian W. B. Pope, 'The sacramental inheritance of the Wesleys both in theology and practice was largely lost' under 'Fear of and attacks by the Tractarians' (p. 164).

The concluding chapters, 'From Lunn to Flew—Methodism and the wider ecumenism 1890–1955,' and 'The walk to Paradise Garden,' bring the story up to date. Methodism's modern ecumenical pioneers—John Scott Lidgett and A. S. Peake among them—are recalled, as are the failed Anglican-Methodist union schemes and the failed English Covenant proposals. The rueful implication is that far from being inadequate as constituting 'reunion without repentance' (L. Newbigin), some form of federal relationship between the English denominations may be the only viable option in the foreseeable future. The author concludes that 'For England it is the end of the Lambeth Quadrilateral as a negotiating base over the ordained ministry' (p. 225). But The (ecumenical) Queen's College, Birmingham, on whose staff John Turner served from its inception in 1970 to 1981, and of which a sketch is provided, serves as a ray of hope—not least because Turner, having emerged from the experience, can still say, 'I . . . cannot and will not do what I cannot believe in' (p. 230).

The book is amply referenced, helpfully indexed and, a few typographical and other slips apart, well produced. Above all, it is provocative of thought. Among our own reflections are the following.

'In the eighteenth century reason and enthusiasm, Butler and Wesley lived in uneasy tension' (p. 2). This polarization requires qualification (a) lest the impression be left that Wesley was something of an irrationalist—that he was not is declared, but not demonstrated, later (p. 57); and (b) because over against certain types of Calvinists, for example, Butler and Wesley shared a certain optimism concerning human ability.

To Turner's well-taken point that 'justification by faith might save us from the awful guilt-ridden "frantic philanthropy" which seems to be a substitute for the gospel these days' (p. 48) we should wish to add that the recovery of the idea of the divine sovereignty might help to overcome ministerial 'burnout,' which is at least in part occasioned by that "frantic activity" (assumed to be necessary by pastors, and sometimes cruelly demanded by congregations) which looks for 'success' and denies God the privilege of being Lord of the harvest.

On page 52 we are informed that 'Wesley, . . . in implying that holiness on earth is necessary to reach heaven not only rules out further progress beyond death, but drives a dangerous wedge between the sacred and the secular if the idea is to be pursued that the world is only to be used, while God is to be enjoyed.' But (a) Wesley did contemplate post mortem spiritual growth—do Methodists still do so in great numbers? (b) Is it not a further problem that with the implication here described Wesley seems to play into the hands of those who misguidedly branded him 'Pelagian'?

Turner notes that Sunday Schools and class meetings turned their attention, respectively, from social control and evangelism to nurture and fellowship. This, he says, is a 'sign of lack of expansion' (p. 61). Can such ecclesiological considerations as nurture and fellowship only come into view when growth is arrested, or when decline has set in? The question has a more than antiquarian interest, for what English churches experienced in the nineteenth century is still being experienced in many parts of the world today. How are we to ensure that we have both church *growth* and *church* growth?

A parallel question is, 'How are we to have both churchly *witness* and *churchly* witness? The 'Nonconformist conscience' exemplifies the problem. John Turner rightly notes its pitfalls of pietism, moralism and self-righteousness (p. 144), but the underlying ecclesiological weakness, so well brought out by H. F. Lovell Cocks in *The Nonconformist Conscience* (1943), requires careful examination. Thus, for example, in nineteenth-century Congregationalism, the church conceived as a covenanted community of saints lost ground before the idea that it is an aggregate of saved individuals; and the notion of the saints' seeking unanimity in Christ at Church Meeting fell before the heresy that the church is a democracy. The difficulty of keeping the prophets accountable to the church remains with us—as any familiar with para-church organizations will testify.

This book is pervaded by a suitably broad view of ecumenism. John Turner would no doubt share the reviewer's opinion that any ecumenists who think in terms of 'recalcitrant fundies' on the one side, 'woolly-minded liberals' on the other, and all the 'ecumaniacs' in the middle, knowing whom they like and not relating to the others, have yet to learn the first lesson in ecumenism. But there are divides; what is to be done? One small step would be taken if we recalled our history. Turner reminds us of the profound impact of the revivalist D. L. Moody on the first generation of modern ecumenical leaders (p. 180). A still bigger step would be a fresh grasp of that gospel of atoning grace which is the bedrock of God's ecumenism, and which puts all our parties, platforms and projects in perspective.

One of Wesley's preachers, John Pawson, burnt Wesley's annotated Shakespeare because he deemed it 'worthless lumber not tending to edification' (p. 52). Many forests-worth of ecumenical literature might cheerfully be consigned to the flames if that were necessary in order to preserve a few books of this calibre.

Mid-Stream 27 (1988) 82–85.

53

English Baptists in the Nineteenth Century

J. H. Y. Briggs. *The English Baptists of the Nineteenth Century*. Didcot, Oxfordshire: The Baptist Historical Society, 1994. Pp. 432.

The Baptists are well served by an historical society which is unusually active in publishing records, monographs and *The Baptist Quarterly*. The editor of the *Quarterly* here contributes the third volume to the series, 'A History of the English Baptists,' and a substantial piece of work it is—and had to be. For the personalities, events and activities of the nineteenth century are many, and the extant sources—printed books, newspapers and periodicals, minute books, manuscripts—are vast. As his ample notes bear witness, Mr. Briggs, Head of History at the University of Keele, has thoroughly immersed himself in the relevant materials.

The author wisely eschews the 'chronological romp' in favour of the patient elucidation of ten themes: Congregational life and worship; Baptism and communion; Ministry and ministerial training; General and Particular [Baptists]; Faith and thought;

Associations, Alliances and the wider Church; Number, class and gender; Mission and evangelism; Baptists and education; Society and politics. We have here a work which is comprehensive in scope and rounded in treatment, and this is all to the good. John Briggs knows the importance of both theological ideas and historical and sociological method—whereas a mere 'number cruncher' might well have missed the sometimes subtle doctrinal nuances by which Baptists lived, and which were the ground of their separation from the world and, on occasion, from one another.

Among many highlights is the thought-provoking comparison of Spurgeon with John Clifford. The former eventually became estranged from the Baptist Union, the latter its most ardent servant; yet Spurgeon retained a high view of the church and of the real presence of Christ at the Lord's Supper, whereas Clifford's ecclesiology was emasculated, and his view of the sacraments was that they were symbols. The increasing importance of an educated ministry is epitomized by the contemporary remark that Regent's Park College, London, set out to show 'that between nonconformity and mental incapacity there is no inseparable relation as is sometimes taken for granted.' The steps towards the union of the New Connexion with the Particular Baptists are clearly traced. I especially liked J. C. Pike's remark concerning his (Arminian) New Connexion: 'We believe that it was ordered by Divine Providence that we should be General Baptists. We are predestinated to be such.' It goes without saying that the issues of open communion, open membership, and the Downgrade Controversy could not be avoided.

The complaint of 1866 that a chapel with over a thousand seats was a denial of basic nonconformist principles (interesting in view of what is said to be a Baptist church of 20,000 members in Dallas—that would be some church meeting!); the way in which Trust Deeds could act as 'a significant alternative authority to that of the church meeting'; Baptist reluctance to assign mission to specialized agencies on the ground that evangelism was the *raison d'être* of the local church; the outlay of five shillings at Haslingden for the purchase of straps with which to discipline erring children; the importance attached by some to both individual philanthropy and social reform; the recognition of the 'Pelagianism' to which teetotalism could lead; F. A. Cox's involvement in the founding of London University; the campaign against the disabilities under which Dissenters suffered—these are among many matters which caught the eye.

In 1892 the *Baptist Magazine* declared that the union of Baptists with Congregationalists was one of the pressing questions upon which the Baptist denomination should make up its mind without delay. Apart from local unions in some ecumenical pastorates, the traditions remain apart to this day. Nevertheless there is much in this book which could fuel faith and order discussions of the widest kind (not surprisingly, since the author is among those who represent Baptists at the World Council of Churches). Certainly it would be a great pity if Baptists alone read it. John Clifford, in the wake of Isaiah Birt, wrote of church Baptism, 'No church is asked to approve a person as fit; the church is not taken into question at all'—and this was not a lament. It was, however, a significant departure from classical Baptist practice. It betokens that blending of post-Evangelical Revival individualism concerning personal experience with the post-Lockean insistence that the church is a 'voluntary society' of those who freely associate together (rather than a covenant people called out by grace). This has devastated more ecclesiologies than the Baptist. Andrew Fuller's caution against restorationism where church polity was concerned is not yet redundant; and Robert Hall's (sadly false) complaint that strict communion Baptists *only* reject at the Lord's Table those whom Christ has received poses a continuing challenge to the Church at large.

The Evangelical Quarterly 68 (1994) 180–182.

54

Strict Communion Baptists in Victorian England

Geoffrey R. Breed. *Calvinism and Communion in Victorian England Studies in Nineteenth- Century Strict-Communion Baptist Ecclesiology*. Springfield, MO: Particular Baptist Press, 2008. Pp. xli + 646.

Over the years Geoffrey Breed has served scholars and others well by the research materials he has brought to light. Many who have no Baptist ancestors, and perhaps a few who keep quiet about them, have been helped by his booklet, *My Ancestors were Baptists* (4th edn., 2002). Then there is *Particular Baptists in Victorian England* (2003), which tells the story of those strict communion Baptists who united with Arminians in the Baptist Union and supported the Baptist Missionary Society.

In the present substantial volume, beautifully produced and offered by the author at half price, Mr. Breed presents documents illustrative of the tensions over communion which flared up between Particular and Strict Baptists in the first quarter of Victoria's reign. The backbone of the volume comprises the Minutes of the London Association of Strict Baptist Ministers and Churches, of which Mr. Breed has the only legible copy, and the Minutes of the Ramsgate Chapel Case of 1862. In addition there are Circular Letters of the London Strict Baptist Associations on 'The scriptural constitution of the churches of Jesus Christ' (1846), 'The privileges and obligations of church membership' (1852), and 'Christian experience' (1853); and seven ecclesiological pamphlets on such matters as strict communion, articles of belief and Baptist Associations. To the Ramsgate Minutes are added articles on the case drawn from *The Times*, *The Primitive Church Magazine*, and *The Gospel Herald*. The third of three appendices is entitled, 'William Hatcher's conversations with C. H. Spurgeon on the subject of church communion and the Strict Baptists of

London.' The author is Terry Wolever, who also transcribed the LASBMC Minutes and, with Gary Long, is co-publisher of this collection.

In a nutshell (and some of these saints were hard nuts), supporters of open communion endorsed the argument of Robert Hall (1764–1831), while the strict communionists followed Joseph Kinghorn (1766–1832) and William Norton (1812–90). The latter urged that to forfeit the belief that the Lord's table was open to baptized believers only was to forfeit the major Baptist distinctive. The case concerning Cavendish Chapel, Ramsgate, was brought by one of its generous benefactors, Mary Spencer. She took the Revd B. C. Etheridge to court, contending that the Trust Deed of 1841 was to be construed as requiring closed communion. The judgement was that the Deed was a Particular Baptist one, and that therefore the church meeting had the right to determine communion practice.

The book opens with Mr. Breed's lucid account of the LASBMC's ten-year history (1846–55). It is a tale of frequently clear convictions and sometimes prickly persons. Not all who wished to join the Association were admitted, and some were expelled. Among the latter was Br. Rothery. He had dared to administer communion in the open communion church at Islington. As if this were not enough, he had withheld £3/0/0 from the Association for an extended period. Mr. Breed remarks, 'A cynic may be tempted to think that the loss of £3 weighed more heavily with the committee than did the communion question.' The problem of duty faith reared its head, and this was a factor in the formation of the London New Association of strict communionists in 1848. None of the internal tensions suffices to explain the demise of the London associations in Breed's view. On the contrary, 'The failure of these associations was caused by their limited vision . . . hardly any concern or responsibility for the struggling masses of London was ever shown.'

The carefully transcribed Minutes of the LASBMC are a mine of information concerning bye-laws, membership, finances, ministers and activities. The addresses given under the Association's auspices largely concern Calvinistic doctrinal points, though Br. Pepper gave a no doubt spicy lecture on 'Priestly assumptions—contrary to the Christian system.' It is not recorded how many in the land trembled when the Circular Letter of 20 October 1846 declared that 'Ecclesiastical establishments, founded in human policy, sustained by human authority, acknowledging another headship than that of the Lord Jesus Christ, by whatever name distinguished, must eventually be overthrown.' And which local church today would not be gingered up if it heeded the injunction in the Third Circular Letter:

> A little more contrivance in the head,
> A little less indulgence in the bed,
> A little more devotion in the mind,
> Would quite prevent you being so behind?

D. Griffiths, writing on articles of belief, was eager to observe that those who endorse Chillingworth's slogan, 'The Bible, the Bible only, is the religion of Protestants,' while they thereby renounce the authority of tradition and abjure the 'dogmas of popery,' do not establish their own orthodoxy.

Enough has been said to whet the appetite for this book which, as well as being a valuable research resource, is more than a little entertaining. Its ease of use is greatly facilitated by the provision of indices of persons, biblical persons, subjects, churches (geographically arranged), and biblical churches; and a number of illustrations and reproductions of some very neat handwriting further enhance the attractiveness of the volume.

It would be an overstatement to say that these Strict Baptists invariably thought theologically; but a number of them thought more theologically about the Lord's Supper in relation to baptism and church membership than some in other traditions, either then or now, and we should be grateful to Geoffrey Breed for bringing them to our attention.

Journal of the United Reformed Church History Society 8 (1009) 306–7.

55

Cambridge Theology in the Nineteenth Century

David M. Thompson. *Cambridge Theology in the Nineteenth Century: Enquiry, Controversy and Truth*. Aldershot: Ashgate, 2008. Pp. xiii + 208.

The wonder is that a book on this subject his not been written before. The blessing is that the task has now been undertaken by one whose knowledge of the field is considerable, and whose association with the University of Cambridge is long. The saving grace is that the integrity of the scholar is at no point compromised by that haze of sentiment which has been known to overtake alumni.

Readers of this tightly packed book will be helped if they bear three considerations in mind. First, most of the Cambridge theologians who pass in and out of these pages did not spend the whole of their working lives within the University. In fact a few, though Cambridge graduates, never held an academic post there. Many held ecclesiastical posts for greater or lesser periods, with all that that entailed concerning patronage (which somehow seems much grander than mere 'networking'). Secondly, undergraduate courses in theology as we should nowadays understand them were not available at Cambridge until the 1870s. Thirdly, it was only gradually that the University became 'institutionally detached' from the Church of England.

Professor Thompson rightly has the 'long nineteenth century' in view, for it was in the latter decades of the previous century that the impetus was given to the apologetic endeavour that in one way or another was the concern of Cambridge theologians until the First World War. We begin with Richard Watson, indebted, like many others, to Locke's epistemology, who elevated testimony as that upon which Christianity's truth depends. He thereby set the stage for an apologetic approach that demanded close attention to the biblical (especially the New Testament) texts—work at which Westcott, Lightfoot and Hort excelled. To the annoyance of some, Watson opposed credal subscription; he swashbucklingly maintained that 'scepticism was even less plausible than Christianity'; and, with reference to Tom Paine's thoughts on religion, he bluntly declared, 'it would have been fortunate for the Christian world, had your life been terminated before you had fulfilled your intention.' Less pugilistically, Watson upheld the right of free enquiry, and in this he was followed by William Paley, who also contended for the full toleration of Dissenters. The logic of Paley's *Principles of Moral and Political Philosophy and Natural Theology* gave the student Charles Darwin 'as much delight as did Euclid,' though Darwin revised his opinion upon the discovery of the principle of natural selection (and not because Hume had demolished the argument from design twenty-seven years before Paley published his *Natural Theology*). Thompson correctly observes that Paley's apologetics influenced not only more liberally-minded clerics, but also a number of Anglican Evangelicals.

Herbert Marsh led the way in biblical criticism as he pondered the evidential value of prophecy and the question whether certain biblical texts were God's *ipsissima verba*. He regarded the British and Foreign Schools Society as a ploy by Dissenters to wean children from the Church of England, and he opposed the British and Foreign Bible Society because, in distinction from the SPCK's policy in England, it did not distribute both the Bible and the Liturgy of the Church of England. The widespread and enduring influence of the preaching of the Evangelical Charles Simeon is duly noted, as is the encouragement given to patristics by John Kaye. The letter argued that where revelation was concerned, 'the greater the distance from the fountain-head the greater the chance that the stream will be polluted' (cf. Locke, *Essay*, IV.xvi.10,11, and Caleb Rotheram's contrary view in his Edinburgh dissertation of 1743).

In H. J. Rose we meet a high churchman who opposed the Reformed view that confessions of faith might be modified in the light of Scripture, believed that church history should be read with the eye of faith and, whilst acknowledging the value of anti-deist writings, nevertheless lamented that 'The perpetual weighing of evidences, the consideration of sophistry, the replying to fallacies, is any thing but a favourable employment for purifying and exalting the heart.' Against Rose we may balance the Evangelical George Corrie, who had no time for the Oxford Tractarians, and, unlike others of his party, maintained that Charles I was a martyr who 'died for the Church of England.'

We come next to the considerable influence of Coleridge. His ideas were propagated at Cambridge especially by J. C. Hare who, like C. Thirlwall, had interests in German theology. Hare argued that since faith was the product of an act of will it was a moral as well as an intellectual matter. His best-known student (though Hare had not taught him theology, and their theologies diverged at many points) was F. D. Maurice. A substantial discussion of Westcott, Lightfoot and Hort introduces their work and explains its continuing influence. With them Thompson properly associates E. W. Benson. Westcott's curriculum innovations of 1871 shaped the study of theology at Cambridge for the next hundred years, while Hort urged the establishment of the Dixie Chair of Ecclesiastical History. The trio were alive to the need to challenge scepticism, but they could adopt neither the Evangelical nor the Tractarian responses to it. Westcott defended miracles, majoring on their moral significance, and echoed Thomas Arnold in maintaining that 'the true revelation of the Bible is original righteousness and not original sin.' He and Hort worked assiduously on the New Testament texts, challenging the dating of them proposed by Tübingen scholars, while Lightfoot and Westcott became renowned biblical commentators.

In his final main chapter Professor Thompson introduces 'some Nonconformist Voices.' He offers brief sketches of James Ward, minister of the Great Meeting who, assailed by doubts, turned to philosophy and eventually became the first holder of the Chair in Mental Philosophy and Logic; P. T. Forsyth, who served at Great Meeting's successor, Emmanuel Congregational Church, from 1894 to 1901; J. Rendel Harris, a Congregationalist who became a Quaker; W. Robertson Smith, deposed from his Chair at the Free Church College, Aberdeen, because of his views in the inspiration of Scripture, who became Professor of Arabic; the text-gathering Lewis and Gibson twin sisters, benefactors of Westminster College, Cambridge; and the Baptist T. R. Glover.

While conceding that theological openness was not exclusive to Cambridge, and that even there Rose and Simeon exemplified divines of a different temper, Thompson is justified in characterizing the general tenor of Cambridge theology as evincing 'the willingness to consider theology as a series of open questions rather than already determined conclusions.' Further, he has clearly shown that as to method, 'History and historical criticism provided the core and strength of the way in which the Cambridge theological tradition evolved during the century.' He amply demonstrates his claim that 'to use high/orthodox and low/liberal as a single catch-all division in which all will turn out to be on the same side on each view does not work.'

In a few places a gloss seems to be required. For example, Thompson boldly affirms that 'The dominating issue raised by eighteenth-century scepticism was the authenticity of the Bible in general, and the New Testament in particular.' Later, however, he rightly supplements this claim by observing that 'the moral objections to some of the aspects of God depicted in the Old Testament, together with the doctrines of hell and everlasting punishment' were also causes of concern. But even this is not enough: there is the apparatus of the scholastic *ordo salutis* which was construed by some in such a way as to induce moral revulsion leading to scepticism regarding Christianity as a whole. Again, Thompson rightly refers to Hort's 'underlying Platonism' which shows him to be 'the typical Cambridge man.' But when he says that this 'explains why [Hort] may be read as being sympathetic to the philosophical idealism which grew in the later part of the century' I demur; for the positions of Plato himself and of the Cambridge Platonists (or Plotinists?) differ in important respects from that of the post-Hegelian idealists (and also, incidentally, from that of Berkeley, whose psychological idealism Cambridge's G. E. Moore, who succeeded to James Ward's Chair, famously determined to refute).

This well produced book is furnished with a bibliography and an index. I noted a few slips. On p. 6 it was the nineteenth, not the twentieth century that turned; and for 'Berkeley' on p. 30 we should, I suspect, read 'Butler' and then delete Berkeley from the index.

PHILOSOPHY, THEOLOGY AND HISTORY

In any work of this kind 'then and now' thoughts will almost inevitably occur to the attentive reader. When in 1764 Richard Watson was elected Professor of Chemistry 'he immediately set about learning Chemistry . . .' I understand that a more recent Cambridge scholar who applied for the Rylands Chair of Biblical Criticism and Exegesis at the University of Manchester and had to confess his innocence of Hebrew at the interview, was not as fortunate. We might ponder whether Watson's observation that 'the taste of the present age is not calculated for making great exertions in Theological Criticism and Philology' applies to our own time, and if it does, how far it matters. When reading Watson's opinion that 'The effect of established systems in obstructing truth, is to the last degree deplorable: every one sees it in other churches, but scarcely any one suspects it in his own,' my mind strangely flew to certain ecumenical consultations in which I have participated. It would be pleasant to think that Herbert Marsh's words would caution those who, even in mainline denominations, seem in danger of succumbing to a creeping anti-intellectualism which is at the top of a slippery slope, at the bottom of which is the declaration, 'I have never sat at the feet of a theological professor, thank God, but I have stood at the foot of the Cross.' Marsh said, 'it is not learning, but want of learning, which leads to error in religion.' Not, indeed, that Marsh was invariably helpful: Isaac Milner had him in his sights when he said, 'I do not dread the dissenters, as if they were infected with a contagion.' Watson may have the last word. He published a six-volume collection of tracts written by others so as to give 'young persons of every denomination, and especially to afford the Students in the Universities, and the younger Clergy, an easy opportunity of becoming better acquainted with the grounds and principles of the Christian Religion than, there is reason to apprehend, many of them at present are.' Googling for a sermon late on Saturday evening seems a poor exchange.

This fine study has left me with two questions which, I readily admit, Professor Thompson was in no way obliged to address given his terms of reference. I mention them merely as a way of illustrating the stimulating nature of the material he has supplied. First, I wonder how far Professor Thompson thinks the apologetic approach of his subjects can take us today? Secondly, although both Hare and Forsyth would have agreed that we must concern ourselves with what Calvin called the whole course of Christ's obedience (*Institutes*, II.xvi.5), I should like to know how the author himself stands in relation to the incarnationalism of most of the Cambridge theologians *vis à vis* a theology centring in the Cross such as was supremely expounded in the twentieth century by Forsyth; and this not least in relation to the claim, trenchantly denied by Forsyth, that the Church is a continuation, or extension, of the incarnation—a topic of some ecumenical importance.

In an Epilogue Professor Thompson recalls the series of lectures on the theme, 'Objections to Christian Belief,' which was mounted by the Cambridge University Divinity Board in 1962, and which he attended. The series was, he rightly thinks, consonant with the enquiring approach exemplified in his book. He also allows himself to say, 'it is not easy to imagine the Oxford Faculty putting on a similar series at that time.' Any reviewers of this book from 'the other place' may make of that what they will: it is a matter on which I cheerfully maintain something approaching Olympian detachment.

Journal of the United Reformed Church History Society 8 (2009) 236-39

Part Two: History

56

A Unitarian Theological College

Leonard Smith, ed *Unitarian to the Core: Unitarian College Manchester 1854–2004* Manchester: The Unitarian College, 2004. Pp. xii + 210.

From an historical point of view the theological colleges of Old Dissent located in Manchester are being well served at the present time. We have already had Elaine Kaye's account of the Congregational/United Reformed Northern College, *For the Work of Ministry* (1999); Peter Shepherd's book, *The Making of a Northern Baptist College*, is eagerly awaited; and here we have a handsomely-produced sesquicentennial celebration of the Unitarian College Manchester. It is fitting that all of these studies are to hand in this year in which the centenary of the Faculty of Theology of the Victoria University of Manchester is being marked—a Faculty of which the denominational colleges were founder-members.

During the nineteenth century Manchester grew in size and prestige, and one by one the Dissenting denominations established their theological colleges there. The Congregationalists moved down from Blackburn in 1843, the Baptists from Bury in 1873, but Manchester was the first and only home of the Unitarian College of 1854.

To R. K. Webb has fallen the task of contributing the backround chapter on 'English Unitarianism in the nineteenth century.' Quite rightly, he has not taken a literalistic view of the topic he was allocated: his scene-setting takes him back *via* 1662 to Socinus. He has clearly been constrained by space, and at certain points his study suffers from undue compression. For example, it is worth noting that while, as Webb says, some eighteenth-century Arians—Micaijah Towgood among them—deemed it appropriate to worship Christ, others, including Richard Price, did not. Again, the non-subscribers at Salters' Hall were doing more than 'reaffirming the old Protestant confidence in private judgement over written creeds'; they were, like divines of all stripes, upholding the principle of the sufficiency of Scripture, in some cases denying all knowledge of Arius in the process. The story from Priestley onwards is well told: the Birmingham riots; the influence of David Hartley; the significance of Robert Aspland in securing denominational Unitarianism, and the determination of Martineau and others to sit loose to it—all of this and more is recounted in relation to rapidly changing times and circumstances. Differences over liturgy, the enthusiasm of some for domestic mission, the impact of biblical criticism, and the transfer of members from other Christian traditions—notably Robert Spears—are among other matters passed in review.

PHILOSOPHY, THEOLOGY AND HISTORY

Geoffrey Head writes on the College's founders, John Relly Beard and William Gaskell. While the former worked for nearly forty years in working-class Salford, the latter was ideally suited to the cultured air of Cross Street Chapel, Manchester. Opposites temperamentally, and with Beard much more the Unitarian controversialist than his more free-spirited co-worker, they nevertheless shared a passion for the education of all classes in general, and for theological education in particular. Beard's socio-evangelical zeal and his burning concern for the underprivileged were, so to speak, built into the very foundations of the College—to the irritation of *The Inquirer*, which contended that 'The ministry should be on a social level with the best families amongst us . . .'—a view utterly disregarded by the Manchester pioneers.

To the editor, Leonard Smith, falls the task of introducing us to the first students. He sets the scene by reference to the Religious Census of 1851, and tells the story of the inauguration of the Unitarian Home Mission Board in 1854. Prominent opponents of the scheme included Martineau, who did not think that the Unitarian denomination would ever 'exercise a wide influence, over the uneducated masses of England.' The early students were required to sign a document containing the promise 'to devote myself to the work of preaching and Extending the Gospel of OUR LORD JESUS CHRIST . . .' The breadth of the curriculum is described, the inadequate educational background of the students acknowledged. Of the mixed bunch of first students William Binns was gifted, but of William Wyn Robinson it was later said that he had been more a devoted musician than a faithful minister.

Principal Alexander Gordon has a chapter to himself, as well he might. A. D. G. Steers outlines his career, paying particular attention to his Irish pastorate and his tutorial apprenticeship in Belfast. Due prominence is given to Gordon's extensive and exemplary contribution to *The Dictionary of National Biography*, note being taken of the prominent ministers of the Non-Subscribing Presbyterian Church of Ireland on whom Gordon did not write. On accepting the Manchester post, Gordon retained his church membership in Ireland, and never became as well known to English Unitarians as he might otherwise have done (though he was an Edinburgh-educated Englishman). In Manchester he played a full part in the infant Faculty of Theology, and we learn that 'His . . . Unitarianism was very precise in its belief and he did not appreciate either those who attempted to dilute it into a nonspecific theism or those who mixed no clear doctrinal positions with an edited Anglican liturgy.' Some found Gordon's sardonic humour disquieting and, an enemy of all presumption, he more than once declined honorary doctorates.

Andrew M. Hill does as well as could reasonably be expected with the 'Too soon forgotten' Sydney Herbert Mellone. The unavoidable conjectures in this chapter remind us how swiftly the details of the careers even of the relatively recently deceased can be forgotten. Mellone, like Gordon before him, had pastoral experience in Ireland, and on arriving in Manchester it fell to him to see the College through World War I, during which period College activities were suspended for one academic session. Mellone was a prolific writer, whose range was wide and whose *Logic* (1902) had passed through twenty editions by 1945, and was reissued in 1950. It is good to have Hill's full bibliography of his works.

Alan Ruston offers us 'A sandwich of principals': McLachlan, Holt and Kenworthy. The first had been Gordon's star student, the last was among McLachlan's stars, while Holt. though a child in Lancashire, was so far exotic as to have been trained and employed for twenty years at Manchester College, Oxford. McLachlan's scholarly industry is recorded, as is his sometimes 'difficult' temperament. He served the College and University tirelessly, though when we are informed that in 1920 he earned the first Manchester D.D. for twenty-one years, we must understand (since the Faculty was by then only sixteen years old) that McLachlan was the first to achieve this distinction, and that the earned D.D. was not subsequently awarded for a further twenty-one years. (I have been told that McLachlan made sure that it wasn't, but I cannot verify this). The next recipient, in 1941, was H. G. Marsh. Among other things we learn that like Principals before and since, McLachlan struggled with the College's finances, and that he was a strong supporter of women ministers. R. V. Holt, an inveterate optimist with an unusual lecturing style, was a man of wide interests: the Holiday Fellowship, the Fabian Society, Oxford City Council, biology, birds, poetry, the playing of Gilbert and Sullivan on the piano and the singing of German songs. To all of which he managed to add a passion for social reform and religious liberty. *The Unitarian Contribution to Social Progress in England* (1938) is an important part of his legacy. In 1955 Fred Kenworthy succeeded Holt. Not to speak of the living, it must be said that of all the Principals Kenworthy seems to have been the most loved: 'who couldn't care for a man with such a pronounced stoop, and such a mangy-looking old dog at his heels?' asked alumnus Graham Murphy. An able scholar with a pastor's heart, Kenworthy published little—a possible explanation being the painting and renovating of the College premises which he and his wife undertook during the vacations. In March 1974, shortly before his planned retirement, Fred Kenwortliv collapsed and died on his way to the University.

Chapter 7 strikes a different note. Sándor Kovács provides a welcome account of the relations between English Unitarianism and the Unitarians of Transylvania, with special reference to Manchester College. Mutual contact began in the 1830s, but from 1860 the first Transylvanian scholars came to Manchester New College, then in London. From 1911, thanks to the generosity of the Sharpe sisters, Transylvanian girls could study at Channing School, London, and Transylvanian ministers, the first of whom came to Manchester in 1906, could qualify for the Sharpe Hungarian Foundation from 1911. The lists of girls and ministers are supplied; the trials of the communist era are noted; and from the concluding chapter we learn that Principals Long and Smith are Honorary Doctors of the Protestant Theological Institute in Cluj, where Unitarians, Lutherans and Reformed study together.

The present Principal, Ann Peart, brings the story up to date. Finance again looms large, the domestic salaries being more than one and a half times those of the tutorial staff. The inauguration of the Northern Federation for Training in Ministry, the evacuation of the College premises and the removal to Luther King House are among significant recent developments. The advent of the Partnership for Theological Education, Manchester and the introduction of a BA in contextual theology are among other changes noted. It is impossible for an outsider to know what Principal Peart means when she says that 'in an ideal world I would prefer to be part of an interfaith group rather than an exclusively Christian partnership.' Is she for a multi-faith context for theological education, or for syncretistic content in theological education, or both?

The book is furnished with appendices listing Unitarian resources at The John Rylands University of Manchester Library, registers of tutors, officers and students from 1854–2004, and an index and a list of subscribers to the volume. The photographic reproductions and illustrations, and the overall design of the book are excellent.

Unlike some institutional histories this one does not have too much of the 'in house' feel about it. Accordingly, it will be warmly welcomed by theological educators and church members from many traditions; and by local historians and historians of education too.

In the body of this review I have concentrated upon the primary information to be gleaned from this book. But there are many miscellaneous items of interest along the way. The Unitarians of Bath who included vaults in their 1795 chapel which could be leased to nearby wines and spirits merchants; the way in which the lack of voice production in ministerial training led to shortened ministerial careers; L. P. Jacks's non-doctrinal trimming when he refused to preach warnings to the rich lest Mr. Thom be upset; Elizabeth Gaskell's turning to novel writing to assuage her grief at the death of an infant son, and her husband's determination to keep her at arm's length from his sphere of work; the uncouth William Binns who, 'When he shook his mane great was the upsetting of china, and great the consternation of "correct" personages'; student Henry McKean who ministered for 41 years at Oldbury, became a prominent Freemason, and did many good works in the district, not least the provision of a billiard table to retain firemen *in situ* between calls; the loss, with the sinking of the Leinster in 1918, of some of the proofs of Gordon's *Cheshire Classis*; Sydney Knight who, failing to gain access to the College by normal means, entered through an upstairs window in order to attend his interview with Principal Holt, and thus 'climbed into the Ministry.'

My favourite comparison concerns the very different interviewing styles of Principals McLachlan and Kenworthy. Of the unsuspecting, Greek-less, candidate Hilton Birtles, McLachlan enquired, 'What is the Greek derivation of the word telephone?' By contrast, John Allerton's interview with the shy Fred Kenworthy, a native of Mossley, went like this: '"Nah then, Mr. Allerton, I gather you want to train for the ministry." "Yes" (Silence). "You're in the UYPL?" "Yes" (Silence). "And you went to Mill Hill?" "Yes" (Long silence). "Aye, well, all right then." End of interview.'

Three overriding impressions are conveyed by this illuminating book. The first concerns the depth of social conscience and evangelistic zeal evinced by the founders and many of the College's alumni. The second is the importance of the relationship with the Non-Subscribing Presbyterian Church of Ireland. The third is the diversity of views, doctrinal and liturgical, which have come to expression in English Unitarianism. Where the string binding those of other traditions has sometimes snapped with secessionist consequences, the Unitarians seem to have patented an elastic which holds together those of sometimes contradictory views. Which thought brings me full circle to the title of this book. In deference to the logical S. H. Mellone I should point out that in 'Unitarian to the core' the 'to' is ambiguous. I quite see that the phrase is intended to mean 'Unitarian through and through.' But it can also mean 'Unitarian up to/as far as the core.' Then what? The thought occurs that those present-day Unitarian students at Luther King House who find 'the exclusively Christian language of the courses difficult to cope with' would have liked even less the promise which their forebears of 1854 were required to make.

Faith and Freedom 57 (2004) 175–79.

57

A Baptist Theological College

Peter Shepherd., *The Making of a Northern Baptist College*, Manchester: Northern Baptist College, 2004. Pp. xvi + 298.

The jigsaw is complete. Elaine Kaye has given us the story of the URC/Congregational Northern College and its predecessors[5]; Leonard Smith and others have this year celebrated the sesquicentenary of Manchester Unitarian College[6]; and with this bicentennial study, Dr. Shepherd has completed the picture of theological education in Manchester as far as the institutions of Old Dissent are concerned—and this in the centenary year of the colleges' junior partner, the Faculty of Theology of the Victoria University of Manchester.

Whereas the Manchester Unitarian College has never been anywhere else, the lineage of the URC/Congregational College reaches back to Ottery St Mary (1752), almost half a century before the New Connexion Baptists opened the senior forerunner of the Northern Baptist College in London (1798). Unlike earlier Dissenting academies which provided a general higher education to youths against whom the university portals were closed—Henry Grove's academy at Taunton and Philip Doddridge's at Northampton, for example—Ottery St Mary and London and their successors were products of the Evangelical Revival and their sole brief was to train ministers.

Dr. Shepherd sets out from the Particular Baptist, John Fawcett, and the evangelical Arminian Baptist, Dan Taylor, both of whom were keen to advance the cause of adequate ministerial training. In the event, the New Connexion was first off the ground with its connexionally-supported institution which found homes successively in London,

---

5. E. Kaye. *For the Work of Ministry: A History of Northern College and its Predecessors*. Edinburgh: T. & T. Clark, 1999.

6. See previous review.

Wisbech, Loughborough, London, Leicester, Nottingham, Chilwell, and Nottingham again. Among its notable alumni were N. H. Marshall and J. H. Rushbrooke, while its most distinguished tutor was T. Witton Davies. The situation of Midland College was ever precarious—especially following the termination of the nationwide General Baptist Association in 1891, when New Connexion churches joined the then existing Particular Baptist regional associations and the Baptist Union of Great Britain and Ireland. It did not survive World War I. The funding of its John Clifford Chair passed to Rawdon College.

Although frequently beset by difficulties, both financial and in terms of personnel, the Particulars' colleges generally fared better and certainly survived longer than their Arminian counterpart. That at Horton, Bradford, and from 1859 at Rawdon, Leeds, opened under the tutelage of that 'great lump of goodness,' William Steadman, who could 'shake a sermon from the sleeve of his coat.' Its succession of principals, including T. V. Tymms, A. C. Underwood, L. H. Marshall and D. S. Russell, ensured a commitment to high academic standards, and the lifetime of service contributed by the devoted William Medley, himself no mean scholar, should not go unremarked.

In Lancashire, David Griffiths conducted an academy at Accrington from 1841 to 1849 and then, following an hiatus, a fresh start was made in Bury in 1866, the College there removing to Manchester eleven years later. Until well into the twentieth century this College upheld strict-communion principles. Among its principals were Henry Townsend and Kenneth Dykes. The latter, though raised among the Strict Baptists, did not allow strict-communion views to prevent the union with Rawdon in 1964.

Dr. Shepherd fully appreciates, but does not shrink before, the difficulty of writing recent history. We are treated to a somewhat breathless account of cylinders firing in all directions during Michael Taylor's somewhat provocative term as principal—a period which saw the complete reorganization of ministerial training, the fostering of ecumenical partnerships, and the converging of the Methodists, URC/Congregationalists and Unitarians on the Baptists' Brighton Grove campus. To Brian Haymes fell the task of integrating new tutors and tidying up loose ends when Taylor transferred his attention to Christian Aid. The former principal, Russell, and the present principal, Richard L. Kidd, contribute a Foreward and Afterword respectively.

The author has juggled with a mass of sources, and has had to balance many judgements passed upon more recent events by those still living. As one who managed to avoid the institutions with which he deals, he has brought a welcome degree of objectivity to the task. There are some cryptic remarks. In what respects, for example, was the theological teaching at the universities of Leeds (p. 205) and Manchester (p. 206) deemed to be deficient by the Baptists? Among a few repetitions, we are twice informed of Townsend's DD and thesis (pp. 160, 178). Some readers might have welcomed a little more information regarding the scholarly work which some of the tutors, including Tymms, Medley, Davies, Marshall and Russell, managed to achieve, their multifarious duties notwithstanding. Small slips include the removal of Leominster to Wales (p. 36); the claim (p. 69) that R. W. Dale was principal at Airedale College (A. M. Fairbairn was); and the mis-naming of Lancashire Independent College (p. 73).

Among many points of interest noted in passing is the information that the saints at the delightfully-named Barton-in-the-Beans, though evangelized by the Countess of Huntingdon's preachers, nevertheless threw their lot in with the Arminian Dan Taylor. Again, we learn that in 1977 a team of inspectors reviewing the educational provision as reformed by Michael Taylor reported (in what seems to be a classic example of 'reference language') that the governors were less than fully involved, something which the governors themselves attributed to 'the cogency and power with which [Taylor] can order the arguments he uses to support his case' (p. 243). Did they live to rue the day, one wonders? In Taylor's root and branch reforms, undertaken in order to inaugurate local-church-based training, there were some curriculum casualties. We are informed that less emphasis was placed upon biblical languages and textual criticism, and that philosophy of religion and systematic theology were 'largely ignored' (p. 230). Writing as an almost exact contemporary of Taylor's on the then formidable postgraduate Manchester BD course, I find it hard to suppress the thought that in all of this there is, on Taylor's part, an element of biting the hand that fed him. The 1950s were a high point for the Manchester Faculty and I, for one, was far from disadvantaged by having the Bible opened, the great Reformation themes enunciated, the English Reformation in its Anglican and Dissenting forms elucidated, Christian doctrine ruminated upon, the nuts and bolts of Christian ethics displayed, and the principles of other faiths expounded by an ecumenical galaxy of scholarly talent: my ministry was greatly assisted by this. As for philosophy of religion, introduced by the logically rigorous John Heywood Thomas, and which, among other things, I have myself sought subsequently to purvey, surely there are few matters of greater *pastoral* importance than the ability to respond sensibly and sensitively when, on an almost daily basis in the pastorate, the problem of evil is raised, death beckons, faith and reason appear to collide, and the Ayers and Dawkinses of this world need to be dealt with; and these are among the fundamental issues in philosophy of religion. It is a paradox that the pursuit of relevance may leave pastors to some extent incapacitated. I do not say that all ministers in training need exactly the same course of study, but I am uneasy about losing core disciplines by appealing to the need to 'professionalize the ministry.' Dr. Shepherd says that the early crusade for ministerial training was 'particularly understandable when the general level of literacy and education was low and congregations needed able teachers and preachers to communicate the message lucidly and persuasively' (p. 2). The need is no less great today. But this is no more than an instrumentalist consideration. How much better if ministers, according to their capacity, had what Dan Taylor and John Fawcett seem to have had: 'a love of learning for its own sake' (p. 51).

On closing Dr. Shepherd's lucid and informative book, the abiding impression is of a devoted struggle, often against formidable odds, to secure the flow of competent and faithful ministers of the Gospel by one means or another. The subjects of this bicentennial volume deserve their memorial, and Dr. Shepherd has served them, and us, well.

The Baptist Quarterly 41 (2005) 53–57.

58

Religion in the West Midlands

Geoff Robson. *Dark Satanic Mills? Religion and Irreligion in Birmingham and the Black Country*. Carlisle: Paternoster Press, 2002. Pp. 294.

On the map, the West Midlands conurbation resembles a large inkblot; from the air it appears as a rather characterless sprawl of houses, industrial buildings and waterways. But peer more closely and you will find fascinating variety, and communities which are, defiantly, the very reverse of monochrome. Where religion and 'irreligion' are concerned, few have peered more closely than Geoff Robson, whose viewing spectacles are of the historical-cum-sociological sort. He is very much at home with tables (of which there are thirty-nine) and statistics; his analyses of a mass of data are perceptive, and his criticisms of other investigators of the scene are acute; his occasional comparisons with findings in other regions are illuminating.

He would have gut off on quite the wrong foot (and risked at least a verbal drubbing had he strayed west of Ocker Bonk (aka Hill) if he had not made very clear the distinction in character, industrial activity and denominational spread as between Birmingham and the Black Country. If the former is the city of a thousand trades, with brass, jewellery and guns prominent, the latter is a constellation of smaller towns and villages, with Walsall (don't yo fergitit) having a much older charter than England's second city. There were nail makers here, saddlers there, locksmiths a mile away, and miners under the ground.

Robson's objective is to account as far as he can for the 'striking difference' in church attendance as between Birmingham and the Black Country, as revealed by the 1851 Census returns. First, however, he sets his discussion in its context. He discusses the economic and social setting of the region: its mineral resources, industrial development, and unusually rapid population growth during the first half of the nineteenth century. He rightly draws attention to the considerable amount of domestic outworking which took place, much of it done by women. The situation regarding parliamentary and local government is described, with Anglican clergy being prominent in the latter. The poor relief system is explained, as are the ecclesiastical arrangements of the Church of England. The Dissenters and Methodists are introduced. Of the latter, the Wesleyans, Primitive Methodists and New Connexion Methodists took root in the Black Country, whereas the Wesleyans alone came to have a significant numerical presence in Birmingham. The advance of the Roman Catholics is marked by new churches across the Black Country, and by the rebuilding of an older Birmingham church as St. Chad's Cathedral in 1841.

Part Two: History

The heart of the book comprises Robson's discussion of the 1851 Census. This is an intricate matter which defies summary here. Two samples will illustrate the kind of information gleaned: church attendances were (atypically) highest in Sedgley and Tipton, where there was the highest proportion of unskilled labourers; and the Black Country had larger proportion of under twenty year-olds in Sunday School than Birmingham.

The impact of the 1832 and 1849 cholera epidemics upon church attendance is next assessed. Some preachers employed the epidemics as a homiletic device to prompt individual repentance or to 'demonstrate' the Almighty's displeasure with Socinianism, or at moves towards Catholic emancipation. During the panics congregations increased; afterwards they declined, though there was still a net gain of attenders, most noticeable among the Primitive Methodists.

A chapter follows on the methods and messages of evangelism. We learn that John Gent Brooks, clearly a victim of attempted 'sheep stealing,' was moved to write, 'You must not think that because I am a Unitarian my soul is bound up in ice . . .[The orthodox] have not been able to draw my people away from me, but I do feel pained at their want of Christian love' (p. 157). If mass evangelism was attempted only by the Black Country Methodists, Birmingham was notable for the number of its denominationally diverse home missionaries, whose achievements, subjected to close scrutiny, elicit Robson's driest remark: 'Death bed conversions . . . were regularly reported by missionaries with the advantage that their reality was not easily denied; (p. 176). More might have been made of methods by which the messages were proclaimed, not least in the rising press. One thinks of the first successful newspaper in Walsall, founded by Edward Myers, the Unitarian minister in the town. Those who were drawn into the churches faced varying degrees of stringency. The Congregationalists of Birmingham thought that the Methodists were too lenient in receiving members, their leading minister, John Angell James, though he was stricter than many, regretting that there were 'many, very many' whom he ought to have rejected.

A chapter on popular religion and the religion of the people follows, which has to do with credulity ghosts, and superstitions, and in which the Methodist situation is to the fore. Robson here betrays his knowledge of 'Aynuk and Ayli' jokes (as well he might—though he resists the temptation to tell us some); and so we come to a summary of his findings and a bibliography, between which are sandwiched all those statistical tables. There are indexes of persons and of places (which might have been fuller) but, sadly, not of subjects.

Within its carefully defined parameters this is a most valuable study. Robson's explanation that he could not analyze the church membership lists and baptismal registers for a region as large as this is quite understandable. He also says that he could not trace the history of every denomination. But in this connection I think that he could have done a little more than he has. We should not expect an amalgam of local chapel and parish histories, but there are readily accessible writings which do not appear in Robson's bibliography which would have helped him to say a little more about the religious beliefs of those he discusses—and this without delving into sermons, biographies, diaries and the like. He does note the inter-Methodist fluidity of membership, and he mentions a few individuals who migrated between other denominations. But entire churches 'came out,' sometimes—a least ostensibly—on doctrinal grounds. Thus, for example, while we are reminded that the Rev. Theodosius Theodosius of Ruiton Congregational church strove to take his members into the Church of England, and failed; the fact that the prominent Robert Street Baptist church came out of the same congregation is passed over. And what of the puzzle concerning the passage of the Independent chapel in Cradley to the Church of England? We are left with the impression that Robson is more adept at counting the religious and describing their social status and conditions than at getting under their convictional skins; yet some of the Birmingham and Black Country saints did some of the things they did because of what they believed.

Robson writes, 'The Birmingham evidence indicates that there was little doctrinal difference between the moderate Calvinism of Anglican, Independent and Baptist and the Arminian theology of the Methodists...' (p. 185). A strong case could be made for saying that in the Black Country doctrinal antennae were more sensitive than this, not only in the first half of the nineteenth century but for generations afterwards. Indeed, in the memory of those still living an allegorical interpretation was given to the geographical fact that at the top of a certain Black Country hill were the hyper-Calvinists, half-way down were the high Calvinists, and at the bottom of the hill were the benighted Arminians. In the midst of such piety, some of it highly introspective, some of it uncomfortably judgemental, there was a certain comfort to be derived from the reminder in the nickname of the Cradley Heath Speedway Club that there were also Heathens around.

Geoff Robson has served us well with this stimulating, carefully argued, study. Thanks are also due to his publisher, who is more prepared than some to take the risk of publishing important specialist studies in British Christian thought and history.

Anyone for pork scratchings?

Proceedings of the Wesley Historical Society 54 (2001) 135–37.

59

Charles Grandison Finney

Keith J. Hardman. *Charles Grandison Finney, 1792–1875, Revivalist and Reformer.* Syracuse, NY: Syracuse University Press, 1987. Pp. xvii + 521.

'We presume that no man . . . has inflicted more injury upon the cause of religion, and especially upon revivals of religion, than Charles G. Finney.' 'He is made for the millions. . . . He is a heaven-born sovereign of the people . . . He seems specially created for oral labour.' Anyone of repute who can evoke such contradictory estimates as these is likely to be of interest to a biographer. But in the case of Finney, the incompatible judgements have spawned such a vast amount of letters, pamphlets and articles that it is hardly surprising that nobody has plunged headlong into this subject since 1891.

The professor of philosophy and religion at Ursinus College, Pennsylvania, who has already introduced us to American revivalists from Stoddart to Moody (*The Spiritual Awakeners*, 1983), now offers this meticulous study of an eminent American preacher, around whom controversy rages to this day.

From Finney's early years the biography progresses *via* his legal training and practice, to his scanty theological education and ordination as a Presbyterian minister, and thence to evangelism in New York State, notably at Rome. Finney was opposed alike by Old School Calvinists who disliked his 'new [revivalist) measures,' and by Unitarians, Universalists, deists and atheists. The contrast between the evangelistically-conservative Asahel Nettleton and Finney (both of whom claimed to be heirs of Jonathan Edwards (and were, but to different parts of him) is especially well drawn. So to the confrontation at New Lebanon between the eminent Lyman Beecher and his fellow easterners (including Nettleton), and Finney, with his western colleagues. The testimony of the latter to Finney's innocence of revivalistic excesses, and their unsatisfied demands for evidence of alleged irregularities, earned Finney a win on points.

Finney's influence grew as he opposed Old School Calvinism on the one hand, and rode the crest of the millennial and perfectionist waves on the other. His work in Philadelphia and New York, though supremely at Rochester, had lasting results. Boston, at once the power base of Beecher and of the Unitarians, proved less receptive to Finney's content and style. Finney increasingly identified himself with the Free Church Movement in New York, working for abolition (while keeping blacks separate from whites inside his church); and in 1836 he left the Presbyterian ministry for the Congregational. Meanwhile, he had accepted a post at Oberlin College, though with the proviso that he might have periods free for evangelism. At Oberlin he developed his 'Pelagian'(as distinct from Wesleyan and antinomian) perfectionism. He visited Britain twice, on the first occasion receiving a particularly warm welcome from Dr. George Redford of Worcester Congregational church.

Finney's long career, of which the above is the baldest summary, is skilfully set in context by Dr. Hardman. The theological changes, the increasing political clout of 'ordinary' people, the humanitarian thrust of the age, the anti-slavery movement, the temperance cause, the anti-Masonry drive, the Civil War—all are here. So too are such prominent Christian businessmen as Arthur and Lewis Tappan, whose stewardship and personal courage in supporting unpopular causes was remarkable; and such intriguing (in both senses) ministers as Lyman Beecher, who secured acquittal at a General Assembly heresy trial by making a strictly orthodox statement, 'having learned that he could get away with no less.'

The strength of this work in part results from the fact that while Dr. Hardman is primarily an historian, he is no mean theologian. If his contrast between rationalistic and evangelical Arminianism is too swiftly drawn to be very helpful, his demonstration of the way in which Finney's gospel elevated sin above grace and, in 'Pelagian' fashion, emphasized human ability to the detriment of the Cross and the Spirit, is superb. From the same 'Pelagianising' root comes Finney's hostility to the Calvinist doctrine of the perseverance of the saints—on which Dr. Hardman's comment is as apt as it is concise: 'to deny the security of the believer is the inevitable tendency of the doctrine of natural ability run rampant.'

But what of the 'new measures'? Finney undoubtedly held that 'A revival is not a miracle . . . It is a purely philosophical result of the right use of the constituted means.' But Dr. Hardman convincingly shows that few, if any, of the 'new measures' originated with Finney (the Baptists and Methodists were already—often literally—in the field); that he used them with discrimination; and that there is a considerable gulf between his practice and that of latter- day mass evangelists, whose harbinger he is sometimes said to be.

Although we are assured that Finney could be tender, and that his affection for his children and for his three successive wives was genuine, 'stern and unbending'are the adjectives which most aptly characterize him. He was a great one for 'agonizing' in prayer, as a student of his recalled: 'When Professor Morgan prays for rain, it just drizzles, but when President Finney prays, it pours!' Finney had no qualms about naming names from the pulpit. On one Sunday he named those who had borrowed his tools and failed to return them. The next day implements arrived at his yard from all quarters—many of which he had never owned or seen before.

This admirable study is furnished with a bibliography and an index, and is enhanced by a number of illustrations. The frontispiece shows Finney wearing an expression calculated to make sinners tremble, and to give even the godly a nasty turn if they encountered him unawares in a dimly-lit alley.

The Baptist Quarterly 33 (1989) 99–100.

Part Two: History

60

Philip Schaff

George Shriver. *Philip Schaff, Christian Scholar and Ecumenical Prophet*. Macon, GA: Mercer University Press, 1987 Pp. 138.

By any standards Philip Schaff (1819–93) was a remarkable, and a remarkably hard-working, man. Born at Chur in Switzerland, he was educated under such varied scholars as Strauss and Dorner at Tübingen, Tholuck at Halle, and Neander and Schelling at Berlin. Following travels in Italy and Sicily he assumed the role of Privatdocent in Berlin. In 1843 he accepted a call to Mercersburg (German Reformed) Seminary, Pennsylvania, where he arrived in 1844. With his colleague, J. W. Nevin, though more temperately, he developed the Mercersburg Theology—that Christologically-grounded version of evangelical catholicism which wished to listen to the ages and revitalize the liturgy.[7] In 1865 Schaff resigned his post at Mercersburg, and became secretary to the New York Sabbath Committee. Five years later he accepted a Chair at Union Theological Seminary, New York (concurrently transferring to the Presbyterian Church USA), where he remained until his death.

Schaff lectured widely; paid fourteen return visits to Europe; made numerous friends in theological and ecclesiastical circles; helped to revive the ailing Evangelical Alliance in 1866; led the North American side of the Bible translation-revision group; wrote extensively in the fields of ecclesiastical history and biblical exegesis; edited and co-edited a number of significant works; and founded the American Society of Church History in 1888.

Shriver's book is a component of the centennial celebrations of the last-named Society and, with the exception to be noted below, Schaff and the Society have been well served. We have here a straightforward account, which makes good use of many of the numerous extant primary and secondary sources. Useful appendices, a bibliography and an index enhance the work.

The author skilfully brings Schaff to life. He emerges as an eirenic person who, in his earlier years, withstood a heresy trial and weathered much misunderstanding with a good grace—and also with some humour. When advocating the use of the Christian Year to his students, Schaff referred to the one who had brought the heresy charge against him thus: preachers 'should be bound to some order and not as Dr. [Joseph F.] Berg who preached against stingyness or something of the kind on Ascension Day.' On the question of liturgi-

---

7. See further reviews 74–77 below.

cal revision, one wishes that Shriver had referred to the conservative case as proposed, for example, by J. H. A. Bomberger, an erstwhile supporter of Nevin.

Shriver's portrayal of Schaff as an 'ecumenical prophet' would have been even stronger had Schaff's pioneering work on behalf of the World Presbyterian Alliance (the first of the modern international confessional organizations) been noted. The Alliance is indeed mentioned, but only within a sentence, the main purpose of which is to inform us that Schaff and his wife and daughter visited Jane Borthwick whilst in Edinburgh for an Alliance meeting. From sources other than Shriver we learn that Schaff was 'untiring in his efforts' to promote the Alliance; that he attended the first four Councils of that body; and that at the first Council (1877) he presented a noteworthy paper on 'The Consensus of the Reformed Confessions,' in which he expressed his evangelical catholic vision in homely fashion thus: 'We want a wall to keep off the wolves, but not a fence to divide the sheep.' Shriver's brief was to write to a specified length, but this important aspect of Schaff's ecumenical work could have taken precedence over some portions of the chronicles of his travels.

Schaff was a prophet who looked to the future but, like all good prophets, he was also firmly rooted in his time. One of the ways in which this emerges is in connection with his post-Hegelian view of history. Shriver mentions Schaff's indebtedness to Baur and also to Schelling, who argued that the process of Christian history was from Petrine objectivity and authority (thesis) *via* Pauline freedom and subjectivity (antithesis) towards a Johannine synthesis in love. Schaff maintained (see *Proceedings of the World Presbyterian Alliance*, 4, p. 363) that the reunion of Christendom was the prerequisite of synthesis, and of the conversion of the world to Christ. Many early ecumenists were fired by the same passion, and inspired by the same philosophy of organic development.

The clamant question thus arises: 'Which philosophy of history undergirds our current ecumenical vision?' Quite apart from its inherent difficulties, it would seem that Schaff's utilization of his philosophy of history is not open to us, in view of more recent biblical criticism, views of mission and perceptions of society. Does more than one understanding of history underlie present-day ecumenical thinking (cf. Schaff's catholicism *versus* that of Pusey)? If so—and having regard to the close link between theories of history and positions on the 'development' of doctrine—may this not go some way towards accounting for the ecclesiological and other road-blocks which beset us in ecumenical discussion? Shall we make much progress unless we articulate, clarify, and attempt to reconcile our often tacitly-held philosophies of history? Here is a huge and (at least relatively) neglected subject for debate in ecumenical circles.[8]

One of Philip Schaff's major works is *The Creeds of Christendom*. He could see, however, that the era of relations with the non-Christian world was fast approaching—as witness his last public appearance at the World's Parliament of Religions (Chicago, 1893). What form will the several churches' 'Creeds of Post-Christendom' take, and how ecumenical will they be?

The Ecumenical Review 41 (1989) 141–2.

8. See further, Alan P. F. Sell, *Enlightenment, Ecumenism, Evangel: Theological Themes and Thinkers 1500–2000*, Milton Keynes: Paternoster, 2005, ch. 6.

Part Two: History

61

Revival in Wales

Eifion Evans. *Fire in the Thatch. The True Nature of Religious Revival*. Bryntirion, Bridgend: Evangelical Press of Wales, 1996. Pp. 234.

There must be many people who go to their graves without knowing that in 1858 seventy-six people were converted at Ystumtuen. Our author will enlighten all who are interested in such matters. Indeed, at first glance this is simply a collection of fifteen papers, ten of them previously published, in which various aspects of the story of revival are recounted. But do not be deceived. Dr. Evans, well known over many years for his interest in, and contributions to, this field is in addition proposing a theology of revival and issuing a challenge to the churches.

As far as the more historical papers are concerned, we set out from Richard Baxter's Kidderminster ministry, noted for its emphasis upon 'The duty of personal catechizing and instructing the flock.' The personal devotion of Griffith Jones, rooted as it was in Puritan and Anglican spirituality, is next considered; and there follows an account of Whitefield's contribution to the eighteenth-century revival in Wales. The sterling work of David Jones in consolidating the fruit of that revival in Glamorganshire is here described, as is the place of the Bible in the Great Awakening. A study of John Davies' mission to Tahiti forms a bridge between the eighteenth and nineteenth centuries, and then we come to the Beddgelert revival of 1817, and the 1859 revival which is represented by pieces on Humphrey Jones and Dafydd Morgan.

As sometimes happened when papers written over a period of years are gathered together, there are a few inconsistencies of historical judgement. While on occasion recognizing that revivals have their shadow side of idiosyncratic excess, Dr. Evans generally paints the gloomiest possible picture of the circumstances into which revivals erupted. 'Revival,' he declares, 'takes place against the background of deadness and barrenness.' Again, 'At the risk of over-simplification it can be maintained that the revivals of the sixteenth and eighteenth centuries came to an apostate, declining, expiring Church, while those of the seventeenth and nineteenth took place against the background of a dormant, listless, and unconcerned Church.' In view of the considerable amount of scholarship which now tells a much more varied story, Dr. Evans should not have taken the risk. On the other hand, he himself, in the chapter on 'Spirituality before the Great Awakening,' refers to a number of cases which demonstrate that to write 'Ichabod' over the period would be premature, and well as dishonouring to a faithful remnant. Furthermore, some of those who rebuked Methodism (of whatever theological complexion) for its 'enthusiasm' deserve to have justice done to their very real fear of fanaticism leading to sectarianism and thence to civil unrest—seventeenth-century examples of which lingered powerfully in the memory.

At times one could wish for fuller explanation of terms—as when eighteenth-century Arminianism is characterized in its rationalist guise only. And since 'Deism' is nowhere defined, it serves simply as a disapproved-of Aunt Sally. Dr. Evans surely goes 'over the top' in declaring that 'Deism, Socinianism and Unitarianism were swept aside as the revival spread,' for in some centres Unitarianism at least was prominent at the end of the eighteenth century.

Nevertheless there is much of interest in the historical studies, and ample and effective use is made of apt quotations from the principal actors and from other relevant sources. Indeed, apart from the distinction in typography it would sometimes be hard to tell when a quotation ends and when the author resumes: he has lived so long with these characters that his style is imbued with their cadences, as when he expostulates, 'Alas! That is it necessary to bemoan in these days the scarcity of such divine visitations as were so frequent in the eighteenth century!' But with this we come to the theology and the challenge. These concerns are to the fore in the Introduction, and in the chapters entitled, What is Revival?; Revivals: their rise, progress and achievements; Preaching and revival; Adding to the Church—in the teaching of the Welsh Calvinistic Methodists; Early Methodist apologetic—explaining and defending revival; and Why no revival?

Dr. Evans is in general clear that whereas revival is the work of God the Holy Spirit, evangelism and preaching are human endeavours. We do not decide to have a revival, neither do we effect it. But ambivalence creeps in from time to time. Dr. Evans can say both that revival is an 'unsought, unexpected' activity of the Spirit, and urge Christians to pray for it expectantly. But in so far as it is sincerely prayed for, it is sought.

Whilst granting that Harris and others were reluctant to appear as sectaries, and resisted separation from the Anglican Church, it must be said that Dr. Evans seems not to be sufficiently alive to the ecclesio-covenantal problem which revivals pose. True, he speaks of revivals as awakening the Church, as increasing its numbers, and as stimulating many varieties of Christian enterprise. But the overriding impression is conveyed that revival has to do with the salvation of individual souls, and that even when the saved come together in fellowship meetings they do so as converted individuals desiring to contribute their testimonies, rather than as those engrafted into the community of the baptized. Indeed, the sacrament of baptism seems often to be a casualty of revivals, as more emphasis is placed upon conversion than upon covenant. Robert Mackintosh's provocative yet perceptive comment of a hundred years ago comes to mind: 'Infant baptism is the great rock of offence to the triumphant revival.'

With this is connected the question of the reception of church members. Dr. Evans recounts the dialogue between John Jones and Dafydd Morgan. The former wanted converts to consider the cost of discipleship for at least one month prior to reception. Morgan retorted, 'Well! well! God's Spirit says, "Today", the devil says "Tomorrow"; but the old evangelist of Blaenannerch says, "A month hence will do".' We are left to guess where the author's sympathies lie; but insofar as both Jones and Morgan might have appealed to Scripture in support of their positions, each had a point. It is hard to believe that that eminent catechist, Richard Baxter (whose ecclesiastical-ecumenical contribution is here largely overlooked), would have wished people to be 'swept in' to the church without due preparation.

In relation to the question, What is to be done today? Dr. Evans suggests that the Gospel needs faithfully to be proclaimed, and prayer needs to be ardent. Who could disagree? But in view of the importance of the question his analysis of the causes of diminishing interest in preaching and revival might well have gone deeper. He observes that churches are turning to newer methods in mission, and that ecclesiastical leaders no longer think in terms of revival. But what of other options currently open to people—the proximity of other faiths and of a variety of spiritualities, for example? What of that societal cynicism and/or apathy which greets not only politicians but also authority figures (not excluding preachers) in general? So one could continue. To plead for such analysis is not to deny that profitable suggestions may be gleaned from the study of past revivals (though we should beware of the restorationist attitude in this field as in others); but it is to suggest that preachers need to know something not only about the seed to be sown, but about the soil in which it is to be sown. Whatever the final prescription might be for today's Church, no one can deny that in 1858 seventy-six people were converted in Ystumtuen . . .

Journal of the Presbyterian Church of Wales Historical Society 20 (1996) 77–81.

62

The Crisis of Belief in Canada 1850–1940

David B. Marshall. *Secularizing the Faith: Canadian Protestant Clergy and the Crisis of Belief, 1850–1940*. Toronto: University of Toronto Press, 1992. Pp. 325.

'Every dinner table was a theological class, and with the pork and potatoes went the Calvinism and Arminanism in due course. The Bible was the family hand-book, and handled reverently, it was the arbiter of the daily discussion.' Such was the experience recalled by a Baptist raised in the Ottawa Valley about one hundred and fifty years ago. The remark calls to mind those Alexandrian barbers who were said to indulge in trinitarian debate (where I live they talk about the Calgary Flames).

One way of describing David Marshall's welcome and informative book is to say that it is concerned with the displacement of such language from common Christian parlance.

Again, this is a work concerned with the decline of mainstream Canadian denominations, especially the United Church and its Presbyterian and Methodist predecessors. Yet again, this is a study of the complex relations of Church and culture. But however we describe major thrusts of the volume, secularization is the running theme which makes a unity of the whole.

That this daunting theme is treated by so balanced a scholar is a relief indeed. Dr. Marshall, of the University of Calgary, neither chortles over the Church's apparently waning influence, nor does he wax apocalyptic concerning the inroads made by the 'world.' He is well aware that no wedge can be driven between 'sacred' and 'secular,' as if the ecclesiastical bodies were wholly in the former realm and not at all influenced, internally as well as externally, by the latter. He does not overlook the fact that people are motivated by their deeply-held convictions, neither does he deny the impact of social, cultural and economic factors upon them. He has not fallen for the notion that statistics will tell us all we need to know (because, for example, churches compute membership in significantly different ways, and with varying degrees of accuracy), though he utilizes such methods where appropriate. This temperate eclecticism is exactly what is required to argue his thesis in a rounded and just manner, for his theme is as subtle as it is multifaceted.

Against the view of some that fully-grown secularization smote the Canadian churches during the 1960s—prior to which time all had been a tale of churchly progress, Dr. Marshall believes that secularization's birth certificate is unavailable. Its emergence was not sudden and cataclysmal; it came without fanfare—here and there, now and then—as Canadians gradually accustomed themselves to changing religious and ethical views of the world, to cultural changes, and to an increasingly hospitable consumer society. Secularization, he declares, has much to do with 'the rise of individualism, a growing sense of personal freedom, and greater tolerance for diversity.'

Dr. Marshall's thesis is that since the middle of the last century the dominant motif in Canadian Protestantism has been that of the accommodation of clergy and churches to an increasingly secular society, 'not a march of progress towards the Kingdom of God.' The argument is mounted by means of a detailed examination of the struggle of ministers to find an adequate and a preachable Gospel.

In prosecuting his case Dr. Marshall harvests the fruits of his extensive archival research, drawing particularly upon the diaries, memoirs, publications and sermons of ministers. His knowledge of secondary sources is likewise impressive, his notes and bibliography are full, and his style is fluent.

The stage set, the author first considers the increase of religious doubt concerning the presence and purpose of God, providence, and the trustworthiness of the Bible. He characterizes evangelical faith as having to do with doctrines, religious experience and social commitment. He finds the view prevalent among the Methodists that perfection was to be sought, and that it was attained, if at all, largely by the believer's own efforts. He notes the spiritual struggles after assurance through which some ministers passed—struggles which sometimes conveyed them from Calvinism towards Arminianism. The doctrines of election and predestination came to be less regularly promulgated from Presbyterian pulpits. Many of the doctrinal concerns were focused in Presbyterian circles by the heresy trial of the Rev. D. J. Macdonnell who, after initial training at Queen's University, imbibed 'advanced' critical notions in Glasgow. In the Macdonnell case more than particular doctrines or the methods of biblical criticism were at stake: the status of the Church's subordinate standards was clamantly raised.

We proceed carefully through such intellectual challenges to the faith as those supplied by the geologists and Darwin, but Dr. Marshall feels that the moral revulsion which was widely felt against older 'immoral' views of God was just as unsettling, as were the societal changes resulting from more adequate transportation and communications systems.

Among those who sought to stem the tide of a more liberal theology was E. H. Dewart, who held the influential post of editor of the Methodist *Christian Guardian*, and whose hostility to scientific materialism, and desire for uprightness of life were not in doubt. He did, however, see the need for some reconciliation of the newer thought with the Christian faith. With the passage of time, and under the influence of historical studies, he deserted the orthodox view of the fixity of doctrine. The intellectual struggles of others are noted—not least those of Nathanael Burwash, as is the cautious stance of William Caven, Principal of Knox College. God became immanent, not remote; Jesus became more the 'Perfect Man' than the divine saviour, and thus 'Conceptions of God were being based, in part, on what people would like God to be.'

The next chapter concerns those who devoted themselves to 'Salvaging the Bible and the evangelical tradition.' There was the Crossley-Hunter revival team; there were the central positions of Caven and Principal MacVicar of Presbyterian College, Montreal; and there was the response of Dewart to his fellow-Methodist George C. Workman's denial that when delivering their messages the Old Testament prophets had Jesus in mind. When John Campbell, professor of church history and apologetics at Presbyterian College, Montreal, declared that his reason and moral sensibilities told him as much about God as the Bible did, this, as we might imagine, was too much for some of his co-religionists to bear, and a further heresy trial ensued. The successes of the Salvation Army and the missions of Moody and Sam Jones sharply posed to Presbyterians and Methodists the question of the content of the message to be preached.

Some began to feel that if the churches heeded the missionary commission to go into all the world, benefits would accrue at home too. There was also a growing concern for the Canadian West. But although much faithfulness—and even heroism, and considerable financial resources were expended in both directions, the results were not generally encouraging as far as the health of Canadian church life was concerned. Once again, the nature of the message to be proclaimed was raised. In the first place, with God increasingly understood in genial liberal fashion, and with hell, as one writer put it 'frozen over, or turned to innocuous ashes,' a powerful motivation to conversion was undermined. It must have been very discouraging to a preacher who took the line, 'If you were to die tonight, where would you go?' to meet with the implicit, bland response, 'Pull the other one!' Not surprisingly, many had recourse to homiletic Plan B. Secondly, it became increasingly impossible to regard those of other faiths as utterly benighted heathens. Some revision of received opinion was required, and George Grant was among the more forward-looking in this matter. The novels of Ralph Conner and the rise of the Social Gospel are all part of the story of the diverse ways in which relevance was sought.

During the period 1890–1914 major emphasis was laid upon stemming the tide of secularization. The churches increasingly began to compete with other educational and social institutions with a view to holding their territory, and combatting increasing consumerism. Not all found it easy (and perhaps some did not try very hard) to hold William Witherow's line: 'The more institutional [the Church] is, the more spiritual it needs to be.' The crusade for Sabbath observance, argued generally on 'good for health' grounds in the political arena, was also motivated by the desire to preserve some Christian distinctiveness and distancing from the 'world.' Family worship diminished mightily. Even S. D. Chown, who had tried so hard to root Christian social concern in the traditional evangel, came to question the Social Gospel on the ground of its theological inadequacy.

Undeniably the theology of the Social Gospel, but also the theologies espoused by more conservative ministers, was sorely tried during the First World War. Dr. Marshall's excellent chapter on the efforts of chaplains and the responses of soldiers, and on the rift between the perceptions of chaplains and others at the front and church leaders at home, makes for poignant reading. On the one hand the Methodist Chown had said 'Khaki has become a sacred colour!' (Presbyterians echoed the sentiment—albeit not at the expense of the real sacred colour, Presbyterian blue) On the other hand some—not least those in the thick of battle— could see no place for such apparent triumphalism. The same Chown, now chastened, came later to see that 'to glorify war again would be like "painting roses on the lid of hell".'

The 1920s are described as 'An era of drift.' After the War the numbers of students signing up for theology did not match those for other disciplines, and financial problems increased. Not even the achievement of church union in 1925 could mask the underlying malaise. Moreover, in the scheme of union discordant theological doctrines were placed side by side with no attempt at resolution. Although the fundamentalist-modernist controversy for the most part passed the United Church by (whereas the Baptists were ravaged by it) it did encourage fresh thought on the centralities of the faith. Prominent here was Richard Roberts, in some ways a Barthian before Barth became widely known in the English-speaking world, who sought a Gospel faithful to the Word, which would hold together the transcendence and the immanence of God, and would not unduly exalt human nature. Walter Bryden expressed similar concerns within the Presbyterian Church.

In the 1930s the economy at large, and not least the coffers of the churches, came under increasing strain, and the thoughts of many Christians turned once more to revival which, they felt, was long overdue. The Oxford Group made a fairly widespread impact, but was eventually weighed and fond wanting by many, not least because it seemed to endorse the transformation of theology into psychology, of sin into weakness. Gradually, and prodded from without by the challenges of the Depression, and from within by the likes of Roberts and E. H. Oliver, some steps were taken towards a more positive theological statement of Christian distinctives. The former urged the need of 'penitence for personal complicity in collective sin,' the latter denied that the Social Gospel contained all the answers sought. Dr. Marshall's rueful conclusion is that neither the more evangelistic, nor the more socially orientated activities of the churches had sufficed to stem the tide of secularization, or to make more Christians.

I proceed now to a few observations. First, Dr. Marshall does not sufficiently probe the allegation that Calvinism was unduly doctrinally harsh, and pays little heed to those who questioned this assertion during the period which concerns him. During the past twenty years lively debate has surrounded the degree to which Calvinism departed from Calvin, and while writers continue to differ, it has at least become clear that even if older caricatures of Calvinism were explicable (there being no smoke without fire), they did not tell the whole story. Secondly, the claim, 'the disestablishment of religion has proven to be an essential pre- condition in the process of secularization,' is one which does not admit of proof in the Canadian context, since we cannot say what would have happened had an established Church continued here to this day. What is clear is that in Germany, the Scandinavian countries and England religious establishments have not been conspicuously successful in countering the process of secularization. Thirdly, I should have welcomed more on the influences upon Macdonnell. Were his views on the eternity of punishment, for example, influenced by the writings of F. D. Maurice, Edward White and others? In the fourth place, while it is true that many theologians and ministers managed to turn the theory of evolution (or, at least, the evolutionary theme—few tarried long in Darwin's works) to good account as indicating the gradual, progressive way in which God had developed his handiwork, more might have been made of the fact that that the sting of evolutionism was to some extent drawn by criticisms of Darwin's explanatory hypothesis in scientific circles themselves. Dr. Marshall properly notes the writings of those theologians (he mentions James McCosh in this connection) who pointed out that, after all, the evolutionary theory had to do with process, not with origin, and hence it left the doctrine of creation intact.

Did Ritschl influence Canadian Social Gospel thinking as he did American? Was appeal made to Hugh Price Hughes, perhaps? On the question of the immanentism of the period, something on Romanticism, the post-Hegelian intellectual climate and, in particular, the contribution of John Watson (Edward Caird's pupil and disciple) would have rounded out the account. Did R. J. Campbell's 'New Theology' make an impact in Canada? To what extent did the Canadian denominations draw succour from the growing Christian internationalism of the times? Certainly the Canadian Presbyterians were involved in the affairs of the World Presbyterian Alliance (1875) from its infancy onwards. By what route did Barth become indigenized—and was Scotland a channel here, as it had been for the transmission of the earlier higher criticism? Was the infant science of psychology deemed to be more of a help than a hindrance in theology and biblical exposition (and not simply in pastoral counselling)? How far has the 'handing over' of the 'family altar' to the minister (which is tantamount to handing the Bible back to the 'priest'— and that's not why we had a Reformation) fostered ministerial 'professionalism' —a mixed blessing indeed? Simply to list the questions is to indicate the degree to which this stimulating book has caused one reader furiously to think.

Of the importance of this study to historians of Canada there can be no doubt, but it is of considerable importance to theologians and church members too. It clamantly raises the issue of the locus of authority in the Church. It cannot be said that the churches have finally answered the questions of the way in which the Bible is to be appealed to, the place of Tradition and of doctrinal standards, the role of the whole people of God *qua* interpretative community. In some circles Ryerson's lament of 1871, with which Dr. Marshall's book opens, that people have only 'the shifting sands of expediency,' and are thus 'blown about by every wind of passion,' has become sanctified as the 'doing one's own thing' orthodoxy. Small wonder that when it is necessary to bring a common Christian mind to bear upon moral, socio-economic or political issues (which, since the Gospel has to do with the whole of life, may from time to time be required) the Church's trumpet makes an uncertain sound; it is as if the players are reading from different scores, and some seem to be improvising as they go along. Related to this is the place of doctrinal standards and church discipline ('Men want convenient comfortable creeds,' declared the Presbyterian James Robertson). Heresy trials, those ecclesiastical soap operas in which Presbyterians have run off with so many of the awards, bear witness to discord within the Church; but they also testify to a deep concern for right doctrine, and to commitment to the view that truth matters. We might pose the questions, Are occasional heresy trials preferable to constant doctrinal muddle? Can things be so open-ended that everything of importance drops out?

What, next, of the viability or otherwise of apologetics? It is currently fashionable to say that we live in a post-Christendom age. To the extent that this is true, it may prompt us to reflect that the context of the mainline churches—minorities in the midst of a multiplicity of world views ranging from the sublime to the bizarre—is much more like that of the early, pre-Christendom, divines than it is like that of Luther and Calvin, for example, who could more understandably make the assumptions of Christendom. Yet in that pre-Christendom period the Church managed to win and retain some of the ablest intellects. Dr. Marshall's study offers scant assurance that the churches in the period he discusses made great strides in this matter, and one may not be sanguine concerning what has happened since. I by no means intend to legitimate an elitist 'gnosticism' according to which those with advanced degrees are more important than those without that sometimes dubious distinction. It is simply that it is part of the Church's pastoral and witness-bearing calling to meet people where they are. Christians frequently beat their breasts concerning the Church's widespread failure with the 'working class'; I am simply suggesting that to those with serious intellectual questions about the faith (and these are to be found across all 'classes' —and not least in childrens' playgrounds), many churchly preoccupation must appear as mightily 'in-house,' and hence as irrelevant. The matter of the content of preaching; the place of family worship—in fact, of families, as we should now have to add: these are among other issues clamantly raised by this book.

Dr. Marshall forces the question upon us: How far is churchly decline related to the neglect of the supernatural? He maintains that belief in the supernatural is a defining characteristic of Christianity. In this connection it is interesting to observe secularization working from within the Church with all the evangelistic talk about 'Only believe . . .'—as if we can, unaided; or what of the 'Pelagian' construction of the doctrine of perfection, to which I referred earlier? This both denies the need of supernatural grace, and is also a most efficient way of heaping up damaging guilt when we fail to hit our target (as we will).

To note one further matter arising: How may we encourage congregations which have inherited a large portion of Enlightenment individualism (a line of enquiry which merits further elucidation) to understand themselves as ecclesial bodies, rather than as aggregates of saved atoms gathering under one roof? And how are local churches (as distinct from local congregational oligarchies) to take their rightful place in the structures of their several denominations? Until this matter is resolved, it is difficult to see how genuine mutual *episcope* as between wider and more local *foci* of churchly life is possible. There is no doubt that where toleration, freedom, and the scuttling of untoward, overweening authorities— whether biblicist or ecclesial—are concerned, the Enlightenment was 'a good thing.' But the ecclesial weaknesses arising from the concomitant individualism (not least in its evangelical guise) have yet to be worked out of the ecclesiastical system.

In this story of change and decline, there is a point which is so obvious that it may be overlooked. Through all of the theological turmoil and social unrest considerable numbers of the faithful seem to soldier on: in the language of the trade, they have the grace of perseverance. In face of 'dry' preaching and sensationalist, 'flash-in-the-pan' theology, the saints have an uncanny knack of knowing when to stay in their trenches with their tin hats on. The same applies *vis à vis* external challenges to the faith. On the same Sunday in the 1960s, in a rural part of England (and I was reminded of this by Dr. Marshall's reference to the homely, acted-out sermons of some of Moody's followers) I both watched a lay preacher acting out his sermon on Jacob's ladder ('Nay, we'll 'ave t'put it on yon' side o't'pulpit, else we'll knock Nellie off th' organ'), and saw A. J. Ayer running circles around one of the most prominent preachers of the day on 'The Brains Trust.' Time-lags play a not unimportant role where the conservation of the faith is concerned.

Half a century has passed since the terminus of David Marshall's admirable study. The religious landscape has changed dramatically. No one queries the term 'multifaith' when applied to our society, and we even seem to be in a period of heightened interest in the spiritual, variously understood. Where mainline churches are concerned, there has been such an ecumenical emphasis on the correct theological notion that the Church comprises its members that many of them have begun to believe it. Woe betide any ecclesiastical apparatus, whether centred in Toronto or Rome or anywhere else, which is perceived by its flock as being so 'advanced' or so 'reactionary' as not to speak for the Church. When sufficiently frustrated the first recourse of the saints is to keep their money at home. When all else fails, they walk. Meanwhile they continue to take their meals. For many, however, the mealtime focus is not the Bible, but the television set; and none of the advertisers peddles Calvinism or Arminianism.

The Literary Review of Canada I (1992) 11–12.

63

The Social Gospel in Canada 1875–1915

Brian J. Fraser. *The Social Uplifters: Presbyterian Progressives and the Social Gospel in Canada, 1875–1915*. Waterloo, ON: Wilfrid Laurier University Press, 1988. Pp. xvi + 212.

We are greatly indebted to Brian Fraser of the Vancouver School of Theology for this rounded and informative study of the Social Gospel among Canadian Presbyterians. The focus is upon the contribution of the "progressives": C. W. Gordon, J. G. Shearer, J. A. Macdonald, G. C. Pidgeon, R. A. Falconer and T. B. Kilpatrick, all of whose roots were in the Free Church Presbyterianism of central Canada, and all of whom strove for the creation of a Christian society *via* the reformation of the individual conscience.

While the importance for the Canadian Social Gospel of the philosophical idealism of Watson and Grant at Queen's University is not denied, Fraser explains that the institutional bases of the progressives' philosophy were the Presbyterian colleges in Toronto, Montreal and Halifax. Edward Caird emerges as the primary philosophical influence upon the progressives, the biblical inspiration came largely from J. E. McFadyen, a pupil of George Adam Smith (Glasgow), while Moody's urban revivalism supplied the evangelistic impetus. To the Presbyterian progressives, the Church's primary task was evangelism leading to moral and social reform: they could not agree with those American Social Gospel leaders who contended that social salvation preceded individual salvation.

The growth of the denomination in which the progressives worked is clearly charted, and the statistical tables are more than decorative. The Presbyterian critique of Canadian society, with its well-heeled, middle-class roots, is usefully contrasted with the urban-slum pastoral experience of other Social Gospellers. The objective of the progressives was the perfection of society—they themselves being the judges of what was necessary to this end—rather than the radical reformation of it. We learn of the many steps taken to meet the needs of the inner city, though all the while the Presbyterians themselves were making for the suburbs. Church union moves were justified as a means of marshalling progressive forces in the land.

The progressives founded their strategy on the sanctity and discipline of the Christian home and on the pulpit. The religious press played its part in transmitting progressive ideas, and J. A. Macdonald's move to the secular *Toronto Globe* was significant. The contribution of schools and Sunday schools is evaluated—though one wonders whether there was any opposition to the latter, as there was in some Free Church of Scotland circles.

Numerous attempts were made to mobilize the Presbyterian Church concerning Sabbath observance, labour relations, immorality, temperance; and through it all the progressives failed to question the Anglo-Saxon moral and social values which suited them so well. The First World War threw the progressives into disarray: their responses to the catastrophe were diverse, and in the aftermath of conflict their progressivism as a cohesive force was no more.

Although on a number of occasions Fraser notes the failure of the progressives to scrutinize their own values and strategies, he does concede that their very moderation forestalled the divisiveness which marred Social Gospel activities elsewhere.

Whereas other North American Social Gospellers exploited Ritschlian theology, the 'Presbyterian progressives drew on different theological sources found in Scotland.' That is, they drew upon philosophical idealism and the new evangelicalism. How far were these genuinely compatible? Fraser mentions the idealistic transformation of the older evangelicalism, but we should greatly have welcomed a discussion of evidence at this point, especially given the traditional importance of the Creator-creature distinction in Reformed theology. Why did those influenced by, and in Kilpatrick's case taught by, A. B. Bruce not adopt a more critical stance towards philosophical idealism—as many contemporary Scottish theologians were doing? Still more puzzling is the silence of the progressives on Ritschl. No doubt the Ritschlian tide flowed up the Clyde shortly after Kilpatrick left Glasgow in 1881; but given the constant flow of books and ideas from Scotland to Canada it is surprising that the work of Ritschl and his critics (many of them with Glasgow connections: R. Mackintosh, J. Denney, J. Orr, A. E. Garvie and Bruce himself) did not make more impact upon the progressives—especially since they valued so highly the anti-individualistic thrust of philosophical idealism. On the evidence presented here it would appear that the progressives neither benefited from Ritschl, nor appreciated how the 'back to Christ' liberalism of Bruce and others sought a *via media* between idealism and Ritschlianism. There is much here to be teased out. Fraser says, 'As yet . . . no one has attempted a synthesis of international influences on the Social Gospel in the North American triangle.' May we hope that this theme is high among his own agenda?

The book is well written, attractively produced and enhanced by a bibliography and an index. The generally thorough notes usefully include references to dissertations.

On p. vii Fraser refers, retrospectively, to 'the turn of the twentieth century.' How's that for a piece of Presbyterian progressivism?

Studies in Religion 18 (1989) 495–96.

Evangelical and Liberal Theology in Victorian England

Mark Hopkins. *Nonconformity's Romantic Generation: Evangelical and Liberal Theologies in Victorian England*. Milton. Keynes: Paternoster, 2004. Pp. xv + 291.

Despite his subtitle Mark Hopkins does not attempt an exhaustive review of evangelical and liberal theologies in Victorian England, but wisely concentrates upon issues which agitated the Congregational and Baptist heirs of Old Dissent. The main protagonists of his 'Romantic generation'—J. Baldwin Brown, R. W. Dale, C. H. Spurgeon and John Clifford—were born between 1820 and 1836. As might be expected, the influence of Carlyle, Erskine of Linlathen, McLeod Campbell and F. D. Maurice was marked upon the liberals of the period, but Hopkins does well to draw attention to A. J. Scott's part in stimulating Brown's intellectual quest. This yielded an incarnational emphasis in Brown's thinking and the elevation of God's fatherhood above his sovereignty, the casualty being scholastic Calvinism. With Dale who, like Brown, studied under Henry Rogers (a missed trick here), came theological adjustments prompted by a strong commitment to moral freedom, the importance of conscience and the authoritative 'Christ within.'

A chapter is devoted to the Leicester Conference controversy (1877–78), when more conservative Congregationalists found themselves at odds with their more 'advanced' colleagues, the most provocative of whom was J. Allanson Picton. Turning to the Baptists we meet C. H. Spurgeon, the best (if only partially) known personage in the book, keen to uphold Calvinism and proclaim the traditional Gospel; and John Clifford, more practical than deeply theological, influenced by immanentist thought and committed to a low doctrine of the Church. Thence to the Downgrade Controversy of 1887–88, an escapade more thoroughly researched by Hopkins than by any previous writer and one which elicits his most judicious analysis. If the denominational problem at Leicester was that of arresting the flight of the liberals towards ever more speculative theology, that in the Downgrade Controversy was the difficulty of holding together a commitment to both evangelicalism and freedom in the absence of an agreed confession. The challenge faced by Congregationalists and Baptists alike concerned the maintenance of both denominational communion and the autonomy of local gatherings of saints.

Not slow to trounce other toilers in this tangled vineyard, quick to denounce unnamed 'historians of limited theological literacy and historically naïve theologians,' as well as those who have appreciated but not understood Forsyth, Hopkins should not object if I gently gloss his account: (1) The most casual reading of Richard Baxter's *A call to the Unconverted to Turn and Live* would suffice to show that Baxter is not to be classed with those who held that 'sensible sinners' only should be invited to believe the Gospel. (2) Too much scholarly water has flowed under the bridge for dated references to 'the eighteenth century's long [religious] drought' to stand. (3) A fuller acknowledgement of those who, before the 'Romantics' hove into view, levelled moral objections against Calvinistic doctrine—not least the oft-despised eighteenth-century 'Arians'—would have been welcome; as would some notice of the Congregationalist Edward Williams, who sought to round the sharper corners of Reformed scholasticism. (4) Against possible misunderstanding it might have been made clear that the post-'conversion' Forsyth did not merely follow the ageing Baldwin Brown in lamenting liberal excesses, but repudiated liberal theology. Happily, I receive only a slight tap on the wrist for a passing reference to Brown as an 'Hegelian Congregationalist.' Even more happily, Hopkins immediately proceeds to specify precisely those Hegelian characteristics in Brown's thought which prompted my remark. But enough of this. Hopkins has given us a stimulating book which contains assessments of persons and events with which scholars in the future will need to wrestle. Running through the work is a question: 'What are the permissible degrees of doctrinal tolerance within the Church, and by what means, by whom, and on what grounds are the boundaries to be drawn?' The 'ecumenical century' which separates us from those here discussed notwithstanding, that question awaits an answer.

Journal of Ecclesiastical History 57 (2006) 791–2.

65

C. J. Cadoux

Elaine Kaye. *C. J. Cadoux: Theologian, Scholar and Pacifist*. Edinburgh: Edinburgh University Press,1988. Pp. xiv + 228.

It is especially important that those who swim against the theological and/or ecclesiastical tide, and who are, for that reason, normally without benefit of churchly publicity machines, should have their testimonies carefully recorded. Only so can later generations make properly balanced and informed judgements of hindsight. C. J. Cadoux, the doughty and learned liberal modernist, the churchman who thought Congregational catholicity the only kind worth having, the pacifist, the total abstainer, the vegetarian, was such a swimmer. We should be grateful to Elaine Kaye, and to the Cadoux family, for making this intriguing story available, and to the Edinburgh University Press for accurate and elegant work.

Cadoux (1883–1947) began his working life at the Admiralty, concurrently gaining his BA, teaching in Sunday School and serving the Boys' Brigade. Called to the ministry, he proceeded to Mansfield College, Oxford, and thence, as professor, to Yorkshire United Independent College, Bradford (1919–33), and Mansfield (1933–47).

Where others caught their modernism from post-Hegelian immanentism and the optimism of evolutionary times, Cadoux's came from close attention to the Gospel records, combined with the repudiation of all authorities save the inner witness of the Spirit. On this basis, and armed with sharp research tools, he defended his version of Protestant catholicity, published studies of the life and ministry of Jesus (his best-seller, *The Life of Jesus*, was posthumous), investigated early Christian attitudes to war, and articulated impressive, and gradually mellowing, statements of the pacifist position. He also wrote the history of Smyrna, in which city he had been born.

Perhaps Cadoux was too much of an independent in the sense of an individualist to be a fully-rounded Independent. Perhaps, like some other liberals, he was too adversely critical of the dogmatisms of others to perceive his own dogmatic presuppositions with due clarity. It would certainly seem that Elaine Kaye's epigram concerning his pacifism has merit: while he was a theorist of pacifism, [his wife] was a practitioner in peace-making. Cadoux's love of truth and his enjoyment of a thoroughgoing intellectual scrap—provided it were scrupulously polite—is epitomized in a letter to his son Theo: 'I am in rather a whirl of controversial articles and *lrs* to press ("spice of life"—what ho!).' It appears that although some controversies—notably one with *The Tablet*—distressed him, Cadoux generally enjoyed the swashbuckling. No doubt this was some consolation: he did not often convert opponents to his views. Stanley Shrubsole, who knew him well, spoke the truth as a friend should: 'there is something characteristically aggressive about you that makes it harder for you to win the hearts and minds of your hearers to doctrines that are distasteful to them.'

Despite staunch friends, respectful students, and happy relations with many churches who appreciated his simple and dignified conduct of worship, a certain sadness hovers around Cadoux as here (no doubt accurately) presented. Passed over in connection with New Testament positions which were nearest to his interests, and for which he thought himself best qualified, he ended in Church History. He was a pacifist through two World Wars—when, least of all, pacifism 'pays.' He was out of step with Principal Micklem's version of catholicity, and even more at odds with the rising Neo-orthodoxy, which he faulted as being a-historical. He saw the convictions which he had laboured hard to justify being opposed or, what is worse, ignored. Distressed by physical and psychological ill-health, he drove himself on, and seemed to come really close to his family only in his declining years. Saddest of all, the impression is conveyed that his disappointments wounded his ego rather than humbled his spirit—a not uncommon result in those who are good at being 'right'.

Despite the inadequacies of his Christology, Cadoux had the pearl of price: 'The Christian who has no use for Calvary, whether in his ethics, his theology, or his devotions, is missing the straightest and plainest path to that ultimate reality which is the heart of God.'

Faith and Freedom 43 (1990) 150–151.

Part Three
Theology

66

Origen

Wilson Trigg. *Origen: The Bible and Philosophy in the Third-Century Church.* London: SCM Press, 1985. Pp. xiv + 300.

This scholarly, comprehensive and eminently readable book is greatly to be welcomed. It keeps close to the texts where there are texts; and where extant written evidence is slight conjecture is sensibly employed—as, for example, in connection with Origen's upbringing, on which subject English-speaking readers are helpfully introduced to the detective work of Pierre Nautin. For good measure we have a map, an appendix on the two Origens, a bibliography, full notes and an index; a preface by Maurice Wiles and a foreword by Robert M. Grant. The work is only very slightly tarnished by a prefatory quotation from Ralph Waldo Emerson which reveals a theological liberal being dogmatic against the 'dogmatism of bigots.'

We are introduced to Alexandria, the pre-eminent intellectual centre of the Roman empire when Origen lived there; to the received canon of faith which Origen made it his business to defend (and which had 'almost nothing to say' on grace, *inter alia*); and to the moral teaching, worship and order of the Church of Origen's day. The kind of education Origen would have received, and the influence upon him of Gnosticism and Platonism—notably in the latter cases of Clement of Alexandria and, in more shadowy fashion, of Ammonius Saccas—are discussed, as is Origen's sojourn in Rome and the linguistic skill which enabled the production of the Hexapla. In the remaining chapters Origen's works are sympathetically analyzed (which is not to say that Dr. Trigg will not reprove his subject where necessary); and his difficulties with Bishop Demetrius and his various controversies—supremely that with Celsus—are judiciously handled.

Perhaps Dr. Trigg's greatest achievement is that he has transformed Origen, the card to be played by students of Christian doctrine, into Origen the man who, though denied 'the crown of martyrdom . . . conclusively demonstrated that his own devotion to Christ was not purely theoretical.'

In his concluding chapter Trigg briefly charts the reception accorded to Origen in subsequent ages, and suggests that he may yet speak to us, especially concerning theodicy and the relation of the intellect to religion. With this we have no quarrel, but there is something more. At the beginning of the first chapter we read: 'When changed conditions call the church's message into question, a theologian must develop an all-encompassing religious vision that enables other Christians to interpret their experience. Two theologians, more than any others, have accomplished this for the entire Christian church. Paul of Tarsus is one of them. The other is neither Augustine, Thomas Aquinas, Luther, nor Schleiermacher, for none of them shaped the entire Christian tradition. The other is Origen, who lived at a time when the church's present divisions were, at most, only incipient.'

As we read scattered references to Alexandrian Christians who felt guilty because of their wealth; to religious pluralism; to converts to Christianity suffering more at the hands of the secular authorities than birthright Christians; and to relatively few Christians attending worship, whilst many maintained a church connection more out of habit than out of zeal, we seem to have come surprisingly close to home. All the more reason for us who inhabit post-Christendom to pay careful heed to one of the greatest pre-Christendom theologians (and, incidentally, to lament the passing of patristics from the purview of so many ordinands). Is 'an all-encompassing vision' still a viable possibility? Does it matter whether it is or not? Has the twenty-first century's Origen yet been born? We can deduce much of his or her job description from this valuable book.

Philosophical Studies 32 (1998–1990) 370–371.

67

Calvin on the Law

I. John Hesselink. *Calvin's Concept of the Law*. Allison Park, PA: Pickwick Publications, 1992. Pp. , xii + 311, £27.90.

The most competent doctoral theses may not succeed as books. Here is one which does. Yielding finally to scholarly pressure, Dr. Hesselink has revised and updated his dissertation of 1961 and by so doing he has placed Reformed and other theologians greatly in his debt. A born teacher, his exposition is so clear and balanced that a readership much wider than the specialist will benefit greatly from his book. Any authors who persist in presenting the hard-nosed, law-bound Calvin of caricature are now entirely 'without excuse,' and we shall wait with interest to see if some may even feel moved publicly to repent.

The work opens with an expression of surprise that notwithstanding the ever-expanding Calvin industry, relatively little detailed study of the reformer's concept of the law has been undertaken. Now this important lacuna is filled; justice is done to Calvin; and any who would probe to the heart of his teaching will need to reckon with this book. The chapter titles indicate the scope of the work: Prolegomena; Creation and the Law; The Covenant and the Decalog; Law and Gospel; The End and Use of the Law; Conclusion: Calvin's Dynamic Understanding of the Law.

Though especially concerned with Calvin's 'third use of the law,' the author is thorough on the other uses too. He demonstrates his argument by ample reference not only to the *Institutes*, but also to the *Geneva Catechism*, the commentaries, and to Calvin's liturgical and pastoral objectives. He graciously yet firmly adjusts himself to the views of others, dissenting where necessary alike from Lutherans and Reformed, both classical and contemporary. Moreover, this being no hagiography, Dr. Hesselink adverts to the blind spots of Calvin himself.

Among the strengths of this work are (1) the way in which Calvin is related to his medieval forebears; (2) the judicious discussion of natural law; (3) the presentation of Calvin as much more the practical theologian than the logic-chopper; and (4) the way in which the relation between the law and the work of the Holy Spirit is clarified.

The following random assertions, albeit shorn of the provided supportive argumentation, will exemplify Dr. Hesselink's style and indicate his position: '[I]t is not true to say that [Duns Scotus] identified God's absolute power with the purely arbitrary (p. 21) . . . Calvin's concept of God—or the law—should not be prejudged by one's evaluation of his doctrine of predestination (p. 25) . . . It must be conceded that . . . in his treatment of reprobation Calvin sometimes seems to speak of a God who operates apart from Jesus Christ (p. 32) . . . [T]he killing, terrorizing work of the law is the consequence of sin and hence "accidental" (p. 55) . . Separated from the Holy Spirit, the law has either a negative effect—rebellion, hardness of heart, greater guilt—or none at all . . . If the law is separated from Christ and does not lead to him, it is horribly perverted (pp. 96–97) . . . The law functions in different ways according to time and circumstances (p. 112) . . . [I]f Christ is the substance and soul of the law . . . then Christ's "faithful interpretation" of the law is nothing other than a self- witness (p. 163) . . . [W]hat separates the law from the gospel like fire and water is the matter of justification (p. 196) . . . [D]espite Calvin's hermeneutical principles and presuppositions he did not choose to develop his *Institutes* in an explicitly and systematically Christological manner (p. 224) . . . When theologians of a later generation developed a systematic *ordo salutis*, they moved beyond the reformers (p. 235) . . . The law has not been rendered obsolete with the advent of Christ . . . Calvin does not have two norms for the Christian life but one (p. 280).'

This admirable work is furnished with full notes, a bibliography and an index.
European Journal of Theology 3 (1994) 175–76.

68

Assurance

Joel R. Beeke. *Assurance of Faith*. New York: Peter Lang, 1991. Pp. xvi + 518.

With this substantial and welcome volume Joel R. Beeke makes a significant and diverse contribution to the history and import of a currently neglected doctrine. The diversity is revealed in his elucidation of the development of the doctrine of assurance through the centuries to the Dutch Second Reformation; his holding together of the British and Dutch aspects of the matter; his engaging in the current 'Calvinism *versus* Calvin' debate; and his pleading for a faith that is biblically-grounded, reasoned, experimental and practical. That he can hold all of these concerns together and leave us with a volume which is a unity is testimony to his considerable organizational skill.

The author's thesis is that 'Calvinism's wrestlings with assurance were *quantitatively* beyond, but not *qualitatively* contradictory to, that of Calvin.' In Part One, 'Assurance prior to the Westminster Assembly,' he outlines the (relatively scanty) treatment of the doctrine of assurance in the early and medieval Church, proceeding thence to 'The Reformation from Luther to Bullinger,' 'Reformed Developments in Calvin and Beza,' and 'The Fathers of English Puritanism and the Dutch Second Reformation.' Dr. Beeke's route may very roughly be charted by the following collage of quotations:

'[F]or Calvin assuring faith compels an indissoluble tie between *saving knowledge, the Scriptures, Jesus Christ, God's promises, the work of the Holy Spirit, and election* . . . Calvin clearly allows for degrees of faith and assurance . . . For Beza and Calvin the critical point is *faith in Christ*. There are no *essential* differences between their views of assurance, though their *emphases* and *methods* vary considerably—no doubt in some measure due to their being in different mileus . . . Teellinck was not simply a duplicate of Perkins. In some senses he "out-Puritaned" the "father" of Puritanism by his intense emphasis on godly living, the fruits of love, the marks of grace, and the primacy of the will.'

The ground laid, the author turns in Part Two to 'Assurance from the Westminster Assembly to Alexander Comrie.' He discusses 'English Puritanism and the Westminster Confession, Chapter 18,' 'John Owen,' and 'Alexander Comrie.' He finds that 'Though the Puritans deny works-righteousness on the one hand against the "legalist", they also reject the notion of assurance which rests on mere doctrine against the cold "professor" of Christianity . . . The organic yet distinct relationship between . . . saving faith in its essence and developed assurance, was critical for the Puritans from a pastoral perspective . . .'

In Part Three, 'Comparison of English Puritanism and the Dutch Second Reformation,' Thomas Goodwin and Owen, and Owen and Comrie are compared, Goodwin being

Part Three: Theology

revealed as the one in whom, above all, English and Dutch teaching on assurance was synthesized.

In his 'Conclusion' Dr. Beeke rehearses the difference of emphasis between English and Dutch Calvinism—for example, the English Puritans emphasized the marks of grace, the Dutch of the New Reformation the steps of grace—and laments the fact that today's Church is 'for the most part, scarcely aware that it is crippled with a comparative absence of strong, full assurance.' There follows a helpful appendix on 'The Second Dutch Reformation.'

This detailed, clearly organized work, reads well (though sometimes the small words let the author down—as in the sentence just quoted; and he is too fond of italics and of the adjective 'renowned'). The notes are a mine of information, and whole courses of lectures could be developed out of some of them. Where necessary Dr. Beeke offers grounds for dissenting from such older scholars as William Cunningham and John McLeod, and from such of his contemporaries as W. Niesel and R. T. Kendall. There are occasional slips, as when in the Bibliography my former esteemed colleague Lawrence Proctor is re-baptized; and the omission of the late Robert Paul's magisterial work on the Westminster Assembly is surprising.

Close analysis of the author's case cannot be entered upon here. Three general remarks may, however, be made. First, Dr. Beeke writes, 'Perkins knew that his hearers would be led to fundamental questions such as these: "Am I one of the elect . . . How may I be sure that I possess true faith . . . ?"' One wonders how many ministers of today face a barrage of such questions. Ought we to be worried if they do not? For the Puritans, 'God's *absolute promises* in election and covenant are solid pillars for increasing weak faith.' If they are right, is it not disturbing that predestination—even as good news—is conspicuous by its absence from many statements and affirmations of faith published by Reformed churches of the past thirty years?

Secondly, there is a welcome recovery of the doctrine of the Trinity in current systematic theology. An intensely practical and pastoral concern for assurance as here discussed—and Trinitarian references abound—would 'warm up' trinitarian discussion and act as a safeguard against the Trinity's becoming simply a systematician's presupposition, or a counter to be played. These writings implicitly question the wedge which is sometimes driven between the so-called 'academic' and the so-called 'practical' in theological education. At the same time, when Dr. Beeke throws down the gauntlet thus: 'saving faith is essential to the true study of Christian theology. When theology is properly undertaken, even its scientific aspect cannot be divorced from faith,' one hesitates over the word 'study.' However it may be with theological construction, I, for one, wish theology to be studied and criticized by believers and unbelievers alike. Accordingly, we must take care that the terms 'true' and 'properly' are not used in such a way as to legitimate a patronizing, falsely proud new Gnosticism in the academy along the lines, 'Lack of comprehension, or of assent, is only what you would expect from the unititiated/unsaved/unsound.'

Thirdly, we are informed that Dr. Beeke is 'pastor of a very large congregation in Grand Rapids, Michigan.' There is reassurance (save the pun) in the fact that while some in comparable positions have, willingly or not, come more and more to resemble directors of corporations, Dr. Beeke continues to exalt the vocation of director of souls.

European Journal of Theology 2 (1993) 81–82.

69

The Existence of God in Dutch Theology

John Platt. *Reformed Thought and Scholasticism. The Arguments for the Existence of God in Dutch Theology, 1575–1650.* Leiden: E. J. Brill, 1982. Pp 249.

Dr. Samuel Johnson, one of the most distinguished sons of Pembroke College, Oxford, said 'A man will turn over half a library to make one book.' Dr. Platt, the present Chaplain of Pembroke has done just that and the result is a notable contribution to scholarship. It is notable for the author's skilful use of the original texts—indeed, he is so at home in one of the necessary languages that his English style at times becomes quaintly Latinate. It is notable for the underlying detective work which has led, for example, to the publicizing of the 1636 sale catalogue of Colonius's library of more than two thousand volumes—'a source hitherto unknown to continental scholarship.' Above all, it is notable for the temperate and fair- minded way in which Dr. Platt picks his way through competing and sometimes contradictory scholarly opinions, ancient and modern, not hesitating to correct the mighty (for example, B. B. Warfield) as he goes.

With sound judgement Dr. Plattt resolves to concentrate upon one geographical area—and that a veritable melting-pot of Reformed theology; upon one major theme, that of natural theology—crucial in view of its implications for the nature-grace question; and upon at period of time which properly terminates at the point of Cartesian impact. These limitations permit the requisite detailed analysis to be undertaken.

We set out, quite properly, from Melanchthon, on whose list of theistic arguments subsequent Dutch theologians most frequently drew. These arguments (no matter how many, or how variously ordered by different writers) reduce to the appeal 'to the idea of the deity inside in man and to the providential ordering of nature and history.' At this point Melanchthon then goes beyond Luther, his mentor in some other respects; and in not utilizing arguments drawn from the non-human natural order (apart from a subsidiary motion-to-first-mover argument on which he places little reliance) he stands apart from Aquinas's five ways. The radical effects of the Fall weigh much more heavily with Melanchthon than with Aquinas, and although he grants the continuance of natural knowledge of God in fallen man, the effect of this knowledge is, in typical Reformation fashion, to render man 'without excuse.' With the passage of time Melanchthon attained a more positive appreciation of natural reason; but whereas he always qualified this reason's competence, some of his successors were not as scrupulous.

The question of the Dutch reception of Calvin's *Institutes* is next considered, and this by means of a discussion which reveals that whereas Colonius remained largely faithful to Calvin, Piscator (under Ramist influence), by introducing theistic arguments into the locus 'De cognitione Dei' gave encouragement to those, like Ursinus, who did likewise in the locus 'De Deo,' thereby facilitating subsequent departures from Calvin in a rationalistic direction.

The *Heidelberg Catechism* (1563), the work of Olevianus and Melanchthon's pupil, Ursinus, did much to mediate Melanchthon's position. Dr. Platt devotes a chapter to commentaries upon it of which that of Ursinus himself is especially important. Where Melanchthon had cautiously allowed a place to theistic arguments as affirming the believer in his faith, Ursinus, though emphasizing the negative function of the arguments in leaving people 'without excuse,' nevertheless opened the door to their use for apologetic purposes. To Ursinus both *a posteriori* arguments drawn from God's works and *a priori* arguments from his nature and attributes 'are demonstrable and are common to philosophy and theology.'

In setting out to prove the existence of Providence, Bastingius shows that he is methodologically closer to Ursinus than to Calvin. The hand of Ursinus is seen in the works of Lubbertus, Kuchlinus and others, though Kuchlinus, in face of the Socinian threat and Roman Catholic scholasticism, was more alive to the perils of rationalism. For his part, Hommius resorts to scriptural evidence before coming to the traditional internal/external natural grounds of God's existence. Two commentaries alone bear no marks of Ursinus's influence: those of William Ames and Hendrick Alting.

The *Belgic Confession* (1561/1566), modelled on the *Gallican Confession* (1559) is next considered. From the fact that its first article begins with God rather than with scripture some, including Barth, have maintained that the *Gallican Confession* reveals a non-Reformed concession to natural theology. Dr. Platt disagrees, pointing to the very strong statement of human inability found in article nine of the *Gallican*, and surmising with P. Courthal that Barth has confused general revelation, which *is* taught in the confession, with natural theology, which is not. In the *Belgic Confession* the inexcusability clause is emphasized, and this became a bone of contention between those who upheld the findings of the Synod of Dort and the Remonstrants. Interestingly, in his commentary on the *Belgic Confession* Maresius accords a place to the innate knowledge of God—something of which the *Confession* makes no mention at all. His later opponents missed this trick.

So to a detailed consideration of the Leiden theologians. Dr. Platt expounds *inter alia* Junius, who maintained the principle of innate knowledge of God; indeed, in confining natural theology to innate knowledge he set his face against the appeal of the Reformation tradition to the external witness of creation and providence. At the same time he followed Calvin in emphasizing the effects of the Fall on human reason, ending with a strong disjunction between nature and grace. So grievous are these effects that Junius's deployment in *De Deo seu Deum esse* of *a posteriori* arguments is but academic in both senses of the term. Our author's gentle conclusion is that Junius 'is a very strange hybrid among natural theologians.' For all that, some other Leiden theologians soon utilized Thomistic arguments themselves. Gomarus, however, remained more faithful to the traditional Reformation appeal to nature and history, and did not reproduce even the few scholastic arguments which Melanchthon, Ursinus and Daneau had used. For his part Vorstius (followed, though more for theological than for philosophical reasons, by Episcopius) denied the innate idea of God, and held a Thomistic (*via* Suarez) view of the nature-grace relation; while Arminius, with his distinction between axioms and arguments, sought to order scholastic and Reformation arguments in a coherent manner. With Coccejus we revert to a conservative 'Reformation' approach to natural theology. Where some Leiden theologians failed even to mention the fact that the natural knowledge of God is designed to render people inexcusable, Coccejus, though recognizing that such natural knowledge is affirmed by Scripture, concentrated on the proofs derived from God's self-revelation.

In his chapter on 'Nature, Grace and Inexcusability' Dr. Platt investigates the light shed by the disputes over predestination upon the nature-grace relation. Many of the issues are epitomized in the Remonstrance of 1610 and the (orthodox) Synod of Dort (1618). Thus we see, for example, that by maintaining that all natural knowledge of God is of grace, Arminius faced the orthodox charge that he had equated 'common grace' with the 'natural light.' The debate between Du Moulin and the Remonstrant J. A. Corvinus is analyzed; and Episcopius's view that though darkened, human reason is not utterly incompetent, is shown to bypass completely the inexcusability controversy. He will accept that sinful men are inexcusable because they have not in fact used their reason aright, but (*contra* the orthodox party) they could have used reason aright had they so chosen.

Under humanist influence there was a return to Aristotle, and this could not fail to affect the way in which theistic arguments were propounded. In a word, Melanchthon's innate ideas were sacrificed to Aristotle's *tabula rasa*. Thus, Vorstius, for example, though he did not capitalize upon the *Belgic Confession*'s silence on innate ideas. Equally, when Hommius condemned Vorstius for his rejection of innate ideas he was undeterred by the *Confession*'s silence on the matter. Episcopius's rebuttal of the doctrine of innate ideas is theological rather than philosophical—even fallen man is free to use his right reason to gain knowledge of God: hence the viability of apologetics. Melanchthonian constraints upon theistic argumentation are thus cast aside. The apologetic task was largely left by theologians (except Vorstius) to laymen, of whom the two most prominent were Du Plessis-Mornay and Grotius.

It is abundantly clear that Dr. Platt has treated ideas which are in the most literal sense seminal. Some of the fruit appears in later Unitarianism—in part a product of concentration upon the *being* of God; some appears in the subsequent divorce of ethics from theology which was one result of the emphasis upon the predestinating work of a sovereign will, at the expense of the Father's grace in creation, covenant and redemption; some appears in eighteenth-century rationalism—and here the earlier role of the Netherlands as a haven for some in the English Dissenting tradition should not be overlooked. The four-centuries-long debate over the human being's ability or otherwise *vis-à-vis* salvation which I have sought to unravel in *The Great Debate: Calvinism, Arminianism and Salvation* (1982/1998) also has roots in Dutch soil. Again, there is a methodological debate within the Reformed family to this day, some espousing a 'scholastic' apologetic whose apex was 'Old Princeton'; others setting themselves up as Christian presuppositionalists whose indebtedness to the Dutchman Kuyper are plain for all to see. Finally, scholars continue to debate the questions which underlie Dr. Platt's work: Was the influence of the methodological changes embraced by Reformed theologians cosmetic only, or was the heart of Reformed doctrine affected? To what extent, if at all, did Calvin's successors leave their mentor behind? Those who wish to take the 'cosmetic' line have had their task made much more difficult by Dr. Platt.

To pursue the matters arising from Dr. Platt's foundational work will require the application of as much philosophical and theological skill to succeeding centuries as he has expended upon his period. It is a prodigious labour. But then, as George Whitefield—another Pembroke man—is alleged to have said, 'I had rather wear out than rust out.'

Philosophical Studies 31 (1986–1987) 429–32.

70

Samuel Clarke and the Trinity

Thomas C. Pfizenmaier. *The Trinitarian Theology of Dr. Samuel Clarke (1675–1729): Context, Sources and Controversy.* Leiden, Brill, 1997 Pp. 235.

Dr. Pfizenmaier's title conjures up a vision of a rather large number of eighteenth-century high Calvinists and evangelical Arminians turning in their graves and expostulating, 'Dr. Samuel Clarke—a trinitarian?' In this Fuller Theological Seminary dissertation Pfizenmaier returns a carefully qualified affirmative response. If it were only because this is the first full-scale published monograph on Clarke since 1976 this study would be welcome. What makes it intriguing is the author's determination to demonstrate a thesis (something not all doctoral candidates seem to do these days) which will require intellectual and doctrinal historians to tread more carefully in the future when attempting to locate Samuel Clarke on the map of theological 'isms'.

Was Clarke an Arian? The label has been frequently attached to him. Is it justified? Pfizenmaier argues that it is not. Indeed, he believes that the customary options: Sabellian (Socinian), Arian, Orthodox, are inadequate, for they do not accommodate the 'Semi-Arian,' *homoiousian*, position which Clarke, in the wake of Origen, Eusebius of Caesarea and the Cappodocian fathers, adopted. Pfizenmaier resolves to restore Clarke to the trinitarian fold by investigating, in good ante-Nicene and eighteenth-century fashion, the relations of the first two persons of the Trinity.

Following an introduction in which he reproduces Clarke's fifty-five Propositions on the Trinity, Pfizenmaier turns to Clarke's intellectual context, with particular reference to the rise of modern science and the Reformation. Homage is paid to Bacon—his books of nature and of God—and to his significance as a pioneer of inductive science. Descartes is presented as one whose sceptical method led him to the indubitable, clear and distinct idea of God. Both Bacon and Descartes maintained a belief in a revelation from God whilst at the same time laying the foundation of ensuing challenges to it. Locke's special contribution was to argue for the reasonableness of Christianity in such a way as to require the rational scrutiny of revelation. With Newton the inductive method reigned supreme and, against Descartes and Leibniz, the universe was conceived as a vacuum, not as 'an enormous plenum filled by visible and invisible matter.'

The post-Reformation fragmentation of the Church prompted Locke and others to seek a rational foundation of belief on which all people of goodwill could stand. This objective was shared by Calvinists, Arminians, deists, and Socinians, though their disparate doctrinal findings were the subject of keen debate. Pfizenmaier's focus is upon deism, Cambridge Platonism and the Great Tew Circle, and Latitudinarianism. The deist Toland, indebted to Locke, surpassed his master in holding that nothing contrary to, *or above*, reason could be part of Christian doctrine. The Cambridge Platonists, supporters of the 'new science,' elevated the 'light of reason,' and sought to avoid metaphysical disputes by grounding theological assertions in the Bible. Chillingworth, a leader of the Great Tew Circle, posited moral certainty grounded in the evidence of testimony as proof of faith—albeit this proof lacked the certainty of mathematical, scientific, or metaphysical proof. This last position became characteristic of the Latitudinarians, of whom some were more, others less, doctrinally orthodox. If Stillingfleet and Thomas Sherlock exemplify orthodox Latitudinarians, Clarke, like Benjamin Hoadly, is among the 'heterodox Latitudinarians.'

The scene set, we turn to 'Clarke within his context.' Clarke holds that the deists' natural reason has been eclipsed by the Gospel—a revelation which does more than clarify (though it does not contradict) reason: it supplies additional information concerning salvation. Influenced by the Cambridge Platonists and the Great Tew Circle, Clarke deems moral virtue to be the heart of natural and revealed religion. Against Hobbes, who contended that the state of nature was a state of war, Clarke maintains that virtue is at the heart of the universe, and that the state of nature is 'a perfect expression of the nature and attributes of God.' Further, Clarke is at one with the Latitudinarians in making an appeal to Scripture alone on controverted points. He bolsters his case for the existence of God with *a posteriori* considerations drawn from Newton, and he understands miracles not as supernatural interruptions of the natural order, but as 'unusual and unexpected exhibitions of God's providence upon an order which was constantly maintained supernaturally.'

Clarke's project now was to apply his rational method to theology. Particularly in respect of the Trinity, his efforts attracted strong opposition. In *The Scripture Doctrine of the Trinity* (1712) he has recourse to patristic authors, and his indebtedness to these

Part Three: Theology

brings us to the crux of Pfizenmaier's case, and to his longest chapter. A careful examination of the relevant texts reveals Clarke to be not an Arian, not a Sabellian, not Orthodox, but a Eusebian. That is, he refutes the Arian idea that the Son was a creature, or work, and that there was 'a time when he was not.' He is not a homoian because he believes not simply that the Son is like the Father, but that he was 'like in all things' except ingenerateness. And he was not orthodox because he retains a certain subordination flowing from Origen, and denies that the Father and the Son are of the same substance (the *homoousian* position). He is a *homoiousian* in the line of Eusebius, affirming the pre-existence of the divine Son, who is of like substance with the Father. Pfizenmaier thus identifies the following relationship as between the early centuries and the eighteenth: neo-Arians / deists; *homoian* Arians / Socinians; *homoiousian* / Clarke; and *homoousian* / 'orthodox' majority. He regrets that both theologians of Clarke's period and their nineteenth-century successors reduced these options by conflating the Arian with the Semi-Arian (*homoiousian*) position.

Clarke also draws upon a wide range of contemporary sources, and in his fourth chapter Pfizenmaier finds himself especially indebted to Newton's view that both Arius and the *homoiousians* had introduced metaphysical considerations into the church's doctrinal teachings. Neither Newton nor Clarke could endorse the Arianism of their friend William Whiston. Pfizenmaier's tentative view—tentative because there is not the hard evidence which correspondence between Newton and Clarke might have supplied—oscillates between saying that the older Newton 'must have been' a key source of Clarke's trinitarianism, and saying that it is probable that he was such a source.

There follows a discussion of the literature of the eighteenth-century trinitarian controversy, which Pfizenmaier dates from Bull's *Defensio* of 1685. He discusses the views of Thomas Burnet, Waterland and others, finding that the 'centrepiece' of the trinitarian controversy is the debate between Clarke and Waterland—the subject of his penultimate chapter. Waterland understands that there are three doctrinal options only where the Trinity is concerned: the Catholic = Athanasian; the Sabellian = Socinian; and the Arian. To him the Son is either God or a creature. Clarke resists this strong disjunction, contending that while the Son is not the supreme God, he is God in all respects save for self-existence and the supremacy. Both appeal to the Bible in justification of their respective positions.

In a brief conclusion, Pfizenmaier summarizes his findings, and expresses the hope that future evaluations of Clarke will be guided by the evidence he has adduced to show that Clarke was in the line of Origen, Eusebius and the Cappodocians, and hence that he was 'within the broad scope of doctrinal orthodoxy.'

A number of comments may be offered on this robust work. First, Pfizenmaier writes, 'Clarke's position on the trinity developed in the midst of the shift from external to internal constructs of authority which took place in the late seventeenth century and early eighteenth centuries in England' (p. 13). As well as overlooking the fact of those timelags which are so prominent a feature of intellectual movements, this sentence is a little unsubtle; for if there was a turn from ecclesiastical authority to the authority of conscience and the right of private judgement, there was also, on the part of orthodox and heterodox divines alike, an appeal to the authority of Scripture. It is not an insignificant that the title words, *The Scripture-Doctrine of...* are reiterated time and again by liberal Anglicans and Dissenters alike. Moreover, in the nineteenth century many apologists appealed eclectically to Church, Bible, conscience, and experience.

Secondly, Pfizenmaier sometimes misleads by offering only partial summaries or incompletely qualified statements of a writer's position. Thus, for example, he tells us that Locke 'helped to complete the demolition of the Cartesian emphasis on innate ideas, and fostered the empirical method.' But Locke did more than this. He made a place for both sensation and reflection in the acquisition of knowledge, and in ethics he appealed, *inter alia*, to intuitive principles. Again, Pfizenmaier skates too swiftly over Locke's 'very significant' ideas on the Trinity, and over the question how far Locke was a trinitarian—matters on which much ink had been spilled before the original submission of this thesis, and between that date and the publication of this book. Yet again, Pfizenmaier refers to 'the Latitudinarian doctrine of toleration' (p. 72). Some readers might take this as implying (*pace* John Owen and countless others) that the Latitudinarians alone advocated toleration, or that they espoused a particular view of toleration.

Thirdly, while it is shown that Clarke is in the wake of Origen, for example, the contrasts between their respective intellectual environments is not brought out. To accommodate a Trinity within the Alexandrian philosophical framework which Origen inherited was, no doubt, a challenging task. But this was not Clarke's intellectual challenge. Why did he and others launch into the trinitarian debate when they did? Was it, perhaps, because of a desire to uphold the principle of the sufficiency of Scripture in the face of a doctrinal scholasticism which seemed to introduce, and to make badges of separation of, terms like 'Trinity,' 'substance' and the like which were unscriptural in the sense that they were not to be found in the Bible?

Fourthly, why, apart from a brief reference in a footnote (p. 208), do the Dissenters not figure more largely in respect of Clarke's intellectual context and the literature of the trinitarian controversy? There is no mention of Salters' Hall, or of John Taylor, or of any of the 'Arian' Presbyterians whose indebtedness to Clarke was so clear, and whose impact upon the ecclesiastical situation in England and Wales was so far-reaching. One might also ask how the Church of England managed to avoid most of the secessionist tendencies which afflicted the eighteenth-century Presbyterians greatly and the Congregationalists and Baptists to a lesser degree?

To offer the above observations is to indicate the stimulating nature of this book. Nor can the question be suppressed (though, given his objectives, Pfizenmaier was in no way bound to address it): How far does Clarke's trinitarian position stand up in the wake of modern biblical criticism, and in relation to the renewed emphasis upon the trinity in current theological discussion?

Some slips were noted, among them: the date of the Toleration Act is 1689 (p. 28); Woolston died in 1733, and his title is mangled (p. 36); read Emlyn for Emlin (p. 51); read McLachlan for McClachlan (p. 53); read Worcester for Gloucester (p. 54); read 1660 for 1160 (p. 231). Some works mentioned in the footnotes do not appear in the bibliography.

Indices of names, places and subjects, complete this sturdily-produced book.
Enlightenment and Dissent 18 (1999) 270–275.

Part Three: Theology

71

Fletcher of Madeley

Patrick Streiff. *Reluctant Saint? A Theological Biography of Fletcher of Madeley.*
London: Epworth Press, 2001. Pp. ix, 406.

For too long readers of English have been denied a full study of Fletcher of Madeley (1729–85). With this fluent translation of a book originally published in German in 1984, and now revised and updated, the omission is splendidly repaired. Patrick Streiff has tracked down a wide range of sources relevant to Fletcher's life and ministry, with the result that Fletcher comes alive as a preacher, pastor and, by eighteenth-century standards, an eirenic controversialist, who normally sought a middle way between opposing points of view. Fletcher is carefully placed in the intellectual context of his Swiss homeland and the influence upon him of 'reasonable [Reformed] orthodoxy' is demonstrated. Contrary to widely received opinion, he did not study philosophy or theology in Geneva but was an autodidact in those fields. Unable to assent to the doctrinal (predestinarian) formulae of the Swiss Church, and after a brief flirtation with the army, he came to England and became first a private tutor and then, for the rest of his life, Vicar of Madeley in Shropshire. He was the most significant second-generation Methodist of the Wesleyan sort. He maintained good relations with the Countess of Huntingdon and the Calvinistic Methodists, and served as president of the Countess's Trefeca College, until controversy over antinomianism and predestination in the late 1760s resulted in a breach which prompted his resignation in 1771. Thereafter Fletcher's contribution was mostly among the Wesleyans. He never swerved in his loyalty to the Church of England, and consistently regarded Methodism as a movement within that Church. Despite the Wesleys' repeated requests, he refused to leave Madeley with a view to succeeding John at leader of the Methodists. In the event the Wesleys outlived him.

Fletcher's ideas are competently expounded: the necessity of the new birth; the work of the Spirit in sanctification; the need for 'enthusiasm' to be tempered by reasonableness; the (somewhat ambiguous) doctrine of perfection; the trinitarian setting of the doctrine of grace; and creation understood in relation to the mediatorial work of Christ. The book's subtitle, 'A theological biography,' however, causes a little concern. In the first place, it is possible to detect in some present-day scholars of the Evangelical Revival an anxiety to show that the early leaders of that movement were (after all/despite everything) theologians; but this card can be overplayed. This is not to deny that Fletcher makes many perceptive theological points. Secondly, and more seriously, in a theological biography we should expect a fuller account of the intellectual environment than is here provided. For example, the reiterated explanation that 'Wesleyan Arminianism was not identical with the original seventeenth-century Arminianism' requires fuller elucidation; the dispute between Wesley and Whitefield over free grace needs more than a passing reference; the influence of Locke, which is here dealt with in a very compressed way, merits greater attention; the blanket references to deism lack discrimination; and when Streiff says, 'The differences between early Enlightenment, deism and scepticism must be kept in mind,' the puzzled may retort, 'but first we need a rounded account of the intellectual movements thus labelled.' Above all, in a theological biography we should expect to hear more of the voices of the 'opposition.' Fletcher's position on antinomianism and predestination, for example, needs to be set against that of the Baptists Gill and Brine; similarly with the Presbyterian John Taylor on original sin. Priestley's position on the person of Christ is briefly outlined, but none of his works are referred to or listed in the bibliography; Toplady on predestination is mentioned but not quoted. On the question of the American colonies Fletcher's Baptist opponent, Caleb Evans, is mentioned and his works listed, but to his Presbyterian target on the same issue, Richard Price, there is no reference at all. Finally, when Streiff declares that 'The doctrine of Christian perfection . . . was as central for the Wesleyan Methodists as it was disputed by the Calvinistic Methodists,' we ask, 'On what grounds did they dispute it? Let us hear them.' The overall impression is thus of a debate with one side only being permitted adequately to present its case, and this despite the fact that underlying many of the controverted points was a concern common to both sides to be true to Scripture. Dr. Streiff tells us that 'use has been made of the most recent material,' but a number of works have escaped his attention, among them the responses provoked by Kendall's 'valuable investigation' into English Calvinism, and Brantley's work on Locke, Wesley and the English Enlightenment.

The above adversely critical remarks notwithstanding, this is a most welcome work which deserves a wide readership. If its hero is Fletcher, its heroine is undoubtedly the patient Mary Bosanquet, whom Fletcher had thought of marrying in 1760 but actually got around to marrying in 1781—'Better late than never,' wrote Charles Wesley to Mary. When reading this biography the thought more than once occurred to this reviewer that in terms of practical outcomes there is not much to choose between saintly caution and ungodly vacillation. But almost certainly that is an unsanctified thought. Here is another: after a number of examples of Fletcher's pious self-examination the down-to-earth information that in his day 40 percent of English pig iron was produced in Shropshire comes as a blessed relief—or should this trophy of grace call it an uncovenanted mercy?

Modern Believing 43 (2002) 54–56.

Part Three: Theology

72

Baptist Theologians

Timothy George and David S. Dockery, eds. *Baptist Theologians*.
Nashville: Broadman Press, 1990. Pp. 704.

Here is a bumper bundle of Baptists! Timothy George, Dean of Beeson School of Divinity, Samford University, who has already written helpfully on major Reformers, here joins with David S. Dockery of The Southern Baptist Theological Seminary in editing this handsomely- produced and encouragingly-priced collection of studies of thirty-three significant Baptists.

The editors contribute a Preface; George follows with a chapter on 'The Renewal of Baptist Theology'; and Dockery closes the work with a survey of 'Baptist Theology and Theologians,' in which reference is made to many not included here. The remaining chapters and contributors are: John Bunyan (Harry L. Poe); Benjamin Keach (J. Barry Vaughn); John Gill (T. George); Isaac Backus (Stanley J. Grenz); Andrew Fuller (Phil Roberts); Richard Furman (Thomas J. Nettles); John L. Dagg (Mark E. Dever); James Madison Pendleton (Keith E. Eitel); Patrick Hues Mell (Paul A. Basden); J. R. Graves (Harold S. Smith); James Petigru Boyce (T. George); Charles Haddon Spurgeon (Lewis A. Drummond); Augustus Hopkins Strong (Kurt A. Richardson); Benajah Harvey Carroll (James Spivey); E. Y. Mullins (Fisher Humphreys); William Bell Riley (Timothy P. Weber); Walter Rauschenbusch (Stephen Brachlow); W. O. Carver (John N. Jonsson); H. Wheeler Robinson (Duane A. Garrett); Walter Thomas Conner (James Leo Garrett, Jr.); Herschel Hobbs (Mark Coppenger); W. A. Criswell (L. Russ Bush III); Eric Rust (Bob E. Patterson); George Eldon Ladd (Molly Marshall-Green); Frank Stagg (Robert Sloan); Carl F. H. Henry (R. Albert Mohler, Jr.); Dale Moody (Danny R. Stiver); George R. Beasley-Murray (R. Alan Culpepper); Bernard Ramm (Alan Day); Edward John Carnell (L. Joseph Rosas III); James Deotis Roberts (Gerald Thomas); Millard J. Erikson (D. S. Dockery); and Clark H. Pinnock (Robert V. Rakestraw).

The above selection at once prompts a number of remarks. First, it is clear that in this volume 'Baptist' both designates a specific Christian communion and a believer-Baptist position. That is to say, such believer-Baptist groups as Mennonites, Pentecostals, and others are not represented here. Indeed, the editors admit that the majority of the entries concern Southern Baptists of the United States (p. xi).

Secondly, there is an apologetic motive at work that has influenced the process of selection. The editors are concerned for their communion, which, according to George, is suffering from 'a crisis of identity rooted in a theological failure of nerve' (p. 13). Baptists are said to suffer from 'spiritual amnesia (we have forgotten who we are) and ecclesiastical myopia (whoever we are, we are glad that we are not like "them")' (p. 13). It soon becomes clear, however, that not any recovery of memory will suffice. George declares that 'throughout our history, Baptists have been explicitly orthodox in our continuity with the Trinitarian and Christological consensus of the early church' (p. 21); yet two pages earlier he has observed the 'There have . . . been several major doctrinal defections such as the Unitarian invasion of General Baptist ranks in eighteenth-century England' (p. 17). George would clearly have his readers recall their orthodox heritage. Accordingly, although, as the editors rightly state, there is variety in this volume—Calvinism, Arminianism, Landmarkism, fundamentalism, liberalism, and ecumenism, for example—one searches in vain for a Unitarian Baptist of the eighteenth-century and, for that matter, for a seventeenth-century Seventh Day Baptist or a nineteenth-century Gospel Standard Baptist. We thus have representativeness within limits; and these limits are geographical as well as theological, there being no subjects drawn from continental Europe, the 'third world,' Australasia, or South Africa. In a word, there is a certain theological and internal-Baptist denominational insularity here.

Thirdly, however, it is hoped that this is the first book of 'many others' (p. xi), and this raises section questions of a different kind. Having determined the meaning of 'Baptist,' what are we to make of 'theologians'? The editors recognize (pp. x–xi) a distinction between 'pastor theologians' and 'professional academic theologians.' Why not a volume for each class? We could then have removed Spurgeon, Criswell, and others from their present company and included them elsewhere with Christmas Evans, Alexander Maclaren, F. B. Meyer, H. E. Fosdick, J. Sidlow Baxter, *et al.* Space would thus have been made here for W. N. Clarke, Shailer Matthews and others, as well as for such earlier theologians as Brine, Wayland, and Hovey ('the foremost theologian of [his] day,' according to Dockery, [p. 688]). The inclusion of some who are primarily biblical scholars —Ladd, Stagg, Wheeler Robinson, Hobbs, and Beasley-Murray—is odd when so many theologians are omitted. Had the biblical scholars a volume to themselves, T. H. Robinson, Aubrey Johnson, Ronald Clements, and, above all, H. H. Rowley, the doyen of Baptist Old Testament scholars in his generation, could have been included. And ought not the fundamentalist Riley ('theologians were among his least favorite people in the world' [p. 351]) to be in a collection of Baptist leaders in which he would rub shoulders, however uncomfortably, with the likes of John Clifford, J. H. Shakespeare, and Ernest Payne? Indeed the last-named could equally well adorn a book of Baptist historians, along with Taylor, Crosby, Whitley, Latourette, and others.

Fourthly, there is a problem of selection even when attention is confined to 'professional academic theologians.' It is not a question of whether a scholar is a systematician, an historical theologian or an apologist—such variety is to be welcomed; it is a question of the requisite degree of recognition required in order to merit inclusion. If the criterion were 'internationally studied across the ecumenical spectrum,' few of the professional theologians here presented (as distinct from one or two of the biblical scholars) would meet the test, since, unlike the writings of Barth, Pannenberg, and Rahner, for example, the writings of a number of these scholars have not, to judge by citations, travelled far outside of their naturally sympathetic (that is, evangelical) audience. (This may, of course, be more an adverse judgement upon other possible audiences than upon the theologians themselves.) Given that the operative criterion is 'influential among Southern Baptists at least,' the inclusion of all is, no doubt, justified.

The above reflections are not prompted by the stock reviewer's complaint, 'I would have done it differently,' but by a strong conviction that the project in hand is so important that if further volumes are to appear efforts should be made to secure a wider representation of the past and present Baptist worlds, and more consistency of subject types (pastors, leaders, biblical scholars, historians).

All of this said, the overall quality of the essays gathered here is high, and the book is warmly to be welcomed. We have a biography, exposition, evaluation, bibliography, and portrait of thirty-three diverse subjects. All of the studies are informative, and all will repay close attention. The following are among thoughts that occurred *en passant*:

1. Poe might have mentioned other Puritans—Howe and Baxter, for example—who, like Bunyan, sought to emphasize Gospel truths shared by all believers and to shun sectarianism (p. 26).

2. Vaughn's suggestion that 'Keach's life [1640–1704] coincided almost exactly with the rise and decline of the Calvinistic (or Particular) Baptists' (p. 49) is odd in view of the fact that the Particular Baptists founded the first modern missionary society in 1792 and lived to unite with the General Baptists of the New Connexion in 1891. He further states that the *Savoy Declaration of Faith and Order* (1658) 'became the confessional document of the Independents (later known as Congregationalists' (p. 56). But, (a) some explanation of the use (or lack of it) of Savoy would have been helpful; and (b) 'Independent' and 'Congregational' were alternative terms from the 1640s onward.

3. In his able account of Gill, George fails to note that the issue at Salters' Hall in 1719 was subscription, not the Trinity as such; indeed, non-subscribers wrote a letter affirming their Trinitarian convictions.

4. Grenz ably shows Backus (1724–1806) as influenced by, and as modifying, Locke, but strangely designates the latter (d. 1704) a contemporary of the former (p. 111).

5. Roberts misleadingly describes the Sandemanians as 'a Scottish Baptist element' (p. 127). The Sandemanians predated the Scotch Baptists, the latter being formed after Alexander M'Lean and Robert Carmichael resigned over a case of church discipline from the Glasite (i.e., Sandemanian) church in Glasgow in 1763, and then espoused believer baptism.

6. The struggles over the Landmarkism of the mid-nineteenth century and the fundamentalism of the earlier twentieth century are well brought out by several writers, as are the ominous continuing influence of Graves (p. 243) and the efforts of Mullins and Hobbs in their respective generations to hold the Southern Baptists together.

7. Strong's attempt to undergird his theology with ethical monism is, philosophically, the most interesting section in the book.

8. The considerable problems associated with the idea that the Church is the continuation of the Incarnation are not hinted at by Jonsson in his account of Carver (p. 394).

9. Day appears to find Ramm reluctant to preach the Gospel for the salvation of the lost (p. 600). Such reluctance is not detectable, however, in Ramm's Paul King Jewett Lecture on *The Theology of Evangelism*, 1978, which does not appear in the bibliography of Ramm here provided.

10. Thomas does well to portray Deotis Roberts as by no means a 'one issue,' revolutionary black theologian. While believing that the black experience in the United States 'deserves theological analysis and interpretation' (p. 630), Roberts is also one of a disturbingly small number of philosophers of religion in American seminaries. We could wish that his work on Pascal, Whichcote, and others had been more fully expounded here.

There are a few slips and infelicities. The word (p. xi) is 'especially.' A quotation (p. 22) should be attributed to H. Richard Niebuhr. It is odd (p. 23) to find English Methodists included among 'dissenting groups.' What does Garrett mean (and why the 'somewhat') when he says of Wheeler Robinson that 'The corpus of his writings, although somewhat redundant, is enormous' (p. 402)? Not even Criswell can have been at Dallas for sixty years (p. 452) when he went there only in 1944. We read (p. 468) of a T. G. and R. G. Collingwood, and both are indexed, though we may suspect that the former never was. Lloyd-Jones is deprived of his 'M' in the index, while an unwanted 'n' is introduced into the name of Glenn Iglehart (p. 448 and index).

These studies are serious but not dry. From time to time the diligent reader is favoured with encouragements along the way. Thus George's description of the doctrine of the priesthood of all believers when individualistically abused as 'every tub sitting on its own bottom' (p. 16) is choice. It was amusing (in a chilling sort of way) to meet the anti-mission 'Hardshell' Baptists. Some may wish to borrow Conner's riposte to students who protest, 'But doesn't the Bible mean what it says?': 'No. It means what it means' (p. 425). One only of these saints' hobbies is mentioned—that of Criswell. He watches the stock market (p. 453). Since, according to J. R. Graves (p. 235), shaving is contrary to the law of God, we may perhaps infer that Carroll is the godliest man in the book, since his beard gives no sign of finishing at the bottom of his portrait (p. 309). Graves further declares, 'To be a full Baptist is the highest glory of man' (p. 230)—so now we know! The same luminary urges his readers to 'Have a real Baptist heart . . . a good round heart—not a flat, slobby, sobby one' (p. 230). By this criterion it is only from the bottom of a heart of the latter kind that your suitably chastened reviewer can thank the contributors to this most stimulating and informative book.

Calvin Theological Journal 27 (1992) 120–125.

Part Three: Theology

73

Charles Hodge

John W. Stewart and James H. Moorhead, eds. *Charles Hodge Revisited: A Critical Appraisal of his Life and Work*. Grand Rapids: Eerdmans, 2002. Pp. x + 375.

To begin at the end: in the concluding sentence of his 'Afterword' James H. Moorhead, writing of Hodge, declares that 'the time has come for serious historical investigation of a figure who has too often been either a bogey or an icon to later generations' (p. 334). This important volume amply demonstrates that the task is well in hand. Nor is the significance of this collection limited to the academic consideration that Hodge (1797–1878), teacher at Princeton Theological Seminary for over 50 years, merits adequate study (which he does). There are sizeable tracts of present-day evangelicalism which are suspicious of, or hostile to, the modern ecumenical movement, and deeply indebted in their theological stance to Charles Hodge and his Princeton successors. To understand them adequately we need to understand him, and this book will take us a long way in that direction.

In these papers Hodge is set in his theological, ecclesiastical and socio-political context. As might be expected, running themes include the influence upon Hodge of Scottish common sense realism and his commitment to biblical inerrancy and the *Westminster Confession* and *Catechisms*. But Hodge's broader interests are covered too. Richard J. Carwardine writes on Hodge's politics, encompassing his views on slavery, public education, Sabbatarianism and the Civil War, while Allen C. Guelzo majors on 'Hodge's antislavery movement,' carefully exposing the way in which biblical, ecclesiastical and moral considerations influenced Hodge's fluctuating stance on the issue. From Louise L. Stevenson we learn that, notwithstanding those Pauline verses which were inconvenient to one committed to an hierarchical view of relations between the sexes, Hodge was a deeply affectionate and greatly loved family man (cf. Noll's paper, n. 85).

Returning to the beginning of the book we find co-editor John W Stewart's paper, 'Introducing Charles Hodge to Postmoderns.' At certain points—for example, concerning Old School/New School Presbyterianism and Thornwell's 'passivity doctrine of the Church—this introduction fails to introduce. There are some slips too. On p. 5 Philip Schaff is described as a German—an error corrected by the next contributor (p. 42); and an author noted as John Hicks on p. 12 is correctly rebaptized Peter in Stewart's extensive bibliography with which the volume closes (sadly, there is no index). Blemishes apart, Stewart helpfully expounds Scottish common sense realism; he notes Hodge's objective of integrating all reasoned enquiry with all human behaviours and piety; he introduces us to Hodge's understanding and use of the Bible, and to his views on the Church and society.

PHILOSOPHY, THEOLOGY AND HISTORY

James Turner writes well on 'Charles Hodge and the intellectual weather of the nineteenth century,' arguing that Hodge's individualism, coupled with his atemporal epistemology inherited from Scotland, led eventually to his worldview's being 'swept under by the tide of historicism' (p. 60). Bruce Kuklick, pointing out that American intellectual life was fertilized by parish ministers and amateurs like Emerson, divinity-school theologians, and holders of chairs of mental or moral or intellectual philosophy, places Hodge in the middle group, and wonders why, unlike Edwards, he is not studied by philosophers today. He attributes this to the fact that Hodge's faculty psychology is now dated, whereas the voluntarist psychology espoused by William James and John Dewey had more in common with that of Edwards; while Hodge's biblicism, which determined his approach to science and entailed the subordination of his own experience and knowledge of his culture, became for him 'the sole measure of what the men in the new universities could know' (p. 75). They, of course, disagreed. Ronald L. Numbers pursues the scientific question further in his paper, 'Charles Hodge and the beauties and deformities of science.' He makes it clear how long-standing Hodge's interest in science was; it was by no means a passing concern prompted by Darwin's theory of natural selection.

E. Brooks Holifield helpfully places Hodge in the American theological succession, and clearly relates him to his theological contemporaries. He notes the wide range of doctrinal issues which engaged Hodge's attention; he brings out the importance to Hodge of the federal theology of the seventeenth century, and emphasizes Hodge's commitment to the defence of theology's cognitive content. B. A. Gerrish writes elegantly on 'Charles Hodge and the Europeans.' He is especially instructive on Hodge's response to Schleiermacher, which was inadequate, thinks Gerrish, because Hodge failed sufficiently to distinguish Schleiermacher's position from Hegelianism.

In a most illuminating essay Mark A. Noll discusses 'Charles Hodge as an expositor of the spiritual life.' He subtly analyses the relationship between Hodge's commitment to the objective ground of truth in the Bible and his equally real subjective experience of Jesus Christ. Although he strongly believed in the unity of doctrine and life, Hodge failed fully to integrate them. David H. Kelsey considers 'Charles Hodge as interpreter of Scripture.' Hodge defends the view that the Bible was inspired by the Spirit, and that it comes home to us by the same Spirit. However, it does not follow from this, Kelsey argues, that Hodge was necessarily committed to pre-critical biblical interpretation.

I set out from James Moorhead's closing sentence; I end with his opening one: 'The legacy of Charles Hodge has been inescapably tied to subsequent Presbyterian controversies' (p. 327). While it is undeniable that the line from Hodge through his son, A. A. Hodge, to Warfield and Machen is clear for all to see, and that a good deal of Presbyterian infighting occurred, Moorhead's assertion seems unduly parochial, and suggests a dimension missing from this collection as a whole. The question arises, how far did Hodge's influence extend? To what extent was his student, J. P. Boyce, able to transplant his mentor's theological approach in the Baptist circles in which he moved? How strong was Hodge's influence in Scotland—especially within the Free Church there? (The passing references to William Cunningham on pp. 7 and 272 do not pursue the link.) How successful was the doughty Irishman, Robert Watts, surely one of Hodge's most devoted students, in propagating his teacher's ideas in his homeland? One could go on, at a further remove, to ask how far such a French theologian as Auguste Lecerf was indebted to Hodge.

For too long Hodge has been among those many divines who from within their gilt frames glower down upon diners in theological institutions. He now steps out of the frame. May others, similarly portrayed and equally neglected, follow.

Modern Believing 44 (2003) 74–76.

74

John Williamson Nevin

Richard E. Wentz. *John Williamson Nevin, American Theologian.*
Oxford: OUP, 1997. Pp. viii + 169.

Richard E. Wentz of Arizona State University, raised in the tradition of which he writes, here adds to the growing body of literature on the Mercersburg movement. Deriving its name from the Pennsylvania location of the German Reformed Seminary, and its intellectual impetus from F. A. Rauch, J. W. Nevin and Philip Schaff, this tradition represents a plea on behalf of the catholicity of the church conceived as an organism, and for a liturgy which draws upon the heritage of the ages and gives due place to the sacraments; and this in face of sectarian attitudes and revivalistic methods current in American in the nineteenth century. The legacy of Mercersburg is a living one, as is evident from the activities of the Mercersburg Society which was constituted in 1983.

The Mercersburg tradition has generally been regarded as rooted in the intellectual soil of the Romantic movement, of which Hegelian and post-Hegelian immanentism is a conspicuous aspect. Under this influence many theologians came to exalt the incarnation of Christ sometimes (as Bomberger and others thought of Nevin, and as James Denney, for example, thought of the idealists of his day) at the expense of the Cross.

Professor Wentz does not deny the importance of Nevin's intellectual inheritance, but clearly feels that some have paid almost exclusive attention to it (though he overlooks a good deal of post-1986 Nevin scholarship, which is unfortunate). He wishes to redress the balance by presenting Nevin as a distinctively American theologian who reacted against the socio-religious trends of his day which, he believed, were fostering the disintegration not only of the churches, but of American culture as a whole. Nevin is thus seen as an 'outsider' to the mainstream of American religious life. To Nevin the culprits are Puritanism, revivalism, individualism and voluntaryism.

An outline of Nevin's life and work is followed by discussions of the nature of systematic theology, the public character of theology, a radical and realized catholicity, the theology of history, nationalism and the American Republic, missions, and liturgy and the American cultus.

Wentz does well to elevate the socio-religious stimulus and challenge to Nevin's received idealism, and some of his assertions are in the best sense provocative, for example: 'The significance of Christianity may well be found in its philosophy of history, not in a salvationism that nourishes believers.' He capably indicates the novelty of Nevin's stance: he opposed American naturalism and rationalism which failed to understand the true nature of the Church, and he was at odds with his theological compatriots in insisting that theology is not a matter of thinking about faith, but of thinking by means of it. It is good to be reminded of Nevin's view of the *Catechism*, which is not without significance as we seek to form Christians for a new millennium: 'The *Catechism* is more than mere doctrine. It is doctrine apprehended and represented continually in the form of life.'

Perhaps as a concession to fashion Professor Wentz declares that his work 'is not an intellectual biography in the modernist sense of that genre but rather a kind of postmodern portrait of Nevin's ideas.' Any proposition which begs three questions tends to obscure more than it reveals. More seriously, Wentz fails to give Nevin's theological opponents a fair hearing: for example, the views of Bomberger are communicated all too briefly, and this *via* a secondary source which mangles them. Again, when Wentz, expounding Nevin's view of the mystical union with Christ, says 'Although he would not have understood it so, there is a sense in which [Nevin's theology, here deemed sophisticated] offers to dialogue with a Buddhism that insists on the necessity of transcending the experience of ordinary, particular selfhood,' there are no balancing words from those who feared for the scandal of particularity in Nevin's hands. Nevin is let off the hook regarding his view of the Church as the extension of the incarnation, and his claim that 'our nature as a whole was lifted from its fallen state, and brought into union with God' demands closer analysis than it here receives.

But there are many good things in this stimulating book, and for reminding us of the Mercersberg witness concerning the importance of the heritage of faith, the catholicity of the Church, and the peril of individualism in religious life, Professor Wentz is warmly to be congratulated.

Journal of the United Reformed Church History Society 6 (1999) 303–5.

Part Three: Theology

75

Mercersburg Theology and American Religion

Linden J. DeBie. *Speculative Theology and Common-Sense Religion: Mercersburg and the Conservative Roots of American Religion*. Eugene, OR: Pickwick Publications, 2008. Pp. xiii + 116.

Dr. Linden DeBie is among the most thoughtful expositors of Mercersburg theology, which originated in the Pennsylvanian village of that name, where Frederick Rauch, John Williamson Nevin and Philip Schaff were seminary professors of the German Reformed Church. We are here offered a lucid, concise, account of the way in which proponents of this theology, indebted as they were to Kant's view that the mind initiates knowing, to Hegelian idealism, and especially to Schelling's efforts in overcoming Kant's phenomena-noumena dualism by emphasizing the organic connectedness of all life; and in general sympathy with those German theologians who mediated between the positions of Schleiermacher and Hegel, clashed with the 'sitting tenant' philosophy of common sense realism which was so widely espoused by nineteenth-century American Protestants—above all by professors at Princeton Theological Seminary, whose leading campaigner was Charles Hodge. The generality of Protestant theologians upheld the body-mind dualism originally propagated by Descartes, but filtered, in the wake of Lockean empiricism by the Scottish realists, Thomas Reid and Dugald Stewart, in reply to the perceived scepticism of Hume. This yielded the nature-spirit dichotomy and a reliance on intuition, or, in more theological contexts, on the Holy Spirit: 'Time and again, in evangelical doctrine after doctrine, the world of heaven and earth were forced apart and held distinct, except through the exclusive intervention of the Spirit' (p. 22).

Over against this the Mercersburg theologians advocated the organic union of will and reason in the mind and, for their pains, they were accused by Hodge of the madness of uniting spirit and flesh. A further charge against them was that their understanding of catholicity, their interest in patristics, and their emphasis upon the sacraments, indicated that they were unduly enamoured of Rome. If such mediating theologians as Dorner, Rothe and Neander were the primary influences upon the philosophical and theological thinking of the Mercersburg theologians, the German 'High Church' neo-pietists were the inspiration of their ecclesiological, liturgical and sacramental standpoints. Some labelled them 'Puseyites,' others (to whom a few defections from the Reformed Church were grist to the mill) regarded them as crypto-Roman Catholics. Nevin, never one to pull his punches, responded to the charge as, for example, when he wrote of the Lord's Supper, 'There is a palpable contradiction in making Christ identical with matter or symbol. This is heathenism.'[1] Hodge repudiated the Mercersburg view of the Church as an organism, and of doctrine as subject to development, on the ground that the Bible's truth is unchanging, and the true Church is a spiritual union of those, known to God, who are its members. Yet another source of tension concerned the Calvinist/continental view of Church-state relations, according to which the state was expected to support the Church, over against American voluntaryism.

Underlying the intellectual strife was the Mercersburg contention that whereas the Calvinistic realists insisted upon maintaining the dualism of the worlds of sense and spirit, they were right to hold them together in accordance with the axiom that 'nature exists only for mind' (p. 66). Their opponents, they were convinced, 'stunted the growth of the kingdom of God by making its appearance in the natural world mechanical and artificial' (p. 95), as when appeal was made to external 'evidences.' In the wake of Rauch, the Mercersburg theologians adhered to the orthodox view concerning the noetic effects of sin. While this was, on the one hand, an implicit concession to dualism, it was also, on the other hand, the route by which they came to appeal, over against Hodge's biblicism, to the person of Christ as the interpreter of Scripture. Furthermore, as if to rebut Hodge's claim that they peddled esoteric, pantheizing nonsense, Nevin's emphasis upon the believer's union with Christ by the Spirit 'allowed full participation in Christ's divinity (and humanity) [at which point Schaff demurred] with no hint of a pantheistic identification of humanity with God' (p. 98). The tussle between Hodge and Mercersburg ended inconclusively because it was a classic case of weighty intellects passing one another on different trajectories; but Dr. DeBie hints that Nevin won the fight on (scholarly) points.

The author carefully unravels a tangled web of influences and arguments, and the above summary merely scratches the surface of this tightly-packed book, which prompts a number of discussion points. First, like many others Dr. DeBie labels Locke an empiricist, but this does not tell the whole story. Locke held that knowledge is gained by sensation and reflection,[2] and in ethics he was on the rationalist side. Again, the author bypasses the question how far Nevin was correct in likening Locke to the medieval nominalists.[3] Secondly, when the author declares that 'America provided the first testing ground of voluntary religion' (pp. 7–8), he seems to sweep the continental Anabaptists and the English and Welsh Separatists out of history. Thirdly, I am puzzled by some oscillations in his remarks on Schleiermacher. For Schleiermacher, we are informed, 'the beginning of the process of discovering God . . . is fundamentally emotion, or emotion's determinative force, will' (p. 41). By contrast, 'a noncognitive approach was unsatisfactory to' Hegel (ibid.). No doubt; but is the author endorsing Hegel's judgement or not? He ought not to, because he has just said that Schleiermacher's 'feeling' 'recognizes its utter dependence

---

1. J. W. Nevin in William H. Erb, ed., *Dr. Nevin's Theology. Based on Manuscript Classroom Lectures*, Reading, PA: I. M. Beaver, 1913, 394.

2. J. Locke, *An Essay Concerning Human Understanding*, ed. Peter H. Nidditch, Oxford: Clarendon Press, 1975, II.i.4.

3. See Nevin's *History of Philosophy Lectures*, transcribed by George B. Russell, [1850], Archives of the United Church of Christ and the Evangelical and Reformed History Society, Lancaster, PA, AMsS, 11–12, 78.

on another as the ground of its existence'—a cognitive operation indeed; but then he cites, with apparent approval, an author who claims that Schleiermacher and others were 'opting for an intuitive grasp, an emotional response, a worship of they knew not what' (p. 41, n.). This is a travesty of Schleiermacher's position. Fourthly, in connection with the Mercersburg interest in, and distinction from, the Oxford Movement, Dr. DeBie explains that the latter 'sought to restore the high-church ideals of the 1600s' (p. 46). I fear that this assertion obscures more than it reveals.[4] Fifthly, Dr. DeBie makes passing reference to the influence upon Nevin of John Owen, other unnamed Puritans, and Coleridge (p. 58). I should have welcomed a fuller statement at this point, not least because of Nevin's remark that John Howe's 'deep Platonizing thoughts took hold of my mind with great force.'[5] How far, one wonders, did these English authors temper Nevin's approach to Hegel? Finally, it is interesting to observe how similar some of Hodge's views on the corruptions of the Roman Church were to those earlier expressed the Unitarian, Joseph Priestley—a bedfellow whose company, one may with some confidence surmise, Hodge would not have relished.[6]

Dr. DeBie concludes that while the Mercersburg movement is now extinct its legacy is impressive. For example, it lives on in some of the heirs of the German Reformed tradition who are now within the United Church of Christ. My own view is that Mercersburg theology raises philosophical, theological and ecumenical questions of considerable importance, many of which await final, or deserve fresh, answers. Dr. DeBie has done well to bring these questions to the fore, and to set them within their multi-faceted intellectual context. I hope that his book will receive the wide and thoughtful attention that it deserves.

The New Mercersburg Review 40 (2009) 52–56.

---

4. See review no.49 above.

5. J. W. Nevin, *My Own Life: The Early Years*, Lancaster, PA: Historical Society of the Reformed Church, 1964, 122.

6. See J. Priestley, *An History of the Corruptions of Christianity*, in J. T. Rutt, ed., *The Theological and Miscellaneous Works of Joseph Priestley*, Bristol: Thoemmes Press, 1999, vol. 5.

Mercersburg Theology and Reformed Catholicity

W. Bradford Littlejohn. *The Mercersburg Theology and the Quest for Reformed Catholicity*. Eugene, OR: Pickwick Publications, 2009. Pp. xvii + 195.

Let it be said at the outset that this well-produced book is a credit to both author and publisher. It deserves to be widely read in theological, historical, and ecumenical circles. It is fluently written, the style oscillating between the elegant and the homely—as when 'Hodge offers his two cents.' Readers of the Mercersburg type will be encouraged, others will be challenged, some (especially historians of philosophy) may wish for more at certain points, and, no doubt, a few will be infuriated; for we are dealing here with nineteenth-century theological-*cum*-ecclesiastical fires the embers of which are still warm and, in some places, are flickering into renewed life, such (to mix metaphors) are the sensitivities of Reformed doctrinal antennae. Littlejohn's objective is by no means antiquarian. On the contrary, his diagnosis is that the several varieties of current American Protestantism have so departed from a true understanding of the Church as to have fallen into fractious sectarianism. Nevin, he declares, foresaw this: he 'knew that the reigning Reformed scholasticism did not possess the theological resources to cope with the swelling tide of subjectivism and arid rationalism, the twin daughters of the Enlightenment which threatened to overwhelm American Christianity" (pp. 1–2). (I pause to observe [a] that there was more than one Enlightenment; and [b] that when Enlightenment thinkers opposed on moral grounds certain ways—notably Reformed scholastic ways—of expounding Christian doctrines, and when they encouraged people to question untoward authoritarianisms whether Biblicist or ecclesiastical, they did well.[7] However it may have been with Nevin, I should not like to think that Littlejohn himself is of the tribe of wanton Enlightenment-bashers). In Mercersburg theology the author finds the remedy for American Protestantism's disarray. More than that: in a fresh departure in Mercersburg studies, he investigates the degree of compatibility between his favoured theology and that of the Anglo-Catholics in England, the Eastern Orthodox traditions and the *nouvelle théologie* of Henri de Lubac and others in the Roman Catholic Church.

Littlejohn first adjusts himself to the positions of D. Hart, R. Wentz and J. Nichols, all of whom have toiled in the Mercersburg field. Not completely satisfied by any of them, he awards the highest grade to the last. He next introduces us to Nevin and Schaff, and also to Charles Hodge of Princeton, whose role in this tale is that of supreme opponent

---

7. See Alan P. F. Sell, *Enlightenment, Ecumenism, Evangel: Theological Themes and Thinkers 1550–2000*, Milton Keynes: Paternoster, 2005, ch. 3.

of Mercersburg. There follows a sketch of the intellectual environment in which the three worked. This takes the form of a breathless scamper through the history of philosophy from Descartes (D- on account of his dualism) to Hegel (A+ for his healing of the Cartesian-*cum*-Kantian breach). On the way we meet Thomas Reid and the Scottish common sense realism, so important for the understanding of nineteenth-century American Presbyterian thought— and hence of Hodge's thought. It is unfortunate that partly perhaps because of compression, partly because at this point he summarizes secondary sources, Littlejohn is less than fully clear on the matter. In the first place the term 'common sense' requires careful elucidation: there is a spectrum of common sense approaches with Oswald and Beattie at one end and Ferrier at the other. Secondly, the judgement that 'Of crucial importance for theology was Common Sense Realism's thoroughly dualistic outlook' (p. 21) needs to be set against Reid's objective of bringing self-consciousness and sense perception together. In the course of doing this he argued that Hume's sensation was an abstraction that could not be dissociated from an experiencing self. This in turn led Andrew Seth to say that 'by maintaining a theory of Immediate Perception, Scottish philosophy destroys the foreignness of matter to mind, and thus implicitly removes the only foundation of a real dualism.'[8] Littlejohn doffs his cap to Schleiermacher, though it is not made clear that in the eighteenth century 'feeling' was understood to concern the whole person and hence had cognitive import, was not a matter of emotion only, and was certainly far removed from present-day feel-good cosy glows.

With a discussion of Hodge *versus* Schaff on the latter's work, *The Principle of Protestantism*, we approach the heart of this book—an account of the tussle between Hodge and Nevin over *The Mystical Presence*. The root of the dispute was Nevin's incarnationalism, which Hodge construed as post-Hegelian pantheizing immanentism. At this point Littlejohn nails his colours to the mast. Hodge's judgement, he declares, is 'skewed and off base,' and is revelatory 'more of Hodge's own presuppositions than Nevin's' (p. 63). For the most part Littlejohn's account of the opposing arguments is judicious and fair, though, if I may emulate the author's style, on occasion Hodge emerges as more of a noodle than Nevin.

As befits one who endorses a theology deemed to have significant ecumenical potential, Littlejohn offers three exotic chapters: the first on. English Anglo-Catholicism ('The dons across the pond'!); the second on Mercersburg and Eastern Orthodoxy, the third on the *nouvelle théologie* of de Lubac as it bears upon the definition of catholicity. I shall refer to these shortly. Meanwhile I note Littlejohn's concluding aspirations. He hopes that 'By exposing the presuppositions of Hodge's system of doctrine, Mercersburg may show many how their "Reformed" doctrine is more a product of the Enlightenment than the Bible or the Reformation' (p. 170); and that Mercersburg theology will be a 'welcome mat' to Anglo-Catholics, the Orthodox, and Roman Catholics influenced by de Lubac. Time will tell.

Before proceeding further I note a few points of detail. Littlejohn writes that Hart 'tends to emphasize Nevin's critique of Protestantism as a critique aimed at recent low-

---

8. A. Seth, *Scottish Philosophy: A Comparison of Scottish and German Answers to Hume*, Edinburgh: Blackwood, 1890, 76–77.

church innovations, rather than a questioning of Protestantism as such (p. 4). But Nevin was more than a little concerned about what he regarded as 'low church' liturgical tendencies within the German Reformed Church, especially as these were represented by J. H. A. Bomberger. Littlejohn somewhat surprisingly passes over this issue, its relevance to the Lord's Supper and the mystical presence notwithstanding. Secondly, he refers (p. 18) to 'the liberal United Churches of Christ.' The plural is a slip, and the adjective is not universally applicable to the members of that denomination. Thirdly, Nevin referred disparagingly to 'The fond notion which some have of a republican or democratic order in Christianity' which relies upon 'the popular vote' (p. 113). It cannot be denied that some in the tradition of those whom Nevin pejoratively branded 'Puritan,' as well as some Presbyterians, have thought of their church order as being democratic—and, sadly, the newly-published *Cambridge Dictionary of Christianity* defines the Congregational order as democratic. But Congregationalism is far removed from democracy, if by 'democracy' we mean 'one person, one vote and government by the majority.' It is not the will of the members that is sought, but the mind of Christ the sole Lord of the Church; and the quest is for, unanimity in Christ, not human majorities.

This is a most stimulating book, and part of its stimulus results from an enthusiasm for Mercersburg which sometimes prevents Littlejohn from guarding his flank. But it is also a modest book in that the author understands that there is more work to be done (p. 172). I hope that he will undertake some of this work, and that in doing so he will derive benefit from K. Penzel on Schaff, J. W. Stewart and others on Hodge, Peter B. Nockles on Anglo-Catholicism, and from a number of those who have contributed articles to this journal. Among the last is Lee Barrett who has admirably demonstrated the illumination to be derived from the bringing together of the theologies of Mercersburg, Berlin, and Basel.[9]

In what follows I shall propose seven discussion points by way of showing how some British Reformed theologians who are not in the line of Hodge or Nevin, might be drawn into the debate. I launch forth from points raised by Littlejohn without in any way implying that in this book he should have extended the discussion in the ways I am suggesting.

1. *Union with Christ*. Littlejohn quotes Nevin as saying that by the 'inward living union between believers and Christ' believers are 'incorporated into his very nature, and made to subsist with him by the power of a common life' (p. 42). This union, he continues, is not spiritual only, but is a union with Christ's manhood (p. 67). Again, Nevin declares that 'The object of the incarnation was to couple the human nature in real union with the Logos, as a permanent source of life' (p. 103); and that 'Humanity, as a single universal fact, is redeemed by Christ, truly and really' (p. 60). It is not difficult to see in such remarks the impetus towards Littlejohn's discussion of *theosis* as adumbrated in Orthodox thought. There does seem, however, to be a puzzling oscillation between speaking of believers as united with Christ and the whole of humanity as being so united. There is also the question of the nature of the union. In a paper on 'Regeneration' Bomberger declares

9. Lee C. Barrett III, 'The Metamorphoses of the Mercersburg Heritage: Mercersburg meets Berlin and Basel,' *The New Mercersburg Review*, 42 (2010), 5–44.

that 'Man is not deified by regeneration. In it men become Christians, but are not made Christs.'[10] With many others on his side the Welsh Presbyterian, Huw Parri Owen, insisted that 'The ontological distinction between the Creator and all creatures is absolute and permanent';[11] and elsewhere he made the logical point: 'It is an obvious self-contradiction to affirm that one experiences an ontologically complete identification with, or absorption into, the Supreme; for one could not have any consciousness of any kind without a distinct, enduring, subject—without *oneself*.'[12] While those who query divinization/ *theosis* are ill advised polemically to brandish 'pantheism' and 'divinization' as pejorative terms, they are entitled to greater clarity on the matter than is sometimes provided, and they need to be shown how the points made by Bomberger and Owen are mistaken, or, if they are not, how they may be circumvented by those who stand for *theosis*.[13]

2. *Word and Sacraments*. A related question concerns the way in which the mystical union of the believer with Christ is inaugurated. In one place (p. 100) it appears that Nevin makes baptism the agent of the union; in another (p. 48) Littlejohn finds him in the line of the 'old Reformed view' that 'the sacrament [the Lord's Supper] accomplishes a real union with the person of Christ.' We are thus confronted by the broader question, How is salvation mediated to us? In this connection the relation of the Word and sacrament is crucial, and it may be suggested that Nevin's sacramentalism discourages him from giving due place to the preaching of the Word. Thus Nevin argues that 'Christ's presence in the Supper was "*specific* in nature, and *different* from all that has place in the common exercises of worship"' (p. 47). Littlejohn expounds the point thus: the Supper 'offers a profound grace and participation in Christ that cannot be found elsewhere in the Christian life' (p. 47), and this he regards as the historic Reformed view which has come to be 'flatly denied' by those who hold that 'the ordinances become merely different instruments for accessing the same grace' (p. 47). Is this the historic Reformed view? Calvin may advise us: 'the sacraments have the same office as the Word of God: to offer and set forth Christ to us, and in him the treasures of heavenly grace.'[14] Indeed, 'the right administration of the Sacrament cannot stand apart from the Word.'[15] It sounds to me as if Calvin would have us understand that the sacraments witness to the same gracious saving activity that is proclaimed in the Word, and that they cannot justifiably be sundered from the Word. It does not seem that Calvin believes that either sacrament as such or in isolation effects the union of the believer with Christ.

---

10. J. H. A. Bomberger, 'Regeneration,' in *Proceedings of the Second Council of the World Presbyterian Alliance* (1880) p. 552.

11. H. P. Owen, *Christian Theism: A Study in its Basic Principles*, Edinburgh: T. & T. Clark, 1984, p. 102.

12. H. P. Owen, *The Christian Knowledge of God*, London: The Athlone Press, 1969, p. 189. For Owen see Alan P. F. Sell, *Convinced, Concise and Christian: The Thought of Huw Parri Owen*, Eugene, OR: Pickwick Publications, 2012.

13. See further Alan P. F. Sell, *Confessing and Commending the Faith: Historic Witness and Apologetic Method*, Cardiff: University of Wales Press, 2002, Eugene, OR: Wipf and Stock, pp. 70–79.

14. J. Calvin, *Institutes*, trans. Ford Lewis Battles, ed. John T. McNeil, Philadelphia: Westminster Press, 1961, IV.xiv.17.

15. J. Calvin, *Institutes*, IV.xvii.39.

3. *The heart of the Gospel*. Littlejohn fairly sums matters up by saying that the Mercersburg theologians 'made as their starting point the Incarnation, in which the infinite became finite, the natural became supernatural, Spirit took on matter, the deathless died and the mortal became immortal' (p. 173). Leaving on one side the question of the analysis of such claims, the nagging feeling persists that Mercersburg theologians are inclined to play down the Cross. Of course the incarnation is temporally and logically prior to the Cross—Christ can do what he does only because he is who he is; but in terms of Good News and the inauguration of the Church the Cross is of central importance: 'The doctrine of the Incarnation,' wrote P. T. Forsyth, 'did not create the Church; it grew up (very quickly) in the Church out of the doctrine of the cross which did create it—in so far as that can be said of any doctrine, and not rather of the act and power which the doctrine tries to state.'[16] For this reason, 'Our approach to Christology is through the office of Christ as Saviour. We only grasp the real divinity of His person by the value for us of His Cross.'[17]

4. *The nature of the Church*. Littlejohn quotes Schaff's opinion that the Church is 'the kingdom of Christ on earth,' and that it is 'the continuation of the life and work of Christ upon earth' (p. 78). The former claim requires to be considered in relation to the widespread scholarly opinion that while the Church is called to witness to God's kingly rule it is not co-terminus with the kingdom. The latter claim requires to be set against P. T. Forsyth's terse judgement: 'It is it regenerated human nature in which Christ dwells. But that cannot be a prolongation of His Incarnation, wherein there was no regeneration.'[18]

5. *The matter of the Church*. Littlejohn shows that at the heart of the running battle between the Mercersburg theologians and Hodge is the former's 'recovery of the centrality of the visible Church' over against 'Princeton's rigorous dichotomy between the true invisible Church and the dubious visible Church' (p. 10). Further, 'Nevin insists that we do not allow [the Church] to degenerate into an ideal abstraction; the Church is the corporate body of believers, and is as visible and real as Christ himself when He walked on earth' (p. 68, cf. p. 167). I suggest that here we have the heart of Congregational catholic ecclesiology: the saints gathered into the Church catholic in the only way possible if the Church is to be visibly embodied on earth—that is, into one of its local expressions. There are not many churches, but one Church in many places; otherwise, as Calvin saw, Christ would be divided, which cannot be.[19] The implication is that on the ground of the Son's saving work the Father, by the Holy Spirit (normally through the preaching of the Word), calls and gathers the saints into a visible company, with the result that while they remain in the world they are not of it: their true citizenship is in heaven. This would appear to be so far compatible with Littlejohn's account of Nevin's 'sharp distinction between the Church, the locus of divine life, and the world, the object that must be transformed by that

---

16. P. T. Forsyth, *The Cruciality of the Cross*, London: Independent Press, 1957, p. 50 n.

17. P. T. Forsyth, *The Church and the Sacraments*, London: Independent Press, 1953, p. 33.

18. P. T. Forsyth, *The Church and the Sacraments*, p. 82. I have elsewhere observed that 'the Mercersburg theologians and Forsyth are nowhere farther apart than here.' See Alan P. F. Sell, *Testimony and Tradition: Studies in Reformed and Dissenting Thought*, Aldershot: Ashgate, 2005, p. 195.

19. J. Calvin, *Institutes*, IV.i.2.

life' (p. 66). But later he reports Nevin's view as being that 'In the Church, as "catholic," the whole of mankind and all of his endeavors are raised up from their fallen state, beyond even the created state, into a new age that brings all to completion' (p. 169)—which is puzzling since the visibility of the Church has just been re-emphasized, yet we now seem have in view more than the saints. In passing I note the Mercersburg (and Littlejohn's) dislike of the idea of the Church as comprising 'voluntary gatherings of individual saints' (p. 169). Certainly the Church is a body, not a collection of isolated atoms; but the word 'voluntary' should hold no fears. When the Separatist, Robert Browne, declared that 'The Lord's people is of the willing sort,'[20] he was not thinking of voluntary membership of darts clubs and suchlike organizations; he was expressing positively what his fellow-Separatist, Henry Barrow, declared with heavy irony of the Act of Uniformity of 1559: 'All this people . . . were in one daye, with the blast of Queen Elizabeth's trumpet, of ignorant papists and grosse idolaters, made faithfull Christianes and true professors.'[21]

6. *Varieties of catholicity*. Littlejohn explains that in Schaff's opinion, 'The Catholic Church, though operating within an Augustinian tradition, had not adequately appreciated the corrupting powers of sin, that man "is unable to produce from himself anything that is good"' (p. 30). Hence the importance of the doctrine of justification, which directs us to God's grace alone for salvation and spiritual growth. Interestingly, the Mercersburg theologians do not seem to be equally troubled by another side of Augustine's thought, namely, a sacramentarianism which, when faced with the necessity of dealing with sins committed after baptism deemed regenerating, concluded that priests were, by ordination, endowed with *potestas* and were thus able to absolve sinners. (I put this crudely for the sake of brevity). From this has flowed the ecclesiastical sectarianism that requires communion with the Bishop of Rome for ministries to be fully recognized and sacraments to be 'valid' or 'regular.' We thus have the separation at the table of the Lord of those who by grace alone God by the Spirit has already made one in Christ and engrafted into the one Church catholic. It is tragic. It is an affront to the work of the triune God. It elevates polity above the Gospel, and it denies the fact that those stand in the succession of the apostles who proclaim the apostles' doctrine. It has always seemed odd to me that Nevin, with his ability to discern sects, did not take the full measure of one to two rather large ones. Much of this applies also to the Anglo-Catholics. In connection with them, Littlejohn explains Nevin's view that 'the visible Church flows out of the authorization of its ministers; rather than its ministers being authorized by the Church which is first instituted generally' (p. 112)—in other words the ministers are above the Church because they inherit the apostles' commission. But according to the Presbyterian scholar, T. W. Manson, there was no 'handing on' of authority from the apostles to their successors such as would justify what Robert Mackintosh, that self-styled 'refugee' from the Hodge-like Presbyterianism of the Free Church of Scotland to Congregationalism, bluntly called

---

20. R. Browne, *A Treatise of Reformation without Tarrying for Anie*, in Leland H. Carlson and Albert Peel, eds., *The Writings of Robert Harrison and Robert Browne*, London: Allen and Unwin, 1953, 162.

21. H. Barrow, *The Writings of Henry Barrow*, ed. Leland H. Carlson, London: Allen & Unwin, 1962, p. 283.

'nonsense about apostolic succession.'[22] Without question both Manson and Mackintosh saw the value of the *pastor pastorum*, but they would have abominated any notion that religion is somehow 'done to' the people by the ministers, and they would have insisted that it is the Church, not the ministers, that celebrates the sacraments. To Mackintosh the problem was not episcopacy as such, but the 'superstitious doctrine of sacramental grace' associated with it.[23] In justice to Schaff and Nevin it must be noted that they were not uncritical of Anglo-Catholicism. In particular, while welcoming its recovery of the early Church, they found it too backward-looking—a judgement that does not prevent Littlejohn from uncritically asserting that Anglo-Catholicism 'put an indelible stamp of the future history of the Anglican Communion, and ensured the survival of that Church by breathing new life into her' (p. 90).

7. *Revivalism*. While it is not impossible to find more charitable responses to Finney than Nevin's, the latter is on firm ground in lamenting revivalism's 'emphasis on the immediate, subjective encounter of the believer with God [which] set the stage for a more anthropocentric, unchurchly, and unsacramental style of religion' (p. 20). Certainly it is possible to demonstrate that in circles in which conversion became the favoured route into the Church, local Congregational covenants declined,[24] mission halls erupted, and baptism was sometimes neglected. It is interesting to compare Nevin's case against revivalism with that of Mackintosh, from whose pamphlet, *The Insufficiency of Revivalism as a Religious System*, I have already quoted. Like Nevin, he laments the individualism that revivalism encourages. Like its parent, the earlier evangelicalism, it 'does not wish to be distracted by any wider moral outlook than the desire to save one's own soul in the first place, and, secondly, to promote the salvation of the souls of other individuals. It has, and can have, no thought of the kingdom of God.'[25] As to the revivalist's procedure—'What counsel does the revivalist offer?,' Macintosh asks. He answers, 'Resolve to be converted tonight, and all must go well.' Could unreality go further? . . . Human souls are not their own, to dedicate or to withhold. Boasting is excluded here.'[26] Again, Mackintosh argues that intellectual and moral considerations prevent educated public opinion from resting in conversionism:

> Apologetic forbids it. The sources of doubt are so many, and so serious, that we are driven to counterbalance them, not by mere force of authority, not by 'miracles and prophecy,' or by machine-made arguments of Paley's school, but by internal evidences—i.e. by a view of the inherent moral probability of the Christian rev-

---

22. See T. W. Manson, *The Church's Ministry*, London: Hodder and Stoughton, 1948, ch. 2; Robert Mackintosh, 'Church Union—Hopes and Cautions,' *The Congregational Quarterly* 11 (1933) 452. Those who enjoy theology of the more bracing sort may care to consult Alan P. F. Sell, *Robert Mackintosh: Theologian of Integrity*, Bern: Peter Lang, 1977. See also my *Aspects of Christian Integrity*, Eugene, OR: Wipf and Stock, 1998, ch. 4.

23. R. Mackintosh, *The Insufficiency of Revivalism as a Religious System*, Glasgow: Maclehose, 1889, p. 13.

24. See Alan P. F. Sell, *Dissenting Thought and the Life of the Churches: Studies in an English Tradition*, Lewiston, NY: Edwin Mellen, 1990, ch. 1.

25. R. Mackintosh, *The Insufficiency of Revivalism*, p. 13.

26. Ibid., p. 22.

elation. But conversionism is absolutely inconsistent with an ethical view of life. If conversionism is right, Christianity cannot be the complete moralising of human life . . . [A] conception of salvation as being a spasm in the individual life does not give us any help towards the kingdom of God.[27]

But the 'decisive [anti- revivalist] consideration' is that 'the Church's tradition is anti-individualistic. Infant baptism is the great rock of offence to the triumphant revival.'[28] One can almost hear Nevin's 'Amen'—though if he knew what was coming on the next page he might have second thoughts about Mackintosh, who there declares that 'The High Churchman, in spite of his tall talk, is as great an individualist as any ranter. His community is the aggregate of baptized individuals, as the other's is of converted.'[29]

I have not been able to develop any of the foregoing seven points. They are no more than hints of trains of thought that have been started by W. Bradford Littlejohn's stimulating volume. At most they suggest that just as Littlejohn has reached out to traditions other than his own (and let there be more of this), so, as Lee Barrett has shown, the enquiry into a wider than American sample of diverse Reformed responses to neuralgic theological and ecclesiastical questions that transcend oceans and channels alike may not be altogether fruitless.

The New Mercersburg Review 44 (2011) 22–30.

77

Reformed Confessionalism in Nineteenth-Century America

Sam Hamstra, Jr., and Arie J. Griffioen. eds. *Reformed Confessionalism in Nineteenth-Century America: Essays on the Thought of John Williamson Nevin.* Lanham, MD: The Scarecrow Press, 1995. Pp. xxii + 257.

Since Reformed confessionalism came in a variety of forms in nineteenth-century America, it is well that the sub-title of this collection of papers clearly indicates the authors' concern with the contribution of the erstwhile Presbyterian, J. W. Nevin (I 803–86) to the German Reformed Church of his adoption. Not indeed that the interest of the

---

27. R. Mackintosh, *The Insufficiency of Revivalism*, p. 27.
28. Ibid., p. 27.
29. Ibid., p. 28.

essayists is antiquarian only. On the contrary, the Mercersburg theology (so named after the seminary of its origin) of Nevin, Schaff and others lives on (especially, but not exclusively, within the United Church of Christ) through the Mercersburg Society, its conventions, regional gatherings and journal; and through the Chair of Mercersburg Theology at Lancaster Theological Seminary. It is a Christocentric, incarnational-catholic theology with strong liturgical implications. It takes its stand not upon subjective experience, but upon Scripture, the confessions and tradition.

In their introduction the editors introduce Nevin, paying special attention to the formative influence upon him of J. A. W. Neander's romantic and dialectical historiography; and to Nevin's theological position, epitomized by *The Mystical Presence* (1846), which emphasizes union with the risen and glorified Christ through the Lord's Supper. Nevin was as opposed to revivalist Arminianism and New England 'Puritanism' (many Congregationalists having by now become Unitarian or gone revivalist) as he was to the decretal predestinarianism of Dort and the scholastic realism of the Princetonian, Charles Hodge.

James D. Bratt writes on 'Nevin and the antebellum culture wars,' showing that *The Anxious Bench* symbolizes Nevin's opposition to both revivalistic 'new measures' and to the cultural invasion of Pennsylvania by New England. In 'Nevin and American nationalism,' Richard E. Wentz discusses Nevin's opposition to four prevalent responses to the religious fragmentation of early nineteenth-century America: restorationism, dispensationalism, transcendentalism and 'the Bible and private judgement.' To Nevin these were vitiated by unhistorical and untheological biases which caused them in their several ways to elevate individualism at the expense of true catholicity. Undergirding Nevin's theology is his adoption—in the wake of his Mercersburg colleague, the philosopher F.A. Rauch (1806–41)—of such neo-Hegelian motifs as organic unity, development and the like—concepts which William DiPuccio discusses in 'Nevin's idealistic philosophy.' However, we are reminded that the influence of 'the deep Platonizing thoughts' of John Howe, and of the Cambridge Platonists, as well as of Coleridge, should not be overlooked.

The early history of the Mercersburg theology is further elaborated by Stephen Graham; while theological and ecclesiological themes are discussed by Walter Conser, Jr.. (the Church), Arie J. Griffioen (the Lord's Supper), John B. Payne (baptism), Glen Hewitt (regeneration) and Sam Hamstra, Jr. (the pastoral office). The paper on baptism by the current Mercersburg professor is of particular interest for its discussion of the divergent positions of Horace Bushnell, Charles Hodge and Nevin.

In 'Nevin's holistic supernaturalism' David Wayne Layman regrets that recent emphasis upon Nevin's ecumenism, sacramentalism, and liturgical practice has obscured what all of these are premised upon: a doctrine of revelation which proclaims that theology 'points toward and is grounded in the radically present *experience* of God's presence and activity.' For Nevin the incarnation is not primarily a doctrine, but an 'historical enduring fact.' Insofar as the Bible is revelatory it 'is Christ as incarnate revelation, now inscripturated.' Finally, Charles Yrigoyen, Jr. writes on 'Nevin and Methodism.' Without much difficulty he clears John Wesley of Nevin's charges against the 'sect system' and 'new measures' revivalism.

The book's usefulness is enhanced by a Nevin chronology, a bibliography, and an index. There are, however, a few slips: William DiPuccio refers, oddly, to 'the Common Sense philosophers (i.e., the Baconians)'; John Payne refers (ambiguously to the uninitiated) to 'the English Baptist W. Noel' rather than to 'the English Baptist, Baptist W. Noel'; and Sam Hamstra Jr. invents the new sin of 'hypocracy.'

Charles Yrigoyen's piece apart, this is not the volume in which to seek correctives to Nevin—though James D. Bratt does regret that Nevin said so little concerning the Church's mission and, as a result of his elevation of the sacred above the secular, left Calvinism's cultural activism to the New Schoolers. But the papers are nonetheless informative and welcome. They deserve to reach a wide audience within the Reformed family (whose member churches can be remarkably ignorant of their sisters and cousins) and beyond.

Journal of the United Reformed Church History Society 6 (1997) 61–63.

78

Reformed Theology in America

David F. Wells, ed. *Reformed Theology in America: A History of its Modern Development.* Grand Rapids: Eerdmans 1985. Pp. xvi + 317.

This collection of essays which is often illuminating, sometimes disappointing and occasionally alarming, is in general to be welcomed. The editor explains that while the main emphasis is upon the Reformed theology of the twentieth century, that theology cannot be understood apart from some consideration of its nineteenth century antecedents. Thus, after an introductory chapter in which George M. Marsden distinguishes three major, overlapping types of American Reformed theology: the doctrinalist, the culturalist and the pietist, we come to the Princeton theology (Mark A. Noll), Charles Hodge (the editor) and Benjamin B. Warfield (W. Andres Hoffecker).

Noll notes the influence of the Scottish common sense philosophy upon Old Princeton, but does not discuss the significant role played in this matter by James McCosh, who is named but not indexed (Cf. the recent work of J. David Hoeveler Jr.). He finds that 'Only a scattering of individuals today combine Augustinian Calvinism, empirical realism, evidentialist apologetics, and piety based on propositions in the manner of the Princeton theologians.' Wells focusses interestingly on the early, polemical, Hodge, whose apologetic method was nurtured in controversy with assorted freethinkers, Unitarians and others. He locates the crux of Hodge's differences with the New School theologians in the former's distrust of happiness as the goal of existence—an idea whose roots might well have been exposed. Wells rightly notes that Hodge 'imbibed the interests of Common Sense realism... almost without recognition on his part.' What, then, are the implications of such dependence upon a philosophical 'ism' for theology? Hoffecker shows how by positing truth prior to both theology and experience Warfield sought to place the conservative (truth first) *versus* liberal (experience first) debate in perspective. Those who think of Warfield primarily as a polemicist will here be reminded of his concern for piety, the Church, and culture. Preeminently Warfield championed the supernatural and waged war upon the naturalistic presuppositions of so many of the biblical scholars of his day. As with Hodge, so with Warfield: common sense philosophy was his bulwark against scepticism and his launching pad against Kantian epistemology and its theological debtors.

We come next to the Westminster School. The School's rise is chronicled by W. Robert Godfrey, and its most prominent founding fathers, J. Gresham Machen and Cornelius Van Til are lucidly treated by W. Stanford Reid and Wesley A. Roberts respectively. The controversy between those in the Old Princeton line of evidentialist apologetics and those in the wake of Van Til and his presuppositionalism continues. It may be, as Hoffecker suggests, that a discussion of what constitutes a fact would indicate a way forward (or, less optimistically, it may show why there can be no way forward).

James D. Bratt characterizes the Dutch School, making clear its indebtedness to Kuyper and Bavinck. Whereas Princeton drew on common sense realism, the Dutch School united continental dialectical idealism with a radical Augustinian psychology: 'There simply was no religiously neutral rational faculty or middle ground.' How the antithesis squares with Kuyper's later invocation of common grace is, in the master's thought, unclear. Henry Zwaanstra writes with integrity on Louis Berkhof. A highly regarded servant of the Church, and an accomplished teacher and packager of theology, he nevertheless joined with others in 'shopping' his colleague Janssen, whose view of Scripture, according to students, was defective; and he was 'pervasively dependent on Bavinck, often to the point of literally reproducing Bavinck's words and phrases.' C. T. McIntire's subject is 'Herman Dooyeweerd in North America.' The chapter is clear and succinct, and the conclusion is: 'No doubt Herman Dooyeweerd has been the most creative philosopher in the Reformed tradition, thus far in the twentieth century.' For good or ill this judgement remains to be endorsed or challenged by many Reformed philosophers, to some of whom Dooyeweerd's name is scarcely known at all.

Morton Smith introduces the Southern Tradition. He begins interestingly, tracing theological developments in the South from the Colonial period onwards; but when he comes to 'Recent developments' his partisan spirit obtrudes. Many will, however, derive solace from his assurance that 'There remain those who are sound in the faith in' the Presbyterian Church USA. Douglas Floyd Kelly presents 'Robert Lewis Dabney' warts and all. Dabney's continuing philosophical importance may be as a bridge between the common sense evidentialists and those of the Van Til school—Kelly is especially perceptive on this matter. Towards the end of his life Dabney lamented, 'I have no audience'—we can but sigh with relief as far as his attitude to slavery is concerned. Luder G. Whitlock Jr.

writes the slightest piece in the book, on James Henley Thornwell. Readers will be better served by J. H. Leith, *James Henley Thornwell and the Shaping of the Reformed Tradition in the South* (1983).

The final section is on neo-orthodoxy—a subject helpfully introduced by Dennis Voskuil, who shows that American neo-orthodoxy 'was not simply a backwoods variety of the European movement, but a genuinely indigenous form of religious thought.' He concedes the right of the movement to be regarded as in many ways Reformed, whilst noting such denials of the right as Van Til's. His verdict is that neo-orthodoxy in America was 'A transitory movement, . . . stimulated and best sustained during an era of social and intellectual crisis.' In more detail Gabriel Fackre writes on Reinhold Niebuhr, and Malcolm Reid on H. Richard Niebuhr. The former uses the theme of divine sovereignty as his key; the latter locates his subject within 'the Reformed tradition in theology and ethics' (though that tradition is not further elucidated), and regrets what he perceives as a Christological weakness in Niebuhr's thought.

The alarming paper is the concluding one. James Montgomery Boice writes on 'The future of Reformed theology,' but what a narrow definition of 'Reformed' he espouses. When cataloguing hopeful signs of inner-Reformed co-operation he does not mention the World Alliance of Reformed Churches (which may not surprise, given his presuppositions) or even the Reformed Ecumenical Synod. But it is his list of emphases required under 'need of the hour' which really disturbs: A high view of scripture as the inerrant Word of God; the sovereignty of God ; the Lordship of Christ ; human depravity; grace; godliness; work to do; security in Christ; discernible love. He then asks 'Will Reformed theology carry the field?' If his list provides the starting-point sequence and definition of 'Reformed theology' it had better not! Certainly, to suppose that the first need is of an agreement upon Biblical inerrancy is to put the indifferent cart before the substantive horse; it is at the same time both to erect a theological 'new circumcision,' and to deny the name 'Reformed' to countless theologians who have adorned the tradition from Calvin's day onwards—including most if not all of those who signed the Barmen Declaration, which Boice cites with approval.

The editor faced a real difficulty in inviting contributions to such a book as this. A principle of selection was required, but 'Reformed' is an ambiguous term. For the most part he has focused upon those who are most consciously Calvinistic, and those who belong to denominations labelled Presbyterian and Reformed. But there are theologians who are Reformed by ecclesiastical allegiance who are, for example, active in process theology and Anglo-Saxon linguistic philosophy of religion (the latter phenomenon is accorded a footnote). Conversely, in the period with which this book deals there have been Calvinistic theologians who were Baptists and Congregationalists (the former are noted twice in passing, the latter are not mentioned at all). The German Reformed tradition and the Mercersberg theology likewise receive only a passing mention. Thus it should be remembered that the scope of this book is somewhat narrow.

Implicit throughout, and with occasional explicit evidence provided, is the fact that theological method has been a church-dividing issue within the Reformed family. As such it stands alongside our differing ecclesiologies (presbyterial/congregational) and our diverse (especially missionary) histories. Perhaps the chief usefulness of this book is that it has posed sharply some of the methodological issues to which a Reformed family which is seriously concerned with the question of its inner unity and union (cf. *The Reformed World* (1986): 585–87) cannot properly neglect.

Reformed World 39 (1987) 738–39.

79

Thomas Chalmers and Mission

John Roxborogh. *Thomas Chalmers, Enthusiast for Mission: The Christian Good of Scotland and the Rise of the Missionary Movement*. Carlisle: Paternoster Press for Rutherford House, 1999. Pp. xiv + 324 pp.

Thomas Chalmers was, without question, the leading Scottish churchman of his generation. His contributions were diverse and, if he did not attain the heights in every field he tilled, many of his insights, some more, some less conservative, were influential for years to come: indeed, they have shaped the face of Scottish Christianity down to our own time. During the past twenty years his life and work have been discussed in a number of articles and, notably, in S. J. Brown's biography of 1982. What John Roxborogh, of the School of Ministry, Knox College, Dunedin, New Zealand, does in this fresh study is to show how the several aspects of Chalmers' work were inspired by a deep and activist concern for the Church's mission. His was a mission to rural areas, to city charges, in the university, to Scotland as a whole, to the world. It was as practical as it was intellectual, encompassing service to the poor supported by the voluntary offerings of Christians and apologetic tomes. It entailed upholding the idea of the national Church but, against the intrusion by patrons of non-evangelical ministers into parishes where they were not welcome, it also necessitated the leading out of the Church of Scotland, Free, in 1843, and the insistence that he and those like him were not Voluntaries. It inspired his commitment to Bible societies, and his view that the primary task of the minister was not to engage in multifarious acts of service and visitation himself, but to 'multiply the workers.'

Neither an hagiographer nor a debunker, Dr. Roxborogh presents a balanced, carefully researched account. He does not hesitate to inform us that the recently-licensed but as yet unconverted Chalmers published his opinion that 'after the satisfactory discharge of his parish duties, a minister may enjoy five days in the week of uninterrupted leisure for the prosecution of any science in which his taste may engage.' He frankly recognizes the difficulties Chalmers faced in his city charges; he records failures as well as successes. We learn that in order to finance the activities of the Free Church, business communities came to predominate over working class members; and that Chalmers did not always get his way with the General Assembly, as when it refused to permit the Free Church as such to join the newly-formed Evangelical Alliance. We see Chalmers sailing close to the wind with such opinions as that justification by faith was not to be found either in Moderate preaching or in the *Westminster Confession*. Through it all, Chalmers made and kept friends of numerous theological persuasions—sometimes being regarded as a fellow-traveller by the more conservative (or suspicious) members of his own Church. His underlying Toryism distinguished him from the bulk of evangelicals, who were Whigs.

As to research: Dr. Roxborogh sets Chalmers' missionary concerns in the wider context of modern missions, and in the process uncovers illuminating material on many topics—not least on the roots of missionary endeavour in Scotland. He thoroughly and usefully combs sermons, minute books, parliamentary papers, archives, magazines, theses and books, all of which activity yields a bibliography of forty-four pages in nine sections. In addition there are tables, among them those concerning the London Missionary Society, church attendance, and the biblical texts on which Chalmers preached.

Of particular interest is Dr. Roxborogh's account of Chalmers the systematic theologian—a guise in which he has not hitherto received due attention. He shows how Chalmers' practical missionary concerns were to a considerable extent governed by his theological exposition, prompting him, for example, against Westminster's teaching on effectual calling, to surmise that a native of China unreached by Christianity would fare better hereafter than 'The nations of Christendom who have been plied with the offers of the gospel.'

Many questions are raised by the information provided. How common were private baptisms such as those conducted by Chalmers at the Tron Church, Glasgow? How many of the sermons one has recently heard might fitly be described as 'preparatives for death?' And how would a Research Assessment Exercise panel respond to the news that one's book (in Chalmers' case, *Astronomical Discourses*) had transported a student 'into a state of chronic ecstasy which lasted all summer'?

The Evangelical Quarterly 74 (2002) 287–88.

God, Grace and the Bible in Scottish Reformed Theology: A Review Article

M. Charles Bell. *Calvin and Scottish Theology: The Doctrine of Assurance.* Edinburgh: The Handsel Press, 1986. Pp. 211.

George M. Tuttle. *So Rich a Soil: John McLeod Campbell on Christian Atonement.* Edinburgh: The Handsel Press, 1986. Pp.174.

Richard Allan Riesen. *Criticism and Faith in Late Victorian Scotland: A. B. Davidson, William Robertson Smith and George Adam Smith.* Lanham MD and London: University Press of America, 1985. Pp. xxiv + 466.

To read these books in sequence is to become acquainted with some of the major theological controversies which have disturbed, and on occasion disrupted, Scottish church life from the Reformation to the early decades of the twentieth century.

Dr. Bell examines the relation of saving faith to assurance—a concern which exercised Scottish theologians for almost two centuries. He contends that whereas to Calvin assurance, grounded *extra nos* in the person and work of Christ, is of the essence of faith, Scottish theology came to teach that assurance is a fruit of faith, grounded *intra nos*, and attained by self-examination and syllogistic deduction. The result, in full-blown Federal theology, was that Calvin's *ordo salutis* was inverted in such a way that law preceded gospel, and legal repentance preceded faith and grace.

Dr. Bell argues his case with such patient examination of relevant texts that would-be refuters (and there will be some, for controversial zeal subsists in some quarters—as witness our author's urgent challenges to Paul Helm) will be able to proceed with integrity only if they too quote chapter and verse.

The drift began with Knox, who elevated discipline to the status of a mark of the Church, thereby fostering the 'legal strain'; and who viewed God's covenant as a national league between God and man which was conditional upon obedience. We covenant with God, whereas in fact the new covenant is made for us in Christ. Robert Rollock introduced the term 'covenant of works' to Scotland, and declared that the ground of our assurance is our 'firm and certain assent' to God's promises. For his part, the supralapsarian Samuel Rutherford (*contra* Calvin) argued from double predestination to limited atonement, while the arch-Federalists, Dickson and Durham, so exalted the individual's faith and self-examination as preconditions of the operation of the covenant of grace as to violate grace. Of their joint work, *The Sum of Saving Knowledge*, C. G. M'Crie declared that 'The blessedness of the mercy-seat is in danger of being lost sight of in the bargaining of the market-place.' The authors of the *Westminster Confession* erred in separating assurance from faith.

In John Brown of Wamphray and Hugh Binning we detect resistance from within to Federal legalism; and Fraser of Brea 'is unique among 17th century Scottish Federalists in that he sought to affirm the universal character of Christ's atonement.' While both Robert Traill and Thomas Halyburton insisted that faith includes assurance, their emphasis upon self-examination as prerequisite effectively torpedoed this insight. Against this Thomas Boston and the Marrowmen protested, though the constraints of Federalism did not permit them to draw all the consequences of that conviction concerning the propriety of the offer of the gospel to which they held so strongly.

One hundred years on, and out of pastoral concern for Christians who were burdened by a less than grace-ful theology, and a damagingly introspective piety, McLeod Campbell urged that the atonement manifests God's forgiving love for all, and that (returning to Calvin) assurance is of the essence of faith. These are the themes explored in detail by Dr. Tuttle in *So Rich a Soil*.

Under the influence of Romanticism, Campbell (a devotee of Wordsworth and Scott) came to the view that the Bible, the vehicle of God's word, is recognized as the Word of God only as conscience responds to it. Certainly he could not recognize the Federal 'deductions' from Scripture as the Word of God, neither could he tolerate their baneful pastoral effects. He objected both to the 'works mentality' and to the limited atonement of Federal Calvinism. Not, indeed, that all would inevitably be saved. This is the day of grace, but we must not presume upon God's grace. Though all are already forgiven, all are accountable as regards the acceptance or rejection of this gift: hence the coming judgement.

In all of this Campbell was turning rich soil, but he was also ploughing a lonely furrow. He was no rationalizing Moderate of the older sort, but neither was he willing to permit the *Westminster Confession* to be the judge of Scripture in the manner endorsed by some of his evangelical contemporaries. The verdict of the 1831 Assembly trial—that Campbell be deposed from the ministry of the Church of Scotland—was, in the circumstances then prevailing, not surprising. Very few supported him; presumably some decided not to oppose him; and Thomas Chalmers, 'the only churchman with sufficient stature to gain a fair hearing for the accused,' absented himself, pleading other business and insufficient time in which to prepare for the trial.

At the heart of Campbell's message was that universal love of God which did not need to be provoked or cajoled into being loving by a penal substitutionary atonement. Far from being the cause of God's love, the atonement was the consequence of it. Received views which turned upon distributive justice (John Owen) or a benevolent governor (Grotius) wrongly laid the emphasis upon our relationship to the divine law, rather than upon the freedom of divine grace.

As the gift of grace the incarnate Christ represents God to humanity and humanity to God; and suffering (which is not in itself the atoning element) is inevitable when holiness and love confront sin. These themes reverberate *in The Nature of Atonement* (the first edition of which appeared in 1856, twenty-five years after Campbell's deposition), and they raise a particularly acute problem: Christ lives and acts on behalf of humanity; we cannot confess our sins and repent as we ought; but can Christ, the guiltless one, do that for us? Can anyone repent on behalf of another? How could the virtue of a vicarious repentance he transferred to a sinner?

Dr. Bell, with some excuse because of his much broader canvas, does not probe these questions in detail, but Dr. Tuttle cannot avoid them. He carefully discusses those who have opposed Campbell's language on these matters, whilst in some cases agreeing that Campbell had introduced insights which are of permanent value in atonement doctrine, and records his own belief that 'Campbell would not entertain the use of the designation "vicarious repentance" if it appeared to bear the substitutionary ideas which had been affixed to the word "vicarious".' It remains unclear, however, that the idea of representative repentance as prospectively facilitating humanity's repentance saves the day, or that Dr. Tuttle has convincingly answered the critic (unquoted here) who protested, 'After having implied that Christ repented of the sins of the race, we do not see why Mr. Campbell should object to the theory that he was punished for these sins.' He has nevertheless shown the considerable impact of Campbell's constellation of ideas not only upon professional theologians (however elusive some of them found his terms), but also upon such a distinguished New Testament scholar as Vincent Taylor. Campbell's influence (at however many removes) upon subsequent generations of preachers is, we may suppose, great, if impossible accurately to compute.

If the books by Bell and Tuttle remind us of the dangers of legalistically-inspired self-examination, they also reveal the Reformed zeal for legalistically examining one another! Further evidence of the latter is provided by Dr. Riesen's able book, *Criticism and Faith in Late Victorian Scotland*. Here the question is 'What happened when the higher criticism of the Bible (paradoxically) began to be pursued in what was ostensibly the most conservative of Scotland's churches—the Free Church of the 1843 Disruption?' The head which rolled is that of William Robertson Smith, who was removed from his Aberdeen Old Testament Chair (though not deposed from the ministry) in 1881; the case against George Adam Smith was dismissed by an Assembly majority of 271 in 1902; and the senior scholar of the trio here considered, A. B. Davidson, 'the power behind the throne,' was pursued in the course of the W. R. Smith trial, but never formally brought before the Assembly.

Dr. Riesen begins with the G. A. Smith case which was occasioned by the publication in 1901 of *Modern Criticism and the Preaching of the Old Testament*. In this book Smith advanced such 'revolutionary opinions' as that there is an 'absence of history' from Genesis 1–9, and declared that 'Modern Criticism has won its war against the Traditional Theories.' This was 'fighting talk,' and when Smith further averred that 'those who have been led into unbelief by modern criticism are not for one moment to be compared in number with those who have fallen from faith over the edge of the opposite extreme,' and set his face against the 'dogmas of verbal inspiration,' conservative feathers were, not surprisingly, ruffled.

In G. A. Smith's writings the ethical interest outweighs the theological, and Dr. Riesen properly notes that whereas Smith could formally articulate an orthodox confession of faith, 'There is apparently nothing, in [his] view, either judicial or ritual or of divine requirement in the death of Christ. It is simply the consequence . . . of the confrontation between good and evil and as such has had its "likeness" both before (e.g., Jeremiah) and since (in war-time).' Keen on the distinction between the law and the prophets (and siding with the latter), and convinced that the ethical teaching of the prophets not only supersedes but nullifies the older sacrificial system, Smith paid little heed to the distinction between law and grace, and thus minimized the meaning of Christ's death. The critical method wedded to practical preaching—especially from the prophets would, he believed, foster a grander vision and a nobler life. So admirable an exegetic, so woolly a theologian!

We are brought up sharp by a decided change of tone as, in chapter two, Dr. Riesen presents a retrospect of those dogmas of verbal inspiration which were espoused by the first generation of Free Church teachers: William Cunningham, R. S. Candlish and James Bannerman. Their theory, differences of emphasis notwithstanding, was that the Bible is verbally inspired in its entirety; they did not, however, believe that the manner of its inspiration had been revealed. Apart from plenary inspiration, they held, we are on a sea of subjectivity: do we have a revelation from God, or not? This position was by no means exclusively intellectualist, for wrong views were often held to accompany a wrong spirit; but their strongly doctrinal emphasis cannot be gainsaid. Textual study is required for exegetical theology, and upon that foundation is erected systematic theology. Philip Doddridge and John Pye Smith had wrongly admitted the presence of errors in the Bible, and Schleiermacher's anti-supernaturalism and subjectivism did not, thought Bannerman, permit a truly objective divine revelation.

Such were the views which were to be challenged supremely by William Robertson Smith, whose life, character, position and trial form the centrepiece of this book. Our author does well to make it clear that not all 'liberals' were of the same hue. Whilst accepting the main findings of critical scholarship, and being utterly committed to the critical method in the interest of faith, Smith uncompromisingly rejected fashionable theories of the organic development of religion as being founded not upon critical scholarship, but upon pantheistic presuppositions. He upheld a supernatural revelation, and regarded rationalism as 'Pelagianism of the intellect.'

As to method, Smith would allow no *a priori* theory or ecclesiastical tradition to determine in advance what the Bible must say. The Bible does not present us with a systematic narrative, but with a collection of varied documents which require close historical analysis, and which are not immediately fodder for dogmaticians. As for saving faith, it is not 'mere intellectual persuasion' nor 'a mere subjective habit of mind,' but 'the intelligent and moral outgoing of the will and personality towards a personal revelation of God.' The revelation is that in Christ God has saved us, and we believe the Bible to be true because it testifies to this; we do not believe that Christ has saved us because we first believe the Bible to be true. Whereas to the traditionalists the content of the Bible was supremely doctrinal and propositional, to Smith it was first intensely personal. The methodological question, as much as if not more than any specific critical findings, lay at the root of the dispute between Smith and the traditionalists—a dispute exacerbated by the sometimes incautious mode of expression of one who did not suffer fools gladly, and who did not seem to have the pastoral sensitivity to anticipate the hurt which his more unguarded language would cause to intelligent Christians of simple faith, who might not normally read technical works of Old Testament scholarship, but who might well browse in that volume of *Encyclopedia Britannica* (1875) in which Smith's offending article on 'Bible' appeared. (Unusually for a Free Church Professor, Smith had not been in pastoral charge prior to his appointment to a Chair).

Dr. Riesen does not hesitate to indicate the enigmas in Smith's work. For example, granted that the older school may have over-emphasized the predictiveness of prophecy, is it not strange that one so committed to the historical should have underplayed the historical rootedness of so much of the prophecy as Smith did? Again, is it not odd that one who wrote so much on sacrifice in the Old Testament should have had so little to say about the sacrifice of Christ—even in *Britannica* articles on 'Epistle to the Hebrews' and 'Sacrifice'? Yet again, how could one so provocative in print be so conventionally, non-didactically, 'devotional' when preaching? When the traditionalist Horatius Bonar heard Smith preach he questioned his sincerity, for what he said was so orthodox!

But the enigmas surrounding Smith are as nothing compared with those attaching to A. B. Davidson. He is commonly regarded as the founder of modern biblical criticism in Scotland, yet his critical views are not altogether clear or consistent. He maintained an almost complete silence during the trial of his pupil W. R. Smith (perhaps because of poor health and a dislike of controversy, perhaps because of distaste for the tone and distinctiveness of some critics). Of him it was said that he possessed 'a strange power of seeing both sides of a question with great intensity in periods immediately succeeding each other.' He shunned the limelight, preferring to preach (when he did preach) in the country, refusing city pulpits. Dr. Riesen justly characterizes him as 'fair, tolerant, perceptive—or alternatively, reticent, indecisive, skeptical.'

Yet on devotional matters Davidson evinced 'the most stringent doctrinal orthodoxy.' Unlike his pupil, George Adam Smith, for example, Davidson held that there was a 'radical distinction' between sacrifice as self-dedication and sacrifice as substitution. On the other hand, Davidson was non-traditionalist in insisting that the Bible be examined in the same way as any other book and in urging that grammar precedes dogmatic: the Bible is the record of religious experience, not a doctrinal manual. At the same time, he was pessimistic concerning the destructive spirit which all too often animated critical scholarship. To him the Bible, human though it was, was superintended by the divine spirit; it is systematic, though in an organic, not a static way. Religious faith grounds not upon an inerrant text, but upon what God has accomplished in history and upon the testimony of religious experience. The latter, however, is to be distinguished from the moral sense— Davidson did not blur this distinction as did G. A. Smith. Unlike W. R. Smith, Davidson did not place faith on a par with criticism—to him the former took precedence.

In chapter five we return to Cunningham, Candlish and Bannerman, who were united in maintaining the plenary inspiration of scripture. By means of a careful analysis, however, Dr. Riesen shows that the critical seeds are present in their defences of their position (though this is least the case with Cunningham). In Bannerman especially (though unnoticed by him) we find the 'solvent ideas' that God is revealed first in history and only later in words, and that in order to discern his mind we have to look beyond the text on the sacred page.

Dr. Riesen concludes by summarizing his contention that 'the change of attitude to the Bible in Scotland' in his chosen period 'was concerned more with the meaning of faith than matters of criticism'; and that what we have is a transition rather than a revolution, for traces of the new are to be found in the old.

The three books under review are greatly to be welcomed. They are impressive in their scholarship, and for the most part balanced in their judgements. Those of Bell and Tuttle would have benefited from indices of names such as Riesen supplies; all carry bibliographies. All display a few slips and infelicities: Dr. Bell means that baptism is complemented (not 'complimented') by communion (p. 27); Dr. Tuttle refers to 'discreet individuals' where he means 'discrete' ones, and notes 'D. W. Simpson' when, as his bibliography records, the name is 'Simon'; and Dr. Riesen has an incomplete sentence on p. 268, and an ugly 'gotten' on p. 263.

More serious is the coupling of Dr. Bell's correct admission that 'Boston and Erskine can only be fully appreciated against the background of 17th century Federal theology and the Marrow controversy,' (p. 168) with his silence on Moderatism as such. Dr. Tuttle's peril is that of stumbling into stereotypes. Without supplying evidence he can assert the universal proposition, 'The cold rationalism of the eighteenth century had starved the human emotions' (p. 14); and, with commendable impartiality and equal lack of discrimination, he can pronounce that 'Evangelicals were narrow and harsh' (p. 34). Dr. Riesen, though the most questingly analytical of the three authors, at one major point fails to play an important card. He concludes that in the debate with which he has been concerned 'What was at stake was the nature of the relationship between God and man' (p. 432). My own suggestion is that what was fundamentally at stake was the doctrine of the nature of God as such, and that herein lies a link between these three books.

Implicit in Dr. Bell's book (and it might have provided more of a running theme) is the realization that distorted theology has its origin in a distorted view of God. Where his themes are concerned, the root of the problem lies in Calvin's 'unbiblical stress on the hidden will of God' which 'runs counter to the biblical truth that God has fully and in utter fidelity revealed himself to us in Jesus Christ as our loving Father' (p. 32). Now if God then comes to be presented as a god of *quasi*-Stoic legalistic conditions, as Dr. Bell maintains, it is not surprising that McLeod Campbell's point of departure was a grievously burdened flock, as Dr. Tuttle shows. Neither (and this is the point which Dr. Riesen should have underlined) would it be surprising if a God of will-issuing-in-legislation left us with a law book—and G. A. Smith drew an analogy between the Koran and the Bible traditionally viewed. We might then speculate that when A. B. Davidson enigmatically declared, 'I dislike the old, I distrust the new,' he meant that he distrusted the scornful tone and unfeeling negations of some modern critics, but that he disliked what the traditionalists had done to God.

But if religion does not begin with the internalization of divinely-revealed inerrant propositions, it also does not begin with 'a certain vague feeling and consciousness of God' as Davidson said it did; neither is it 'absolutely a thing of the heart' as W. R. Smith said it was. At this point traditionalist and 'advanced' critic alike are trapped in individualism—a further theme which runs through the three books under review. Thus, Dr. Bell shows that 'the corporate dimension of the believer's life as a member of the body of Christ was eclipsed by the individualistic nature of the Federal theology' (p. 104); and Dr. Tuttle reminds us that Calvinist and Arminian alike 'were forever searching within themselves for the evidence of conversion experience' (p. 25). The Unitarian James Martineau certainly had a point when, in his review of *The Nature of the Atonement*, he said that 'the doctrine of *mediation*—in the strict sense implying transitions with God on behalf of men, *as well as* in the opposite direction, cannot be harmonised with the modern individualism.'

So pervasive is the individualism that we might almost speak of an 'ecclesiology-shaped-blank'—and this despite W. R. Smith's strong assertions of the necessity of churchly fellowship. While believing that there was a common faith, and that the Church is not simply an aggregate of individuals, he yet remained individualistic at heart. In his preaching individual piety and personal faith were dominant themes. One might have expected something more of an Old Testament scholar, given the importance of the concept of 'covenant'—but, as Dr. Bell reminded us, that venerable term had been grievously misapplied in Scottish religion from Knox onwards.

This extended review is justified by the fact that these three books raise issues of wide and continuing significance. How is it with the doctrine of God? Do present-day biblical inerrantists need to examine this question afresh? Can present-day Roman Catholics find any similarities between Scotland's theological struggles and their own post-Vatican II adjustments and reappraisals? Is the gospel of grace still being distorted into a new law by those who make their own competence in *glossolalia*, or their predilection for specific language or programmes the test of another's status as a Christian or right to fellowship? Which ecclesiology (and what kind of Christian education) will most effectively carry forward the idea that the Bible is the book of the people of God, and not exclusively that of the 'priest' whether traditionalist or critic? What kind of God are we tacitly proclaiming in our theological systems and our churchly discipline—or lack of them?

So we could go on; but we must allow William Robertson Smith the last word: 'God has placed us so, that round the central verities, and inmost convictions, there lies a margin that is debatable, in which we are denied the satisfaction of final and absolute certainties.' That should caution both traditionalist and critic alike. Of course, it begs the question, 'What are the 'central verities'?

The Irish Theological Quarterly 54 (1988) 66–71.

Part Three: Theology

81

Theology through the Theologians

Colin E. Gunton. *Theology Through the Theologians.*
Edinburgh: T. & T. Clark, 1996. Pp. xi + 228.

In general and in particular, Professor Gunton is an enthusiast (I eschew Dr. Johnson's pejorative definition of that term). He writes with restless energy of the importance of systematic theology, and he wishes us to share his great if, on occasion, qualified appreciation of such ancients and moderns as Augustine, Anselm, Calvin, Coleridge, Irving, Barth, Hardy, Jenson, Zizioulas; and, from his own tradition, John Owen, R. W. Dale and P. T. Forsyth. The mere recitation of these names prompts the suspicion that the author's expression of his objective, 'this book is intended as an introduction of a kind to systematic theology' (p. x) may be turned around: this book is an introduction to a kind of systematic theology. It is none time worse for that. On the contrary, the selection of a manageable set of theologians, and the admission that not all of theology's central topics are to be treated, strengthen the book by facilitating an unusual degree of coherence between the several chapters, many of them previously published.

We are first introduced to the sorry state into which, from the nineteenth century onwards, systematic theology has fallen in England, and especially in the Church of England. Professor Gunton seeks a systematic theology understood as 'the articulation of the truth claims of Christianity, with an eye to their internal consistency, on the one hand; and, on the other, to their coherence with Scripture, the Christian tradition and other truth . . .' (p. 5). Coleridge, pitted against Newman, is applauded for his obsession with truth as a systematic theological quest in which the thinker is untrammelled by a given system, and for his ability (like Irenaeus) to see the whole as well as the parts. There follows chapter on the nature of dogmatic theology, in which the 'sins' and 'vices' of rationalism are announced and denounced, and the strengths and weaknesses of Newman's critique are weighed. Then comes the author's prescription: 'What is needed to engage with the challenge of the end of modernism, if it is the end, is a combination of Newman's firm hold on the tradition with Coleridge's willingness to engage with any thought that came his way' (pp. 32–33).

In the next four chapters the author turns to Barth and Jüngel. He discusses the development of Christian doctrine; the knowledge of God, the distortions of Enlightenment individualism, and the need of an epistemology in which the relational is understood as being prior to the conceptual; the being and attributes of God; and Barth's doctrine of election. In these chapters, as in the seventh, on Augustine and his successors, pneumatology is a prominent linking theme. Indeed, perhaps the most valuable feature of the book are Professor Gunton's suggestions as to how pneumatology may be brought to the rescue of systematic theology at critical points.

The doctrine of creation is next in view, and then we come to Christology, where help towards a Spirit Christology is sought from Irving; Dale on the atonement; Owen and Zizioulas on the Church; Niebuhr on human nature; and Forsyth on authority and freedom. Pneumatology is again invoked, and the entire collection is informed by the author's strong trinitarian stance.

These stimulating papers prompt many observations and queries, among them the following: (a) given the terms of reference of the volume as an introduction, a glossary of technical terms wound have assisted some readers. (b) Inadequately documented complaints are made from time to time—for example, against theological rationalists (p. 21) and foundationalism (p. 52). (c) Torpedoes are occasionally launched against the likes of Bonhoeffer (p. 53) and Moltmann (p. 72) without the targets being heard on the complained-of issue, and as if all readers were conversant with the stances to which exception is taken. In this connection Professor Gunton's introductory lament that the blank dismissal of opposing positions . . . often happens' (p. 16) is something of a hostage to fortune. (d) To attribute the sorry state of English (especially Anglican) theology to nationalism (pp. 1-4) is to tell less than half of a very complicated story. (e) Novices may well find Professor Gunton's insufficiently indiscriminating references to the Enlightenment (pp. 23, 50, 188) puzzling; and scholars will feel that his compressed references to Locke (pp. 20, 208) are unsubtle.

The above remarks are those of one who has, through this book, greatly enjoyed sitting at the feet of Professor Gunton; and to sit at the feet of theologians is, as he rightly says (albeit not with reference to himself), 'One of the ways of learning to write theology' (p. ix).

The Scottish Journal of Theology 52 (2000) 262-64.

Part Three: Theology

82

John and Donald Baillie

George Newlands. *John and Donald Baillie: Transatlantic Theology.*
Bern: Peter Lang, 2002. Pp. 451.

Those who facilitated the access of the Glasgow professor of divinity to the letters and papers of John and Donald Baillie of Edinburgh and St. Andrews respectively, did well. For George Newlands has produced a book which affords a comprehensive insight into the often intertwined lives of these distinguished brothers. As all too infrequently happens, we are taken behind the scenes of the published writings and are introduced, substantially from original sources, to the cultural milieu from which their work emerged. It is the world of the children of a Calvinistic manse, whose theology underwent change, but for whom the centrality of the experience of God's grace remained. It is the world of classically-educated bright boys with poetic instincts; of university students whose education under such luminaries as A. S. Pringle-Pattison and H. R. Mackintosh was topped off in Germany; of music and, in John's case, amateur dramatics; of bridge and tennis parties; of widely-travelled lecturers and preacher, in and out of whose homes flit many of the most notable theologians of the day; of two World Wars; and of dedicated churchmen, whose dismay at the slow progress of the ecumenical horse never tempted them to put it out to grass. Not all was plain sailing. John was subject to periods of ill health; his wife was at death's door for an extended period; and Donald was an asthmatic subject to depression. Both knew the gnawings of doubt.

So alike were John and Donald in spirit and in theology that Donald was sometimes hesitant to write on themes which John had treated lest they be accused of copying one another. But their experience was not identical in all respects. Whereas Donald knew Europe and North America as a student and visitor, John studied in Europe but lived for fifteen years in North America—at Auburn, Toronto and New York. John's circle of friends included Reinhold Niebuhr, Henry Sloane Coffin and H. P. Van Dusen, and it appears that he enjoyed a liberation of spirit in America which eluded him on his eventual return to Edinburgh. Meanwhile, until his appointment to St. Andrews, Donald was the faithful minister, ever juggling the claims of the pastorate with his desire to make a serious and sustained contribution to theology. John and Jewel had a son, Ian; Donald never married. Their friend, the poet Andrew Young, remarked that whereas he was 'frightened' by John's considerable learning, Donald had the sharper mind.

Professor Newlands deftly deploys his materials in such a way as to sustain his thesis that particular theologies take their flavour and shape from the culture within which they are nurtured. Not surprisingly, the Baillies' contribution was urbane in tone, and revealed a breadth of sympathy, a concern for the social implications of the gospel, and, over all, a liberal attitude in the evangelically-anchored sense of that oft-abused term.

But this does not exhaust the author's case. In the light of his examination of their lives and works, Professor Newlands argued that while we cannot simply reproduce their theology today—not least because of the new challenges, social and intellectual, which have come our way during the past fifty years—we may nevertheless learn from their openness and catholicity of spirit as we seek to produce theologies which are culturally relevant. Further, we may be cautioned by them that our theologies are never the last word: this was, indeed, the burden of John Baillie's criticism of the older theological liberalism.

There are some repetitions in the book. The President on p. 303 is presumably Johnson; the 'k' is sometimes omitted from H. R. Mackintosh's name. The Baillies clearly had something against Professor G. T. Thomson, but we are not told what. Many names are dropped—Dodd, Lightfoot, W. Manson, for example—and some readers would have been helped by a clause to locate them. No doubt in eternal terms R. W. Hepburn's critique of John Baillie's encounter theology came 'soon' after the latter's book of 1939, but in earthly terms there was a gap of nineteen years. The book is illustrated by photographs, and furnished with three appendices and an index. Appendix I (pp. 321–420) comprises 'Selected additional entries from John Baillie's diaries and from his letters.' The other appendices are bibliographical in nature.

The narrative is enlivened by many an item of interest. Some may draw consolation from the fact that John's DPhil thesis was referred in 1917, though he did manage the DLitt eleven years later. There are the chairs they did not secure, and the less than flattering (albeit atypical) reviews their books attracted. Due attention is paid to Donald's use of the concept of paradox, and to Donald MacKinnon's querying of it in the interests of *kenosis*. Then there are the brothers' frankly-expressed opinions of others, Donald emerging as the more trenchant of the two: 'I must say I'm sorry that [T. F.] Torrance is being nominated for the systematic theology chair. New College will become even more conservative-ultra-Barthian than ever' (p. 182). Yet Torrance preached at John's memorial service in St. Giles Cathedral. Equally, neither of the brothers was bowled over by Barth, but Donald in particular had little good to say of him—in private: 'I can't see what contribution he makes to theology . . . [Anti-liberalism] seems to he the one thing that unites Communists, Fascists, Barthians, Roman Catholics, Fundamentalists, Agnostics, Imperialists and all other pestilential persons whatsoever' (pp. 144, 162). In public, however, Donald delivered the oration when Barth was awarded the St Andrews DD in 1937—and for this Barth wrote to thank him.

Occasionally Professor Newlands' dry wit shines through. On an American student's report from Germany in 1923 that 'The University professors were standing in line for a little horse flesh,' Newlands comments: 'Somewhat reminiscent of Britain under the Thatcher government' (p. 72). More worthy of serious consideration are some of his judgements: 'In my view Barth was right to emphasise the distinctiveness of Jesus Christ, but wrong to set this in opposition to culture in an exclusive view of revelation' (pp. 317–18). 'The postmodern is valuable as an extension and development of the modern, not a denial' (p. 298). 'My own conviction is that a multilayered strategy is usually more effective in deploying theology in relation to the need for social change along the lines of an agonistic liberalism' (p. 114). To hazard a paradox of my own: there is much to he said for taking up cudgels on behalf of Professor Newlands' irenic approach.

Irish Theological Quarterly 68 (2003) 400–402.

82

The Centenary of *Lux Mundi*

Geoffrey Wainwright, ed. *Keeping the Faith: Essays to Mark the Centenary of Lux Mundi.* Philadelphia: Fortress Press and Allison Park, PA: Pickwick Publications, 1988. Pp. xxv, 399.

Geoffrey Wainwright here gathers sixteen authors between the covers of a book which is substantial in bulk and in content. The objective is both to commemorate *Lux Mundi* and, more importantly, to interpret the catholic faith in our day as the authors of a century ago did in theirs.

Whereas the eleven authors of *Lux Mundi* were Oxford Anglicans, the present contributors include six Anglicans, three Reformed, two Lutherans, two Methodists and a Roman Catholic; they are drawn from a number of universities on both sides of the Atlantic. It is especially cheering that each has something which is at worst interesting, and at best important to say: Dr. Wainwright does not succumb to 'tokenism'.

Authors and titles are as follows: Stephen Sykes, 'Faith'; Robert W. Jenson, 'The Christian Doctrine of God'; Brian Hebblethwaite, 'The Problem of Evil'; Richard Norris, 'Human Being'; Alasdair Heron, 'The Person of Christ'; Paul Avis, 'The Atonement'; David N. Power, 'The Holy Spirit: Scripture, Tradition and Interpretation'; George Lindbeck, 'The Church'; Theodore Runyon, 'The Sacraments'; Keith Ward, 'Christian Ethics'; Duncan B. Forrester, 'Christianity and Politics'; Daniel Hardy, 'Rationality, the Sciences and Theology'; Lesslie Newbigin, 'The Christian Faith and the World Religions'; Geoffrey Wainwright, 'The Last Things'; and Dikran Y. Hadidian, 'A Bibliographical Epilogue: Before and After *Lux Mundi*.'

The following random notes may whet the appetite and, in one case, make the blood boil. In his lucid paper Stephen Sykes reminds us of the way in which the content of the idea of faith has 'swung uneasily' between those theologies which emphasize divine grace, and those which seek to do justice to human freedom. His call to theologians to pay due heed to the differences between their dilemmas and those of laypeople is timely. The trinitarian thrust is strong in Robert Jenson's essay. Here are references to Jonathan Edwards *qua* anti-mechanist, and to Barth in connection with Jesus Christ's eternal actuality as the ground of creation. He is needlessly disjunctive, if fashionable, in asserting (without argument) that 'the real God is not the securely persisting Beginning; he is the triumphing End.' He introduces the term 'deification' without the qualifications it requires; and at times he lapses into rhetoric: 'Western Christendom is now baffled by its God'—to which one possible retort might be, 'Large tracts of Western Christendom are insufficiently baffled by their God: they know exactly where they have him; he endorses their favoured set of doctrines, or he reads the Bible as they do, or be joins them on their socio-political platform.'

Alasdair Heron quotes A. M. Fairbairn's perceptive remark upon *Lux Mundi*: 'Curiously the Incarnation is the very thing the book does not, in any more than the most nominal sense, either discuss or construe,' and demonstrates its validity by reference to the contributions of Moberly, Talbot and Illingworth. They failed, he declares, 'to develop the idea of a *trinitarian theology of the crucifixion*' (author's italics). In the course of his account of the church as 'the messianic pilgrim people of God typologically shaped by Israel's history,' George Lindbeck makes one astonishing, and one strangely insensitive, claim. First: 'Until a hundred years before *Lux Mundi*, a chapter of the kind that Walter Lock wrote [on ecclesiology] would have been a novelty. Specific topics such as ecclesiastical structures and discipline were addressed at length . . . but separate treatments on the church as a whole are modern phenomena.' Readers of this *Journal* may feel tempted to force-feed Dr. Lindbeck the *Works* of John Owen, to name but one. Secondly: 'The historic episcopacy . . . is the only ministry that exists to promote the unity and responsibility of the worldwide church. Those churches which lack it have no substitute. To the degree that they are concerned about unity and mutual responsibility, it is to this ministerial ordering of the church they need to turn.'

Having no space for detailed rebuttal, we simply inquire, where now is the Trinity?

If Dr. Lindbeck overlooks the Trinity at a crucial point where reference to it might have been expected, Duncan Forrester builds strongly upon it in a context from which it is sometimes banished—political theology. He expounds his view that 'the most politically relevant and distinctive element in Christian faith is its trinitarian nature,' and warns us against 'the twin seductive perils of a privatized and a politicized Christianity.' Indeed, it is not too much to say that the Trinity, historical particularity (strongly asserted in different ways by A. Heron, D. Hardy and L. Newbigin), and eschatology are the recurring themes in this collection. To the last-named the editor devotes his attention. He has considerable recourse to the Bible— except at a notable point where he writes, 'If there is to be progress in the heavenly service and enjoyment of God, there is no reason why the earlier stages may not be "purgatorial."' In which connection he allows himself the cheekiest remark in the book: 'Apart from some of us Methodists, few attain on earth even to that carefully limited perfection which Wesley preached.'

An index at least of names would greatly have assisted the student. But the more serious lack is of a carefully analytical 'then and now' paper relating the intellectual environment of *Lux Mundi* to that of the present day. Undeniably, many pointers are to be found throughout the book, and D. K. Hadidian's bibliographical epilogue touches upon some of the sources, but the deficiency remains. What would we make of the presuppositions of the *Lux Mundi* divines —for example, that philosophy and theology are partners; that Christianity is the culmination of the world's religions; that evolutionary development cashed in incarnational terms is the key to theology? Moreover, we have to articulate the catholic faith not only in a context of religious pluralism, but in relation to cultural expressions of Christianity which sometimes appear only tenuously related to certain catholic verities, and in face of new sectarianisms, whether 'issue-based,' or deriving from theologico-ideological method. Geoffrey Wainwright alludes to the cultural factor in his preface, and David N. Power raises the hermeneutical issue. But a probing and sustained concluding discussion along the lines indicated would have rounded off what is, even as it stands, a most stimulating and welcome volume.

Journal of the United Reformed Church History Society 4 (1990) 397–99.

84

Donald MacKinnon as Theologian

Donald M. MacKinnon. *Themes in Theology: The Three-fold Cord*. Edinburgh: T. & T. Clark, 1987.

Our distinguished author's deep commitment to the traditional scheme of the Trinity and incarnation, conceived as a base to be maintained and not abandoned, unites the essays collected in this stimulating volume.

Part A comprises six papers on problems within philosophical theology, with special reference to *theologia negativa*. In 'The inexpressibility of God' we are warned against 'reducing the divine eternity to terms of the recognizable.' The transcendent is not to be levelled down 'to the form of a magnified supra-human reality.' We pass to 'Kant's philosophy of religion,' and are reminded that it was in the context of competing religious authoritarianisms that Kant insisted that no form of religion could be valid which failed to acknowledge the sovereignty of moral principles. Kant is found to end the tradition of negative theology in that he 'can neither accept a religious faith that presupposes a divine self-revelation nor completely subordinate the entertainment of its possibility to morality as an instrument that serves the effective extension of the latter's authority.' Kant reappears in the third essay, 'Reflections on time and space,' as treading 'the narrow path between idealism and realism,' and profound questions concerning the relation of the temporal to the eternal are raised. In addition to recalling some unjustifiably neglected thinkers, the paper on 'Some aspects of the treatment of Christianity by the British idealists' adverts to the service performed by Green and Edward Caird on behalf of those post-Tractarians whose teleological inheritance from Butler had been eroded by Darwin. The investigation of 'Metaphor in theology' which follows is notable for its insistence upon the fact that 'the saturation of our religious and theological speech by the consciously or unconsciously metaphorical, is perfectly compatible with the allowance that such speech is intentionally referential.' The section ends with 'Reflections on mortality.' Since death deprives us of the context of genuinely human life, 'any hereafter which we can represent to ourselves in significantly human terms is inadmissible.' Here 'an essentially negative theology must be enabled to have the last word.'

Part B contains two essays: 'Power, politics and religious faith,' and 'Creon and Antigone,' which endorse Dr. MacKinnon's contention that 'any serious theological work must take account of the over-all ecclesial and human context in which it is carried on.' We thus proceed from an historical study in which righteous anger is displayed against Constantine's slogan, *in hoc signo vinces*, to a discussion of nuclear power which tends in the direction of unilateralism, whilst appreciating the statesman's responsibilities.

Part C gathers pieces on *The Myth of God Incarnate*,' 'The relation of the doctrines of the Incarnation and the Trinity,' 'Prolegomena to Christology,' 'Teilhard's *Le Milieu Divin* re-considered,' 'Crucifixion and resurrection,' and 'Edward Schillebeeckx's Christology.' The author confesses that this group of essays is informed by an impatience with those who shrink from the task of theological reconstruction, and with those who are unwilling to re-think *ab initio* the proper relations of church and state. He concurs with Charles Raven that we may not think of the universe as no more than the state set for the drama of redemption—a point at which he feels Teilhard may still assist us; he urges a fresh view of *kenosis* as 'the conception which alone enables us to approach the *arcana* of the divine condescension'—and he will not permit 'the rhetoric of *Christus Victor*' to obscure that reality. In the review of Schillebeeckx he underlines the importance of a 'proper hermeneutics'.

Part D, 'Epilogue,' resumes the theme of the vulnerability of God as expressive of his essential being, and reminds us that all our thinking about the transcendent yet involved divine being must take due account of the fact that we are those who live in the century of Auschwitz.

Dr. MacKinnon is appreciative of all he has learned from others, but he remains his own man, correcting and reproving where necessary. Thus, he finds the authors of *The Myth of God Incarnate* 'by no means at ease in handling the history and sense of such notions as substance' (which, given the subject, some may consider an understatement as fatal as a tap from an elephant's paw); and he can descend upon Schillebeeckx from a great height thus: 'The way in which Schillebeeckx has recourse to this particular phrase [i.e., 'Jesus as eschatological Lord'] is neither worthy of his stature as a theologian, nor indeed required to get him out of difficulties that he is treating more effectively elsewhere.' Profoundly aware of mystery, and of the consequent limits of human awareness and understanding, Dr. MacKinnon is not one to invent mysteries. Never afraid to nail his colours to the mast, he will, above all, permit no skirting of the scandal of particularity where the incarnation is concerned.

In passing, a formidable agenda of work to be done is presented: on Teilhard's vision; on the place of silence before mystery and *contra* idolatry; on the analysis of 'fact'; on Kant and eschatology; on the Holy Spirit and the mission of the Incarnate; on Moltmann *vis-à-vis* the idealist-realist debate; on Christ and time. In return, I presume to ask Dr. MacKinnon for more. There is, as I have said, much here on God's condescension (which *is* grace—than which, *pace* the quoted Newman, there is no higher gift); there is also the spectre of Auschwitz and all it represents. What, then, needs to be *done* in the God-ward direction in order to atonement, having special regard to God's holiness? At this point, P. T. Forsyth, to whom passing reference is made, may come to our aid. Again, I should welcome Dr. MacKinnon's observations upon James Denney's remark that it is 'the doctrine of the Atonement . . . which makes it inevitable that we should have a Christology.'

With our author, I regret that so many in the West have discussed the attributes of the one God independently of the fact of the divine tri-unity; and with him I urge a close *theological* (not simply a missiological/pragmatic) investigation of church establishments which, incidentally, are varied and not Anglican only. The issue should be pressed to the Trinity itself, for only when we take full account of the fact that God calls his Church into being by the Spirit through the Word, and gives it to his Son as bride, shall we have the basis for a proper consideration of church order, and the resources for witnessing to and, if need be over against, the powers that be.

For all the modesty with which he presents his deepest convictions, there is a steadiness of course here which would regard alien gusts as merely providing further occasions of wrestling. At the end of 'Power politics and religious faith,' Dr. MacKinnon observes that 'we have all of us to reckon with the fact that for all our boasted openness of mind, we are likely to continue to prefer the quick, seemingly satisfying answers of the *simplificateur*, whether theoretical or practical or both, rather than acknowledge the tragic stuff of which human existence in its simultaneous *grandeur et misère*, is fashioned.' Perhaps; but Donald MacKinnon will be among the last to succumb to the preference here described.

King's Theological Review 11 (1988) 71–72.

85

Liberation Theology

Juan Luis Segundo. *A theology for a New Humanity*. Translated by John Drury. 5 volumes, Dublin: Gill and Macmillan, 1980. Pp. 172, 213, 206, 154, and 148.

This is no ordinary systematic theology. It is far removed in content, format and style from the dogged plod through the 'departments' from God to eschatology. Indeed, Fr. Segundo disclaims any intention of presenting a complete theological system, and modestly regards his work as a first attempt to write a theology for a new humanity. The five volumes are entitled, *The Community Called Church*; *Grace and the Human Condition*; *Our Idea of God*; *The Sacraments Today*; and *Evolution and Guilt*.

The work is not only less comprehensive than a traditional systematic theology, it has two further distinguishing features. The first concerns the process of gestation and the resulting format. The material has been devised in collaboration with the staff of the Peter Faber [Pastoral] Centre in Montevideo, and has been tested out on and by lay Christians. We thus have series of lectures interspersed with 'clarifications' and followed by accumulations of pertinent Conciliar texts (except in vols. 3 and 5), biblical passages and expositions, and 'springboard questions' (except in vol. 5). A disadvantage of this as a final form of presentation is that necessary qualifications of what is said in the lectures are sometimes delayed until we reach subsequent (not always immediately following) clarifications. The references provide a useful means of keeping up with the debate in Latin American theology, though there is surprisingly little reference to Protestant contributions to that debate. Perhaps, in a series originally published in 1968, the author felt that he had enough on his hands in communicating Vatican II and Medellin to a Church which both holds and at times exasperates him. The work would have benefited from an index—at least of names.

The second distinguishing feature is the theological method adopted. Fr. Segundo follows the path of liberation theology, though in a subtle and discriminating way—this makes him at once easier to sympathize with and more difficult to pin down. He will tolerate no absolute dualism as between sacred and profane history (4: App. 2), and he insists that theology begins not from ideas but from praxis: 'the truth that brings freedom is not a matter of theory but a matter of praxis' (5: p. 52). Like many liberation theologians Fr. Segundo has a good deal of theorizing to do about praxis—a fact which in itself suggests that the theory-praxis distinction should not be pressed too far. I shall return to the methodological question after making a number of general points.

Part Three: Theology

The series is pervaded by genuine pastoral concern—a concern made urgent by the conviction that 'among many Christians the process of growing into mature human beings is estranging them from the faith' (1: p. i). But Fr. Segundo's hope is not quenched—even by the possibility of nuclear war, for man 'may well celebrate the day on which [he] acquired this dreadful power to destroy himself. Why? Because from that day on, even though we may not have realized it then, no spot on this planet could be disregarded and no facet of mankind could be overlooked without danger of igniting the spark that could destroy the whole world' (1: p. 101). He welcomes Vatican II as evidence that the Church now, for the first time, enters into dialogue with the world *of which it is a part* (1: pp. 128–32); and while he believes that 'Our unjust society and our perverted idea of God are in close and terrible alliance' (3: p. 8), he can yet believe that 'Liberty is a possibility given and a value to be won by handling an ever increasing number of determinisms' (2: p. 33).

Fr. Segundo has many criticisms to make of his Church, and not least of Vatican II (2: pp. 131–36), but his are not the shrill protests of the debunker. He opposes magical views of the sacraments; emphasizes the communitarian nature of the Church; and goes so far as to say that 'In principle, and for deep and sound theological reasons, we would have preferred to replace *priest* with some such term as *elder* or *director*, since this term ties in with a profound and decisive experience lived by the early Christian community' (4: p. 28 n. 5). His understanding of the Church as a community of priests, and of the Eucharist as presupposing community, might have found support in a covenant ecclesiology. Such an ecclesiology would also have enabled his to speak more positively about infant baptism (4: p. 6). He does not wish to espouse a mechanistic view of the sacraments (2: p. 162), but he can still speak of 'channels' of grace (1: p. 39). With my in-bred suspicion of 'pipe-lines' I should much prefer him to speak of *means* of grace. He has pertinent comments upon the Church's practice of canonization, but does not relate them to the New Testament understanding of 'saint' (2: pp. 92–94).

The volumes contain many illuminating discussions: of mass-directed media and the work of grace (2: pp. 50–55); of Thomas à Kempis's classic, the full title of which (*Imitation of Christ and Contempt for the World*) helps Fr. Segundo to make his point (2: pp. 86–94); of the 'death of God' theology in relation to the Medellin documents (3: pp. 12–18); and of Bultmann. In this last he challenges that 'empiricism' of modern man which does not accept the transcendent: 'this stance does not come from experience but from an attitude. And it is in fact an attitude for which any sort of revelation would lack meaning. So this modern man is opposed to accepting the transcendent, not because of his modernity, but because of an attitude that is as old as the world itself' (3: p. 49). In a manner reminiscent of certain Anglican theologians of the earlier part of this (the twentieth) century, Fr. Segundo defends Trinitarian theology and claims that 'the God Jesus revealed to us is a God who is a society' (3: p. 66); but he draws a more modern conclusion: 'all theology, even when it is concerned with the Trinity, is political. And doubly so when it does not seek to be political' (3: p. 73 n. 23). There is an extended discussion of the place of reason in theology in which the author is, perhaps, too quick to give advice and too eager to win a victory: 'the philosopher must give up opposing the Christian God to the God of the philosophers. We must be bold enough to describe the latter as the God of bad philosophers' (3: p. 140). The 'laicist' conception of liberty, according to which an individual's mind is held to be a *tabula rasa* on reaching choice-making maturity is rightly denounced (4: p. 80); and the crisis of confidence of the priesthood, which is deemed to turn on the fact that sacraments are not rites but signs, is discussed (4: pp. 104–13).

Apt use is made of illustrations drawn especially from modern novels. We are not surprised to find Sartre, Camus and Gide; but the use of Rodó and Carlos Martinez Moreno is refreshing. The volumes contain some spelling errors; some battered letters; some ugly words, of which the worst example is 'unbeknownst'; and some slipshod writing, as when we are told that something is 'fairly worldwide.'

Returning now to Fr. Segundo's methodology, we find that it turns upon the view that salvation/liberation is a matter of God's action in history, and that it involves the whole person in his social context (2: pp. 37, 39 etc.). At this point Fr. Segundo is subtler than some liberation theologians, who have embraced Marxist epistemology less critically than he. But although he criticizes Marxism (5: pp. 96–101), and submits the crucial concept of violence to close analysis (5: p. 121), he does not follow through to the eschatological clash as between Marxism and Christianity. On the other hand, he does not identify the cause of God with that of the poor after the extreme manner of some liberation theologians. In fact, in an important note (3: p. 160 n. 7), he points out that many in his own day are poorer than the artisan Jesus, and that 'The poverty of Christ was a relative and ambiguous value, if it is taken independently of his concrete mission.'

The crux of the methodological issue is the assumption of liberation theology that the gospel and socio-political analysis are equally informative and, indeed, that the latter is the source of the former. Fr. Segundo does allow that man 'will not manage to lay hold of the living God solely *by starting from* the history of man. God reveals himself *in history but he does not surface from* history' (3: p. 175); but the force of this comment is not consistently allowed. It is thus hard to see how, on this theory (mark the word) some aspects of man's life can be subject to the judgement of the gospel. Recourse is had to a hermeneutic of history rather than to one of scripture. Hence the tendency for compatibility with 'the modern mentality' (itself an abstraction) to become the criterion by which the propriety or otherwise of the Church's formulations are to be judged (Introduction to vol. 2). This is not to deny that there is a considerable amount of biblical exegesis in these volumes, but the use of Scripture tends to be selective and subjective, and on occasion contrary cases are overlooked. Paul, for example, has more positive things to say about law than is allowed in volumes 2 and 3; and in connection with heaven the positive aspects of New Testament teaching on reward are not given due place (2: p. 163).

I suspect that the lack of eschatological clarity in these volumes, as well as their optimism, derives in part from the influence of Teilhard de Chardin. The universe is Christified; the Church is self-consciously Christified; and the process of humanization cannot but succeed. The various determinants of human life must and will be transformed into servants of liberty (1: pp. 120–124; 2: pp. 82–86; 5: *passim*). It thus transpires that universalism is permitted to tone down the crisis of the Kingdom, to remove the scandal of the Cross, and to evacuate the concept of the sons or people (as distinct from the children) of God of its proper significance. There is a biblical particularity of which proper account is not taken here. Or, at least, in an ambiguous way, Fr. Segundo does recognize the Church's minority position, whilst upholding the salvation of those outside its fellowship (3: p. 102; 4: p. 78); but his is the strangely gnostic particularity of those who are in the know concerning salvation (1: chapters 1 and 2, and pp. 89–91).

The universalistic thrust is intensified by Fr. Segundo's horror of religious individualism. He rightly protests against this, and especially at the sacramental abuse to which it can lead (3: p. 18; 4: p. 35). But we must not minimize the challenge of the gospel to the individual, but rather encourage him to realize that while his relation with God is a personal matter it is not a private one. Fr. Segundo can sound orthodox enough, as when he says 'in Christ and through Christ . . . the plan of God is fully realized in us human beings' (1: p. 15); but if this happens merely by the fact that we are born, we have an inevitability here which sits lightly both to human responsibility and to atoning grace—and this despite oft-reiterated opposition to Pelagius.

I cannot believe that the fact that it was not Fr. Segundo's intention to cover the whole of Christian doctrine excuses the lack of attention to Christ's atoning work, and (surprisingly in Latin America with its phenomenal Pentecostalism) to the regenerating work of God the Holy Spirit.

One way of expressing my disquiet at the apparent destination of Fr. Segundo's methodology is in relation to the classic question with which the *Westminster Shorter Catechism* opens: 'What is the chief end of man'? Fr. Segundo replies: 'Turning ourselves into *persons* . . . was the end goal of hominization. And turning ourselves into *persons* also seems to be the end goal of our elevation, our divinization' (2: p. 70). The *Catechism*'s answer is: 'Man's chief end is to glorify God, and to enjoy him for ever.' My 'springboard question' which I address to this series is: 'How, if at all, are these answers related—and does it matter if they are not'? I do not find an unambiguous answer in Fr. Segundo's books, but I am sure that the new humanity needs one.

Philosophical Studies 28 (1981) 270–273.

The Atonement

John Driver. *Understanding the Atonement for the Mission of the Church*. Scottdale, PA: Herald Press, 1986. Pp. 286.

Colin E. Gunton. *The Actuality of Atonement: A Study of Metaphor, Rationality and the Christian Tradition*. Edinburgh: T. & T. Clark, 1989. Pp. 222.

Since the original publication some years ago of F. W. Dillistone's *The Christian Understanding of the Atonement*, there has been something of an 'atonement-shaped-blank' in serious theological writing in the English-speaking world. The two books here under review are welcome signs that the silence is being broken. Professor Driver is a Mennonite teacher of Bible and church history, with missionary experience in Latin America. Dr. Gunton is in the line of historic orthodox dissent; he is Professor of Christian Doctrine, and his mission field is King's College, London.

The two books complement one another in style and content. An historical thrust is common to both, but where Dr. Gunton is more tough-mindedly the systematic theologian, Dr. Driver presents a good deal of biblical material which students of doctrine would do well to master.

Dr. Driver advocates what he calls a radical evangelical approach to the atonement. The disciples of Jesus experienced atonement before they understood it, and the New Testament refers to the work of Christ *via* a range of pictures, analogies and images. The metaphors used are not to be regarded as alternatives to literal meanings of Christ's work; rather, images are 'terms or concepts whose meanings are not exhausted by the strictly literal sense of the term.' We must resist the strong disjunction which avers that terms must be either metaphorical or ontological.

With the passage of time certain metaphors have received privileged status, and Constantinian ecclesiastical attitudes have adversely affected the presentation of atonement doctrine. Dr. Driver supports these claims by an analysis of Christus Victor, Abelardian and Anselmian themes.

The heart of Dr. Driver's book comprises chapters on the principal biblical images for understanding the atonement: conflict-victory-liberation; vicarious suffering; archetypal images; the martyr, sacrifice, expiation, redemption-purchase, and justification motifs; and the adoption-family image.

Turning to contemporary implications of atonement doctrine, Dr. Driver discusses the work of Christ *vis-à-vis* the messianic community and the idea of cosmic restoration, and comes finally to some missiological reflections which revolve around the themes of communion, peace, justice and love.

At certain points in Dr. Driver's exposition questions are raised, of which I have space to mention two. First, it must be said that he wields an unduly blunt instrument against the satisfaction theory of the atonement. On this matter Dr. Gunton is much more sensitive—and accurate. Secondly, Dr. Driver devotes only two paragraphs to what he calls the incarnational (that is, the Eastern) theory of the atonement. It is not that one wishes to exalt incarnation above atonement, or to divorce the one from the other. But in a book on the work of Christ which has a missiological emphasis, the lack of detailed analysis of the mission of God the Holy Trinity (on which subject the East is considerably illuminating) is regrettable. Nevertheless, Dr. Driver has done well to bring the work of Christ and the mission of the Church into mutual relation to the extent that he has.

Dr. Gunton's method requires him to confront us directly with three intellectual giants, all of whom are weighed and found wanting. Their good points notwithstanding, Kant transmogrified the Christian gospel into its opposite; as a result of his elevation of the aesthetic dimension of human experience, Schleiermacher diminished Christian claims; and Hegel's idealism is reductionist. In the hands of all three the doctrines of sin and atonement become casualties. Dr. Gunton seeks to go beyond, and in some respects against, these thinkers. He sets out to counter rationalism, and to advocate the view that atonement language is metaphorical. This, he considers, will enable us to take due account both of the concreteness and mystery of atonement: 'Metaphor,' he declares, 'is a supreme instance of the harmony that can be attained between language and the world.'

Thus equipped, Dr. Gunton explores the atonement metaphors of victory (Aulèn), justice (Anselm), satisfaction (Forsyth), and sacrifice (the Bible), and Edward Irving (qualified 'substitution'). He shows that the metaphors are ineradically relational. Hence to a chapter on 'The atonement and the Triune God,' in which he works towards 'a non-interventionist concept of the atonement which yet maintains the utter uniqueness and definitiveness of the career of Jesus,' and elucidates the eschatological dimension of the metaphors—all of which focus upon both God and the world.

So, finally, to 'The community of reconciliation.' Here the running theme is that 'language takes shape, remains alive, in a community speech.' Constantinianism is denounced, and the (entirely appropriate) suggestion is made that the 'traditions of dissent' may prove illuminating concerning the Church-state relation. The atonement metaphors are discussed with reference to the life of the Christian community, special attention being devoted to the dominical sacraments. The 'ecclesiological outcome' is that Christ and the Spirit 'create, in time and space, a living echo of the communion that God is in eternity.' The eschatological unity of nature and grace, realized in Christ's atoning sacrifice, is the ground and inspiration of the Church's praise.

Dr. Gunton skilfully juggles with a number of balls. He wishes to accord due place to reason without becoming a rationalist; he analyses Christian discourse with a view to reinstating metaphor as the appropriate way of speaking of matters divine, human and real; he dusts down the traditional atonement metaphors, seeking to anchor them all in a trinitarian base; and he emphasizes the inescapability of the Church as the community of reconciliation. All of this is woven into a cumulatively persuasive case. The argument moves at a brisk pace—at times, perhaps, it is a little too brisk; some assertions could be given a closer analysis. But here a general point only can be made. It concerns Dr. Gunton's tendency occasionally to tilt at the Enlightenment. (I recognize that in other writing he has done more than tilt at it, but tilting is what sometimes happens here). It may be that even Enlightenment rationalism is preferable to the sectarian violence which so often preceded it. It is conceivable that the excesses of rationalism are the price we pay for our release from *pseudo* authorities, whether written or institutional, which would usurp the Gospel. Further, there is something in Locke's cautionary word in one of his letters: 'To be rational is so glorious a thing, that two-legged creatures generally content themselves with the title.' The something has to do with truth.

Our two authors converge at many points. They both abhor Constantianianism; they share a cosmic view of redemption; they underline the importance of the Church as the community of reconciliation. If Dr. Driver needs to 'beef up' his Trinitarian-patristic content (to borrow a technical term from Dr. Gunton!), it is quite clear that he is entirely in accord with Dr. Gunton on this point: 'The Christian church still stands or falls by whether it proclaims and lives by the Gospel of the liberating grace of God, or whether its life degenerates into some form of self-salvation. For that reason, the doctrine of the atonement must continue to be at the heart of Christian theology.' Only so will 'Christianity's orientation to the action of God in re-establishing free human life . . . be maintained and articulated.'

The Irish Theological Quarterly 57 (1991), 82–84.

87

Models of the Church

Avery Dulles. *Models of the Church*. Dublin: Gill and Macmillan, 1976. Pp 216.

Since the Church is a mystery, we cannot speak about it directly. Rather, we must resort to models (pp. 7, 8). These models, which 'speak to man existentially and find an echo in the inarticulate depths of his psyche' are more than metaphors (p. 18). A vital key to the interpretation of religious symbolism, which is both functional and cognitive, is provided by religious experience (pp. 18–19). Models help us both to explain and to explore (p. 22).

From this anchorage Fr. Dulles launches into a critical review of some of the more important models of the Church. He treats of the Church as institution; as mystical communion; as sacrament; as herald; and as servant. There follow chapters on 'The Church and Eschatology,' 'The True Church,' 'The Church and the Churches,' 'Ecclesiology and Ministry,' and 'The Church and Revelation.' The work ends with 'The Evaluation of Models'.

This stimulating book is marked by five characteristics in particular:

1. It is lucidly written, and although good use is made of sources ancient and modern, Catholic and Protestant, we can always see the shape of the argument.

2. It is a very fair book. Fr. Dulles is quick to note both the strengths and the weaknesses of every model he passes in review. To take one example: the advantages of the model of the Church as mystical communion are said to be that it builds upon the biblical idea of *koinonia*; that it is ecumenically fruitful; that it is well grounded in the Catholic tradition; that its emphasis upon 'the personal relationship between the faithful—individually and collectively —with the Holy Spirit, helps to revivify spirituality and the life of prayer' (p. 55); and that interpersonal models are calculated to meet a need expressed by many of the faithful. On the debit side is the absence of a clear statement of the relationship between the Church visible and invisible; the tendency to over-exalt and to divinize the Church; the failure of this ecclesiology to provide Christians with a clear sense of identity or mission; and the tension (ambiguously, but not always prudently covered by *koinonia*) 'between the Church as a network of friendly interpersonal relationships and the Church as a mystical communion of grace' (p. 56). The book's fairness emerges too in Fr. Dulles's kindly and generally accurate exposition of Protestant views. He even (and this does not always happen) understands the position according to which 'apostolic succession' means 'continuity with the faith and proclamation of the apostles' (p. 127).

3. This is an eirenic book. This is manifest in many places, not least in Fr. Dulles' quest of a 'theology of ministries that is free from the juridicism that characterized the Roman thinking of the late nineteenth century' (p. 140; cf. chapter X).

4. It is an honest book. The author unhesitatingly criticizes his own Church where he thinks it has been in the wrong—notably in connection with imperialistic institutionalism (e.g., p. 121).

5. Much of the book's honesty is a function of Fr. Dulles' desire to ground his work in the Bible (cf. the quotation from G. Weigel, p. 17). Thus, for example, 'The New Testament, at least, does not impose the three-tier hierarchical system (bishop, presbyter, deacon) today familiar to us' (p. 154). At times, perhaps, Fr. Dulles is not yet biblical enough. The ecclesiology of Küng in particular, which removes from the ministry 'the cultic element that has caused it to be called "priestly"' (p. 156), is said to be influenced unduly by modern democratic theories. But may it not be that Küng is just being more radically biblical? 'The bishop or pastor,' Fr. Dulles declares, 'should not be allowed to turn into a mere business manager or personnel officer' (p. 158). Quite so; but there is an unhealthy sacerdotalism which is equally to be shunned. I should greatly have welcomed the author's comments on T. W. Manson's *The Church's Ministry* (1956) and *Ministry and Priesthood: Christ's and Ours* (1958).

After analysing the models and dealing with the matters arising, Fr. Dulles concludes that there cannot be a supermodel; that no model may be accepted without qualification; and that of the five models studied the institutional model alone cannot be taken as primary, for 'institutions are subservient to persons, structures are subordinate to life' (p. 187).

So much for the contents and characteristics of this book which, from the typographical point of view, is marred only by the failure of italicize foreign phrases on pages 137 and 143–44. I can think of no more suitable fate for it than that it should become required reading at ecumenical fraternals and study groups. If I were present at any such gathering I should be inclined to make the following points:

1. The view cited by Fr. Dulles that 'Christ is the foremost recipient of revelation' (p. 170) should be handled with great caution. The attenuation of the Gospel which resulted when some older Protestant liberalisms spoke in these terms prompt the protest—against the possibility that Christ may be demoted to 'the first among equals'—that Christ *is* the revelation.

2. I endorse Fr. Dulles' view that for all the defects of the institutional model, the Church needs to be visible in the world (pp. 8, 32). (Dare I recall, *in this journal*, Dr. John Whale's comment that 'It would be an Irish result if the only discernible mark of the Church were its invisibility'?) I would add that there is an interdenominational testimony within evangelical Protestantism to the effect that we are 'All one in Christ Jesus' (in one sense gloriously true) which softens, if it does not deny, the challenge and the affront of a divided Table.

3. Fr. Dulles declares that the Catholic Church 'must at all costs avoid falling into a sectarian mentality' (p. 8). I confess that it is hard for me to resist the temptation to advert to some further words of his when I see (chapter 11) the pickle into which Rome gets when wondering what to do about the likes of non-Roman me! Against the wrong kind of institutionalism Fr. Dulles writes, 'The gifts and graces of the Holy Spirit, it would seem, must wait upon the approbation of the official leadership' (p. 41). (Cf. from the Reformed side, B. L. Manning, *Essays in Orthodox Dissent*, 1953).

4. I am somewhat reluctant to think of the Church as a sacrament (chapter 5). It is partly that the word 'sacrament' can (like 'love,' 'fellowship,' etc.) all too easily be devalued: the slogan 'All life is sacramental' comes to mind.[30] More seriously, the underlying idea here is that of the Church as being the continuation of the Incarnation. Fr. Dulles ought to take more account than he does of possible objections to this view. At one level the objection is that since the Incarnation is a mystery we have not done a great deal to elucidate the nature of the Church (also a mystery) by speaking of the latter in terms of the former. But the fundamental protest against the view is that of P T Forsyth: 'That which owes itself to a rebirth cannot be a prolongation of the ever sinless.'

5. In a few places I would recommend a balancing-up of testimony. It is true that there is a tendency in Protestantism 'to say that the Church exists wherever there is a community that believes in Christ. "Where two or three are gathered in my name, there

---

30. So, more recently, does my parody of W. S. Gilbert: 'When everything is sacrament, then nothing's sacramental.'

am I in the midst of them'" (p. 78). (Incidentally, *pace* the quotation on page 80, Jesus here announces a fact, he does not make a promise.) On the other hand there is a strong Reformed emphasis which would find the quoted words of Jesus more applicable to a prayer meeting than to the Church. The marks of the Church, it would be maintained—as, for example, in John Craig's crisp *Catechism* of 1581—are 'The Word, the Sacraments, and Discipline rightly exercised.' Again, while it is true that much Protestant practice has all but demoted the sacraments (I put the point more strongly than Fr. Dulles does on pages 77, 127, 159), the best Protestant theory has ever held that Word and Sacrament belong together. As is well known, it was Calvin's desire—a desire thwarted by the Genevan magistrates—that the bread should be broken every time the Word was preached. Finally, it is true that there have been Congregationalists who have sought wider fellowship on utilitarian grounds only (pp. 77, cf. 143). Once more I go further and say that some have been downright isolationist in spirit. But at its best this form of church order has recognized the need of inter-dependence, and that not only because it is desirable, but because it is right. The local church is the local expression of the Church catholic; hence it may not unchurch the latter, or proceed as if it did not exist. The classic here is John Owen's *The True Nature of a Gospel Church and its Government* (1689).

6. When Fr. Dulles has given us so much it may appear churlish to ask for more. But I should have welcomed a more extensive discussion of the Church as the priesthood of all believers. The idea is there, and it is correctly construed in a non-individualistic way (p. 152). But the idea of the Church as a community of believers raises a number of thorny question which have relevance not only to discussions between Roman Catholics and others, but also to those discussion within Protestantism between those who do, and those who do not, ally themselves with the World Council of Churches. Such question include the following: 'What is the source of belief?,' 'What is a Christian?,' 'Is there an indispensable minimum of belief?,' 'What is the place of ecclesiastical discipline in relation to belief?,' 'What are the grounds of separation?'

Two Puritans may pose the general dilemma for us. 'What!' expostulated John Flavel, 'at peace with the Father and at war with His Children? It cannot be.' But, averred Walter Cradock, 'It is better to have division than an evil uniformity.' The dilemma is painful, but I am glad that the prevailing mood enables me to be a separated *brother* rather than a *separated* brother.

Philosophical Studies 27 (1980) 348–51.

On Being the Church

Colin E. Gunton and Daniel W. Hardy, eds. *On Being the Church: Essays on the Christian Community*, Edinburgh: T. & T. Clark, 1989. Pp. 263.

The six authors gathered here have German, American, Irish or English origins; with the exception of one who teaches in the Republic of Ireland, they hold posts in English universities; they speak out of Roman Catholic, Anglican or Reformed commitments; and two of them are ordained, four are lay—or, depending upon one's ecclesiology, all are both. Although they do not wish to be regarded as a theological 'school,' their volume is by no means a casual set of musings upon a theme. They have worked as a team and, differences of perspectives notwithstanding, are united in the conviction that there has been a 'massive loss in recent years of a theological basis for a doctrine of the Church.' Their proposed remedy is to affirm and restore what they (and C. C. J. Webb before them) call created 'sociality,' of which the church is the redeemed fulfilment (not replacement). For them this concern is more pressing than that of ministerial orders, on which so much energy has been expended. They concur in the lament that the church too often utilizes a secularized conception of authority, and this, they believe, contributes to the lack of sustained attention to the constitution and being of the church.

I shall briefly indicate the main contentions of the authors, and then seek to enter into conversation with them on a number of points of importance which they have raised.

Daniel Hardy writes on 'Created and Redeemed Sociality.' With indebtedness to Coleridge and over against Kantian and Hegelian individualism, he exalts sociality as a transcendent universal, between which and empirical reality there is (*pace* Kant as often interpreted, and Bonhoeffer) no necessary cleavage. The social transcendental manifests the Divine Trinity, and forbids us to 'privatize' the Christian contribution to sociality by setting Christian faith apart from common sociality: in which connection P. T. Forsyth and Bonhoeffer are weighed and found wanting.

Colin Gunton discusses 'The Church on Earth: the Roots of Community.' His thesis is that 'the manifest inadequacy of the theology of the Church derives from the fact that it has never seriously and consistently been rooted in a conception of the being of God as triune.' Professor Gunton suggests that in the East, the influence of neoplatonism encouraged the view of the world as hierarchically structured—with consequent ecclesiastical implications, despite the general tendency of Christological and Trinitarian theology. In the West, the 'dismal' ecclesiological development was on analogy with earthly empire. The deeply disturbing result of this is the institutionalizing of the Spirit, whereby 'in place of the free, dynamic, personal and *particular* agency of the Spirit, he is made into a substance which becomes the possession of the Church.' The remedy? Less Christologically-grounded universalizing, and a greater emphasis upon 'the action of the Holy Spirit towards Jesus as the source of the *particularity* and so historicity of his humanity.'

But this alone will not suffice. We must move forward to an ontology of the church, and the route to this is *via* a Trinitarian theology of creation. Professor Gunton expresses reservations concerning Augustine's conception of the Trinity, the direction of which is said to be modalist. He prefers the Cappadocian insight that there is no being of God anterior to the persons: 'The being of God *is* the persons in relation to each other.' Turning to his own heritage, Dr. Gunton invokes John Owen's witness to the fact that as the hypostases in relation constitute the being of God, so the relation of concrete historical persons constitutes the primary being of the church. Such an ecclesiology challenges any ordained caste, as well as the subordination of any (not least women) in the church.

Werner G. Jeanrond writes on 'Community and Authority: the Nature and Implications of the Authority of Christian Community.' The bases of Christian faith are political, social, public, historical and eschatological, and all of these are encompassed by the eucharist. This communitarian stance was, he argues, denied by the medieval clergy/lay dualism, the results of which are still with us. Indeed: 'The tragedy of the Second Vatican Council lies in its failure to agree wholeheartedly on the redefinition of the Church as *communio* and to abandon the concept of the Church as *societas*. As long as the final power over the community remains only in the hands of one section of the community, the essence of *communio* authorized by God is destroyed in favour of an ecclesial society authorized only by itself.' Churchly authority requires a communal organization, an elected leadership, and 'the ongoing prophetic critique of both.' In fact, however, we witness a plurality of churches: hence to an enumeration of the difficulties in ecumenical dialogue, and of the problems posed when local churches are unaware of, or wish to proceed faster than, the deliberations of their several— and constitutionally *different*—representative bodies. Dr. Jeanrond ends with a call to hope, and an exhortation to participate in the ecumenical quest.

In 'The Creature of the Word: Recovering the Ecclesiology of the Reformers,' Christoph Schwöbel observes that the political character of the English Reformation led to the treatment of the church from the point of view of church polity rather than that of its nature and mission. He proceeds to a careful exposition of Luther and Calvin on the nature of the church. The crux is that the '*communio sanctorum* as the *creatura verbi divini*, is the *catholic* Church.' The church's basic ministry is to witness to the Gospel: it cannot 'create faith or effectively administer the grace of God —God alone can do this. To which Calvin adds his views on the ordering of the church's ministry of the Word. From the Reformers we may learn the art of distinguishing and relating *opus Dei* and *opus hominum*, thereby avoiding two 'heresies.' The first is that orthodoxy in which 'a particular doctrine or set of doctrines . . . is identified with the truth of revelation.' The second is that orthopraxis which becomes heretical when 'the work of God is identified with a specific form of human action . . . God's work cannot be embodied in any human act.' The recovery of the fundamental distinction between God's work and ours would, Schwöbel believes, encourage the church in its witness, and save it from undue preoccupation with the preservation of its own identity.

Then Dissenting Christian tiptoed timorously along Anglican Alley and, behold, an altercation before the house of the Professor. Such Bunyanesque language comes *initially* to mind as we turn to Richard H. Roberts on 'Lord, Bondsman and Churchman: Identity. Integrity and Power in Anglicanism.' But the initial reaction must be modified, for it is soon clear that what we have here is a 'reading' of two books by Stephen Sykes (*The Integrity of Anglicanism* and *The Identity of Christianity*) after the manner of the those literary theorists by whom some are currently enraptured and who, to others, seem to have wandered into By-Path Meadow. Dr. Roberts is in fact arguing against a position which lies at the bottom of a slippery slope upon which he conceives Professor Sykes to stand, but to the bottom of which he has not as yet descended. (This being so, the editors are perhaps a little oversensitive in advising us that this paper caused the group some controversy because of the 'highly critical discussion of the ecclesiology of a colleague.' We are reassured that the original draft of the paper was seen by Professor Sykes, though what he thought of it is not disclosed). Dr. Roberts contends that Professor Sykes' understanding of 'authority' is ultimately in terms of power— this in defiance of the 'invisible' laity, and in disregard of 'the universal fallibility of all human agency.' In which connection Hegel's parable of the Lord and Bondsman is invoked as a cautionary tale.

The concluding paper is 'Faith in the Cities: Corinth and the Modem City,' by David F. Ford. Dr. Ford finds that the report of the Archbishop of Canterbury's commission on urban priority areas, *Faith in the City* (1983), is ecclesiologically deficient. For all its proper social concern, it lacks an explicit doctrine of the Church. Moreover, its implicit ecclesiology fails to challenge the Church of England's ways of distributing power and authority. In addition, the report underplays the dimension of Christian hope. The discussion of Paul's Corinthian letters suggests that although the Church of England cannot imitate the Corinthian church, it should be warned by Paul lest it purchase relevance at the cost of its true identity.

I now presume to enter into conversation with my six friends. I welcome their book. Seldom does a collection of papers trigger so many discussion points: I must be highly selective. The authors have, in fact, been so provocative (in the best sense) that I shall not only offer reflections upon what they have done, but shall assign topics for their next volume.

First, as to the editorial claim that there has been a 'massive loss in recent years of a theological basis for a doctrine of the Church.' The term 'recent' may be queried—and is strongly queried by Professor Gunton himself: to him the Trinitarian basis of ecclesiology has never yet been firmly in place. John Owen eventually saw the point, but the communion whose greatest seventeenth-century theologian he was progressively lost the vision. If the weakness of Trinitarian theology is the remote cause of the ecclesiological malaise, what is the proximate? I should wish to propose post-Enlightenment individualism as one candidate for consideration. This is by no means to jump upon the bandwaggon of those to whom the Enlightenment is solid mud—how, for example, could one learn from modern biblical criticism and consistently do that? Nevertheless, the 'evangelical' individualism which finds the whole of Christianity in the salvation of my soul; the 'catholic' piety which devoutly makes *my* communion; the 'liberal' mindset which so strenuously exalts *my* interpretative right —these and their variants have been corrosive of Christian community, and have done more than a little to feed that consumerism which afflicts church life in some parts of the world. I should like to hear from Richard Roberts on 'The power of the individual Christian as destructive of communion.'

With the insistence of the authors upon the need to revitalize ecclesiology I have every sympathy. I have myself detected a reluctance in some ecumenical circles to see the point of deeply theological study, or of the detailed analysis of the philosophical presuppositions which underlie the several churchly standpoints. Some appear to find it more convenient, or more 'relevant,' to concentrate upon questions of ministry and sacraments at the expense of other themes. With Colin Gunton I regret this. Even so, the idea, for example, that specific orders are integral to the being of the church must be responded to with the utmost seriousness, for at stake are divergent understandings of the Gospel. Until these are probed there will be no resolution of questions of ministry and sacraments.

The editors assure us that their 'work began as an attempt to bridge the gap between the academic study of theology . . . and the often narrowly focused and pragmatically oriented [*sic*] procedures of official church conversations and committees.' Because they have largely ignored the findings of the latter (Dr. Ford is an exception) we are left with two piers and no bridge. The fact is that some studies by ecumenical bodies (the Christian World Communions as well as the World Council of Churches) would be found to be on the side of these authors in their appeal for a grounded ecclesiology. Other productions are, admittedly, less satisfactory in this respect. But given that these authors are not of that breed of academic theologian whose proudest boast is that he or she has never stooped to 'committee theology,' still less sullied his fingers with *Baptism, Eucharist and Ministry*, they should not, by lack of engagement with ecumenical materials, encourage those who wish to drive a wedge between 'academic = *bona fide*' and 'ecumenical = bogus' theology.

I therefore wonder whether Colin Gunton could be persuaded to write a critical analysis of some major ecumenical documents from the point of view of their ecclesiological adequacy or otherwise? Were he to do this, he may need to guard his own flank by making out a fuller case for the social Trinity than was possible in the present paper. I endorse his resistance to monism and pantheism as alike blurring the Creator-creature distinction; he does acknowledge the pitfalls in the Trinity-church analogy. He is thus well placed to scrutinize the findings of others in this important arena of debate.

I now turn to the editors' observation that 'it is a constant temptation for theologians and other élites to suppose that they can create their own sociality apart from the rest of humanity'; and they recognize this tendency as a contributing factor to the current ecclesiastical malaise. How, then, are the theologians to serve in and with the whole people of God (of whom this book makes so much)? We need not join our voices with those who somewhat hysterically protest that the theologians have 'stolen the Bible' from the people. Surely not all of them have—those of my acquaintance seem to be quite above such dastardly acts. But there is a serious question, as the editors recognize, concerning the gulf which sometimes yawns between the 'professionals' and the majority of those in the pews. Would Werner Jeanrond be willing to help us further here? The editors note that he, a Roman Catholic, writes the most 'congregationalist' paper in this book—hence my request to him. The six contributors will not be surprised by my deep regret that the idea of the progression from sitting under the Word, to receiving the bread and wine, to gathering in Church Meeting, in order to discern, by the Spirit through the Bible, the mind of Christ and to seek unanimity in him—the very essence of classical congregationalism (whether Baptist or Congregational) —has faded so seriously within the tradition itself (for reasons in part connected with the individualism mentioned above, and partly owing to a weakening of the idea that there is an eternally significant distinction between those who are Christ's and those who are not), and hence is so weakly (if at all) present in the united churches into which so much of congregationalism has flowed. Could it be that the Congregationalists had the ecclesiological pearl of price which the current jargon concerning the 'doing' of contextual theology sometimes seems to lack?

However this may be, and in honour of my saints and martyrs, I must record my regret that Christoph Schwöbel omitted the ecclesiology of the radical Reformation from his otherwise excellent paper. Since the positions of Drs Jeanrond and Roberts and, in a different way, that of Professor Gunton, seem to be fuelled by insights drawn from that ecclesiology, some account of its historical roots would have been most helpful.

I have adverted to the importance of the hearing and study of the Bible by all the saints. What might such attentive listening and reflection teach us concerning ecclesiology? It is well known that past advocates of the several polities—episcopalian, presbyterial/ consistorial, congregational—resorted to the Bible in order to prove the authenticity of their way alone. This can no longer be done with integrity. But with what should we replace it? What of the so-called 'argument from silence'? What of the restorationist position, so productive of new denominations? What of its polar opposite —the view that nothing of importance has ever been lost from the (that is, our) church? Here, I respectfully suggest, is an admirable theme for Dr. Ford.

I come finally to Professor Hardy's paper. He presents Bonhoeffer and Forsyth as holding that 'social community is the response to the gift of God, fulfilled in his achievement in Christ.' They thereby 'lose their commonality as created social beings with the society to which they speak,' and they unwarrantably narrow down the work of God by failing to relate it to God's work in creation. I believe it could be shown that neither charge is sustainable, though I cannot produce the textual evidence here. Professor Hardy concludes that the features of human society (which he enumerates) 'not only come into existence but also achieve a qualitative difference in the history of the Jews and the redemptive work of Christ. This is what forms from *created sociality* a truly *redeemed sociality*. And the one is necessary to understand the other.' I hardly think that Forsyth would be at odds with this, though he certainly had a much keener sense of the tragedy of our sinful alienation from holy God, and hence of the radical nature of the atonement required to make the 'qualitative difference' than Daniel Hardy expresses here. The renewed community is a created and an acquitted community. But, for Forsyth, it is a sign of that larger renewal of the whole creation—a point upon which he insisted especially in his theodicy. ('Nature, if not the mother, is the matrix of grace.') Perhaps I have misunderstood Professor Hardy;

but whether I have or not I should be most interested in a dialogue between him and Christoph Schwöbel (who underlines the asymmetrical nature of the Creator-creature relation) on 'the relevance of soteriology to the doctrines of creation and the church.'

If a bonus request be permitted, I should opt for Colin Gunton on 'Making the Trinitarian claim in a pluralist world.'

All of this would still leave the ordering, discipline and mission of the church for a third volume!

The Ecumenical Review 41 (1989) 626–29.

89

Advancing Ecumenical Thinking

Gerard Kelly. *Recognition: Advancing Ecumenical Thinking.*
New York: Peter Lang, 1996. Pp. 312.

To express the point in homely terms, the term 'recognition' is like a snowball which over the past seventy-five years has been rolling down the ecumenical hill, gathering size and momentum as it goes. Gerard Kelly is the first to arrest its progress and to subject it to close scrutiny. By so doing he has served us well. With detailed reference not only to published texts but also to drafts of texts and minutes of meetings, he offers a careful study of the usage of the term in ecumenical discourse, and of the subtle variations in meaning to which it is susceptible. In particular he shows how the term, which had primarily a juridical connotation in earlier days of comparative ecclesiology, has latterly acquired theological significance as indicating the acknowledgement by Christians of one tradition that doctrine embraced by others is integral to the apostolic faith. Each chapter is furnished with ample references; the bibliography is full and helpful; but in an appendix listing the respondents to *Baptism, Eucharist and Ministry* (BEM) the section on united churches is confusing, since the Union of Welsh Independents is not a united church but a denomination of largely Welsh-speaking Congregationalists, and it, together with three of the others listed which are inter-Reformed unions, belongs to the World Alliance of Reformed Churches.

Kelly finds that while Catholics emphasize the recognition of communion grounded in fidelity to the Tradition flowing down from the undivided church, Protestants emphasize the recognition of confessional diversity which requires the reconciliation of several denominational heritages. No doubt his sources at this point (Paul VI, Athanagoras and

Harding Meyer among them) conduce to such a conclusion; but it is equally open to Protestants to recognize both the given unity of all who are in the succession of the apostles' Gospel, and the reality of 'denominations construed as aberrations which—especially if they sanction a divided Lord's table—require urgently to be dealt with.' In making this point I fully grant that Kelly is not to be blamed if his sources on occasion lead him to conclusions which are too disjunctive. Again, he says that 'because of the emphasis on catholicity and apostolicity, the Catholic approach to recognition is more clearly theological than the Protestant approach' (p. 28). But surely many Protestants would respectfully and honestly contend that their approach to recognition is very clearly catholic, apostolic and deeply theological.

Again, when pitting the Anglican Charles Gore against the Congregationalist J. Vernon Bartlet (who is here given an additional 't') Kelly claims that whereas Gore speaks of faith in relation to creeds, Bartlet seems to restrict the term to the moral life of the believer. In respect of Bartlet's view he asks, 'What function can such a recognition play as a possible instrument of unity? The answer is very little, if any at all' (p. 40). One need not conclude that Bartlet has the whole truth, but nevertheless it may be suggested that since, as Kelly points out, reception is frequently associated with recognition, and since we are speaking of the unity of the church, and not simply of its percipient intellectuals, the recognition by one (perhaps unlettered) Christian that another person, from however 'alien' a tradition, nevertheless shares an experienced faith-commitment to Christ is a discovery by no means insignificant. Certainly the choice which Kelly offers between the faith recognized in creed, sacraments and ministry, and the faith recognized only in the invisible church (p. 40) is a false choice since it is too strongly disjunctive: it fails to allow for other alternatives. Thus, for example, speaking of the ecclesiology of the visible saints of orthodox Dissent, Bernard Lord Manning writes, 'Where we found grace we recognized the one catholic and apostolic church which with all Christians we confessed' (*Essays in Orthodox Dissent*, 1939, p. 109). Perhaps recognition as thus conceived needs to qualify recognition construed as the endorsement of credal assertions and ministerial arrangements, lest the church become 'Pelagian' in an intellectualist or constitutionalist way. There is, after all, more than a hint in the New Testament to the effect that it is possible to have all the right credentials and yet be far from the Gospel of God's grace.

These considerations assume considerable importance in relation to the question which the authors of BEM posed to the ecumenical constituency concerning 'the extent to which your church can recognize in this text the faith of the church through the ages.' Kelly thoroughly discusses BEM and its reception, and in the process reveals himself as being at least faintly peeved by the Reformed response to this question, feeling that that communion's way of answering the question sets up 'a confrontational situation where it is the Reformed tradition against the rest' (p. 173). As my own published analysis of Reformed responses showed,[31] there was overwhelming gratitude for the contribution BEM had made, coupled with a variety of responses (some of them mutually contradictory, some incisive, a few cheeky) to particular parts of the document. But on the question

---

31. Alan P. F. Sell, 'Some Reformed Responses to *Baptism, Eucharist and Ministry*,' in *Reformed World* 39 (1986) 549–65.

of the recognition of the faith of the church through the ages, it is difficult to see how this can honestly be answered without reference to a church's understanding of what that faith is, and this understanding is inextricably interwoven with the extent and manner of that church's reception of the apostles' Gospel.

This seems to be the point at issue between the prominent ecumenists Gunther Gassmann and Mary Tanner—a matter to which Kelly devotes a good deal of attention. The latter argued that in searching for 'the common faith, the period of the undivided church was of "peculiar and special importance, not just for some churches but for all of us"' (p. 196); whereas the former contended that 'there is no "faith of the church through the ages" . . . in abstraction from the confessional and ecclesial traditions through which this faith comes to expression' (p. 197). (One might gently note in passing that 'undivided' in the term 'undivided church' is susceptible of more stringent analysis that it customarily receives.) Kelly goes on to explain that the Faith and Order study of the apostolic faith was intended to show that 'the content of this faith was identifiable and normative' (p. 205). Nevertheless the implied adverse criticism in Kelly's claim that the churches which responded positively to BEM were those who 'grasped the nature and purpose of the text, understood the idea of recognition and made use of the questions in the preface' (p. 160) should be tempered in view of the differences of emphasis within impeccably ecumenical circles. The repetition of the claim (p. 180), compounded by the swingeing declaration that 'an important group of churches have rejected the process . . . [T]here is no real will to work towards unity. These churches did not understand recognition nor did they want to' is, if the reference is to the Reformed, inaccurate, unjust (which communion has spawned more united churches'?), and, as J. M. R. Tillard notes in his generally appreciative foreword, unduly pessimistic (p. xxvii). After all this, Kelly's admission that 'there is no doubt that recognition should have been better explained to the churches . . ."' (p. 180) comes a little late.

At a number of other points Kelly's contentions seem careless. Thus, commenting on J. N. Shaw's remark that a reunited church might embrace an episcopacy regarded not as the *esse* but as the *bene esse* of the church, he says, 'in other words, agreement about organic unity does not require agreement on theological principle' (p. 45). But (a) this is a *non sequitur*; and (b) that episcopacy is the *bene esse* only of the church is the received doctrine of a number of episcopal churches.

So one might go on; but I do not wish to close my review of this important book on a negative note. I repeat that Kelly has done well to bring us face to face with the semantics of 'recognition' through his detailed study of the (twentieth) century's ecumenical literature. He properly highlights such discussions as those concerning the nature and purpose of the church, scripture, and tradition and, as my critical comments above imply, he leaves us with important agenda for further discussion. He also prompts in this reader the question, how much further shall we go without serious analysis of the concept of doctrinal development?

This book is far more than a trudge through a soggy field of documents. It is a stimulating work which should be required reading for all who are concerned to manifest the Church's unity. I suspect that some of Kelly's 'over-the-top' judgements are a function of his frustration that things are not moving faster. I am therefore happy to recognize him as a concerned ecumenist. More than that, I recognize him as a Christian. The fact of the mutual recognition of those who are one in Christ seriously challenges our ecclesiastical divisiveness. The gospel, I believe, requires that as a matter of urgency we face up to this challenge, to the end that our churchly treatment of one another may accord with the mind of him in whom we are already one.

The Ecumenical Review 51 (1999) 315–17.

90

Methodists in Dialog

Geoffrey Wainwright. *Methodists in Dialog*.
Nashville: Kingswood Books, 1995. Pp. 340.

Geoffrey Wainwright is a wise and balanced person. More than that, he is among the most judicious and perceptive ecumenists alive today. No doubt he can hold his own with ecumenical veterans; but he can do much more than this because his reading is broad and his learning deep. He can, in the nicest possible way, inform both Methodists and those of other traditions of parts of their heritage of which they are ignorant, or which they have overlooked, or which they would prefer to forget. These characteristics are clearly displayed in this stimulating collection of papers, most of which comprise Wainwright's contributions to ecumenical discussions from the 1980s onwards.

Following a general introduction on 'Methodists in Dialog,' Wainwright gathers his papers under six headings: 'Methodists and Roman Catholics,' 'Methodists and Lutherans,' 'Methodists and Reformed,' 'Methodists and Orthodox,' 'Methodists in multilateral dialogue,' and 'Methodist principles of ecumenism.' A conclusion entitled 'Continuing a Methodist Voice,' a list of abbreviations, copious notes, and a list of sources and acknowledgments complete the work. Would that there were an index of persons at least.

The collection shows how a theologian who has been in dialogue with more traditions than most adjusts himself to the diverse agenda proposed from very different ecclesiastical quarters. From the papers we may deduce the general rule that the older a particular Christian communion is, the more obstacles lie in its ecumenical path: for example, the role of 'anathemamonger' is one from which the relatively youthful Methodists have been spared, and hence they are not called upon to 'reconcile memories' with others to the extent, or in the way, that is appropriate elsewhere. Historically, this has not, of course, prevented them from being irritants to the Church of England in whose bosom they were nurtured, or to Old Dissent, to some sections of which they were upstart enthusiasts who eventually came alongside as more or less reluctant Nonconformists.

It would be quite impossible here to analyze each of Wainwright's chapters in detail, but it will be in keeping with the spirit of the book if I enter into dialogue with him at certain points. He writes, 'In the modern ecumenical movement, the aim has been to discern, and then to achieve, whatever is necessary and sufficient for unity among Christians and among the churches' (p. 13). Admittedly the reference is to what Wesley called 'external union,' which presupposes belief in Christ and love of humanity; but as it stands the sentence has a pragmatic, anthropocentric ring, and I do not think it pedantic, especially given Wainwright's strongly trinitarian thrust, to propose such a revision as would make it plain that union with the Father through the Son by the Spirit, as a gift of God's prevenient grace, is already given to Christians and that their calling is to manifest the fact.

When Wainwright explains (p. 19) that owing to the disproportionate size of the Roman Catholic Church as compared with others, 'it has seemed wiser that Rome should engage in a variegated series of relationships with other Christian world communions as best fits the particular histories and traditions,' one wonders whether that is exactly the ground on which the Roman Catholic Church itself justifies non-membership of the World Council of Churches.

There are, as one might expect given the occasional nature of these papers and the time-lags between their delivery, differences of emphasis from time to time. Thus when expounding the report of the Roman Catholic-Methodist dialogue Wainwright quotes the view that 'the succession of bishops through the generations serves the continued unity of the church in the faith handed on from the apostles.' He further notes that some Methodist respondents to *Baptism, Eucharist and Ministry* might accept episcopal succession as 'a sign, though not a guarantee, of the continuity and unity of the church,' adding that 'the Roman Catholic response to BEM judges this to be inadequate' (p. 54). He does not pursue the point here, but in the following paper he records an important outstanding question: '*Who* identities and conserves the marrow of Christian truth?' (p. 69). He proceeds to refer to the Methodist tradition of conciliarity, pointing out that along such lines 'there is no simple distinction between the teachers and the taught' (p. 70). In yet another paper he suggests that 'bishops (and their successors) serve the proclamation of the true gospel *as long as they remain faithful to it* (p. 85, his italics)—a significant qualification indeed. I would welcome a more coordinated statement of Wainwright's position concerning episcopal succession, one which queried the kind of 'handing on' that one may appropriately speak of where the apostolic succession is concerned, and which asserted the role of God the Holy Spirit as the supreme guardian of the faith.

Wainwright advises us that 'it remains characteristic of Methodism that all church structures, including the ordering of the ministry, will be tested by their contribution to communion with God and among Christian' (p. 75). What role, if any, do Methodists accord to the Bible in the ordering and critique of church structures? Wainwright elsewhere grants that creeds 'must, theologically, be seen as summaries of scripture before they can he seen, as it were independently, as their hermeneutical key' (p. 134), and this position I endorse.

A number of interesting remarks on baptism are made *en passant*. Wainwright thinks that the Roman Catholic-Methodist Joint Commission 'will sooner or later need . . . to grasp more firmly the nettle of baptism and its relation to faith and ecclesial belonging' (p. 55). In conversation with Lutherans, Wainright sets Luther's *baptizatus sum* over against Wesley's exhortation to 'lean no more on the staff of that broken reed, that ye were born again in baptism' (p. 111). He suggests that the difference in context may facilitate mutual rapprochement here, for Luther was thinking of tempted believers, Wesley of wayward believers or non-believers. But might not Wesley's guidance fuel requests for so-called 'second' baptism?

Notwithstanding his 'catholic spirit,' Wesley, we are reminded, 'refused his hand to Arians, semi-Arians, Socinians and Deists, for their heart was not right with his heart' (p. 192). Wainwright later presents two options: 'Some people hold that the church can believe a wrong thing and be the church, others that one cannot believe the wrong thing and be the church' (p. 221; cf. p. 262). Thus is opened up the vexed question of the degrees of tolerance within the church, and I should like to have heard more about this. If we are to follow the New Testament (cf. Heb 5:12–13) in giving milk to 'baby' Christians whilst reserving the hard rusks of doctrine to older hands, what should happen if one of the latter declines to swallow? How far may we go along the line: 'The individual believer is free to be conscientiously in error, but the church as church declares the following . . . ?' And what Olympian vantage point may we occupy so as to judge the 'hearts' of others accurately and compassionately?

There are many other points at which it would be profitable to engage Wainwright in discussion, but enough has been said to indicate the stimulating nature of these papers. I should now like to draw attention to the strength of the trinitarian thread which holds the papers together. In particular I note the author's caution that Methodists (and, I should add, others) 'must not acquiesce in, let alone create, patterns of understanding, speech and prayer that some are proposing in an effort to overcome "patriarchy" but which in fact threaten the Trinity' (p. 192, cf. p. 204).

Were I asked to grade Methodism's contribution to matters ecumenical in the light of the material here presented, I should presume, noting Wainwright's prominent doxological interest and on analogy with the one-to-five-star grading system for hotels, to award Methodism four 'alleluias'! Clearly any tradition can offer only what it has first received, and Wainwright's book admirably illustrates his claim that Methodism contributes doctrinal responsibility, spiritual engagement, a missionary orientation, and aims at the glorification of the triune God. To say that an emphasis upon ecclesiology in relation to polity and the ministry of the whole people of God is also required is to advert to something dear to the hearts of Methodism's (now) close neighbours within Orthodox Dissent. It is not surprising, given that its inspiration was religious and evangelistic rather than ecclesiological, that Methodism has not majored upon this—indeed, terms which suggest a 'society' within the Church of England linger in British Methodist discourse to this day.

Nevertheless, Wainwright clearly sees the question which Old Dissent would pose (however inadequately it witnesses to its churchly understanding in practice): 'Where is "the church" located? How is it composed? Who are the members of it?' (p. 66, cf. pp. 67, 221). To use the language of the old divines, it is the question of the 'matter' of the church.

In this connection the following quotation is of particular interest: 'Orthodoxy ... witnesses to the *visibility* of the church which is credally confessed as "One", in harmony with the Word who was made *flesh* and the Holy Spirit who descended upon a *flesh-and-blood* community of believers' (p. 180). These words would seem to apply equally to the witness of the visible saints of the congregational traditions, though their application in polity differs considerably as between the Eastern Orthodox and the Orthodox Dissenters. Much more could be said, but here I simply record my judgement that there is little point in rhetoric concerning the ministry of the whole people of God; what is required is the involvement of the members corporately (not in the individualistic sense of each one doing his or her thing), and this has implications for polity. I here think of Church Meeting construed not as a democratic assembly, but as the saints gathered under the Lordship of Christ to seek his will for their witness and mission. But, of course, this presupposes that we know who the saints are; and that—with all its implications for church discipline—returns us to Wainwright's pressing question.

The question 'Who are the church?' is also raised by the ecclesiology of the state church (variously developed in a minority of Lutheran, Anglican and Reformed circles). In my experience this is the question most readily sidestepped in ecumenical discussion. There appears to be considerable reluctance to address this matter in a deeply theological way. Wainwright appreciates the importance of the issue, but refers to it only in a footnote (p. 316).

Having been given so much on which to reflect, it is perhaps churlish to ask for more. But I wish that the conclusion had been strengthened by reference to the significant results of many of the dialogues in which Wainwright has been engaged. It is always useful to have something to point to when the activist brigade mutters, 'Ecumenism is all talk and no progress.' For example, Wainright's paper on 'Perfect Salvation in the Teaching of Wesley and Calvin' contributed to the finding of the Reformed-Methodist dialogue commission that the traditionally neuralgic doctrinal points at issue between the two families should no longer be regarded as church dividing. It is worth recording such milestones.

It was a happy thought on Wainwright's part to dedicate this book to Joe Hale, secretary for many years of the World Methodist Council.

At the end of his introduction, Wainwright quotes John Wesley's sermon on 'The new creation': 'There will be a deep, an intimate, an uninterrupted union with God; a constant communion with the Father and his Son Jesus Christ, through the Spirit; a continual enjoyment of the Three-One God, and of all creatures in him.' 'That,' adds Wainwright 'is the final vision held out also by the classic ecumenical movement, and it remains vital to authentic Christianity in our time' (p. 35). What needs to be shown (if indeed this is possible) is that those, whether Protestant or Catholic, who debar Christians who sincerely share this vision from the Lord's Supper, which is an earnest of the vision's realization, and/or who decline to share in the Lord's Supper at their invitation in Christ's name, are not behaving in a sectarian, 'Galatian heresy', manner. Or, to return to Geoffrey Wainwright's roots, shall we for ever have to express our emotions—whether of puzzlement, exasperation or sorrow—in those immortal English North-country words, 'There's nowt so queer as folk'?

The Ecumenical Review 51 (1999) 224–27.

91

Art, Modernity, and Faith

George Pattison. *Art, Modernity and Faith*.
London: SCM Press, 2nd edn., 1998. Pp. xiii + 208.

When his book was first published in 1991 the Dean of King's College, Cambridge, established himself as one of the most thoughtful explorers of the relatively neglected borderland of art and theology. In his new preface he expresses himself as still committed to the general line expounded, though he adds a chapter in which he seeks to 'tie up some loose ends.' In particular, while 'I still wish to insist on the unsurpassability of seeing itself as a mode of interaction between self, society and world that is distinct from and not entirely translatable into the mode of language, . . . I no longer regard religion as capable of securing its own ontological foundations, neither by reason nor by revelation, neither by theology nor by faith. Neither art nor religion tell us how things "are": they simply and supremely show us meaning, value and virtue' (p. xiii). (One immediately wonders whether all examples of either necessarily/invariably do this).

According to Pattison, it is characteristic of modern art that artistic autonomy is sought and established reality critiqued. The challenge of modernity arises from within as well as from without the Church. Pattison gives an early indication of his stance, namely that, while religion and art are not identical, and while neither can be reduced to the other because whereas religion deals in concepts the field of art is that of vision, nevertheless there are paths connecting them. He propounds his thesis with reference to the history of art and of its interpretation; and his seventeen illustrations permit visual art to 'speak' for itself.

A mere list of persons and topics must here suffice to indicate the breadth of Pattison's treatment: iconoclasm; Augustine, Calvin, the Romantics, Kierkegaard; the interestingly different interpretations of Thomism proposed by Maritain, Eric Gill, Umberto Eco, and

Gilson; Ruskin, P. T. Forsyth, and Tillich; and icons. In all of his expositions, Pattison is balanced and fair. We might, indeed, borrow the phrase 'construction through criticism' to characterize his method.

In advancing his case that 'the processes of seeing are of irreducible value in human life' (p. 135), the author adjusts himself to the views of Wolterstorff, Heidegger, and Merleau-Ponty, ever seeking a theology of art in which art does not merely point to something else, but understands that the visual image itself is that which makes visible the invisible depth of God.

In the ninth chapter Pattison reviews his position in relation to faiths other than the Christian, finding in Zen a clue to that holy worldliness which forbids the dualism of nature and grace which has so influenced Western theologies of art. He looks forward to 'a more open theology in which the Church does not imagine itself as the sole purveyor or channel of grace, but as responding, with all sentient being, to the structural grace of life itself' (p. 189).

The heart of Pattison's case is summed up in these words: 'it is precisely the knowledge of God the redeemer which enables us to recognise the goodness and the beauty and the sublimity of nature, and it is in such a recognition and in no other way that we show our knowledge of God as redeemer' (p. 175).

Pattison is occasionally prone to unelucidated rhetoric whose impact is more on the ear than the intellect: 'Modernity is not simply an ideology or a programme to be refuted on the plane of ideas. It is a destiny to be lived, and only so "overcome"' (p. xi). On the next page he assails the eye with the coinage, 'utopistic.' At times one wishes that he had cross-examined his subjects more closely, as when, for example, he expounds Merleau-Ponty as teaching that: 'Vision itself interprets vision' (p. 146).

Pattison properly draws attention to those points of distinction between Forsyth and Hegel which are the crucial spur to Forsyth's constructive theology (as well as to his aversion to monism). However, when the author asks: 'Can the thoroughly individualised faith which [Forsyth] commends, without the support of the solid ecclesiastical tradition on which, for instance, Neo-Thomism draws, weather the historical, cultural and intellectual storms of modernism?'(p. 98), I should wish to challenge the phrase 'thoroughly individualised' in view of Forsyth's high churchmanship, and to suggest that Forsyth thinks that in the Gospel of the Cross (construed in his portmanteau way) he has an anchorage more fundamental than the ecclesiastical tradition, which it transcends, originates and judges.

A recurring question is: Does a piece of visual art carry its own significance with it, or do we need knowledge gleaned elsewhere in order to decipher and interpret it? On the one hand Pattison declares that 'the visual image makes visible the invisible depth of God' (p. 149); on the other hand he grants that Thomas Merton was not ignorant of Buddhism when confronted for the first time by Buddhist art. Again, in what ways does understanding relate to aesthetic judgements of value, and to what extent is the artist's intention, so far as it may be known, relevant here? What is the status of an uninformed response to a work of art originating within a particular tradition? Do all aesthetic judgements, however diverse and even contradictory, have equal validity, or is it possible (as art criticism seems frequently to presuppose) to rank them; and if so, in accordance with which criteria?

Here is an author who both raises intricate philosophical questions and addresses issues which are fundamental to theology, worship, and life itself. Pattison does not only advocate a relational approach, he exemplifies one such approach. May he receive the attention he deserves.

The Irish Theological Quarterly 64 (1999) 83–84.

92

On Christian Ethics

Robin Gill, ed. *The Cambridge Companion to Christian Ethics*.
Cambridge: CUP, 2001. Pp. xv + 290.

The first part of this collection concerns *The Grounds of Christian Ethics*. It opens with Rowan Williams' sensitive paper, 'Making moral decisions.' He is puzzled that some Christians cannot see that their favourable view of the arms trade is obviously wrong, but advocates soldiering on (save the phrase!) in fellowship rather than secession. This, surely, should be the normal response, though one may ask what are the criteria for determining that an issue is *status confessionis*—that is, one which requires some sort of ecclesiastical discipline lest the Gospel be compromised? Williams concludes that the only 'real and effective motive for the making of a Christian moral decision' is 'the vision of a living Lord whose glory I must strive to make visible' (p. 14). Since motives are among the *differentiae* of Christian ethics the question arises: how does the Archbishop's statement of the motive relate to that of Richard Baxter, for example: 'Let Thankfulness to God, thy Creator, Redeemer, and Regenerator, be the very temperament of thy soul, and faithfully expressed by thy tongue and life' (*Works*, 1830, 2: p. 421)?

For Gareth Jones ('The authority of Scripture and Christian ethics') the Bible is (mercifully) not 'a repository of correct answers to ethical questions' (p. 24); indeed, in his last paragraph we see (belatedly, for the point requires elucidation and development) that 'God's self-revelation in Jesus Christ' is primary, and to this 'the New Testament as scripture witnesses' (p. 26). In a particularly helpful study of 'The Old Testament and Christian ethics, John Rogerson contrasts Jewish and Christian ways of approaching the texts the two traditions share, and argues that the Old Testament best contributes to Christian ethics 'by example rather than precept' (p. 37). Given his title, the most idiosyncratic piece in the book is Timothy P. Jackson's on 'The gospels and Christian ethics.' He discusses the teaching of canonical and gnostic gospels on love, sin and salvation, and the former win on points. Writing on the New Testament epistles, Stephen C. Barton emphasizes the fact that 'early Christian ethics is communal or ecclesial ethics set within the broader horizon of God's covenant love for the world' (p. 64).

There follow six papers on *Approaches to Christian Ethics*, in which natural law (Stephen J. Pope), virtue ethics (Jean Porter), gender (Lisa Sowle Cahill), liberation ethics (Tim Gorringe), Jewish perspectives (Ronald M. Green) and other faiths (Gavin D'Costa) are discussed. All of these are informative. Porter's is noteworthy for demonstrating the variety of approaches to virtue ethics; Gorringe's is particularly judicious; and it may be hoped that Green's reference to modern Jewish 'quivering' in the face of some current criticisms of the Enlightenment will give pause to more ignorant iconoclasts.

Part Three concerns *Issues in Christian Ethics*: war (R. John Elford); the arms trade (Robin Gill); social justice and welfare (Duncan Forrester); ecology (Michael S. Northcott); business and economics (Max L. Stackhouse); world family trends (Don Browning); and medicine and genetics (James F. Childress). Particularly helpful is Forrester's holding together of God's justice and mercy, and his recognition of the eschatological setting of justice in the Bible (in which connection a little more on the scuttling of the 'principalities and powers' would have been cheering). Northcott provides a model of theological reflection on an ethical issue, which makes the resurrection of Jesus central; and Max Stackhouse, querying what in some hands seems like the ghettoization of Christian ethics, determines to keep the communicating door open between Church and world.

Since the editor modestly and accurately described the *Companion* as 'fairly comprehensive' (p. xiii), 'selective' as to the issues treated (p. xiv) and 'only a taster' (p. xv), it may seem churlish to advert to lacunae. Certainly it would not be appropriate to complain that specific issues in practical ethics had been omitted, or to suggest that the papers here gathered do not merit close attention. But I refer to two *dimensions* which are largely missing, or at least which do not have specific chapters devoted to them. The first concerns the relations between Christian ethics and contemporary and recent moral philosophy (we do have references to classical authors, to traditional natural law theory, and the statutory invocation from time to time of A. MacIntyre). It really does seem odd that Christian ethicists will talk at length with geneticists, business magnates and the like, but (to judge from this book) hardly at all with contemporary moral philosophers. Apart from such chestnuts as 'Is *x* good because God wills it, or does God will it because it is good?,' and the deontology-teleology debate, there are the implications of anti-foundationalism for Christian ethics, and the revival in some quarters of naturalism—not least in relation to sexual ethics. Further, what, if any, is the relation between 'covenant' in theology and 'collective responsibility' in ethics? So one might go on. Secondly, one might have expected more than passing references to that mass of corporate ethicizing done under the auspices of Christian world communions and wider ecumenical bodies. The competing methodologies involved (themselves the subject of lively current debate) and the questions of the viability and reception of such work are matters which merit close attention.

The book includes a useful bibliography, an index, and biographical notes on the contributors. We thus learn that the editor is also the series editor of the present publisher's *New Studies in Christian Ethics*. In view of the lacunae detected here, the titles in the series will be perused with more than ordinary interest.

Modern Believing 42 (2001) 68–70.

93

Confusions in Christian Social Ethics

Ronald H. Preston. *Confusions in Christian Social Ethics: Problems for Geneva and Rome.* London: SCM Press, 1994. Pp. xiii, 202.

Before the 1950s had run their course, your reviewer was among a select group who toiled over Ronald Preston's merry ethical posers in BD finals. His zeal for setting questions has clearly not diminished with the passing of the years, but now he challenges the ecumenical 'trade' in both its World Council of Churches (WCC) and Roman Catholic manifestations. In a reversal of roles I presume to place the examiner in the first class. For this is a book which demands attention, and presents ecumenical social ethicists with a number of significant challenges.

Professor Preston first defines 'ecumenism' and describes the organization and composition of the WCC. He then traces the Council's work in social ethics from Stockholm (1926) to Canberra (1991) and beyond. This will greatly help all who from time to time meet old ecumenical campaigners, the chapters of whose lives appear to have been marked by such obelisks as Amsterdam, Nairobi and the rest, and who speak of these in tones of mingled pride and reverence. In the third chapter the socio-ethical contribution of the Roman Catholic Church in its pre- and post-Vatican II *personae* is described.

But description, useful though it is, is not the author's main objective. He comes to the point in his opening sentence: 'The immediate context of this book is dissatisfaction with the quality of the social theology and ethics coming in recent years from the World Council of Churches' (p. 3). Since these are not the words of a sniper from the sidelines, but of one who has given a life-time of service to the ecumenical cause, they are to be taken with the utmost seriousness. By using the WCC as a case study Professor Preston hopes to show how Christian social ethics may most satisfactorily be done. In his view the Zagorsk consultation of 1968 was on the right lines, for it yielded the conclusion that (in the author's words) 'Christian faith, continually being thought through afresh, provides the criteria by which empirical evidence on "what is going on" is acquired and assessed' (p. 28). It did not, however, proceed to the consideration of specific ethical problems. Where method and results are concerned, 'empirical' is one of Professor Preston's watchwords. He likes ethicists to have their feet on the ground, and his own training in economics, Bible and theology give him some right to insist upon this. Thus, for example, while welcoming Moltmann's eschatological ethics as a corrective to that endorsement of the *status quo* which has characterized much Christian social ethics, 'it is no direct help in making practical decisions' (p. 28; cf. ch. 7).

Although he recognizes that 'consensus, and even dialogue, was to become more difficult as the "western" character of the WCC began to change' (p. 22), the author nevertheless levels the following charges against that body:

1. It is too susceptible to sloganizing—for example, 'without justice for all everywhere we shall not have peace anywhere.' On which Wayside Pulpit gem Professor Preston remarks, 'Short of the *parousia*, or final triumph of Christ, it is vacuous' (pp. 31–32; cf. p. 37).

2. 'It has been too sanguine about the participation of "the people" on the large technological and economic issues, and too open to pressure groups' (p. 33).

3. The influence upon the WCC of liberation theologies, whose exponents too uncritically endorse the Marxist view of the unity of theory and practice, militates against the recognition of our need of 'the renewal of forgiveness, and a radical vision transcending the present state of affairs to prevent us settling down complacently as forgiven sinners' (p. 68).

4. While not denying that the invocation of *status confessionis* may, on rare occasions, be appropriate, it is in general 'much too blunt an instrument to cope with issues which need a closer analysis' (p. 69), and the WCC tends to resort to it too quickly.

All is not lost, however. The WCC has given a platform to the marginalized—both those who are not generally heard within established church circles, and those experts who are too often marginalized by being ignored. Nevertheless ecumenical memory— that accumulated wisdom from the past—must not be lost under the pressure of current issues, and 'the WCC has to survive by excellence; otherwise it will be ignored' (p. 58). While it is right to hear the voice of the oppressed, it is not necessarily wise to meet all of their requests, some of which may prove to be counter-productive (p. 71).

Among pressing matters requiring considerable expertise are the collapse of the Soviet system; economic growth and sustainability in a global context; and technology, humanity and the environment. In the course of discussing these Professor Preston laments the way in which racism, classism, and sexism have been linked by the WCC as species of a common evil. This, he feels, obscures more than it reveals. There follow discussions of Christian realism, biblicism, liberation theology, orthodoxy and social trinitarianism, and eschatological realism. In view of the current resurgence of interest in the doctrine of the Trinity, it is noteworthy that the author finds the social Trinity of some Anglican and Protestant theologians (not excluding Moltmann) 'dangerous, especially in contacts with Jews and Muslims. The threefold nature of God must be subsumed within the divine unity without equivocation' (p. 140). He further regrets the association of the present General Secretary of the WCC (Konrad Raiser) with eschatological realism, because of its disparagement of the judicious application of instrumental reason. Two Realm ethics, natural law, and the contributions of J. H. Oldham and Paul Ramsey are among many other topics on which the author has instructive comments to make.

Concerning the method of Christian social ethics, Professor Preston sets out from the centrality of worship, queries the WCC's over-emphasis upon the prophetic role of the Church at the expense of her conserving function, and rehabilitates middle axioms—on condition that high calibre work goes into their formulation.

This last consideration recalls a running theme of the book. It is not that the author is elitist, but he does seek responsible Christian social ethics, and he feels that this objective is threatened: 'The attempt within the [WCC] staff to be representative of area, sex, confessional tradition—and even of causes—means that it is not all of the highest quality. Yet the WCC can only survive by excellence' (p. 167).

While the WCC is predominantly in Professor Preston's sights, he nevertheless has pertinent things to say concerning Roman Catholic social ethics. He ponders the silence of Roman Catholic ecclesiology on the curia, whose role, he is convinced, requires scrutiny. He also wishes that the Roman Catholic Church would come to grips with the fact that she is part of, and not above, the problems she addresses.

Not the least stimulating feature of this book are the agenda it bequeaths us:

1. When discussing the Canberra Assembly, and the contribution to it of Latin American liberation theologians, Professor Preston observes, in what is almost a throwaway line, 'The need for liberation from sin was not denied, but it was not in the forefront' (p. 25). There is a balancing task to be done here lest 'salvation' become a too narrowly politicized concept.

2. Professor Preston regrets the anti-Enlightenment bias against universal reason, declaring that 'the status of reason in humans, not possessed by any other species, is basic to our commonality, and fundamental to both our Greek and Judaeo-Christian roots in the "west," together with the possibility of communicating with those of other faiths and philosophies' (p. 111; cf. p. 142). A good deal of work will need to be done if some are to be convinced of this. It is not simply that blanket attacks upon the Enlightenment are philosophically dubious (and frequently unsupported by evidence that those who mount them are acquainted with the relevant texts); the integrity of the theological and religious conviction that we are one in Christ Jesus is seriously called into question unless there are conditions in humanity for such a unity—a unity which will stand as a bulwark against contextual theology gone parochial and possibly sectarian.

3. Professor Preston asserts that 'Christian moral reasoning cannot afford to set itself apart from Moral Philosophy, as it is tempted to do (and much WCC work in this area does...)' (p. 144). Here is a matter on which one could wax lyrical—and occasionally has. Matters are not helped by the demotion in many British universities of the postgraduate BD to a first degree (which precludes the prior study by at least some ordinands and others of philosophy, including moral philosophy); and by the increasing 'professionalization' of the North American MDiv, whose syllabi are frequently innocent of philosophy of

religion, let alone moral philosophy. The rueful conclusion is that within Christian ranks the philosophical acumen for which Professor Preston calls may increasingly be hard to find. (Biblical scholars may be trusted to utter similar laments concerning languages.)

4. A further matter arises which is not directly addressed by Professor Preston. What would be revealed by a comparative study of the Christian socio-ethical pronouncements of the WCC and the Vatican with those of other major Christian world communions? Would the latter employ less rhetoric? Would they make better use of the Bible? Would they be more inclined to reach happy accord because of narrowed-down ecclesiastical allegiance? Would they make a more thorough assault on the empirical factors in the situation? Are they more philosophically skilled? There is no guarantee in advance of the investigation that affirmative answers are appropriate.

There are a few slips. The United Reformed Church in the United Kingdom has, since 1981, included the majority of the former Churches of Christ (some of whom were in Scotland) (p. 7); for Duckrow read Duchrow; some italics are absent on p. 180; the Index is not entirely accurate.

But all of this pales into insignificance in face of the importance of this book. Since the author hints in his Preface that this contribution may be his last for the SCM Press, perhaps one who is not given to 'gushing' may pay well-deserved tribute to his former teacher for the stimulus here provided in characteristically down-to-earth fashion, and for the invaluable service Ronald Preston has rendered as an academic pioneer of Christian Ethics.

Modern Believing 36 (1995) 63–67.

94

Protestant Worship

James F. White. *Protestant Worship: Traditions in Transition.*
Louisville: Westminster/John Knox, 1989. Pp. 251.

Only a bold person would undertake a description of the worship of one quarter of all Christians. Even the professor of liturgy at Notre Dame University draws back from his declaration on the opening page that 'a global setting must be surveyed,' to the realization on the next page that Europe and North America will provide a sufficient, and still a considerable, challenge.

Convinced that Protestant worship cannot adequately be studied by reference to liturgical texts, which are infrequently used, and do not cover all that takes place in church services,

Professor White offers an account of the historical backgrounds to, and current expressions of, the worship of the Lutheran, Reformed, Anabaptist, Anglican, Separatist and Puritan, Quaker, Methodist, Frontier and Pentecostal traditions. The worship of these traditions is studied by reference to seven categories which are deemed to be applicable to the phenomena under review: people, piety, time, place, prayer, preaching and music. The author's stance is that of the 'impartial historian,' who makes no normative judgements as to how Christians ought to worship, and for whom 'Survival is our only criterion for value' (p. 15).

A chapter on 'Late medieval worship and Roman Catholic worship' provides a point of departure for accounts of the nine specified traditions. A considerable amount of historical information precedes the description of contemporary worship in each of the main chapters. There are important reminders along the way, of which I offer a random selection: 'Frequent communion was the most difficult reform for Luther or anyone else to accomplish' (p. 42); 'What Luther did not appreciate was that Zwingli was stating in a new way the reality of Christ's presence as a transubstantiation of the congregation rather than of the elements' (p. 59); 'the early Anabaptists found profundities in believers' baptism as life-and-death commitment that had rarely been known in traditional Christianity since the early church' (p. 91); 'If we concern ourselves with the theology of the sacraments in general and the eucharist in particular, Calvin stands closer to the medieval tradition than does Cranmer' (p. 94); 'The Anglican tradition, more than any other, is a tradition of a book, single book, the prayer book' (p. 95); 'the Quakers were the first to insist that in worship there is neither slave nor free, male nor female, laity or clergy' (p. 139); 'Wesley observed that for many lukewarm Christians (i.e., not for the unconverted, as has sometimes been supposed) the eucharist could be both a confirming and a converting ordinance' (p. 154); 'Having originated in preparations for the Lord's Supper, camp meetings gave the sacraments a major role and always ended with the baptism of converts and the eucharist' (p. 173); 'An important ingredient of their piety is the millennial hope that resonates in most Pentecostal worship' (p. 199).

At this point the rest of the world is in view once more, and the question arises, How far has Christian worship become adapted to the cultural contexts in which it is now found? This might be a question addressed to Professor White, whereas a theologian might wish to ask, How far can/ought Christian worship to be adapted? Again, can we realistically speak of the nine liturgical traditions in contexts where, denominational labels notwithstanding, the American frontier has triumphed. We may hope for further assistance from Professor White on such matters in due course.

For the present I take this book seriously by making a number of remarks in ascending order of importance.

First, Professor White recognizes that the term 'Protestant' has become opprobrious to many Anglicans, but does not indicate the discomfort which some Protestants may feel on finding Mormons and Christian Scientists (and if these, why no many more?) treated in this book.

Secondly, there are a few slips. For example: (a) *contra* p. 80, the General Baptist strain of English Unitarianism only perpetuated believers' baptism, and this only until the middle of the nineteenth century. (b) Hymn singing in England was pioneered by the

Baptist, Benjamin Keach, closely followed by Watts; the Methodists came later (pp. 104, 129). (c) *Pace* p. 150, the Uniting Church in Australia was formed in 1977.

Thirdly, some statements are insufficiently balanced—a function, no doubt, of the need to compress so much material into a relatively small compass. Thus, (a) when we are told (p. 16) that 'The people who form Quaker worship are not the same as for classical Pentecostalism,' an anlaysis of 'same' would have been helpful. (b) Similarly, we could wish that some reasons for the insistence upon exclusive metrical psalmody in some Presbyterian circles had been specified (p. 76). (c) Why did the Plymouth Brethren consider ordained clergy superfluous? (p. 131). (d) Why was 'enthusiasm' so suspect in the eighteenth century? (p. 108). It was not simply or primarily that 'it made religion a matter of the heart rather than the head' (p. 152). What was feared was a return of the sectarian strife of the preceding century. (e) It is not correct to imply that all 'English Methodists kept a strong affinity for the worship forms of the established church' (p. 153).

Fourthly, given that the author has both Europe and North America in mind, some of his universal propositions ring strangely on the ear, and require qualification. Thus (a) the statement that most ordained Protestant ministers are referred to as 'preacher' (p. 20) is not true of Europe. (b) 'Kingdomtide' is not a festival of British Methodists (p. 166). (c) The statement 'Other traditions (than the Frontier) have not found ways of inviting worship through the airwaves' (p. 191) does not apply to Europe.

Fifthly, the author is somewhat at sea in regard to the Separatist tradition. (a) It is unfortunate, in the first place, that he designates the tradition hyper-Calvinistic (p. 118); that term, so often used pejoratively, obscures more than it reveals. (b) To state that the Independents' (only?) ground for free worship was that 'liturgical autonomy had the benefit of making worship more immediately relevant than worship using fixed forms' (p. 119), makes the Independents sound much more like those worshippers of the god Relevance in today's 'me' generation than in fact they were. Moreover, it obscures their primary grounds: they were against the 'vain repetition' to which they thought set forms could lead; they objected to some of the content of the *Book of Common Prayer*; and they denied that it was the monarch's prerogative to prescribe the worship of Christ's Church. In all, they were more concerned with the Lordship of Christ than with what was meaningful to themselves. (c) To brand Separatist congregations 'sectarian' (p. 120) overlooks the catholicity of their ecclesiology, and minimizes the extent of their interdependence (as far as circumstances permitted). (d) It is surely an understatement to say that they 'found it safer to flee to the Netherlands' (p. 120). (e) The importance of the church polity question is played down (p. 123). In fact a revised (and widely unacceptable) understanding of the 'matter' of the Church, and of Christ's Lordship over it, was being proclaimed by more radical Puritans.

Finally, the weakest historical references in the book are to the Enlightenment. Indeed, it is not too much to say that on occasion Professor White caricatures that phenomenon. Thus (a) he appears, mistakenly, to equate 'Enlightenment' and deism's 'watchmaker God' (p. 52), whereas deism was no one thing, and there is much more to the Enlightenment than deism. (b) Hence his strictures (p. 107) against the alleged antisupernatualism (and so weakened sacramentalism) of latitudinarians and others. But, for example, such eighteenth-century Protestant 'Arians' as John Taylor and Micaijah Towgood were staunch upholders of both baptism and the Lord's Supper (*pace* p. 152), and even Priestley did not altogether repudiate the supernatural. (c) It is simply not true that the 'liberal tendencies of the time' moved 'many' English Congregationalists in a Unitarian direction (p. 130). A few Congregational individuals (some of them prominent), but only about six churches, went over. (d) The assertion that 'Methodist worship was a counter-cultural movement in the midst of the English Enlightenment' (p. 152) overlooks the extent to which Methodism, with its early emphasis upon the conversion of souls is, to a degree, 'Enlightenment individualism gone religious.' Hence a number of the ecclesiological problems which beset us today, including that religious consumerism and subjectivism which threatens the understanding of the Church as a covenant people, and prompts many to thing of it as an aggregate of saved atoms. That is to say, we conclude from the conviction, 'Christianity is all to do with my soul' (which it is not), to 'The churches exist to suit my taste' (which they do not).

I should not like my observations to obscure the general usefulness of this book—a usefulness enhanced by a glossary of terms, a select bibliography, and two indices.

National Bulletin on Liturgy 23 (1990) 253–55.

95

Pulpit, Table, and Song

Heather Murray Elkins and Edward C. Zaragoza, eds. *Pulpit, Table, and Song. Essays in Celebration of Howad G. Hageman.* Lanham, MD and London: The Scarecrow Press, 1996. Pp. xi + 286.

Gregg Alan Mast. *The Eucharistic Service of the Catholic Apostolic Church and its Influence on Reformed Liturgical Renewals of the Nineteenth Century.* Lanham, MD and London: Scarecrow Press, 1999. Pp. ix + 183.

Howard G. Hageman was President of New Brunswick Theological Seminary of the Reformed Church in America, and a founding member of Drew University's Graduate Program in Liturgy. His thought and liturgical practice were grounded in Scripture, moulded by the Reformation, and fertilized by the evangelical catholic thrust of the Mercersburg theology of Nevin, Schaff and their heirs.

Part Three: Theology

The papers in this memorial volume fall into three categories. Under the heading, 'Reformation to Evangelical Revival,' Dirk W. Rodgers, writes on the content and influence of John à Lasco's liturgy of public repentance; Horton Davies shows that Zwingli's 'memorialism' concerning the Lord's Supper, though it played down the sense of the eternal priesthood of the Son of God, nevertheless recovered for worshippers the truth that through their obedience to the dominical command the Lord would reveal himself to them; A. Casper Honders encourages us, when pondering the Reformers and music, to distinguish carefully between their attitudes to music within and without worship; Kenneth E. Rowe writes on the Palatinate liturgy of the Pennsylvania German Reformed, remarking that it has suffered undue neglect (though see now Deborah Rahn Clemens' dissertation on the topic); Robin A. Leaver discusses the preaching lectionary of the Dutch Reformed Church (1782); and Randall Balmer reflects upon the historiographical neglect of religion in the Middle Colonies—New York, Pennsylvania, Maryland and Delaware.

Part Two concerns '19th-Century Revivals/20th-Century Renewals.' Gregg Alan Mast shows how, despite Irving's departure from the Church of Scotland, the Church Service Society was strongly influenced by the liturgy of the Catholic Apostolic Church; Martin L. Cox investigates the largely urban sacramental revivalism of the Anglo-Catholic Ritualists, as exemplified by their Twelve Day London Mission of 1869; Fred Kimball Green discusses some hymn tunes loved by members of the Methodist Episcopal Church; Daniel Kames Meeter answers his question, 'Is the Reformed Church in America a Liturgical Church?' by saying, 'Constitutionally, yes; in practice, by no means always'— and he quotes Hageman's fine invitation to communion; and Edward C. Zaragoza offers a structural analysis of the sacred space at St. Mary's [Benedictine] Abbey, Morristown, New Jersey.

The theme of Part Tree is 'Professor Hageman and his Contributions.' Heather Murray Elkins considers Christ's presence in both preaching and sacraments, showing how some United Methodists are learning from the Mercersburg tradition, the founders of which regarded the Methodism of their day as exemplifying much that was wrong with worship; Norman J. Kansfield disusses Hageman and the hymnology of the Reformed Church in America, and refers to the contribution of Erik Routley; Hageman's own hymn, 'And as this grain has been gathered,' is set to music by David M. Tripold; and a chronological bibliography of Hageman's writings, and brief biographical notes on the contributors, complete the work.

Many matters for further reflection arise from this stimulating volume, among them the fact that ministers and elders, not the people, are asked in John à Lasco's liturgy whether an individual's public confession is acceptable; and the way in which the rite makes a serious attempt to affirm both Christian freedom and ecclesiastical discipline. The German Reformed held communion seasons, often lasting from Friday to Monday. The Dutch Reformed preaching lectionary sought to balance the claims of the major seasons of the Christian Year against the Reformed principle of *lectio continua*. The religiously pluralistic Middle Colonies were in advance of (Congregational) New England in the matter of toleration. R. W. Dale thought that Nonconformists might learn something from the use made by Anglo-Catholics of the heritage of liturgical and devotional literature. Meeter confesses that the four smallest American Reformed churches of Dutch heritage rally 'around one or two doctrinal issues which are virtually impossible to explain to those outside the tradition'—in which connection Hageman's own words are pertinent and of wider application:

> Would the preaching in the Reformed Churches have become so loosely connected with the gospel, as it has in some places at least, if every Sunday it had been followed by the proclamation of the Lord's death till he come? Or could the Reformed churches have proved such fertile ground for the growth of sectarianism, producing one schism after another in their history, if every week they had reminded themselves that 'we being many are one bread, and one body; for we are all partakers of that one bread?'

Hageman's quoted lament that so many of the popular evangelical hymns are not addressed to God, but are all about ourselves, is also worthy of note: 'When we have been singing about nothing but ourselves and our needs for a long time, it can get pretty boring. It really is a relief to sing about a good and gracious Father. Perhaps I should say more accurately, to sing *to* a good and gracious Father. For that is basically what a hymn is.'

There are a few misprints, and one or two clumsy sentences. Cox has a statutory remark about 'arid' deism, and uses 'imminent' for 'immanent.' But overall these are thought-provoking papers which may even stimulate liturgical reform and renewal in some quarters. Nothing would have pleased Howard Hageman more.

Gregg Alan Mast's book introduces the Catholic Apostolic Church and its founders, Edward Irving, Henry Drummond and John Bate Cardale, and shows how its liturgy influenced the German Reformed Church through Schaff and the Mercersburg divines, the Church of Scotland (this chapter being largely a reprint of Mast's paper in the Hageman *Festschrift*), and, to a lesser extent, the Dutch Reformed Church in North America. The influence flowed from Albury, Surrey, to Mercersburg; thence to Scotland, and from there back to the Dutch in America. Mast concludes that the nineteenth-century liturgical renewals provided the foundation of inter-Protestant dialogue and for (later) Roman-Protestant rapprochement. In an appendix he suggests that Joseph Wolff, who moved from Judaism to Roman Catholicism and thence to the Church of England, may have been among Cardale's liturgical mentors.

Mast records the judgement of Horton Davies that whereas such revivalists as the Oxford Tractarians and the Cambridge Ecclesiologists focused upon institutional issues, while Plymouth Brethren, Primitive Methodists and the Salvation Army emphasized the charismatic, the Catholic Apostolic Church uniquely combined the charismatic, millennial, institutional and liturgical motifs. But this means that the liturgical-institutional Mercersburgers, Scots and Dutch shunned a good deal of what the Catholic Apostolic Church had to offer. Some explanation of this would have been welcome (though guesses come easily). The oddest statement in the book is that in which we are informed that the incarnation, Mercersburg's central theme, was 'drawn from German idealism.'

This work is based on the author's Drew dissertation of 1985. One could wish that the bibliography had been updated, and that account had been taken—at least in the notes—of important relevant books and articles published since that date.

These liturgically and ecumenically suggestive books are sturdily and attractively produced, albeit at prices which place them beyond the reach of many who would benefit greatly from them.
Journal of the United Reformed Church History Society 6 (1999) 377–79.

96

Theology for Pew and Pulpit

Bassett, Joseph A. *Theology for Pew and Pulpit. The Everlasting Song.* Shippensburg, PA: Ragged Edge Press, 1996. Pp. xiv + 184.

To judge by this book, the saints who gather in the First Church of Chestnut Hill, Massachusetts, are fortunate in having Joseph Bassett as their pastor. He brings worship, preaching and pastoral care together in such a way that they mutually inform one another. He is rooted in Scripture, nourished by the heritage of Christian testimony, sensitive to the rhythm of the Christian year, alive to ecumenical trends and alert to pastoral needs. He can write too, and has produced a book of unusual quality and worth. It is scholarly yet accessible, at times prophetic but not hectoring, serious but not without humour. Ministers and preachers of many traditions will be enlightened, challenged—even at some points reproved—by this stimulating volume.

We follow a local congregation through prominent moments in worship and the liturgical calendar, and a dialogue is initiated between the gathered saints, their heritage (Reformed in particular), and the world in which they are set. Recurrent voices from the past are those of John Calvin, Edward Taylor (1671–1725)—the minister-poet of Westfield, Massachusetts, and Taylor's friend Samuel Sewall (1652–1717), who speaks through his diary and notes. Karl Barth hovers.

Each chapter opens with a pastoral situation to which Word, tradition and liturgy speak. The author's scholarship emerges in his thoughtful discussion of the doxology, where God-language cannot be avoided. In this connection a statement of the obvious is made which would seem redundant were it not (sadly) so pertinent: 'A sung doxological opening of worship stands in marked contrast to opening greetings like "Good morning"' (p. 21). Again, 'Many in the congregation are surprised at how much can be said about baptism from Scriptures other than Jesus taking children in his arms and blessing them'

(p. 42). Yet again, 'The language used to describe the resurrection is not the language of the on-the-spot reporter' (p. 119).

The pastor's kindly humour bubbles up in the chapter on the children's Christmas Pageant: 'Pageant scripts come in three basic forms: Bathrobe Drama, Bathrobe Drama Plus, and Creative . . . In a Creative Pageant . . . the wise men stop at a gas station for directions, Herod smokes a big cigar, Spider Man costumes are allowed because there were spiders in the manger. Usually after a Creative Pageant a return to Bathrobe Drama is all but mandatory for the next year' (p. 68).

We proceed through Lent and Easter and, perhaps surprisingly, we end at 'The test of the hospital.' But is it so surprising? Is not the whole of life intended to be a sacrifice of praise to God—not least the act of dying? Have the Word and the liturgy nothing to say to the crises of life? Mr. Bassett is convinced that they have, and he skilfully addresses the needs of all whose 'sense of the Lord who gives and takes away not only humbles [them], it gives them what one minister called "the ontological shakes" (p. 159).

Read the book; praise the Lord; prepare for the test.

Epworth Review 24 (1997) 126–27.

97

Reformed Spirituality

David Cornick. *Letting God be God: The Reformed Tradition.*
London: Darton, Longman and Todd, 2008. Pp. 171.

It is becoming increasingly difficult to avoid spirituality. In view of the plethora of available retreats, quiet days and workshops, it might even be said that spirituality is big business. Certainly publishers great and small are being tempted to cash in on the phenomenon as they supply ever more tomes and tracts to feed the interests of those on the numerous well- and less-trodden spiritual 'pathways.' There is evidence to suggest that while some enthusiasts thrive on the more glutinous passages in the medieval mystics, others give themselves to the under-energized chanting of words to waly-waly tunes that are alleged to have something to do with Celtic spirituality. Yet again, we find those who have taken an eastern turn. They may be seen walking, sockless, in the chilliest of weather in (designer) sandals, brandishing little bells as they advance towards their gas-guzzling Chelsea tractors in which they transport their Tarquins and Jonquils a few hundred yards to school.

Then there are those who find much inspiration in nature, interspersing their collecting of litter at beauty spots, which is highly commendable, with fairly frequent bouts of tree-hugging, which is more puzzling to the uninitiated. Finally, there is an evangelical spirituality the tentacles of which reach far and wide. Its cosy, sentimental unitarianism of the second person ('Jesus is my boyfriend') is, mercifully, frequently scuppered by the thumping drums (the volume of Gene Krupa minus the skill).

Lest the foregoing gentle teasing fail to convey my conviction that we should do well to approach some of what passes for spirituality with activated theological antennae, I resort to the stern denunciation of any spirituality that is self-serving, world-denying, doctrine-shunning, and mind-disengaging. Spirituality being the multi-faceted phenomenon that it is, I think that a case can be made for the recall of the term 'piety,' which does at least suggest an appropriate attitude before Another, rather than, for example, a quest to 'find' myself. Genuine spirituality, I believe, concerns the head, heart, hands and feet, and when they have behaved themselves the Reformed have understood this very well.[32] Dr. David Cornick knows it very well, and that is why it is a pleasure to welcome this scholarly, accessible and, above all, *sensible* book.

Tackling first things first, Dr. Cornick discusses the terms 'Reformed' and 'spirituality.' He notes the origins and diversity of the international Reformed family, and points to 'the danger for the Christian theologian after Einstein . . . that "spirituality" might be cast adrift from its ethical and political moorings into a sphere of pure interiority.' He adverts to the work of Rowan Williams, whom he reports as arguing that Calvinism and Lutheranism 'are in essence about worldly spirituality in the sense that the division between "sacred" and "secular" has been broken down.' This, I think, is a rather bald assertion, and a little discrimination is called for. While the whole cosmos, and not just the decent religious bits of it, is God's, we do need to recognize the biblical ambiguity of 'world' and 'worldly.' Christians are called to be leaven in the (territorial) world, but separate from the (naughty) world; furthermore they are strangers here, heaven is their home. These ideas underlie the ecclesiology of a not insignificant strand of the Reformed family, as J. Guinness Rogers saw long ago: the 'ideal Church is a body of spiritual men [and women] converted by the grace of God, and living by faith in the Lord Jesus Christ. This is something radically different from a society of truth-seekers resolved to live up to their light and to wait in the hope that more light will come.'[33] The bearing of this upon the sometimes loose talk we hear today about our all being on a journey is clear. Am I a seeker on a journey towards faith, or a saint on the journey of faith?

The first main chapter, 'Who are the Reformed?,' is a marvel of compression in which due place is accorded to humanism, the place of Scripture, simplicity, clarity, and to the educative role of the numerous confessions of faith. We meet the major founders of the Reformed tradition, and the important point is made that their intentions were catholic: they sought not to fragment, but to reform the one Church of Christ. The correct claim

---

32. See further, Alan P. F. Sell, *Enlightenment, Ecumenism, Evangel: Theological Themes and Thinkers 1550–2000*, Milton Keynes: Paternoster, 2005, ch. 8.

33. J. G. Rogers, *The Church Systems of England in the Nineteenth Century*, London: Hodder and Stoughton, 1881, p. 644.

that 'The heart of Calvin's theology and spirituality is the mystical union between Christ and the believer,' may be news to those who always thought it was predestination. Diverse interpretations of this latter doctrine fuelled the debates between Arminius and Gomarus and their respective followers, and of this episode a balanced account is provided. We then touch down briefly on English soil; hop across the Atlantic to notice the 'exciting and beautiful' synthesis of Calvinism, revivalism and Newtonian order offered by Jonathan Edwards; and thence back to Germany in order to doff our caps to Schleiermacher. Post-Enlightenment critiques of scholastic confessionalism and the Barthian response, the international expansion of Christianity through modern missionary movements, and the commitment to ecumenism are shown to be prominent influences upon the Reformed family to this day.

In his chapter on 'A speaking God and a listening people,' Dr. Cornick discusses Reformed worship. He refers to prayer, preaching (the brief reference to the Spirit's interpretative role is rounded out in the following chapter), and the sacraments, and he then jumps nimbly from Calvin to Walter Brueggemann. He does well not to overlook 'the spirituality of the listener' (which, in my opinion, is nowhere more concisely summed up than in the answer to Question 160 of the *Westminster Larger Catechism*); and he properly distinguishes between conceived or free, and extempore prayer. George MacLeod and John Baillie are invoked as exemplary authors of prayers. There follow accounts of Calvin on prayer, and Calvin and others on the Lord's Prayer, the concluding ascription of which informs Reformed spirituality which is 'captivated by the glory and the graciousness of God,' which cannot be 'snatched away' from the 'Father.' Predictable though the remark may be as coming from me, I cannot suppress the feeling that a passing reference to Church Meeting would have been appropriate in this chapter, for there the saints, as 'a listening people,' await God's guidance as to their mission—don't they?

Chapter three, on 'A choosing God and a chosen people,' opens with the first verse of George Matheson's paradox-replete hymn, 'Make me a captive. Lord/And then I shall be free.' In this context Dr. Cornick introduces a sensitive discussion of predestination and election, the former of which, he reminds us, 'is not a Reformed invention.' Supralapsarianism and infralapsarianism pass before the reader's eyes, and we learn that Calvin 'never intended [election] to become the lens through which the purposes of creation could be read.' Rather, 'In classical Reformed thought, election is a celebration of the purposes of God, a delight in the love and mercy that received supreme expression in the cross of Christ'—all of which is underlined in Watts's great hymn, "When I survey the wondrous cross."

'A holy God and a worldly people' is the title of chapter four. The second commandment, iconoclasm, liturgical space and social and political space all come under review, and the contrasting approaches to the last of R. W. Dale, Reinhold Niebuhr and John de Gruchy are discussed. Reflections on art follow, and the chapter ends with remarks on liturgy in relation to architectural shape.

In the concluding chapter, 'A loving God and a catholic people,' we meet John Williamson Nevin who, together with Philip Schaff, developed the Mercersburg theology with its emphasis upon catholicity, the Church as an organism, and the sacraments (and with its unfortunate declaration that the Church is a continuation of the Incarnation—a matter here passed over[34]). George MacLeod of the Iona Community, and Brother Roger of Taizé and Grandchamp represent those who have drawn upon a wide range of resources in developing their spiritualities. We are informed that 'The Church, for the Reformed, is defined not in terms of doctrine or structure, but of the activity of God in Word and sacraments'—hence the Reformed ability to recognize 'the ministries, sacraments, and memberships of other churches.' We need to unpack this claim. In the first place, to say that God is active in Word and sacraments is to articulate a rather important doctrine. Secondly, if, as we have earlier learned, the Church comprises those united by grace to Christ (mystical union) and called (election) into fellowship with one another—to use the shorthand: visible saints—structure of some sort is inevitable. Thirdly, the Reformed recognize the ministries, sacraments and memberships of others because they are already one in Christ with them, and their catholicity forbids sectarian division from them.

It will have become apparent that there are many good things in this book. Dr. Cornick has served his own tradition and others well. He has a pleasant way with words, as when he says that 'If the first manifestation of Reformed spirituality was iconoclasm, its midwife was humanism'; or again, 'Bullinger was graciously reticent before the ambiguity of Scripture, refusing to make neat hospital corners out of the ragged edges of the sheets of the story of salvation.' For the most part he writes with care. Thus, for example, he says that in Calvin's high doctrine of the Church 'the union between the believer and Christ is given expression in baptism'—that is, it is not *effected by* baptism. When quoting from older writings there is, in my judgement, no need to follow the generic "man/men" with [*sic*]; it smacks of toadying to radical feminists (or of thanking God that we are not like other men [*sic*]!), who actually know perfectly well what those writers meant when they, as children of their time, innocently followed the linguistic convention of their day. (What is it that we in our time do not see? We do not know, but we may be sure that our successors will proclaim it from the housetops or on the internet). On one occasion Dr. Cornick waxes impatient. With reference to inner-Reformed divisions he writes, 'The causes of division range from the weighty and majestic like the spiritual independence of the body of Christ, to the absurd like the use of musical instruments in church.' The fact is that some sincere Reformed folk disagree with the use of musical instruments in church, and a minority of them write substantial pamphlets against the practice. I suspect that we shall not win hearts and minds if we begin by dismissing positions unpalatable to ourselves as absurd. Dr. Cornick more than redeems himself when, against any who would fashionably denounce all missionaries as stooges of imperialistic states, he declares that 'The legacy of the missionary movement is ambiguous, yet at its best the Reformed mission was acutely aware of the radical challenge of the Gospel to the structures of colonialism,' in evidence of which he cites John Philip and others in the nineteenth century who fought for native rights, and those in the twentieth century who set their faces against apartheid.

I turn briefly to three more technical observations. First, in connection with Calvin's understanding of our knowledge of God, we should do well to hold together observations

---

34. See further, Alan P. F. Sell, *Testimony and Tradition*, Aldershot: Ashgate, 2005, ch. 8.

that Dr. Cornick makes in two different places. On p. 33 he says that Calvin 'is insistent that human beings cannot know God. God cannot be encompassed by human reason ..' The latter assertion correctly captures Calvin's thought and that of the Reformed tradition at large (and not only that tradition); but the former sentence is corrected on p. 101 where Calvin is accurately said to teach that 'Knowledge of God is both planted in the human mind and written into the structure of creation.' As a result of the noetic effects of sin, human beings suppress the knowledge of God that they have (cf. Rom 1: 19–21) or, as Dr. Cornick puts it, 'the human mind is blinded.' Secondly, it is sad to find that Schleiermacher's epitaph is, 'the *éminence grise* behind the development of twentieth-century liberal theology.' This does not take the measure of his achievement, a significant part of which was to show the 'cultured despisers' of religion that the demonstrations sought by those who advanced the failed theistic arguments did not capture the heart of genuine religion. Finally, Dr. Cornick thinks that debates over predestination can appear 'arcane and absurd. We "do" theology and spirituality very differently ... Thanks to Barth, we also understand election christologically'—and, it might be added, confusingly—'Very few modern confessions refer to predestination ...' I fear that some modern confessions are innocent of a number of important doctrines; but as to predestination, why may we not recover the good news in it? It is the joyous recognition of the fact that we did not get to where we are under our own steam, but that God had an eternal purpose for us. Of course, to bring out this Gospel we shall have to unscramble predestination from philosophical determinism—an intriguing, but not an impossible, task.[35]

This stimulating book prompted me to doodle with the idea of a further chapter which might be entitled, Cornick fashion, 'A challenging God and a disciplined people.' In such a chapter one would adumbrate the Spirit's resources for the life of discipleship. Furthermore, because the saints are also sinners, one would advert to that Gospel discipline, the objectives of which are the glory of God, the integrity of the Church and the restoration of the wayward; and would discuss church discipline in relation to baptism, the reception of members and the 'godly walk' in general. Notwithstanding the fact that they have on occasion badly bungled it, to such corporate spirituality the Reformed have traditionally paid more than lip service, and it is not inconceivable that the rediscovery of it, where that is required, would reinvigorate our mission.

The book is furnished with notes and a wide-ranging bibliography, but would there were an index. Its publisher would perform a signal service if an accompanying anthology of Reformed spirituality not otherwise readily available were to be commissioned.

Journal of the United Reformed Church 8 (2008), 155–60.

---

35. See further, Alan P. F. Sell, *Enlightenment, Ecumenism, Evangel*, pp. 325–38.

Index of Authors/Editors of Books Reviewed

Bassett, Joseph A., 295
Beaty, Michael, 93
Bebbington, David W., 140
Beeke, Joel R., 208
Bell, M. Charles, 244
Boucher, David, 59, 64
Brantley, Richard E., 147
Breed, Geoffrey R., 169
Briggs, J. H. Y., 167

Carr, Brian, 97
Collini, Stefan, 121
Connelly, James, 64
Cornick, David, 296

DeBie, Linden J., 227
DeWeese, Charles W., 128
Dockery, David S., 219
Driver, John, 264
Dulles, Avery, 266
Dunn, David, 135
Durnbaugh, Donald F., 131

Elkins, Heather Murray, 292
Evans, Eifion, 189

Fisher, Carlton, 93
Fitzpatrick, Martin, 111
Fraser, Brian J., 198

Gale, Richard M., 82
George, Timothy, 219
Gill, Robin, 284

Gouldstone, Timothy Maxwell, 56
Grave, S. A., 18
Griffioen, Arie J., 237
Gunton, Colin E., 251, 264, 270

Haakonssen, Knud, 35
Hamstra, Sam, Jr., 237
Hardman, Keith J., 185
Hardy, Daniel W., 270
Harris, James F., 76
Hebblethwaite, Brian, 88
Hesselink, I. John, 206
Hoeveler, J. David, 53
Hopkins, Mark, 200

Johnson, Mark D., 160
Jones, Peter, 111
Jones, R. Tudur, 124

Kaye, Elaine, 201
Kelly, Gerard, 275
Knellwolf, Christa, 111

Lewis, Donald M., 137
Littlejohn, W. Bradford, 230
Locke, Don, 47
Lund, Roger D., 119
Luscombe, David, 101

McCalman, Iain, 111
MacIntosh, J. J., 86
MacKinnon, Donald M., 257
McNaughton, William D., 153, 155, 157

Index of Authors/Editors of Books Reviewed

Mahalingam, Indira, 97
Marshall, David B., 191
Marshall, John, 25
Mast, Gregg Alan, 292
Meynell, H. A., 86
Modood, Tariq, 64
Moorhead, James H., 223

Nelson, Mark, 93
Newlands, George M., 253
Nockles, Peter Benedict, 151
Nuovo, Victor, 20

Parker, Kenneth L., 109
Patrick, James, 62
Pattison, George, 282
Peach, W. Bernard, 43, 45
Penelhum, Terence, 32
Peters, R. S., 66
Pfizenmaier, Thomas C., 213
Platt, John, 210
Pope, Robert, 124
Preston, Ronald H., 286
Price, John Valdimir, 28
Pyle, Andrew, 7

Quinn, Philip L., 72

Rack, Henry D., 145
Raeder, Linda C., 50
Rican, Rudolf, 105
Riesen, Richard Allan, 244
Robson, Geoff, 182
Rogers, G. A. J., 9
Roxborogh, John, 242

Schlesinger, George N., 80
Segundo, Juan Luis, 260
Shepherd, Peter, 179
Shriver, George, 187
Smith, Leonard, 175
Spellman, W. M., 22
Stephens, John, 28
Stewart, John W., 223
Stewart, M. A., 13
Streiff, Patrick, 217
Sutherland, Stewart, 88

Taliaferro, Charles, 72
Thomas, D. O., 37, 43, 45
Thompson, David M., 171
Trigg, Wilson, 205
Turner, John Munsey, 164

Tuttle, George M., 244

Vickers, John A., 143
Vincent, Andrew, 59
Von Rohr, John, 126
Vos, Arvin, 103

Wainwright, Geoffrey, 255, 278
Wells, David F., 239
Wentz, Richard E., 225
Whatmore, Richard, 121
White, James F., 289

Yolton, John W., 15, 17, 28
Young, Brian, 121

Zaragoza, Edward C., 292
Zuck, Lowell H., 135

Index of Sources

Baptist Quarterly, 130, 139, 147, 164, 181, 186
British Journal for the History of Philosophy, 59, 61, 120, 123
Calvin Theological Journal, 76, 111, 222
Congregational History Circle Magazine, 128
Critical Review of Books in Religion, 82
Ecumenical Review, 109, 188, 275, 278, 282
Enlightenment and Dissent, 25, 28, 118, 142, 150, 152, 217
Epworth Review, 296
European Journal of Theology, 207, 210
European Legacy, The, 12
Evangelical Quarterly, 169, 243
Faith and Freedom, 102, 179, 202
Friends of the Congregational Library Newsletter, 126
International Journal of Philosophical Studies, 9, 31, 37, 47, 52, 66, 85, 87
Irish Theological Quarterly, 250, 255, 266, 284
Journal of Ecclesiastical History, 201
Journal of the Presbyterian Church of Wales Historical Society, 191
Journal of the United Reformed Church History Society, 106, 134, 136, 155, 157, 159, 171, 174, 226, 239, 257, 295, 300
King's Theological Journal, 259
Literary Review of Canada, 197
Locke Newsletter, The, 21
Mid-Stream, 167
Modern Believing, 98, 218 225, 286, 289
National Bulletin on Liturgy, 292
New Mercersburg Review, The, 229, 237
Philosophical Books, 79
Philosophical Studies (Ireland), 18, 19, 35, 42, 45, 50, 55, 63, 71, 92, 104, 206, 213, 263, 269

Proceedings of the Wesley Historical Society, 145, 184
Reformed World, 242
Scottish Journal of Theology, 252
Scriblerian, The, 16
Studies in Christian Ethics, 96
Studies in Religion, 199
Transactions of the Unitarian Historical Society, 15

General Index

Abelard, 101
Abbott, Benjamin, 138
Abercromby, David, 7
Abernethy, John, 31
Accrington Academy, 180
Acland, James, 138
Adams, Marilyn McCord, 93
Adams, Robert M., 93
Adams, William, 44, 45, 46
Adams-Acton, John, 144
Addison, J., 7, 31
Adorno, Theodor W., 116
Aesthetics, 64, 282–4
African religions, 72
Aikman, John, 155
Airedale College, 161, 180
Albert the Great, 101
Alcuin, 101
Alexander, W. L., 156
Al-Ghazālī, A. H. M., 98
Allegro, J. M., 3
Allerton, John, 178
Alsop, Ada, 144
Alston, William P., 73, 77, 84, 87
Alting, Hendrick, 211
American Civil War, 223
American Council of Churches, 133
American Independence, 36, 38, 39, 43–4, 218
Ames, William, 8, 211
Ammonius Saccas, 205
Amory, Thomas, 31
Anabaptism/ists, 107, 131, 145, 228, 290
analogy, 89

Andover Seminary, 127
Anglicans/ism, 56–9, 62, 73, 119, 120, 138, 139, 140, 141, 146, 149, 151–2, 158, 162,164–5, 171–4, 182, 184, 189, 190, 216, 229, 231,232, 235–6, 251, 252, 255, 259, 261, 270, 272, 276, 279, 281, 293
Annet, Peter, 31
annihilationism, 44
Anselm, 83, 101, 251
apologetics, 33, 35, 49, 174, 196, 213, 239, 240
Arch, Joseph, 144
Arendt, Hannah, 67
Arians/ism, 18, 21, 30, 31, 38, 46, 52, 57, 120, 125, 201, 213, 214, 215, 216, 280, 292
Aristotle, 3, 62, 101, 212
Arius, 175, 215
Arizona State University, 225
Arminians/ism, 21, 27, 28, 30, 49, 125, 132, 140, 141, 144, 150, 154, 156, 158, 165, 168, 169, 179–80, 184, 186, 190, 191, 192, 197, 213, 214, 218, 220, 238, 250
Arminius, J., 212, 298
arms trade, 284, 285
Arnold, Thomas, 56, 173
art, 282–4
Arthur, John, 155
Asbury, Francis, 139
Ashcraft, Richard, 11, 27, 119
Ashurst, Miss, 44
Aspland, Robert, 175
assurance, 208–10, 244, 245
Astell, Mary, 8, 30, 116
Athanagoras, 275

General Index

atheism/ists, 46, 48, 74, 77, 113, 141, 185
atonement, 57, 149, 244, 245–6, 248, 252, 259, 263, 264–6, 274; see soteriology
Augsburg Confession, 135
Augustine, 83, 91, 95, 101, 235, 251, 283
Aulèn, G., 265
Auschwitz, 259
Austin, A., 139
Austin, J. L., 3, 76
Authority, 104, 112, 196, 215–16, 252, 270, 271, 272
Averroes, 98
Avicenna, 98
Avis, Paul, 255
Axon, Ernest, 41
Ayer, A. J., 63, 149, 197
Aylmer, G. E., 3

Bacon, Francis, 8, 31, 112, 214
Bacon, Roger, 101
Backus, Isaac, 219, 221
Bagshaw, Edward, 8
Baier, Annette C., 86
Baillie, Donald M., 253–5
Baillie, Ian, 253
Baillie, Jewel, 253
Baillie, John, 73, 78, 253–5, 298
Balmer, Randall, 293
Bannerman, James, 247, 248
baptism, 107, 125, 127, 132, 144, 154, 158, 168, 171, 190, 221, 233, 238, 243, 261, 280, 290, 292, 299
Baptism, Eucharist and Ministry, 273, 275, 276–7, 279
Baptist Missionary Society, 169
Baptists, 40, 128–30, 138, 139, 146, 149, 153, 157, 165, 167–71, 173, 175, 179–81, 184, 186, 200, 218, 219–222, 224, 239, 241, 274, 290, 291
Baptist Union of Great Britain and Ireland, 180
Barbauld, Anna Laetitia, 38
Barlow, Thomas, 8
Barmen Declaration, 241
Barrett, C. K., 144
Barrett, Lee C., III, 232, 237
Barrow, Henry, 124, 235
Barrow, Isaac, 8, 118
Barth, Karl, 125, 194, 195, 211, 220, 251, 254, 256, 295, 300
Bartlet, J. Vernon, 276
Barton, Stephen C., 285
Bascom, H. B., 139
Basden, Paul A., 219

Basel Mission, 136
Bastingius, Jeremias, 211
Battles, Ford Lewis, 233
Bauer, F. C., 188
Bavinck, H., 240
Baxter, Andrew, 30
Baxter, J. Sidlow, 220
Baxter, Richard, 8, 24, 189, 191, 200, 221, 284
Bayes, Thomas, 39, 41–2
Bayle, P., 117
Beaham, William, 132
Beard, John Relly, 176
Beasley-Murray, George, 219, 220
Beattie, James, 30, 231
Bebbington, David W., 137
Beccaria, C., 115
Beckerlegge, Oliver, 143
Beddoes, Thomas, 31
Beddome, Benjamin, 139
Beecher, Henry Ward, 128
Beecher, Lyman, 185, 186
Beeson School of Divinity, 219
Beet, J. Agar, 144
Beissel, Johan Conrad, 133
Belben, Howard, 144
Belgic Confession, 211, 212
Benezet, Anthony, 138
Bennett, James, 142
Benson, E. B., 172
Bentham, Jeremy, 51, 115
Bentley, Richard, 17
Bereans, 153, 158
Berg, Joseph F., 187
Berkeley, George, 3, 29, 37, 173
Berkhof, Louis, 240
Berlin University, 187
Bethel, Slingsby, 8
Betjeman, John, 123
Betson, A., 31
Beza, Theodore, 110, 208
Bible, 125, 132, 141, 144, 145, 152, 170, 172, 173, 175, 191, 193, 196, 197, 212, 214, 216, 218, 222, 223, 224, 228, 233, 238, 240, 245, 246–7, 251, 256, 262, 273, 279–80, 287, 289; see also inerrancy
Bicheno, James, 116
Binney, Thomas, 160
Binning, Hugh, 8, 245
Binns, William, 176, 178
Birmingham riots, 175
Birt, Isaiah, 168
Birtles, Hilton, 178
Blackburn Independent Academy, 142

General Index

Black Country, 182–4
Blake, William, 31, 147, 150
Blasius of Parma, 102
Blaurock, Georg, 107
Blount, Charles, 7, 20
Blundeville, Thomas, 8
Boehme, J., 150
Boethius, A. M. S., 101
Bogue, David, 157
Bohemian Confession, 106
Boice, James Montgomery, 241
Bold, Samuel, 20
Bomberger, J. H. A., 136, 188, 225, 226, 232, 233
Bonaventure, 101
Bonhoeffer, D., 252, 270, 274
Book of Common Prayer, 291
Book of Sports, 110–11
Borthwick, Jane, 188
Bosanquet, Mary, 218
Boston, Thomas, 245, 249
Boucher, David, 64, 65
Bourne, Hugh, 144
Boyce, James Petigru, 219, 224
Boyle, Robert, 10
Boys' Brigade, 202
Brachlow, Stephen, 219
Bradford Baptist College, 138
Bradley, F. H., 62–3
Bradley, James, 63
Bradwardine, Thomas, 22, 102
Braithwaite, R. B., 91
Brandon, S. G. F., 3
Brantley, Richard E., 218
Bratt, James D., 238, 239, 240
Bray, Billy, 144
Brennan, Andrew, 87
Brethren churches, 131–4
Brett, Thomas, 151
Brewster, William, 126
Briggs, William, 139
Brine, John, 218, 220
British and Foreign Bible Society, 165
British and Foreign Schools Society, 172
Broglie, G. de, 104
Brooks, John G., 183
Brown, Antoinette, 127
Brown, James Baldwin, 160, 200, 201
Brown, John, of Wamphray, 145
Brown, S. J., 242
Brown, Stuart, 7
Brown, Thomas, 55
Browne, Peter, 8, 148
Browne, Robert, 124, 235

Browne, Simon, 31
Browning, Don, 285
Browning, Margaret, 64, 65
Brown's covenant, 130
Bruce, A. B., 142, 199
Brueggemann, Walter, 298
Bryden, Walter, 194
Brunner, Emil, 162
Bucer, Martin, 106
Buchanan, George, 31
Buckley, J. H., 58
Buddhism, 75, 97, 98, 226, 283
Bull, William, 142
Bullinger, H., 208, 299
Bultitude, Elizabeth, 138, 144
Bultmann, R., 261
Bunhill Fields, 38
Bunting, Jabez, 144
Bunyan, John, 7, 219, 221
Buridan, Jean, 102
Burke, Edmund, 38, 40, 116, 165
Burnet, Thomas, 17, 18–19, 215
Burrell, David, 72
Burrow, John, 121, 123
Burtt, Shelley, 120
Burwash, Nathanael, 193
Bury Academy, 180
Bush, George H. W., 51
Bush, L. Russ, III, 219
business, 285
Bushnell, Horace, 238
Burrows, A., 44
Butler, Joseph, 29, 30, 31, 32–5, 38, 39, 166, 173, 258
Butterfield, Herbert, 144
Byron, George, 48

Cadoux, C. J., 2, 162, 201–2
Cadoux, Theo, 202
Cahill, Lisa Sowle, 285
Caird, Edward, 61, 65, 73, 195, 198, 258
Caird, George, 162
Calvin, John, 3, 42, 78, 103–4, 110, 174, 195, 196, 206–7, 208, 211, 212, 213, 233, 234, 241, 244, 245, 249, 251, 269, 271, 281, 282, 290, 295, 298, 299, 300
Calvinism/ists, 14, 20, 21, 23, 24–5, 26, 28, 30, 35, 37, 42, 46, 48, 49, 53, 55, 75, 106, 112, 125, 126, 127, 132, 140, 144, 146, 149, 154, 158, 165, 170, 179–80, 184, 185, 186, 191, 192, 195, 197, 200, 201, 208, 209, 213, 214, 220, 221, 228, 239, 250, 291, 297, 298
Calvinistic Methodism/ists, 125, 143, 190, 217, 218

307

General Index

Cambridge Platonists, 10, 23, 173, 214, 238
Cambridge University, 56, 171–4
Campbell, Alexander, 134, 154
Campbell, J. A. I., 7
Campbell, John (1766–1840), 155
Campbell, John (1795–1867), 160
Campbell, John, of Montreal, 193
Campbell, John McLeod, 55, 141, 142, 154, 160, 200, 245–6
Campbell, Mary, 155
Campbell, R. J., 195
Camus, A., 262
Canada, 191–9
Candlish, R. S., 139, 247
Cane Ridge, 134
Cappadocian fathers, 214, 215, 271
Cardale, John Bate, 294
Cardiff University, 59
Carey, William, 138
Cargill, David, 138
Carlson, Leland H., 235
Carlyle, Thomas, 48, 121, 122, 123, 200
Carmarthen Academy, 42
Carmichael, Gershom, 8
Carmichael, Robert, 221
Carnell, Edward John, 219
Carroll, Benajah Harvey, 219, 222
Carter, David, 143
Cartwright, Thomas 110, 124
Carver, W. O., 219
Carwardine, Richard J., 223
catechetics, 226
Catholic Apostolic Church, 293, 294–5
Catholicity, 202, 225, 226, 235, 269, 271, 276, 291, 299
Caton, John, 43
Cave, Sydney, 24
Caven, William, 193
Cavendish, Margaret, 8
Celsus, 205
Chalmers, Thomas, 53, 140, 242–3, 245
Chamberlain, Jeffrey S., 120
Chambers, Ephraim, 114
Chambers, Robert, 54
Chandler, Samuel, 31
Channing School, London, 177
Chappell, Vere, 7, 15
Charles I, 121, 172
Charles II, 22
Charleton, Walter, 8
Chatham, see Pitt, W., the Elder
Chaucer, G., 3
Chauncy, Charles, 44

Chelcicky, Petr, 105
children, 296
Childress, James F., 285
Chillingworth, William, 8, 10, 20, 170, 214
Chomsky, Noam, 70
Chown, S. D., 194
Christian Science, 290
Christology, 91–2, 252, 259
Chubb family, 144
Chubb, Thomas, 30
Church
  and state, 163, 170, 195, 228, 259, 281
  covenants, 128–30, 236
  discipline, 133, 250, 269, 275, 281, 284, 300
  doctrine of the, 132, 221, 226, 228, 234–5, 238, 252, 256, 259, 261, 266–75, 299
  matter of the, 163, 234, 269, 281, 291
  meeting, 125, 127, 154, 166–7, 274, 281, 298
  membership, 130, 144, 170
  polity, 127, 132–3, 134, 153, 232, 235, 256, 270, 271, 273, 274, 277, 279, 280, 291
Church Building Society, 151
Churches of Christ, 289
Church of Scotland, 245, 293
Church Service Society, 293
citizenship, 61
Civil War, 116
Clarendon, Earl of, 121
Clarke, Adam, 141
Clarke, Samuel, 8, 21, 29, 30, 31, 38, 83, 112, 120, 213–17
Clarke, W. N., 220
class, 287
class meeting, 144, 166
Clement of Alexandria, 205
Clemens, Deborah Rahn, 293
Clements, Ronald, 220
Cleves, 26
Clifford, John, 168, 180, 200, 220
Clifford, W. K., 85
Coakley, Sarah, 75
Coccejus, Johannes, 212
Cockburn, Catharine, 8, 12, 20, 30
Cocks, H. F. Lovell, 166
Coffin, Henry Sloane, 253
Coke, Thomas, 146
Cole, Thomas, 8
Coleridge, S. T., 48, 49, 52, 57, 147, 162, 172, 229, 238, 251, 270
collective responsibility, 285
College of William and Mary, 78
Collingwood, R. G., 62, 63, 64–6, 73, 222
Collini, Stefan, 121, 123

General Index

Collins, Anthony, 21, 30
Colonius, Daniel, 211
Comenius Faculty Prague, 105
Comenius, J. A., 7, 106
common grace, 240
common sense philosophy/realism, 7, 30, 61, 140, 150, 223, 227, 231, 239, 240
Commonwealth sects, 116
Comrie, Alexander, 208
Comte, A. 2, 51
Confucianism, 72, 98
Congregationalism/ists, 21, 36, 122, 129, 138, 139, 142, 160, 161, 162, 163, 165, 166, 168, 173, 180, 183, 184, 186, 200, 201, 221, 232, 234, 235, 236, 238, 241, 269, 274, 276, 291, 293
   in America, 126–8
   in Scotland, 153–9
   in Wales, 126–8
Congregational Union of England and Wales, 122
Connelly, James, 64, 65
Conner, Ralph, 194
Conner, Walter Thomas, 219, 222
conscience, 19, 33, 39, 117, 245
Conservative Congregational Christian Conference, 128
Conser, Walter, Jr., 238
Constable, John, 123
Constantine, 258
Copleston, F. C., 83
Coppenger, Mark, 219
Corrie, George, 172
Corvinus, J. A., 212
Cotton, John, 126, 127
Coulson, C. A., 144
Courthal, P., 211
covenant theology, 127, 224, 244–5, 249, 250
Cowper, William, 148
Cox, F. A., 168
Cox, Martin L., 293
Cradley Heath Speedway Club, 184
Cradock, Walter, 124, 269
Craig, John, 269
Cranmer, Thomas, 290
creation, 83, 218, 275
creationism, 132
Creator-creature distinction, 53, 233, 273
Creel, Richard E., 74
Crews, C. Daniel, 106
Crisp, Tobias, 15
Criswell, W. A., 219, 220, 222
Croce, Benedetto, 62
Crocker, John William, 122
Crombie, I. M., 77

Cromwell, Oliver, 122
Crosby, Thomas, 220
Cudworth, Ralph, 8, 17, 30
Culpepper, R. Alan, 219
culture, 114–15, 117, 125, 224, 225, 238, 239, 240, 254
Cumberland, Richard, 13
Cunningham, R. L., 91
Cunningham, William, 42, 209, 224, 247, 248
Cunningham, William (Stewarton), 159
Cupitt, Don, 89
Curteis, Thomas, 119, 120
Czech Reformers, 105–6

Dabney, Robert L., 240
Dagg, John L., 219
Dale, R. W., 160, 161, 162, 180, 200, 251, 252, 293, 298
Daneau, L., 212
D'Arcy, Charles, 57
Darwin, Charles, 78, 172, 193, 224, 258
Davenport, James, 127
Davidson, A. B., 246, 248, 249
Davidson, Alexander, 158
Davidson, Samuel, 142
Davies, Horton, 293, 294
Davies, John, 189
Davies, Pryce, 42
Davies, T. Witton, 180
Davies, W. T. Pennar, 42
Dawson, George, 160
Day, Alan, 219, 222
D'Costa, Gavin, 285
death, 296
De Dominis, D. A., 7
Dee, John, 8
Defoe, Daniel, 7
Deism/ists, 11, 15, 18, 20, 23, 29, 30, 32, 34, 46, 48, 112, 115, 120, 150, 185, 190, 214, 218, 280, 291–2
Demetrius, 205
Denis the pseudo-Areopagite, 101
Denison controversy, 151
Denney, James, 61, 140, 199, 225, 259
Dent, 4
depravity, 22–5
Derrida, J., 76, 116
Descartes, R., 10, 44, 46, 112, 214, 227, 231
determinism, 39, 44, 45, 55, 60, 75
Dever, Mark E., 219
Dewar, James, 155
Dewart, E. H., 193
Dewey, John, 224
Dick, Francis, 156

309

General Index

Dickson, David, 244
Diffey, T. J., 64
Dignāga, 97
Dillistone, F. W., 264
DiPuccio, William, 238, 239
Disciples of Christ, 134
dispensationalism, 238
Disruption, 154
Dissent/ers, 12, 24, 26, 31, 35–7, 42, 43, 46, 120, 125, 160–164, 165, 168, 172, 175, 179, 182, 200, 213, 216, 264, 265, 276, 280, 281
Dobson, William, 156
Dockery, David S., 219, 220
Dodd, C. H., 162, 254
Doddridge, Philip, 17, 29, 139, 179, 247
Dods, Marcus, 142
Dodwell, Henry, 8, 150
Dooyeweerd, H., 73, 141, 240
Dorner, I. A., 187, 227
Dowes, Mannaseh, 31
Downgrade Controversy, 168, 200
Dray, W. H., 67
Drew University, 292, 294
Drummond, Henry, 140, 294
Drummond, Lewis A., 219
Drury, John, 122
Dryden, John, 3
Duckworth, Francis, 144
Duff, Alexander, 139
Dugmore, C. W., 3
Dumouchel, Paul, 13
DuMoulin, Pierre, 212
Du Plessis-Mornay, Philippe, 212
Duns Scotus, John, 72, 102, 207
Durham, James, 244
Dussen, Jan van der, 64
Dutch Reformed Church in America, 293, 294
Dutch theology, 210–13
duty faith, 141
Dykes, Kenneth C., 180
Dyson, R. W., 8

Eco, Umberto, 282
ecology, 285
ecumenism, 126, 142, 144–5, 161, 163, 165–6, 167, 174, 188, 220–31, 238, 273, 275–82, 286
Eden Theological Seminary, 136
Edinburgh University, 53, 176, 253
education, 61, 66, 71, 114, 118, 127, 141, 168, 250; see also philosophy of education; theological education
Edwards, John, 20, 23, 24
Edwards, John (actuary), 43

Edwards, Jonathan, 44, 126, 127, 138, 148, 185, 224, 256, 298
Edwards, Paul, 83
Einstein, Albert, 297
Eitel, Keith E., 219
election, 208, 209, 251, 298, 299
Elford, R. John, 285
Elgar, Edward, 63
Elkins, Heather Murray, 293
Elizabeth I, 109, 235
Emerson, Ralph Waldo, 205, 224
Emmet, Dorothy, 3
empire, 122
Enfield, William, 36
Enlightenment, 13, 28, 35, 37, 53, 72, 111–18, 122, 130, 140, 142, 163, 197, 218, 230, 251, 252, 266, 272, 285, 288, 291, 292, 298
Ephrata Community, 133
Episcopius, 212
Erasmus, D., 14
Erastianism, 13
Erb, William H., 228
Erbury, William, 124
Erikson, Millard J., 219
Erskine, Ebenezer, 249
Erskine, Thomas, of Linlathen, 55, 141, 160, 200
eschatology, 90, 116, 259, 262, 285, 287
establishment, 55; see also Church and state
Etheridge, B. C., 170
ethics, 74, 77, 90–91, 181, 241, 246, 284–89; see also morality; philosophy, moral
eucharist; see Lord's Supper
Euclid, 172
Eusebianism, 215
Eusebius of Caesarea, 213, 215
Evangelical Alliance, 141, 243
Evangelical Alliance (U.S.A), 188
Evangelical and Reformed Church, 126, 135–6
evangelicalism, 53, 55, 137–42, 151, 152, 160, 165, 172, 193, 200–202, 236, 245, 249, 268
Evangelical Revival, 49, 125, 146, 148, 153, 168, 179, 217
Evangelical Synod, 135
Evangelical Union, 154, 155, 158
Evans, C. Stephen, 93, 95
Evans, Caleb, 218
Evans, Christmas, 220
Evans, Owen E., 3, 144
Evens, G. B., 144
Everett, J., 144
evil, problem of, 74, 75, 77, 79, 80, 81, 113, 181, 274
evolutionary thought, 54, 56, 60, 78–9, 195, 257

Ewing, Greville, 154, 155, 157, 159
existentialism, 76
experience, 77, 84, 192, 224, 238, 240, 276

Fabian Society, 177
Fackre, Gabriel, 241
Fairbairn, A. M., 156, 158, 161, 162, 163, 180, 256
faith, 12, 27, 54, 86–7, 245, 248, 276, 282
Faith in the City, 272
Falconer, R. A., 198
Farmer, H. H., 73, 78, 162
family, 185
Farr, George, 3
Farrer, Austin, 63, 78
Fawcett, John, 179, 181
federal theology; see covenant theology
Fellowship of the Kingdom, 144
feminism, 75
Ferguson, Adam, 30, 113, 150
Ferrier, J. F., 231
fideism, 74, 75
Fielding, Henry, 119
Filmer, Robert, 8, 27
Finney, Charles Grandison, 126, 127, 138, 154, 185–6, 236
Firmin, Thomas, 27
First Church of Chestnut Hill, 295
Fitzpatrick, Martin, 36, 49, 116, 118
Flavel, John, 269
Fletcher, David B., 93
Fletcher, John W., 3, 217–18
Fletcher, Joseph, 142
Flew, A. G. N., 74, 77, 87
Flew, R. Newton, 165
Flint, Thomas P., 74
Flory, P. J., 133
Foot, Michael, 144
Ford, David F., 272, 273, 274
Forrester, Duncan B., 255, 256, 285
Forster, E. M., 123
Forsyth, P. T., 79, 136, 162, 172, 174, 200, 201, 234, 251, 252, 259, 265, 268, 270, 274, 283
Fosdick, H. E., 220
Foucault, Michel, 116
Franke, A. H., 116
Franklin, Benjamin, 39, 43, 45, 118
Franks, R. S., 162
Fraser, James, of Brea, 245
Frazer, J. G., 140
Frederick the Great, 115
Free Church College Aberdeen, 246
Free Church College Glasgow, 198
Free Church Federal Council, 144

Free Church Movement, 185
Free Church of Scotland, 53, 55, 154, 198, 224, 235, 242, 246, 247, 248
freedom, 252
Freewill Baptists, 129
French Revolution, 36, 38, 45
Frontier religion, 290, 291
Frost, David, 144
Froude, R. Hurrell, 151
Früe, Jörg, 108
Fuller, Andrew, 157, 169, 219
Fuller Theological Seminary, 213
fundamentalism, 220, 254
Furman, Richard, 219

Gadamer, H-G, 76
Galileo, G., 78
Gallican Confession, 211
Galloway, Nisbet, 159
Gambold, Anna, 138
Garber, Samuel, 134
Garcia, Jorge, 96
Gardiner, Allen Francis, 138
Garrett, Duane A., 219, 222
Garrett, James Leo, Jr., 219
Garvie, A. E., 61, 152, 199
Gascoigne, John, 36
Gaskell, Elizabeth, 178
Gaskell, William, 176, 178
Gassendi, P., 14
Gassmann, Gunther, 277
Gay, Peter, 35
Geach, Peter, 93
gender, 285
General Baptist Association, 180
General Baptists, 220, 290
genetics, 285
Gentile, Giovanni, 62
George III, 151
George, Timothy, 219, 221
German Reformed Church, 135, 187, 225, 227, 229, 237, 241, 293, 294
Gerrish, Brian A., 224
Gerson, Jean, 102
Gibbon, Edward, 113, 122, 123
Gibson, Margaret Dunlop, 173
Gide, A., 262
Gifford, Andrew, 31
Gilbert of Poitiers, 101
Gilbert, W. S., 268
Gill, Eric, 283
Gill, John, 218, 219, 221
Gill, Robin, 285

General Index

Gilman, Eric, 3
Glanville, Joseph, 8
Glasgow City Mission, 158
Glasgow Theological Academy, 153, 154
Glasgow University, 53, 61, 193
Glasites, 153, 158, 221; see also Sandemanianism
Glover, T. R., 173
gnosticism, 205, 263
Godwin, J. H., 95
Godwin, William, 23, 47–50
Gomarus, Francis, 212, 198
Goodman, Len E., 75
Goodwin, A., 3
Goodwin, Thomas, 208
Gordon, Alexander, 41, 176
Gordon, C. W., 198
Gore, Charles, 276
Gorham controversy, 151
Gorringe, Tim, 285
Gospel Standard Baptists, 141, 220
Gother, John, 20
Göttingen University, 115
Gottschalk of Orbais, 22, 101
government, 115
grace, 218, 241, 245, 247, 250, 261, 265, 266, 271, 274, 276, 279, 283
Graham, Stephen, 238
Grant, George, 193
Grant, George (philosopher), 198
Grant, Robert M., 205
Grave, S. A., 17
Graves, J. R., 219, 221, 222
Grayston, Kenneth, 144
Great Awakening, 126, 189
Great Ejectment, 124
Great Tew Circle, 214
Grebel, Conrad, 107
Green, Fred Kimball, 293
Green, Ronald M., 285
Green, T. H., 56, 57, 58, 62, 258
Green, V. H. H., 150
Greene, Richard, 17
Greenwood, John, 124
Grenz, Stanley J., 219, 221
Grew, Nehemiah, 8
Grieve, A. J., 4, 160
Griffionen, Arie J., 238
Griffiths, D., 170
Griffiths, David, 180
Griffiths, Paul J., 75
Griffiths, Vavasour, 42
Grosseteste, Robert, 101
Grotius, Hugo, 212, 245
Grove, Henry, 95, 179

Gruchy, John de, 298
Guelzo, Allen C., 223
Gunton, Colin E., 270, 271, 272, 273, 274, 275

Haakonssen, Knud, 13, 30
Haas, William, 3
Habermas, J., 76
Haddock, B. A., 64, 65
Hadidian, Dikran Y., 255, 257
Hageman, Howard G., 292, 293, 294
Haldane, James A., 140, 153, 155, 156, 157
Haldane, Robert, 140, 155, 157
Hale, Joe, 281
Hales, John, 8
Hall, Robert, 169, 170
Hall, Westley, 145
Halle University, 115, 116, 117, 187
Hallow, 4
Halyburton, Thomas, 245
Hamilton, William, 53, 55
Hamlyn, D. W., 70
Hamstra, Sam, Jr., 238, 239
Happy Union, 21
Hardshell Baptists, 222
Hardy, Daniel W., 251, 255, 256, 270, 274
Hardy, Thomas, 57
Hare, J. C., 172, 174
Hare, R. M., 3, 85, 91
Harrington, James, 115
Harris, H. S., 64
Harris, Howel, 42, 138, 143, 190
Harris, Ian, 14
Harris, J. Rendel, 173
Harrison, Jonathan, 4
Harrison, Robert, 124
Hart, D., 230, 231
Hartley, David, 18, 44, 52, 112, 114, 175
Hartley, W. P., 144
Hartshorne, Charles, 77
Harvard University, 54, 79, 127
Harvey, William, 8
Hatcher, William, 169
Hauerwas, Stanley, 93, 94, 96
Haymes, Brian, 180
Hazlitt, William, 47, 48, 148
Head, Geoffrey, 176
Hebblethwaite, Brian, 73, 91–2, 255
Hagel, G. W. F., 2, 54, 57, 60, 97, 227, 228, 229, 231, 265, 272, 283; see also Hegelianism
Hegelianism, 161, 173, 195, 201, 202, 224, 225, 227, 238
Heidegger, Martin, 75, 283
Heidelberg Catechism, 132, 135
Helm, Paul, 244

General Index

Helwys, Thomas, 40
Henry VIII, 124
Henry of Ghent, 102
Henry, Carl F. H., 149, 219
Henry, D. P., 3
Henry, Philip, 24
Hepburn, Ronald W., 4, 78, 89, 90, 254
Herbert, R. T., 87
Herbst, P., 67
Heron, Alasdair, 255, 256
Herrnhut, 106
heterodoxy, 119–20; see also Arianism, Socinianism, Unitarianism
Hewitt, Glen, 238
Heylyn, Peter, 109, 110
Heywood, Oliver, 24
Heywood Thomas, John, 3, 4, 78, 181
Hick, John H., 77, 86, 87
Hicks, Peter, 223
Higgins, Ian, 8
Hignett, Dorothy, 3
Hill, Andrew M., 176
Hill, Christopher, 110, 119
Hill, Thomas, 142
Hilton, Boyd, 123
Hincmar, 101
Hinduism, 72, 97, 122
Hirst, Paul, 68, 70–1
historiography, 121–2, 123
Hoadly, Benjamin, 29, 30, 31, 36, 46, 214
Hobbes, Thomas, 8, 10, 13, 95, 113
Hobbs, Herschel, 219, 220, 221
Hodder, Ian, 64, 65
Hodge, A. A., 224
Hodge, Charles, 3, 223–5, 227, 228, 229, 230, 231, 232, 234, 235, 238, 239–40
Hoeveler, Mrs., 55
Hoeveler, J. David, Jr., 239
Hoffecker, W. Andres, 239, 240
Hogarth, William, 119
Holiday Fellowship, 177
Holifield, E. Brooks, 224
Holt, R. V., 38, 177, 178
Holy Spirit, 190, 202, 207, 208, 217, 227, 228, 235, 251–2, 259, 263, 265, 267, 270–1, 274, 279, 281, 298
Homerton Academy, 142
Hommius, Festut, 212
Honderich, Ted, 32
Honders, A. Casper, 293
Hooker, Richard, 8, 14, 164
Hooker, Thomas, 128
Hooker-Stacey, Morna, 144
Hope, William J., 142

Hopkey, Sarah, 145
Horkheimer, Max, 116
Horne, George, 151
Hort, F. J. A., 172, 173
Horton College, Bradford, 180
Horton, Douglas, 126
Horton, R. F., 161
Hovey, A., 220
Howard, John, 44
Howe, John, 221, 229, 238
Hoxton Academy (1701–85), 49
Hoxton Independent Academy (1788–1850), 142
Hughes, Hugh Price, 195
Huguenots, 112–13, 117
Hull, J. H. Eric, 3
humanism, 77, 90, 102
Hume, David, 17, 29 30, 32, 37, 38, 41, 44, 48, 61, 72, 81, 86, 95, 112, 113, 121, 150, 227, 231
Humphreys, Fisher, 219
Hungary, 106, 107
Hunt, Jean, 61
Hunter, Ian, 116, 117
Hus, Jan, 105
Hussites, 105
Hutcheson, Francis, 29, 30, 31, 38, 39, 53, 112, 150
Hutter, Jakob, 107
Hutterian Brethren, 107–9, 133
Hutton, Sarah, 7
Hyman, John, 73
hymns, 133, 291, 293, 294, 298

iconoclasm, 283
icons, 283
idealism, 54, 56–64, 65, 76, 79, 173, 198, 199, 225, 226, 238, 240, 257, 259, 265, 294; see also Hegelianism
Iglehart, Glenn, 222
Illingworth, J. R., 58, 256
immortality, 19
incarnation, 56, 57, 83, 92, 174, 200, 221, 226, 231, 234, 238, 256, 257, 258, 259, 268, 294
Independents; see Congregationalists
inerrancy, 132, 141, 142, 223, 241, 265, 267, 284–5
Ingram, George S., 158
Inquirer, The, 176
intuitional realism, 54
International Congregational Council, 127
Iona Community, 299
Irenaeus, 24, 251
Irving, Edward, 140, 141, 142, 251, 252, 265, 293, 294
Islam, 88, 97, 288
Islip, Simon, 110
Israel, Jonathan, 116

313

General Index

Jacks, L. P., 178
Jackson, Timothy P., 285
Jackson, Thomas, 95
Jacob, Margaret C., 117
James I, 110
James, John Angell, 160, 183
James, William, 77, 224
Jasper, John, 138
Jeanrond, Werger G., 271, 274
Jefferson, Thomas, 45
Jellema, W. H., 73
Jenson, Robert W., 251, 255
Jeremy, Walter D., 41
Jessop, T. E., 144
Jesuits, 8, 107
Jewish ethics, 285
John à Lasco, 29
John of Jandun, 101
John of Salisbury, 101
John Scotus Erigena, 101
Johnson, A. R., 162, 220
Johnson, Samuel, 31, 210, 251
Jones, David, 189
Jones, Edgar, 3
Jones, Gareth, 284
Jones, Griffith, 189
Jones, Henry, 59–61, 65, 73
Jones, Humphrey, 189
Jones, John, 190
Jones, Peter, 117, 118
Jones, R. M., 8
Jones, R. Tudur, 124, 125
Jones, Sam, 193
Jones, Samuel, 31
Jonsson, John N., 219, 221
Joseph, H. W. B. 62
Jowett, Benjamin, 57, 162
Judaism, 88, 288, 294
Judson, Adoniram, 138
Jump, J. D., 3
Jüngel, Eberhard, 251
Junius, Franciscus, 211–12
justice, 48, 285, 287

Käls, Heironymus, 108
Kansfield, Norman J., 293
Kant, I., 2, 3, 41, 60, 77, 89, 97, 113, 114, 118, 227, 257, 259, 265, 270
Kaye, Elaine, 175, 179
Kaye, John, 172
Keach, Benjamin, 219, 221, 291
Keats, John, 147
Keble, John, 151

Keeble, N. H., 7
Keele University, 9, 167
Keller, James, 93
Kelly, Douglas Floyd, 240
Kelsey, David H., 224
Kendal Academy, 43
Kendall, R. T., 209, 218
Kendall, Willmore, 63
Kennedy, James, 155
kenosis, 254, 258
Kenrick, Samuel, 36
Kent, John, 144
Kenworthy, Fred, 177, 178
Keswick Convention, 141
Keys, Mary, 48
Kidd, Richard L., 180
Kierkegaard, S., 72, 85, 282
Kilham, Alexander, 142, 144
Kilpatrick, T. B., 198, 199
Kilwardby, Robert, 102
King, William, 29
Kinghorn, Joseph, 170
King's College Cambridge, 282
King's College London, 264
Kippis, Andrew, 36, 46
Kirk, John, 156, 159
Knight, Sydney, 178
knowledge, 19, 211, 300
Knowles, Vincent, 3
Knox College, Dunedin, 242
Knox College, Toronto, 193, 198
Knox, John, 53, 244, 250
Knox, T. M., 79
Körner, S., 79
Kovács, Sándor, 177
Kraemer, H., 77
Kralice Bible, 106
Kromeriz, Milicof, 105
Kuchlinus, Johannes, 211
Kuklick, Bruce, 224
Küng, Hans, 267
Kuyper, Abraham, 73, 141, 213, 240

Ladd, George Eldon, 219, 220
Lamb, Charles, 48, 148
Lambeth Quadrilateral, 166
La Mettrie, J. O. de, 113
Lampe, G. W. H., 88
Lancashire Independent College, 4, 163, 180
Lancaster Theological Seminary, 238
Landmarkism, 217, 221
Langerak, Edward, 74
Lansdowne, Marquis of, 45, 46

Lash, Nicholas, 89
Latitudinarians/ism, 26, 27, 36, 112, 214
Latourette, K. S., 220
Laud, William, 22
law, 206–7, 247, 249, 262
Law, Andrew, 156
Law, Edmund, 21, 30
Law, William, 30
Layman, David W., 238
Leahy, Desmond, 3
Leaver, Robin A., 293
Lecerf, Auguste, 224
Leechman, William, 36
Lees, F. N., 3
Leibniz, 8, 214
Leicester Conference, 160, 161, 200
Leich, F. William, 136
Leith, John H., 241
Lenwood, Frank, 161
Leslie, Charles, 8
Leslie, R. F., 3
Levine, Joseph M., 120
Lewis, Agnes Smith, 173
Lewis, C. S., 62
Lewis, H. D., 73, 79
liberal theology, 200–202, 220, 240, 254, 268, 292
liberation theology, 260–263, 287, 288
Lidgett, John Scott, 165
Lightfoot, J. B., 172
Lightfoot, R. H., 254
Limborch, P. van, 20, 23, 27
Lindbeck, George, 255, 256
Lindsey, Theophilus, 41, 45, 46
linguistic analysis, 76–9, 94, 241
liturgy, 226, 238; see also worship
Livingstone, David, 159
Lloyd-Jones, D. Martyn, 126, 222
Llwyd, Morgan, 8, 124
Llwynllwyd Academy, 42
Lock, Walter, 256
Locke, John, 2, 7, 8, 9–28, 29, 30, 31, 38, 40, 46, 74, 112, 113, 117, 119, 142, 145, 147–8, 150, 165, 171, 172, 214, 216, 218, 221, 227, 228, 252, 265
Lockhart, J. G., 122
logical positivism, 76
London Association of Strict Baptist Ministers and Churches, 169
London Missionary Society, 136
London Strict Baptist Associations, 169, 170
London University, 168
Lonergan, Bernard, 73, 90
Long, Arthur, 177

Long, Eugene T., 76
Long, Gary, 176
Lord's Supper, 107, 125, 127, 132, 154, 158, 168, 170, 171, 227, 232, 233, 238, 261, 271, 282, 290, 292, 293, 294
Louis XIV, 113
Lukas of Prague, 105
Love feast, 132
Low, Thomas, 159
Lubac, Henri de, 230, 231
Lubbertus, Sibrandus, 211
Lund, Roger D., 120
Lunn, Henry S., 165
Luther King House, Manchester, 177, 179
Luther, Martin, 104, 110, 196, 206, 208, 210, 271, 280, 290
Lutherans/ism, 26, 106, 255, 278, 280, 281, 290, 297
Luther's Catechism, 135
Lux Mundi, 255–7
Lyell, Charles, 123
Lyons, William, 87

Mabbott, J. D., 64
Macaulay, Catherine, 116
Macaulay, T. B., 121
MacBride, John, 36
McCalman, Iain, 36
McCloskey, H. J., 83
McCosh, James, 53–5, 195, 239
M'Crie, C. G., 244
Macdonald, J. A., 198
MacDonnell, D. J., 193, 195
McFadyen, J. E., 198
McGavin, William, 155
Machen, J. G., 224, 240
Machiavelli, N., 11
Mackie, J. L., 83
McInery, Ralph, 73, 93
McIntire, C. T., 240
McIntire, Carl, 133
Macintosh, J. J., 86, 87
MacIntyre, Alasdair, 86, 87, 285
Mack, Alexander, Jr., 134
McKean, Henry, 178
MacKinnon, D. M., 64, 65, 88–92, 254, 257–9
Mackintosh, H. R., 253
Mackintosh, Robert, 61, 190, 199, 235–7
McLachlan, Herbert, 177, 178, 216
Maclaren, Alexander, 220
M'Lean, Alexander, 221
MacLeod, George, 298, 299
McLeod, John, 209

315

General Index

McNaughton, David, 29
McNeil, John T., 233
McPherson, Thomas, 77
MacVicar, Donald H., 193
Madan, Martin, 31
Madell, Geoffrey, 87
Maimonides, 98
Malan, César, 138
Malcolm, Norman, 77, 83
Mallett, Sarah, 144
Malthus, T. R., 49, 52
Manchester Baptist College, 180
Manchester New College, London, 177
Mandeville, Bernard, 8
Mandler, Peter, 123
Manning, Bernard Lord, 268, 276
Mansel, H. L., 54, 56
Mansfield College Oxford, 160, 161, 162–3, 202
Manson, T. W., 3, 162, 235–6, 267
Manson, William, 254
Mantz, Felix, 107
Marchant, Henry, 43
Marischall College, Aberdeen, 41
Maritain, J., 96, 282
Marlow, A. N., 3
Marrowmen, 245, 249
Marsden, George M., 239
Marsh, H. G., 177
Marsh, Herbert, 172, 174
Marsh-Green, Molly, 219
Marshall, I. Howard, 144
Marshall, John, 14, 15, 21
Marshall, L. H., 180
Marshall, N. H., 180
Marshall, P. H., 49
Martin, C. B., 78
Martin, John, 123
Martin, Michael, 74
Martin, Rex, 64
Martineau, Harriet, 36, 48
Martineau, James, 162, 175, 176, 250
Marxism, 262, 287
Mascall, E. L., 73, 90
Mascall, William, 151
Masham, Damaris, 8, 30
materialism/ists, 113, 193
Matej of Janov, 105
Mather, Increase, 24
Matheson, George, 298
Mathews, H. F., 144
Matthews, Shailer, 220
Maurice, F. D., 55, 139, 141, 160, 161, 162, 172, 195, 200
Maurice, Thomas, 122

Mead, Joseph, 8
Meade, Thomasia, 138
Medellin Conference, 260, 261
medieval thought, 101–2
Medley, William, 180
Meeter, Daniel Kames, 293
Meister Eckhart, 102
Melanchthon, Philipp, 135, 210, 211, 212
Mell, Patrick Hues, 219
Mellone, Sydney Herbert, 176, 178
memory, 109
Mennonites, 107, 111, 132, 219, 264
Mercersburg Seminary, 187
Mercersburg theology, 3, 136, 187, 225–241, 293, 294, 299
Merleau-Ponty, M., 283
Merryweather, Mr., 165
Merton, Thomas, 283
metaphysics, 79, 89
Methodism/ists, 31, 138, 141, 143–5, 162, 164–7, 180, 183, 186, 192, 193, 194, 217, 238, 255, 256, 278–82, 290, 291, 292, 293
   Bible Christians, 144
   Methodist New Connexion, 142, 182
   Primitive, 138, 144, 165, 182, 183, 294
   Wesleyan, 165, 182, 217, 218
Methodist Philatelic Society, 144
Methodist Sacramental Fellowship, 144
Meyer, F. B., 220
Meyer, Harding, 276
Meynell, Hugo A., 86, 87
Miall, Edward, 160
Micklem, Nathaniel, 202
middle axioms, 288
Midland Baptist College, 180
Milburn, Geoffrey, 143
Mildmay Circle, 141
Mill, Harriet, 52
Mill, James, 51
Mill, John Stuart, 50–52, 54, 57, 58, 97, 121
millennialism, 141, 290
Miller, Hugh, 54
Miller, J. Peter, 133
Milne, A. J. M., 64
Milner, Isaac, 174
Milton, J. R., 14, 21
Milton, John, 7, 24, 31, 46
Mirabeau, Comte de, 45
miracles, 40–41, 44, 49, 74, 81, 214–15
missionaries/mission, 117, 122, 125, 126, 127, 133, 138, 165, 168, 193, 221, 222, 225, 239, 242–3, 264, 265, 275, 280, 293, 298, 299–300
Mitchell, Basil, 75, 86, 87
Moberly, R. C., 255

modernity, 282–4
Modood, Tariq, 64
Mohler, R. Albert, 219
Molnár, Amédeo, 106
Moltmann, J., 252, 259, 287, 288
Molyneux, William, 12
Monboddo, Lord, 45
monism, 273
Monro, D. H., 49
Montague, Mary, 116
Montesquieu, C-L de Secondat, 115, 117
Moody, Dale, 219
Moody, Dwight L., 141, 167, 185, 193, 197, 198
Moore, Aubrey, 57
Moore, G. E., 3, 57, 76, 173
Moore, James, 7
Moorfields Academy, 42
Moorhead, James H., 223, 224
morality, 19, 32–3, 34, 38–9, 42, 57, 81, 84, 113, 120, 173, 193, 257; see also ethics; philosophy, moral
moral sense, 150
Moravcsik, Julius M., 93
Moravians, 106, 116, 138, 140
More, Hannah, 30
More, Henry, 8, 10, 11
Moreno, C. M., 262
Morgan, Dafydd, 189, 190
Morgan, John, 186
Morgan, William, 41
Morgan, William (Welsh Bible), 124
Morison, James, 154, 156
Morison, John, 154, 158
Mormons, 290
Moule, C. F. D., 88
Moulton family, 144
Müller, George, 138
Mure, G. R. C., 63
Mullins, E. Y., 219, 221
Murphy, Graham, 177
Murray, A. Victor, 144
Murray, John, 122
Murray, Len, 144
music, 293, 299
Myers, Edward, 183
mystical union, 226, 232, 233, 238, 298, 299
Myth of God Incarnate, The, 258

Nasmith, David, 158
National Association of Congregational Churches, 128
National Council of Churches, 133
National Society, 151
naturalism, 74, 77, 226, 240, 285

natural law, 24, 96, 113, 115, 123, 207, 285
natural theology, 73, 78, 87, 123, 211; see also theism
Nautin, Pierre, 205
Neander, J. A. W., 187, 227, 238
negative theology, 89
Nelson, John, 164
neo-orthodoxy, 202, 241
neoplatonism, 270
Nettles, Thomas J., 219
Nettleton, Asahel, 185
Nevin, J. W., 136, 187, 225–39, 292, 298
Newbigin, J. E. Lesslie, 165, 255, 256
New Brunswick Theological Seminary, 292
New College, Edinburgh, 254
New College, Hackney, 64
New Connexion General Baptists, 168, 179, 221
New Divinity, 127
Newman, J. H., 56, 151, 152, 251, 259
Newton, Isaac, 7, 10, 29, 46, 112, 113, 117, 151, 214, 215
Newton, John, 143
Nicholas of Cusa, 102
Nichols, J., 230
Nicholson, Francis, 41
Nidditch, Peter H., 228
Niebuhr, H. Richard, 136, 222, 241
Niebuhr, Reinhold, 136, 241, 252, 253, 298
Nielsen, Kai, 74, 86, 87
Niesel, W., 209
Nietzsche, F., 72
Nockles, Peter B., 232
Noel, Baptist W., 239
Noetics, 56
Nonconformist conscience, 166
Non-Subscribing Presbyterian Church of Ireland, 176, 178
Norris, John, 8, 23
Norris, Richard, 255
Northampton Academy, 179
Northcott, Michael S., 285
Northern Baptist College, 179–81
Northern College, Manchester, 175
Northern Congregational College, 4
Northern Federation for Training in Ministry, 177
Norton, David Fate, 87
Norton, William, 170
Notre Dame University, 289
Noyes, Moses, 128
Numbers, Ronald L., 224
Nuovo, Victor, 14, 15
Nuttall, Geoffrey F., 4, 9, 24, 42, 165
Nye, Stephen, 20

General Index

Oberlin College, 127, 185
Ogborn, M. E., 41
Oldfield, Adrian, 64
Oldham, J. H., 288
Oldmixen, John, 31
Old Scots Independents, 153, 158
Oliver, E. H., 194
Oman, John, 162
Ombersley, 4
Onely, Rev. Mr., 42
Orchard, W. E., 141
Oresme, N., 102
Origen, 3, 205–6, 213, 214, 215, 216
Orr, James, 61, 199
Orthodox Churches, 231, 232, 278, 281
Orton, Joseph, 144
Osborn, Sarah, 127
Osler, Margaret J., 7
Oswald, James, 30, 231
Owen, H. P., 78, 233
Owen, John, 8, 22, 28, 208, 229, 245, 251, 252, 256, 269, 271, 271, 272
Oxford Group, 141, 142, 194
Oxford Movement, 151–2, 165, 172, 229, 231, 232, 294
Oxford University, 56, 62–4, 151, 161, 174
Oxford University Nonconformists Union, 161
Oxlee, John, 151

Pacific School of Religion, 126
pacifism, 202
Pailin, David, 144
Paine, Tom, 48, 115, 172
Palatinate Liturgy, 135, 293
Paley, William, 55, 123, 172, 236
Pannenberg, W., 220
pantheism, 48, 57, 228, 231, 233, 247, 273
paradox, 254
Parker, Joseph, 122
Parker, Samuel, 119
Parry, Joseph, 125
Partnership in Theological Education, 177
Pascal, B., 81, 222
pastoral office, 238
Paton, H. J., 63, 79
Patronage Act 1712, 53
Patterson, Bob E., 219
Pattison, Mark, 55, 151
Pauck, Wilhelm, 126
Paul VI, 275
Paul, Robert S., 209
Paulson, Ronald, 119
Pawson, H. Cecil, 144

Pawson, John, 167
Payne, Ernest A., 162, 220
Payne, John B., 238
peace churches, 131, 133–4
Peach, W. Bernard, 45
Peake, A. S., 165
Peart, Ann, 177–8
Peel, Albert, 162, 235
Pelagius, 263
Pembroke College Oxford, 210
Pendleton, James Madison, 219
Penelhum, Terence, 75, 86–7
Penry, John, 124
Pentecostals/ism, 219, 263, 290
Penzel, K., 232
Pepper, Mr., 170
perfection, 146, 165, 196, 218
Perkin, H. J., 3
Perkins, William, 23, 208, 209
Perry, Charles, 138
personal identity, 77, 86–7, 96
persons, 15–16
Peter Faber Centre, 260
Peters, R. S., 66–7, 71
Peters, Rik, 64, 65
Peterson, Michael L., 74
Philip, John, 300
Phillips, D. Z., 74, 77, 85, 89, 91
Phillips, George, 3
Phillips, Mark Salber, 121
philosophers
    17th century, 7–9
    18th century, 28–31
philosophes, 48, 114, 115
philosophy
    and Christian theism, 93–6
    and theology, 88–92
    and world religions, 72
    Asian, 97–8
    of education, 66–71
    of history, 226
    of religion, 72–85, 181
    moral, 93–6, 221, 285, 288–9; see also ethics, morality
Piaget, J., 70
Picton, James Allanson, 161, 200
Pidgeon, G. C., 198
pietism/ists, 113, 131, 166, 239
Pike, J. C., 168
Pilgrims, 126
Pinches, Charles, 93, 94, 96
Pine Hill Divinity College, 198
Pinnock, Clark H., 219

Piscator, Johannes, 211
Pitt, William, the Elder, 40, 43
Pitt, William, the Younger, 45
Plantinga, Alvin, 73, 77, 83, 94
Plato, 3, 65, 89, 101, 173
Platonism, 89, 102, 173, 205, 238; see also Cambridge Platonists
Plymouth brethren, 138, 141, 291, 294
Pocock, J. G. A., 119, 120, 122
Poe, Harry L., 219, 221
politics, 123, 125, 168, 223, 256
Pollard, Arthur, 3
Pompa, Leon, 64, 65
Pope, Alexander, 3
Pope, Robert, 124, 126
Pope, Stephen J., 285
Pope, W. B., 162, 165
Popkin, Richard H., 7
Porter, Jean, 285
Powell, Enoch, 123
Powell, Vavasor, 124
Power, David N., 255. 257
pragmatism, 76
preaching, 234, 294
predestination, 23, 38, 74, 75, 207, 212, 217, 218, 238, 298, 300
Presbyterian Church of Wales, 143; see also Calvinistic Methodism
Presbyterian College, Montreal, 193, 198
Presbyterians/ism, 20, 21, 36, 38, 55, 119, 124, 127, 134, 137, 138, 142, 143, 149, 154, 158, 185, 187, 192–3, 194, 195, 196, 198, 199, 218, 223, 224, 232, 233, 235, 240, 241, 291
Prest, Wilfrid, 36
Preston, Ronald, 3, 4
presuppositionalism, 213, 240
Price, Rice, 38
Price, Richard, 3, 30, 31, 37–47, 165, 175, 218
Price, Samuel, 42
Prichard, H. A., 62, 64
Priestley, Joseph, 17, 18, 29, 30, 36, 37, 39, 41, 44, 45, 48, 116, 118, 122, 165, 175, 218, 229, 292
Princeton College, 53, 54
Princeton Theological Seminary, 223, 227, 230, 234, 239
Pring, Richard, 69
Pringle-Pattison, A. S.; see Seth, Andrew
Proast, Jonas, 8, 27
process theology, 85, 241
Proctor, Lawrence, 209
Protestant Theological Institute, Cluj, 177
providence, 44, 113, 123, 210, 211, 215

publishing, 122, 141
Puritans/ism, 39, 149, 189, 209, 226, 229, 290, 291
Pusey, E. B., 151, 188

Quakers, 22, 127, 138, 141, 173, 290, 291
Queen's College, Belfast, 53
Queen's College, Birmingham, 166
Queen's University, Kingston, 193, 198
Quinn, Philip L., 84, 93

racism, 287
Rack, Henry D., 144
Racovian Catechism, 20
Radhakrishnan, S., 97
Rahner, Karl, 77, 220
Raiser, Konrad, 288
Rakestraw, Robert V., 219
Ramm, Bernard, 219, 222
Ramsey, Ian, 77
Ramsey, Paul, 288
Rank family, 144
Raphael, D. D., 47
Ratramnus, 101
Rattenbury family, 144
Rauch, F. A., 225, 227, 228, 238
Rauschenbusch, Walter, 219
Raven, Charles, 258
Rawdon College, Leeds, 180
Ray, John, 8
Redford, George, 186
Reformation, 24, 195, 214
    Dutch second, 208–10
    first, 105–6
    Scottish, 53
Reformed Baptists, 141
Reformed Church in America, 293
Reformed Ecumenical Council (formerly Synod), 55, 241
Reformed epistemology, 73, 74, 77, 78
Reformed theology/tradition, 3, 24, 73, 135–6, 188, 210, 223–42, 255, 276–7, 278, 281, 290, 296–300
Regent's Park College, London, 168
regeneration, 217, 232–3, 234, 235, 238, 263
Reid, George, 157
Reid, Malcolm, 241
Reid, Thomas, 29, 30, 37, 44, 53, 140, 150, 227, 231
Reid, W. Stanford, 240
Religion of Humanity, 50–52
Religious Census 1851, 176, 183
religious language, 74, 77, 78, 89, 91
Remonstrance, 212
republicanism, 115

319

General Index

restorationism, 238, 274
Reublin, Wilhelm, 108
revelation, 34, 112, 123, 173, 211, 212, 238, 247, 261, 262, 268, 282
revival/ism, 127, 134, 137, 185–6, 189–91, 225, 236–7, 238, 293
Richards, 'Bob', Robert, 134
Richardson, Kurt A., 219
Richmond, James, 4
Riedel, Georg, 108
Riedemann, Peter, 108
Riley, William Bell, 219, 220
Ritschl, Albrecht, 61, 161, 195, 199
Ritualists, 293
Roberts, J. Deotis, 219, 222
Roberts, Phil, 219, 221
Roberts, Richard, 194
Roberts, Richard H., 272, 273, 274
Roberts, Wesley A., 240
Robertson, James, 196
Robertson, John, 158
Robinson, H. Wheeler, 162, 219, 222
Robinson, T. H., 162, 220
Robinson, W. Gordon, 3, 4
Robinson, William Wyn, 176
Rochefoucauld, Duc de la, 45
Rodgers, Dirk W., 293
Rodó, J. E., 262
Roger, Brother, 299
Rogers, G. A. J., 7, 8, 30, 119
Rogers, Henry, 139, 200
Rogers, J. Guinness, 297
Rogerson, John, 284
Rollock, Robert, 244
Roman Catholics, 26, 73, 74, 91, 96, 105, 107, 152, 154, 164–5, 182, 183, 211, 227, 229, 231, 235, 250, 254, 255, 267, 268, 269, 270, 274, 275, 278, 279, 280, 281, 286, 288, 290, 294
Romanticism, 140, 141, 147–8, 195, 245, 282
Rooker, James, 139
Roots, Peter Philanthropos, 129
Rosas, L. Joseph, III, 219
Rose, Alan, 143
Rose, Geoffrey, 144
Rose, H. J., 172, 173
Rothe, Richard, 227
Rotheram, Caleb, 41, 44–5, 172
Rotheram, John, 45
Rotheram Independent Academy, 142
Rothery, Mr., 170
Rousseau, J. J., 113, 114, 115, 116
Routley, Erik, 293
Rowe, Kenneth E., 293
Rowe, William, 83
Rowland, Daniel, 42, 143
Rowley, H. H., 3, 162, 220
Ruddiman, Thomas, 31
Rudolph II, 8
Runyon, Theodore, 255
Rupp, E. Gordon, 3, 162
Rush, Benjamin, 45, 46
Rushbrooke, J. H., 180
Ruskin, John, 62, 122–3, 283
Russell, Bertrand, 57, 76, 83
Russell, D. S., 180
Russell, George B., 228
Russell, John, 138
Rust, Eric, 219
Ruston, Alan, 177
Rutherford, Samuel, 244
Rutt, J. T., 229
Ruysbroek, Jan van, 102
Ryan, Alan, 51, 52
Ryerson, William, 196
Ryle, Gilbert, 2, 64, 79, 142

Sabbath observance, 194, 198, 223
Sabbath, the English, 109–11
sacraments, 149, 152, 165, 233, 235–6, 238, 262, 299
Saint-Simon, Henri de, 51
Salters' Hall, 175, 216, 221
Salvation Army, 193, 294
sanctification, 217
Sandemanianism, 48, 49, 221; see also Glasites
Sanders, Alan, 36
Śaṅkara, 97
Sankey, Ira D., 141
Sannox Training College, 154
Sartre, J. P., 68, 75, 262
Savoy Declaration of Faith and Order, 124, 221
scepticism, 86–7, 112, 122, 150, 172, 173, 218, 240
Schaff, Philip, 136, 187–8, 223, 225, 227, 228, 230, 231, 232, 234, 235, 236, 292, 294, 298
Schelling, F. W. J. von, 187, 188, 227
Schemer, I., 67–8
Schillebeeckx, E. C. F. A., 91, 258
Schleiermacher, F. D. E., 3, 49, 206, 224, 227, 228–9, 231, 247, 265, 298, 300
Schochet, Gordon, 119
Schofield, Robert, 18
Schwöbel, Christoph, 271–2, 274, 275
science, 78–9, 113, 214, 224
Scotch Baptists, 221
Scotland, 153–9
Scott, A. J., 200

General Index

Scott, Walter, 245
Scottish Congregational Theological Hall, 161
Scottish Congregational Union, 153, 156, 158
Scottish Moderatism, 36, 53, 54, 153, 157, 243, 245, 249
Scottish Temperance League, 158
Scottish theology, 244–50, 253–5
Secker, Thomas 31
Second Great Awakening, 126
secularism, 119
secularization, 192, 194, 195
Sedbergh, 4
Sedgwick, Adam, 123
Seed, John, 36
Selbie, W. B., 156
Selina, Countess of Huntingdon, 138, 143, 181, 217
Sell, Alan P. F., 12, 58, 129, 188, 230, 233, 236, 276, 297, 299, 300
Sell, James Arnold, 132
Separatists, 145, 153, 228, 235, 290, 291
Sergeant, John, 8, 13
Seth, Andrew, 61, 73, 231, 253
Seven Day Baptists, 129, 133
Seventh Day Baptists, 220
Sewall, Samuel, 295
sexism, 287
Shaftesbury (Anthony Ashley Cooper), 23, 27, 30, 53
Shakespeare, J. H., 220
Shakespeare, William, 3
Sharpe Hungarian Foundation, 177
Shaw, J. N., 277
Shearer, J. G., 198
Shelburne, Earl of, 43, 44, 45
Shelley, Percy Bysshe, 48, 147, 148
Shepherd, Peter, 175
Sherlock, William, 14, 21, 30, 214
Shrubsole, Stanley, 202
Sidgwick, Henry, 57
Sidney, Algernon, 46
Simeon, Charles, 165, 172
Simon, Caroline J., 93. 96
Simon, David Worthington, 161, 249
Simpson, Robert, 30
Simpson, Robert (Hoxton Academy), 142
sin, 228, 288
Skelton, Robin, 3
slavery, 45, 134, 138, 223, 240
Sloan, Robert, 219
Smith, Adam, 113, 115, 150
Smith, D. Howard, 4
Smith, George Adam, 198, 246, 248, 249

Smith, Harold S., 219
Smith, J. A., 62, 63
Smith, John Pye, 142, 247
Smith, Leonard, 176, 177, 179
Smith, Morton, 240
Smith, W. Cantwell, 91
Smith, William Robertson, 142, 173, 246–8, 249, 250
Snaith, Norman, 162
Social Gospel, 127, 194, 195, 198–9
Society for Promoting Christian Knowledge, 151, 172
Society for Propagating the Gospel at Home, 153, 155, 157
Society for the Propagation of the Gospel, 151
Socinus, Fausus, 175
Socinians/ism, 14, 15, 18, 20, 21, 27, 38, 46, 48, 49, 117, 183, 190, 211, 214, 215, 280
Sockett, Hugh, 69
Soskice, Janet, 77
soteriology, 79, 92; see atonement
South, Robert, 14, 30
Southern Baptists, 219, 221
Southern Baptist Theological Seminary, 219
Southey, Robert, 48
Southgate, Beverley C., 8, 13
Spears, Robert, 38, 41, 175
Spencer, Herbert, 97
Spencer, Mary, 170
Spinoza, B., 49, 112, 117
spirits, 15–16
spirituality, 224, 296–300
Spring Hill College, 161
Spivey, James, 219
Spurgeon, C. H., 168, 169, 200, 219, 220
Stackhouse, Max L., 285
Stagg, Frank, 219, 220
Stapleton, Juliet, 123
status confessionis, 284, 287
Stead, Christopher, 89
Steadman, William, 180
Steers, A. D. G., 176
Stennett, Samuel, 122
Stephen, Leslie, 48, 56
Stephens, John, 30
Stephens, W. Peter, 144
Stevenson, Louise L., 223
Stewart, Dugald, 29, 30, 53, 227
Stewart, John W., 223, 232
Stewart, M. A., 7, 8, 36, 37
Stewart, Michael, 144
Stiles, Ezra, 45

General Index

Stillingfleet, Edward, 8, 10, 11, 15, 23, 27, 29, 30, 214
Stiver, Danny R., 219
Stoddart, Solomon, 185
Stoker, H., 73
Stone, Barton W., 134
Strauss, D. F., 187
Strawson, Peter, 84
Strict Baptists, 138, 140, 169–71, 180
Strong, Augustus Hopkins, 219, 221
Stubbes, George, 31
Studebaker family, 133
Student Christian Movement, 161
Stump, Eleonore, 75
Sum of Saving Knowledge, The, 244
Sunday schools, 125, 133, 166, 183, 198, 202
supernatural, 197, 247
Surman, Charles E., 4
Sutherland, Stewart, 90
Suzuki, D. T., 98
Swansea University, 59
Swift, Jonathan, 29
Swinburne, Richard, 75, 77
Swyneshead, Roger, 102
Sykes, Stephen W., 90, 255, 272
Synod of Dort, 212, 238

Taizé, 299
Talbot, E. S., 255
Talgarth Academy, 42
Tanner, Mary, 277
Tappan, Arthur, 186
Tappan, Lewis, 138, 186
Tapper, Alan, 36
Taunton Academy, 43, 95, 179
Tawney, R. H, 123
Taylor, A. E., 73
Taylor, Adam, 220
Taylor, Edward, 295
Taylor, John, 216, 218, 292
Taylor, Michael, 180, 181
Taylor, Dan, 179, 181
Taylor, Vincent, 162, 246
Teellinck, W., 208
Teilhard de Chardin, Pierre, 258, 259, 262
temperance, 125, 158
Temple, Frederick, 57
Tenison, Thomas, 8
Thatcher, Margaret, 254
theism, 74, 77, 80–87, 92, 176, 210–13, 214
Theodosius, Theodosius, 184
theological education, 141, 161, 177–8, 181, 209
theological realism, 91, 92

theologia negative, 257
theology, 117, 251–2, and *passim*
theosis, 143, 232–3, 256
Thiel, Udo, 14
thinking matter, 17–18, 19
Thirlwall, C., 172
Tholuck, F. A. G., 187
Thom, John Hamilton, 178
Thomas à Kempis, 261
Thomas Aquinas, 3, 91, 93, 101, 103–4, 206, 210, 211
Thomas, D. O., 11, 47
Thomas, George, 144
Thomas, Gerald, 219, 222
Thomas, J. W., 144
Thomas, William, 122
Thomism, 73, 102, 282
Thompson, Peter, 144
Thomson, G. T., 254
Thorne, James, 144
Thornwell, J. H., 223, 241
Tillard, J. M. R., 277
Tillich, Paul, 77, 78, 283
Tillotson, John, 8
Timpson, Thomas, 42
Tindal, Matthew, 8, 30, 31
Toland, John, 8, 11, 23, 30, 214
toleration, 10, 14, 24, 26, 27, 31, 40, 74, 112, 117, 172, 216, 294
Toleration Act (1689), 113, 125, 149, 216
Tomassi, Paul, 7
Toplady, A. M., 165, 218
Torrance, T. F., 91, 254
Toulmin, Joshua, 20
Towers, Joseph, 36
Towgood, Micaijah, 31, 175, 292
Townsend, Henry, 180
Tracy, Thomas F., 75
trade, 115
tradition, 75, 109, 196
Traill, Robert, 245
transcendentalism, 238
Transylvania, 177
Trefeca College, 217
Trevelyan, G. M., 123
Trevor-Roper, H. R., 14
Trigg, Roger, 74
Trinity, 11, 14, 20, 21, 27, 91, 141, 209, 213–17, 221, 255, 256, 257, 258, 259, 261, 265, 270, 271, 272, 273, 280, 287–8
Tripold, David M., 293
Tübingen University, 187
Turnbull, George, 29
Turner, J. M. W., 123

Turner, James, 224
Twelve Day London Mission, 293
Tymms, T. Vincent, 180

Underwood, A. C., 180
Uniformity, Act of, (1559), 235
Union of Welsh Independents, 125, 275
Union Seminary, New York, 187
Unitarian College Manchester, 175–9
Unitarian Home Mission Board,
Unitarians/ism, 14, 20, 27, 36, 37, 41, 49, 54, 126, 160, 161, 175–9, 180, 183, 185, 190, 212, 220, 229, 238, 239, 250, 291, 292
United Church of Canada, 192, 194
United Church of Christ, 135, 228, 229, 232
United Kingdom Alliance, 158
United Reformed Church, 134, 180, 289
United Secession Church, 156, 158, 159
Uniting Church in Australia, 291
Unity of Brethren, 105–6
Universalists, 185
University College of Wales, Aberystwyth, 60
University of Alberta, 86
University of Calgary, 86, 192
University of Leeds, 180
University of Manchester, 3, 151, 163, 174, 175, 176, 177, 178, 179, 180, 181
University of Nottingham, 4
University of Paris, 101
University of St. Andrews, 253, 254
University of Sheffield, 101
University of Sussex, 49, 121
University of Warwick, 47
Urey, H. C.
Ursinus College, 136, 185
Ursinus, Z., 211, 212
Utraquists, 106

Valla, Lorenzo, 102
Vancouver School of Theology, 198
Van Dusen, H. P., 253
Van Til, Cornelius, 240, 241
Vatican II, 250, 260, 261, 271, 286, 289
Vaughan, Robert, 122
Vaughn, J. Barry, 219, 221
verification principle, 149
vicarious repentance, 246
Vico, Giambattista, 62
Victoria, Queen, 169
virtue, 39, 285
Voltaire, F. M. Arouet de, 113
Vorstius, Conradus, 212

Wainwright, Geoffrey, 144, 145, 255, 256, 257
Wainwright, William J., 84
Wakefield, Gordon, 143
Waldensians, 105
Wales, 124–6, 189–91
Wallace, Alfred Russel, 55
Wallin, Benjamin, 139
Walsh, John, 144
Walpot, Peter, 108
war, 285
Warburton, William, 30, 44
Ward, Mrs. Humphrey, 57
Ward, James, 173
Ward, John, 159
Ward, Keith, 255
Ward, W. Reginald, 3, 144
Ward, William, 122
Wardlaw, Ralph, 153, 154, 155, 156, 157, 158
Warfield, B. B., 210, 224, 239, 240
Warnock, Mary, 68–9
Warrington Academy, 43
Washington, George, 46
Waterhouse, E. S., 145
Waterland, Daniel, 21, 30, 151, 215
Watson, John (Musselburgh), 156
Watson, John (philosopher), 73, 195, 198
Watson, John James, 151
Watson, Richard, 122, 171–2, 174
Watts, Isaac, 8, 17, 29, 42, 46, 111, 150, 291, 298
Watts, Robert, 224
Waugh, Edwin, 143
Wayland, Francis, 220
Webb, C. C. J., 62, 63, 270
Webb, R. K., 35, 175
Weber, Timothy P., 219
Weigel, G., 267
Wells, David F., 239
Wells, James, 139
Wentz, R., 230, 238
Wernberg-Møller, P., 3
Wesley, Charles, 138, 144, 146, 164, 217, 218
Wesley, John, 30, 138, 139, 141, 143, 144, 145–50, 164, 217, 218, 238, 256, 279, 280, 281, 290
Wesley, Kezzia, 145
Wesley, Martha, 145
Westcott, B. F., 172
Western Kentucky University, 103
West Midlands, 182–4
Western, R. G., 3
Westminster Assembly, 208
Westminster College Cambridge, 173
Westminster Confession, 223, 245
Westminster Shorter Catechism, 263

General Index

Westminster Theological Seminary, 240
Westphal, Merold, 72
Wetenhall, Edward, 21
Whately, Richard, 56
Whewel, William, 57
Whichcote, Benjamin, 9, 23, 25, 222
Whiston, William, 8, 215
Whitby, Daniel, 24
White, Edward, 161, 195
White, Pat, 71
White, Roger, 91
Whitefield, George, 30, 138, 139, 143, 146, 149, 157, 189, 213, 218
Whitehead, A. N., 79
Whitehouse, Mary, 122
Whitgift, John, 110
Whitley, W. T., 162, 220
Whitlock, Luder J., Jr., 240
Whyte, Charles, 154
Wignall, Paul, 92
Wiles, Maurice F., 205
Wilkes, John, 115
Wilkinson, John, 162
Wilks, Matthew, 156
William of Conches, 101
William of Ockham, 102
Williams, Bernard, 90
Williams, C. J. F., 75
Williams, Daniel, 20
Williams, Edward, 125, 142, 201
Williams, Roger, 127
Williams, Rowan, 284, 297
Williams, William, 143
Wilson, Mr., 159
Wilson, A. J. N., 3
Wilson, J. Cook, 62
Winch, David, 121
Winslow, Octavius, 139
Winthrop, John, 44
Witherow, William, 194
Wittgenstein, L. 65, 73, 76, 77, 91
Wodrow, James, 36
Wolever, Terry, 170
Wolff, C., 116
Wolff, Joseph, 294
Wollaston, William, 8
Wollstonecraft, Mary, 30, 116
Wolterstorff, Nicholas, 73, 283
Womersley, David, 122
Woods, John, 67
Woodward, Linda, 78
Woolston, Thomas, 31, 119, 120
Worcester, 4

Worden, Blair, 122
Wordsworth, William, 147, 245
Workman, George C., 193
World Alliance of Reformed Churches, 55, 241, 275
World Communion of Reformed Churches, 55
World Council of Churches, 133, 168, 273, 286, 287, 288, 289
World Methodist Council, 144, 281
World Parliament of Religions, 188
World Presbyterian Alliance, 188, 195
worldviews, 94, 117
World War I, 58, 60, 125, 176, 194, 199
Worn Out Ministers Fund, 144
worship, 127, 146, 288, 289–96, 298; see also liturgy
Worster, Benjamin, 31
Wrede, G. F. E. W., 91
Wright, W. D., 144
Wroth, William, 124
Wykes, David L., 36
Wyclif, John, 105

Yale University, 128
Yeo, Richard, 111
Yoder, J. H., 93, 95
Yorkshire United Independent College, 4, 163, 202
Young, Andrew, 253
Young, Brian, 122
Young, Frances, 144
Yrigoyen, Charles, 238, 239

Zaragoza, Edward C., 293
Zen, 283
Zinzendorf, Nicholas L. von, 106, 135, 138
Zizioulas, John, 251, 252
Zwaanstra, Henry, 240
Zwingli, H., 135, 290, 293
Zwinglians, 107

www.ingramcontent.com/pod-product-compliance
Lightning Source LLC
Chambersburg PA
CBHW060507300426
44112CB00017B/2579